VÁCLAV HAVEL

To the CASTLE and BACK

Václav Havel was born in Czechoslovakia in 1936. His plays have been produced around the world, and he is the author of many influential essays on totalitarianism and dissent. He was a founding spokesman for Charter 77 and served as president of the Czech Republic until 2003. He lives in Prague.

Paul Wilson lived in Czechoslovakia from 1967 to 1977. Since his return to Canada in 1978, he has translated more than twenty books of Czech literature into English, including novels by Josef Škvorecký, Bohumil Hrabal, and Ivan Klíma, and most of Václav Havel's prose works. He is based in Toronto and works as a freelance writer and editor.

TO THE CASTLE AND BACK

To the CASTLE and BACK

VÁCLAV HAVEL

Translated from the Czech by Paul Wilson

VINTAGE BOOKS

A DIVISION OF RANDOM HOUSE, INC.

NEW YORK

The Library of Congress has cataloged the Knopf edition as follows:
Havel, Václav.
[Prosím stručně. English.]
To the castle and back / by Václav Havel ; translated by Paul Wilson.
p. cm.
Includes interview with Karel Hvížďala.
1. Havel, Václav. 2. Czechoslovakia—Politics and government—1989–1992.
3. Czech Republic—Politics and government—1993–. I. Hvížďala, Karel, 1941–.
II. Wilson, Paul R. (Paul Robert), 1941–. III. Title.
DB2241.H38A25 2007
943.7105092—dc22
[B] 200704413

Vintage ISBN: 978-0-307-38845-2

Book design by Virginia Tan

www.vintagebooks.com

Printed in the United States of America
10 9 8 7 6 5 4 3 2 1

For Dáša

Preface

I am delighted that this strange little book of mine is now available to English-speaking readers. I was unable, nor did I wish, to write a full-blown memoir, but after everything I have lived through, I felt I owed people an account of some kind. So I decided to fashion a special kind of collage. It has its own architecture, one that unfolds and interweaves themes and motifs and time periods. It builds slowly, gathering momentum as it goes. I wrote it quickly, without a specific reader in mind. As a result there are some passages that may not interest all of my fellow citizens, and others that non-Czech readers may find hard to follow. Still others refer to events that have long since been carried away by time. And yet, rather than make cuts, I let these passages stand because they belong to the flavor and the fabric of the times, and because I wanted to remind readers that I was not just taking part in routine changes of government; we were building a new democratic country, as it were, from the ground up.

If you occasionally feel like putting the book aside because it seems to skirt some of the world-shaking events that I lived through, or to burrow too deeply into exclusively Czech or Czechoslovak matters, I urge you to skip ahead. It's easy to do because the book is divided not only into chapters, but into short sequences, separated by horizontal lines. But whether you read it whole or piecemeal, I will be satisfied if you feel this book has given you something of value.

Václav Havel

To the CASTLE and BACK

CHAPTER ONE

Washington, April 7, 2005

I've run away. I've run away to America. I've run away for two months, with the whole family; that is, with Dáša and our two boxers, Sugar and her daughter Madlenka. I've run away in the hope that I will find more time and focus to write something. I haven't been president now for two years, and I'm starting to worry about not having been able to write anything that holds together. When people ask me, as they do all the time, if I'm writing something and what I'm writing, I get mildly annoyed and I say that I've already written enough in my life, certainly more than most of my fellow citizens, and that writing isn't a duty one can perform on demand. I'm here as a guest of the Library of Congress, which has given me a very quiet and pleasant room where I can come whenever I want, to do whatever I want. They ask nothing from me in return. It's wonderful. Among other things, I would like to respond to Mr. Hvížďala's questions.

I'd like to start the conversation with a question that touches on the second half of the 1980s, when you became the most famous dissident in Central Europe, or—as John Keane wrote—"a star in the theater of opposition." Do you remember the moment when it first occurred to you that you would have to enter into politics, that your role as a playwright, essayist, and thinker would no longer suffice?

In the first place I'd take issue with the designation "star in the theater of opposition." We did everything we could not to separate ourselves into the "stars" and the others. The better known someone among us became, and thus the better protected from arbitrary repression, the more he tried to come out in defense of those who were less known and therefore more vulnerable. The regime, after all, held to the principle of "divide and conquer." To some they said: "How can you, sir, an educated man respected by everyone, demean yourself by associating with such losers?" To others they said: "Don't get mixed up with those guys; they're a protected species. They're always going to lie their way out of trouble, and they'll go scot-free and leave you to pay the price." It's understandable that in such circumstances we placed a special emphasis on the principle of the equality of everyone who somehow expressed opposition to the regime.

In the second place, you know very well that I have constant doubts about myself, that I blame myself for everything, plausible and implausible, that I'm not very fond of myself. An individual like me finds it very hard to accept, without protest, the claim that he is a "star."

On the other hand, I have to admit that I probably do have a certain ability to bring people together. As someone with a visceral aversion to conflict, tension, and confrontation, especially if they are pointless, and moreover, as someone who hates it when the conversation goes around in circles, I have always tried to contribute to a consensus among people and to find ways to transform a common position into visible action. Perhaps it was these qualities of mine that in the end—without my wanting to or trying to—brought me to the forefront and made me seem, to some, like a "star."

And now, finally, to the nub of your question: I don't think you can find any clear demarcation line in my life separating the time when I did not devote myself to politics from the time when I did. To some degree I have always been concerned with politics or public affairs, and to some degree I have always—even as a "mere" writer—been a political phenomenon. That's the way it works in totalitarian conditions: everything is political, even a rock concert. There were, of course, differences in the nature or the visibility of the political impact my activities had: in the 1960s, that impact was different from what it was in the 1980s. From that point of view, the one genuine watershed in my life was November 1989, when I agreed to become a candidate for the presidency. At that point the issue was no longer just the political impact of what I did; it was a political function, with all that that job entailed. I hesitated until the last minute.

Did the prospect frighten you or entice you?

I found it more frightening than enticing. It was something completely new. I hadn't prepared myself for a presidential role from my schooldays the way American presidents do. I had only a few hours to make a decision that would fundamentally change my life. In the end what probably won me over was the appeal to my sense of responsibility. People told me exactly what I would later often say to others when trying to draw them into politics: you can't spend your whole life criticizing something and then, when you have the chance to do it better, refuse to go near it. This appeal, moreover, was accompanied by an attempt to persuade me that my candidacy was the only possible solution in this particular revolutionary situation and that had I—as the central figure in this process—suddenly refused any further engagement, refused to bear the consequences of my own previous actions, it would have turned all our efforts upside down and been a slap in the face to everyone.

What did your wife at the time, Olga, who was known for her sharp judgments, have to say about it?

I have to say that she had unconditionally supported my previous "dissident" activities, but as far as running for president was concerned, she had the same misgivings I did, perhaps even stronger. But in the end she gave me her blessing.

In the mid-1980s, some of your colleagues, immediately after reading our book, *Disturbing the Peace,* began to suspect that you would enter politics. If I remember correctly, Milan Kundera shared that thought with Václav Bělohradský at the time. I first heard the idea that you ought to become president from Pavel Tigrid, who asked me in early

January 1989 what my response to that would be. When did you first learn of these opinions, and what did you think of them?

I'm not surprised that Milan Kundera said that. I think he's always considered me a more political person than I did myself. When Pavel Tigrid wrote in his exile quarterly, *Svědectví*, that I should be the president, I took it as a joke, as I did later that summer when Adam Michnik said the same thing to me. If I'm not mistaken, it was my friend the rock-and-roller Michael Kocáb who first began to speak in all seriousness, during those revolutionary days, about the need for me to stand for president. In retrospect I seem to have been the very last to have taken the idea seriously.

Washington, April 8, 2005

I remember my previous visits to America. I was here for the first time for six weeks in the spring of 1968. In Prague, the Prague Spring was in blossom and the opportunity to travel came up, and so I immediately took up Joe Papp's invitation to attend the premiere of my play The Memorandum *at the Public Theater in New York. At the time I was chairman of the Circle of Independent Writers, which we had set up shortly beforehand to counterbalance the party cell in the still all-powerful Union of Czechoslovak Writers, and I wrote our program on the plane, while drinking whiskey. (It would be worth looking up sometime; I daresay it would still seem relevant today.) There were many rural people on the plane with me, mostly from Slovakia, and many of them were flying for the first time in their lives. They were probably taking advantage of the favorable political climate to visit their rich American relatives.*

The descent into Kennedy Airport at sunset was fascinating. I'll never forget the experience. Someone was waiting for me at the airport and took me directly to a rehearsal of The Memorandum. *I couldn't believe my eyes: here I was on the other side of the world, suddenly seeing my play being staged exactly as I had imagined it and the way we had presented it in the Theater on* the Balustrade in Prague. People laughed or applauded in the very same places, which particularly surprised me given the fact that the translation was probably not great and there are some things in my plays that are simply untranslatable. After the rehearsal they took me to my hotel and I slept like a log. The next day I looked up my old friend and fellow student Miloš Forman and I moved in with Jiří Voskovec, a wonderful man with whom I stayed for the rest of my visit.

The days I spent there were important in my life. The hippie movement was at its height. There were be-ins in Central Park. People were festooned with beads. It was the time of the musical Hair. (Joe had presented it in the Public Theater before my play opened, and because it was so successful it moved to Broadway, where I saw the premiere.) It was the time when Martin Luther King Jr. was killed, a period of huge antiwar demonstrations whose inner ethos—powerful but in no way fanatical—I admired; it was also the heyday of psychedelic art. I brought many posters home, and to this day they are hanging in Hrádeček. And I brought home the first record of Lou Reed with the Velvet Underground.

My stay in the United States influenced me considerably. After I returned, my friends and I experienced a very joyful, albeit a somewhat nervous, summer, which could not have ended well; on August 21, the Soviet troops arrived. And then, seeing long-haired, bead-festooned young people waving the Czechoslovak flag in front of the Soviet tanks and singing a song that was a favorite among the hippies at the time, "Massachusetts," I had a truly strange sensation. In those circumstances it sounded a bit different from how it had sounded in Central Park, though it had essentially the same ethos: the longing for a free and colorful and poetic world without violence.

The second time I visited America—after a long and gloomy twenty-two years—I was president of my country. The former hippies were now no doubt respected senators or bosses of multinational corporations. Since then I've been here at least ten times; I've become close to three American presidents and to many American politicians (a special role among them was played by my compatriot the marvelous Madeleine Albright), as well as to important people and to many famous stars. These working or state or official visits, however, were brief and the program was always full, so that I only saw America from a speeding limousine. I sometimes found time to go for a walk or visit a rock club, but it was never easy. And so now, here I am on my second long visit almost forty years after the first one. In the meantime, I've lived through quite *a bit, and perhaps precisely for that reason—paradoxically—I long for the freedom of movement I once enjoyed here when I was in my thirties.*

Why is it that after *Slum Clearance*, which you wrote in 1987, you didn't write another play until the Velvet Revolution, unless I count *Tomorrow*, which you wrote on commission for the Theater on a String and which was performed at the time, obviously, under a pseudonym? Before that, you had written a new play almost every two years. It makes me think that by then you had already been drawn too deeply into politics to write.

I admit that as time went on, I had less and less time to write plays. After all, by the late 1980s I had almost become a kind of public institution, so much so that I had to have a full-time secretary—my friend Vladimír Hanzel—which was not common for someone in the opposition. Still, I don't think there was an exceptional hiatus in my playwriting at that time. In any case the revolution caught me at a time when I had a new play already half written, even though it was only a first and very rough draft.

(October 4, 1993)

(. . .)

5) In the morning I am going to have to issue a statement on the situation in Russia. Have Messrs. S. and Š. come by and we'll write something. The prime minister called me: he wants to coordinate our statements. We'll get in touch with him when we've written it, but perhaps he'll call before that. Or Zieleniec.

If so, put me on the line. (. . .)

9) Please have Mrs. M. or E. prepare the pike from Lány that was given to me in some very original way, with unique spicing, so that the parliamentary five will never forget it. (. . .)

(October 17, 1993)

(. . .)

2) Would someone please prepare, from our various tape recordings and from the notes taken by Mrs. B., a complete transcript of the conversations with Kohl. At the dinner, you made notes (and there too some very important things were said, about Poland for instance). The transcript will be top secret and it will be for our use only, and we will give it to someone from the outside to read only after very serious consideration.

3) It's an even more urgent task to write the first version of the letters of invitations for the Central European presidents. I've been asking for them since July, and now it's high time. I should have them by next weekend for editing.

Next weekend I should also have all the source materials for a letter to Zieleniec that I want to write over the weekend. (In my own way I have an idea about how to go about it; I only need all the source materials: for example, a few sentences on every event, its genesis, its political significance, its context, etc.).

4) I'm going to try tomorrow, that is, on Sunday, to work on the speech to be delivered in the Vladislav Hall on October 28, and the one I'll give during the oath-taking. If I manage to draft them I'll send them immediately for consultation. (. . .)

(October 24, 1993)

(. . .)

2) I am including the text of a speech to the military that I will make during their oath-taking on October 28. (. . .) I would like L., Mr. M., and General T. to look it over. I am prepared to make or approve (by telephone) minor changes; please do not make any major edits to the text. When it's approved, I would ask V. to print it out as usual in large type on small cards and give it to me in the afternoon.

3) I would ask V. to ask Mr. D. if there will be a lectern in the Vladislav Hall or not, and if so whether it would be better to have the

speech on large-format paper, or on small cards. If the latter, could he please print it out on the cards and give them to me this afternoon. (. . .)

(November 14, 1993)

(. . .)

3) Can anyone confirm whether the letters of invitation to Litomyšl were properly delivered and whether there is any reaction to them? Is there anything new in the matter of Clinton's visit? Should we be taking some initiative or just waiting? In his time, the minister of foreign affairs asked me to tell him what should be the theme of the first meeting of the foreign policy eleven. I think it should be one of the following two themes: reparations, a dialogue with the Sudeten Germans, and our relationship with Germany as a whole; or our relationship with the European Union and NATO and toward European integration. Some formulae should be found that will be suitable for everyone. At the same time we should make the plan for my foreign policy activities more precise for the minister. (Slovenia has already happened. Munich won't happen. Presidents invited to Litomyšl. Setting the exact dates for visits by foreign heads of state and if necessary of my own trips. Etc.) (. . .)

(December 12, 1993)

(. . .)

6) Clinton. The written material is very good. I would ask Mr. S. and Mr. V. as soon as possible—i.e., before the arrival of the advance team— to meet with a representative of the MFA to discuss it with him, to make any additional explanations, to establish a common strategy for negotiating with the advance team. If it's not necessary, I'd rather not have very many consultations with senior government officials. They would only make things more confused. In this connection I would ask Mr. V. to contact Láďa Kantor or Michal Prokop. Both are suggesting that if Clinton wants to play his saxophone in a jazz club, they would take over Reduta for that purpose and get Vikličky, Stivín, Hammer, and other top jazzmen

with whom it is a pleasure to play. (Kantor is also offering the participation of the Czech Filharmonia in Litomyšl. (. . .)

12) I have the uneasy feeling that the prime minister will ask me, at the Council for Foreign Policy or by telephone or otherwise, to let him see my New Year's speech. I can't claim that it doesn't yet exist, but at the same time I don't feel like giving it to him. Please come up with some appropriate strategy to avoid a pointless confrontation.

13) On the basis of the assembled notes I have done the final edit of my New Year's speech. I include the final draft. (. . .)

(December 18, 1993)

(. . .)

7) I had a visit today (i.e., Saturday) from Messrs. Lux and Kalvoda. It seems that there is going to be a minor standoff this Tuesday during the coalition negotiations. I promised that I would be available if things got rough. If they want to call me, please put them through. Otherwise it would be a good idea to find out from them something about the backroom negotiations on Tuesday and the cabinet meeting on Wednesday and to keep me informed. My priority: that my New Year's speech will sit well in the situation, will not seem like a repetition of what's already been said or a reaction to a passing situation; nor, on the other hand, do I want it to come like a bolt out of the blue, but rather like a program for the "state" articulated at just the right moment and articulated as far as possible independently of momentary party bickering. (. . .)

9) I urgently request Mr. D. to go himself, or to send someone, to Litomyšl. All the presidents have promised their attendance, and even the Prague Filharmonia is offering its services and it's high time to get going on that. (. . .)

(December 25, 1993)

(. . .)

If possible I would prefer to write only when I feel an irresistible need to say something; but that's not very likely to happen. Right now, for example, I'd be delighted to write about a particular theme that I can hardly write about, certainly not for the purposes of our trip to India or Thailand, and that theme is—to put it simply—the reemergence of Czech small-mindedness in Czech politics as our own version of post-communism. I would illustrate it using many examples from our domestic and foreign policy. (. . .)

2) (. . .) It once happened that by mistake, they broadcast Kohl's old New Year's speech instead of the right one for that year; I don't think there's any real danger of that happening to us, but even so I would welcome it if Mr. Š. could view the final draft of the speech before it's broadcast, if that's possible. (. . .)

5) If there is no way a compromise can be found between the ideas of the Ministry of Foreign Affairs concerning Clinton's visit and our own, I would consider it the best possible solution if I were to write a strongly worded letter to the minister, which I would fax to you. It would be better than a telephone call. It's the only way to get them to bend a little. (. . .)

A very strange coincidence: the prince just called me from Vienna with a message from Michael Ž. (. . .) It seems that Michael is a little unhappy with the positions and activities of the Ministry of Foreign Affairs in the matter of Clinton's visit and in general about the atmosphere around it. I understood this only from hints. But there is something more important: Madeleine is arriving incognito a day before the American delegation, and she wants to have a dinner (in secret) with me and Michael Ž., just the three of us. I think that this is very important not only because of the specific scenario of the whole visit but also because I'll probably get the freshest information about the course of the NATO summit and about the apparent and hidden intentions of the USA. (. . .)

In the 1980s you remarked that you preferred a politics that grows from the heart and not from a thesis. "One simple electrician with his heart in the right place," you wrote, "can influence the history of his nation." Did you begin to realize back then that your remarks about the heart were in direct conflict with practical politics, which on the contrary have to be very pragmatic?

Every expression—word, sentence, or concept—is highly situational, and you have to be aware of the circumstances in which it was uttered. What you've quoted is something I wrote in an essay about the political impact of taking a moral stance in totalitarian conditions. In such circumstances, a single courageous word from Solzhenitsyn can have a greater political impact than the votes of a million electors in democratic circumstances. But I mention that only in passing. The main thing is that I still stand behind what I said. In the last fifteen years I've been persuaded on countless occasions that in democratic conditions, too, it's important that politics be more than just a technology of power, but that it provide a genuine service to citizens, a service that is as disinterested as possible, based on certain ideals, a service that follows the moral order that stands above us, that takes into account the long-term interests of the human race and not just what appeals to the public at any given moment; it's a service that resists becoming no more than the interplay of particular interests or pragmatic schemes that ultimately conceal a single aim: to remain in power at all costs. Of course it's one thing to philosophize independently, just for the sake of it, and something else altogether to achieve real things in politics. That I admit. But that doesn't mean that politics must surrender all its ideals, deny its "heart," and become a mere self-propelled, technocratic process.

By the way, if we think of Lech Wałęsa or Mikhail Gorbachev, who along with you probably contributed most decisively to the changes at the end of the last century, we see that in the end they didn't enjoy much gratitude from their fellow citizens. Why do you think this is? Does gratitude have no place in politics? Why do people forget so quickly?

I don't know if it's the rule, because we may also observe the exact opposite phenomenon: someone who has been harshly criticized throughout his political career can, years later—most probably after his death—be practically deified, a figure about whom not a critical word may be said. Whatever the case, the phenomenon of forgetting or even of ingratitude certainly turns up in politics, and it can have a thousand causes. For example: modern media often live from one day to the next, from one flashy headline to the next, so it's no surprise that they can be so mesmerized by today that they forget about yesterday. I would even go so far as to say that the media often behave like a willful little girl; for instance, as I write this, the Czech Republic has a prime minister whom the media turned into the most popular man in the country by far for quite a while, and then recently, in a matter of days, they turned him into the most hated. Neither view had much to do with his real qualities, good or bad. Further: many politicians—thanks to a combination of fortunate circumstances—play a key role at a particular moment when they have, as they say, their moment in the sun, and what they did before or after it may not be interesting at all. Is it any wonder that a long, dull life can sometimes erase the memory of that exceptional moment? Again, many politicians—unconsciously, of course—do everything possible to make people loathe them, for example by becoming absurdly vain. At other times, someone who is no longer in office may have his legacy subtly erased from history by his successor, or rather by those who prefer the favor of politicians in power to those in power no longer. Moreover, politics is a peculiar area of human endeavor: a politician seldom attains a really unambiguous, clearly visible goal that he can then notch up once and for all as an unqualified success. The opposite is more likely to be true: politics is a kind of dough that one is eternally kneading; one can almost never say: the objective has been achieved; I can now cross it off my list and turn to other matters. In any case it's no accident that politicians who govern in times of peace, stability, and order are more likely to be forgotten than those who hold office in turbulent, revolutionary times. How good or bad these politicians are is secondary.

But you mentioned Gorbachev: he is a special and, in his own way, a tragic case. He tried to lift up the lid to let some of the steam out of the pot, and it clearly never occurred to him that a lid, once lifted, can—and, given the magnitude of the pressure, must—be blown away forever. His historical achievement is enormous: communism would have collapsed without him anyway, but it might have happened ten years later, and in God knows how wild and bloody a fashion. Nevertheless, for obvious reasons, this type of achievement does not and cannot entitle him to play an active political role in entirely new circumstances, particularly when those circumstances were not something he sought in the first place.

(January 16, 1994)

(. . .)

1) I am sending a new version of my speech for India. Could Mr. Š. kindly correct any grammatical or spelling mistakes (Indian names). (. . .)

2) I see from my program that I am going to name the university chancellors. Will a speech be necessary for this? Written, or improvised? I'd be grateful for any timely advice so that I could write it. If anyone has any idea or information about this, please send it to me in writing.

3) This week the government should be informed about my trip to the European Parliament. I am probably going to make a major speech, which I must also write in time. In this case, however, I would like to get from the Ministry of Foreign Affairs, in addition to their standard notes, on time (!), on paper (!), the minister's idea of what I should say there. After all, the Ministry of Foreign Affairs came up with the idea for this trip and put it forward. (. . .)

6) I haven't written my speech for Thailand, partly because of the pressure of time, but mainly due to my poor state of mind and body after a party at the restaurant Na slamníku, which was otherwise wonderful and meant a lot to me.

(January 23, 1994)

(. . .)

1) I managed (to my great surprise) to write three short texts: a speech for the naming of the chancellors, a speech for Thailand, and a message for International Theater Day. All three have one thing in common: they are rush jobs. Therefore I would urge my Castle colleagues to make time on Monday to read through the speeches and provide their comments, which I might then work in on Tuesday. (. . .)

(February 5, 1994)

(. . .)

3) In Hrádeček I intend mainly to write a speech for the European Parliament. I don't rule out reading it in English if it is translated in time and M. can coach me on the delivery. (. . .)

4) The second theme that I've broached, and which I would like in some form (an article?) to really sink my teeth into, is the electoral system for the higher governing bodies. To do that I would need Dr. Ch. to coax out of Dr. A. the expertise he once promised to provide. The request is roughly as follows: the regional representative bodies should have between fifteen and thirty members (according to population). I would like to know whether such a representative body could be elected according to the combined system once suggested by Dr. K. for parliamentary elections. It ought to work; every region would then only have to be divided into the appropriate number of single-seat districts, which would be—if my calculations are correct—roughly one third the size of the electoral districts for the Senate. That would bode well for strengthening the relationships between voters and their representatives. (. . .)

(February 17, 1994)

1) I am exceptionally satisfied with the conceptual, political, and organizational preparation for this trip, as well as how the trip itself went. The journey had what I always ask for: i.e., an idea, an ethos, an architecture, a style, a mission, etc. Understandably, I had no proper insight into the backstage and the inner workings of the trip, but it seemed to me very well organized, and everything clicked. In its importance and in how it played out, it exceeded all my expectations. So I repeat my thanks to all the employees of the OPR who made it happen. I am not going to belabor my praise and will merely focus on several minor details about which, despite everything, I have some critical reservations or, at the very least, some questions.

2) Every extra member of the entourage naturally makes the trip more complicated. Therefore, I ask myself whether there were not too many of

us along. At the same time I can't think of anyone who was unnecessary. Mr. S. and Mr. Š. were my political team; they were present and took notes at every event, and they can testify to everything that went on. Stašek was the heart and soul of the expedition as the main—if not the only—expert on the world that we visited. Mr. Š. looked after the press like a father, which everyone appreciated. S. looked after me. There were three people from the Protocol Office. Someone said that three was exactly the right number: someone else felt that two would have been enough. I have no way of judging. Iva looked after Olga. The two translators were absolutely essential, and two doctors were also essential (though I continue to think that one could have done the job).

3) I would rather leave an evaluation of the level of cooperation with the ministers and their teams for an oral debriefing. Kočárník and Sabela did a lot of work and didn't complicate matters: there was no problem with them. What their assistants did I don't know, but I would like to believe that they were doing something important. With Zieleniec it was more complicated. Politically we worked well together; there wasn't the slightest friction; on the contrary we complemented each other. But otherwise he played a rather ambiguous role (backroom gossip about all the people from the OPR, dirty little tricks, the mysterious role of his entourage, his occasional annoyance that he was in my shadow, his unforthcoming manner, his side attempts to increase his visibility). In fact, I would even say that behind the scenes he tried to have a negative influence on Kočárník and Sabela (in the sense that he encouraged them to do spiteful things to me also and to pit them against the OPR).

4) At a reception hosted by the Thai prime minister the whole government, the parliamentary leadership, the entire diplomatic corps, the army high command, Supreme Court judges, bankers, businessmen, etc., etc. In short, everyone who was anyone in that country was present. Even so I noticed that Czechs were standing around talking mainly to Czechs. This is highly inappropriate and in fact almost boorish. Anyone from the OPR who feels hurt by this remark because he also engaged in conversation with Thais, please don't be upset because the exception proves the rule. It certainly didn't apply across the board. But it was my misfortune that wherever my glance fell, there, amid a dozen Thais, was a Czech talking to a Czech, if not standing completely alone. (. . .)

6) As you all know, I'm a pub person, I'm curious about everything,

nothing can shock me. Therefore, when I walked down that famous avenue in Bangkok which you all know, it deeply pained my heart to have to avoid the little lanes of the red-light district. How happy I would have been to have seen this just once in my life! But I knew that I was a guest of the king, that the king is informed of my every movement, and that I simply couldn't permit myself to do it. Why am I mentioning this? I consider it unfortunate that almost all of my delegation, with the minister of finance in the lead, ventured into these places (. . .) and that moreover they took pictures of each other there. (. . .) What the Thai king thought about it I don't know. (. . .)

(February 21, 1994)

(. . .)

5) I haven't had the mental or physical strength to write my speech to the European Parliament. Nevertheless I have diligently read everything I have received on the subject. From various pieces of advice and suggestions it's pretty clear to me what ought to be in the speech: Europe as a political reality that is seeking a new (nonviolent) way of being; West and East; the spiritual and intellectual, nontechnocratic side of integration. The problem is this, that I have already written and talked many times about precisely this subject. Does that matter? Further, I have a question: Is it possible to broach certain topics? A reading of all the documents of the European Community and the European Union has persuaded me that it is an immensely complicated and confused package full of administrative *ptydepe* that can be understood only by professional bureaucrats, not citizens. It cries out for a simple European Union charter and a simple, clear constitution that would somehow underpin or cover this package (in no way changing it): it would simply make it a comprehensible thing. At the same time it occurred to me that unlike other great European empires of the past, the EU doesn't have its own obvious and single head, as a result of which it seems like an amorphous monstrosity composed of many different intertwined institutions and bodies. It clearly needs the office of a president (if it can no longer be an emperor), which would be purely representative and would provide a solid center for the whole structure. He could be nominated by the Euro-

pean Council and elected by the European Parliament. The European Union will be a formation more confederate in nature, but even such a formation should have its own clear head, its apex. The European Union consists entirely of collective organizations and rotating functions, a phenomenon typical of countries on the point of falling apart (Yugoslavia). Perhaps it's inappropriate for me to expand on such thoughts, and I mention it only because it occurred to me. Be that as it may, we must have a meeting about this before next weekend, when I have to write it. (. . .)

(February 27, 1994)

1) I attach the speech to the European Parliament. (. . .) The deadline for any final comments is Monday afternoon so that Monday evening I can incorporate them into the text and then send the definitive version to the Castle Tuesday morning. (. . .)

5) More about the trip to Rome and Strasbourg: from the beginning I had imagined that it would be a small working trip, not a monstrous State Visit, and that all of us, with a few reporters, would fit into the Challenger. I was somewhat taken aback to discover how many of us were going and that we were going to fly again in that big monster. I gave my assent—what else could I do when it was already decided and when, moreover, it was explained to me that everyone's participation was essential? It's probably too late to change it now, but I confess that it makes me wonder more and more. We are going to have to learn someday to fly in small numbers! For example, for the D-Day celebrations I definitely want to take the Challenger with a minimal delegation. My co-workers should probably learn multitasking: they should be interchangeable; they should take turns; and those who've already been somewhere should provide exhaustive written information to all the others so that the sum of acquired experience becomes the property of all. The larger the delegation, the more work it has to look after itself and the more extraneous people it needs—and of course, the more it costs. I am expecting that the government, which, as is well known, is not especially fond of me, will sooner or later begin to draw attention to the size of my entourages. (. . .)

Washington, April 9, 2005

Yesterday I watched the pope's funeral on television. It was a grand and moving spectacle. I knew the pope, and I'd even dare say that we were friends, and perhaps for that very reason I was incapable of experiencing any great sorrow at his death. The thing is, I had a visceral feeling that, with great peace in his soul, he was departing for a place he knew he was going to, a good place. But America is a rather odd country. It's very religious, and at the same time it allows the broadcast of the pope's funeral to be interrupted by advertisements, many of which were the direct embodiment of what he had criticized for his entire life. I found it truly hard to understand, and it made me more and more uncomfortable, until I finally switched the television off.

In the years before 1989, whom did you talk about politics with and in what way? And who was your strongest opponent? What did you argue most about?

In the Czechoslovak antitotalitarian opposition, which means chiefly the members of Charter 77, there were people with a broad range of positions, from Trotskyites to reform communists, various types of socialists, people who declared themselves liberals, Christian Democrats, or conservatives, as well as many people who refused to be put into any kind of predefined political pigeonhole. They all, of course, discussed things among themselves, frequently very passionately, but it was fascinating to see how the existence of a common enemy, and a common antitotalitarian program based on the idea of human rights, led to everyone pulling on the same end of the rope in certain fundamental matters. These political discussions, in other words, never aroused antipathy, enmity, or hostility among the participants. For example, I remember vividly the endless political sparring that went on between two of the most active and perhaps the most closely cooperating chartists, the Catholic conservative Václav Benda and the inveterate left-winger Petr Uhl. They were a welcome and sometimes rather suspenseful fixture at many of our dissident meetings or parties. I myself often felt inclined to play the devil's advocate—that is, to put forward arguments opposing the one who happened to have the upper hand.

Washington, April 9, 2005

Two days ago the new Ukrainian president, Yushchenko, was here on a work-ing visit. I was invited to one of the larger meetings with him, a very cordial encounter where I was asked to speak off-the-cuff. I delivered a shorter version of what I have been thinking for some time now: after the fall of communism, or rather of the totalitarian system of the communist type, there arose in most countries of the former Soviet bloc a transitional phase that we might provi-sionally call "postcommunism." It's a period of unprecedented and rapid pri-vatization not yet contained within a solid, tried-and-true legal framework and in which, naturally, the former communist nomenklatura, or commu-nist enterprise managers, took a significant part. These people had the appro-priate information and contacts (those who had been excluded, of course, could not have such information and contacts), which meant that they formed the core, or at least an influential sector, of the new entrepreneurial class. They know that democracy means freedom of expression and political association, but they are clever enough to impose limits on these freedoms. The system they favor is, therefore, not truly open but rather has a tendency to close in upon itself. In subtle ways, the economic power links up with political power and the power of the media to create something I once called Mafia-capitalism, though it could equally be called Mafia-democracy. (I refer to Zakaria's dis-tinction between democracy and freedom or Popper's analysis of open and closed political systems.) In every country that has rid itself of communism, postcommunism takes on a different form, but very few countries can avoid it altogether.

But as the years go by and a new generation comes to maturity, the public gradually begins to lose patience with that state of affairs, until one day it revolts. And what happens then is a kind of second-generation revolution or— more precisely—a completion of the original revolution. The issue is no longer a settling of accounts directly with communism, but rather with this out- come—this postcommunism (in the sense that I speak of it here). And just as postcommunism has a slightly different form in each country, the revolts against it are different as well: revolt can sometimes take the form of a surpris- ing shift in voter support (that's how the Slovaks settled with Mečiarism), at other times the peaceful pressure of popular demonstrations (Georgia, Ukraine). The particular importance of the Ukrainian Orange Revolution is not, however, that it took place in such a large and important country in the former Soviet empire or that it inspired many countries still burdened with postcommunism, but in something perhaps even more significant: that revolu- tion gave a clear answer to a still open question: where does one of the major spheres of civilization in the world today (the so-called West) end, and where does the other sphere (the so-called East, or rather Euro-Asia) begin? I recall— and I mentioned this during my meeting with Yushchenko—that an important American politician once asked me where Ukraine belongs. My impression is that it belongs to what we call the West. But that's not what I said; I said that this was a matter for Ukraine to decide for itself.

But this all requires a small proviso: today, if you say a country is part of the West, it sounds like a mild form of approval; on the contrary, if it is part of the East, it sounds like mild condemnation. But all of that is the typical expression of a Western sense of superiority. There is no shame attached to being part of the East, just as being part of the West is not automatically a virtue. Simply put, the global world of today can hope for a decent and peace- ful life only if, among other things, there is an absolutely evenhanded coopera- tion among various large supranational or regional entities, defined in terms of their civilization, their history, their culture, and their geographical posi- tion. A necessary condition for such cooperation, however, is a clear agreement on where a particular sphere begins and where it ends. In short, there must be a clear agreement on mutual borders. Only clearly delineated and defined enti- ties can be genuine and creative partners; in the future, any vague or blurred or disputed border can only be—as it was with nation-states in the past—a source of instability, tension, and ultimately war. That's why I think that the creation of a new political world order requires that special attention be paid to the problem of borders between individual spheres of civilization, a problem that can be solved only if the spheres that are momentarily wealthier cease to consider themselves superior to those that are momentarily poorer.

And this brings me back to Ukraine: after the fall of the Iron Curtain, all of Central Europe, and the Balkans as well, declared themselves part of the West. It was undoubtedly the right decision, growing out of a proper understanding of their own history and culture. Where, however, does this West, defined by its values but also by its geography, end on the eastern flank? How can it cooperate meaningfully with anyone else when it is not clear about its own borders, that is, in essence, its own identity? A justified feeling that it's important to decide clearly on the mutual borders of these newly arising supranational political entities—and thus as well on the proper limits to the eventual expansion of their structures and organizations—clearly lay behind the question that American politicians once asked me.

A glance at the map, and at history, will tell us clearly where Ukraine belongs, but I genuinely believed that Ukraine itself should have the deciding word. Now, to my delight, it has given it, fifteen years after the old world order collapsed.

After your return from prison in 1983, you were given one prestigious prize after another: in the United States, three Obies; in 1986, the Erasmus Prize; in 1989, the Peace Prize awarded by German booksellers at the Frankfurt Book Fair; and so on. Did you ever start worrying that you were becoming more of a political icon than a writer? That the West, by giving you all these awards, was, in fact, driving you away from art and into politics?

For the sake of precision: I won my first two Obies in the 1960s, that is, at a time when I certainly could scarcely have been an "icon." I admit that later, when I was in prison or after my release, the various honorary doctorates and prizes I received might have been conferred less as an expression of admiration for my work and more out of respect for something I might call my "story." I was seen as someone who had held to his own truth, who had been willing to go to prison for it, who had turned down an offer of emigration and then come out of prison and begun doing exactly what he had been doing before. That's a nice, understandable story. I can smile at it, and I can tell myself as often as I want that I'm not as nice as my story and therefore not entirely worthy of all these prizes, but at the same time I have to admit that it's actually a very good thing that a story like mine is noticed, respected, and rewarded. On the one hand, it contributes to the general good by confirming certain values or standards, or rather the meaning of a certain kind of work; on the other hand, it represents a very concrete form of support for that work, which, because of this recognition, is taken ever more seriously. Who knows whether, without that international attention, I would have survived my prison sentence or whether I might not have gone to prison for fifteen years instead of five.

The continuation of my story was a little different: I received most of the honorary doctorates and prizes when I was president, when the arc of my story was completed in a way that was almost like a fairy tale, if not pure kitsch: little Honza—although everyone tells him it's hopeless—beats his head against the wall for so long that the wall eventually collapses and he becomes king and rules and rules and rules for thirteen long years. Yes, this "fairy-tale" aspect of the story can naturally make it seem that I have enjoyed, and still enjoy, more admiration than I deserve, but I wouldn't make light of that either. After all, why shouldn't such a story with such a happy ending be exalted? Might it not be a source of hope for others who have not yet experienced the fall of their wall? My own personal feelings about it are not important. And something else: I also saw these awards, among other things, as a kind of caress that balanced the endless, invisible, and exhausting tribulations that lay hidden behind the presidential part of my story.

You were nominated several times for the Nobel Peace Prize. Does it bother you that you never received it?

Every real man is a little bit ambitious. I'd be lying if I pretended that I didn't care whether I got the prize or not. Of course it would please me; indifference or contempt on my part would only be an expression of great vanity. I remember, for example, how annoyed I felt when Jean-Paul Sartre refused the Nobel Prize in Literature. Maybe I'm doing him an injustice, but at the time I saw it as a form of grandstanding, a way of playing the rebel.

In the period of communism the Nobel Prize would have considerably invigorated our struggle, that's obvious. During my presidency, however, I would have felt awkward about accepting it. I think that politicians in office have a duty to work for peace and for a better and more just world; you might say that's what they're paid for, and so it's better that the prize go to someone who works for a good cause voluntarily, and possibly at great risk. That kind of recognition always emboldens such people and their struggle in very concrete ways, and therefore it must not merely be a reward for past merits.

Washington, April 11, 2005

We've rented a nice little house in Georgetown. Almost every evening we go to a local bar; yesterday we went to one with Madeleine, who lives around the corner. Before that we visited some acquaintances who have a beautiful house in the middle of the countryside just outside Washington, and earlier we accompanied Martin Palouš, my longtime friend and now the Czech ambassador to the USA, to an unbelievable Sunday religious service. It was a black congregation. There was a tremendous sense of community. They sang magnificently and, in a kind of ecstacy, communicated not only with their Christian God, but through him perhaps with all the deities that humankind has ever had. The atmosphere of friendship, mutual respect, and solidarity was fascinating.

After several days in Washington it seems to me that people here are, on the whole, far kinder to one another than back home. They are long-suffering (the hours that they sit patiently behind the steering wheel during rush hour moving forward a couple of meters at a time!); they are considerate (you can tell the nature of a society by the way drivers behave toward pedestrians; I remember how in Moscow the drivers thought of pedestrians as insects who either had to get out of the way or get run over); they are cheerful, good-natured, understanding, they have smooth complexions, they have nice haircuts; it's obvious that they have time to look after themselves. They all say hello to each other, and the main thing is—they're hardworking! People here actually do a full day's work.

After September 11 things have obviously gotten much stricter here; you're continually running up against bureaucracy. There are forms to fill out, police checks, baggage inspections, and so on, but the most interesting thing is that absolutely no one complains about it, as would be the case back home. Not only does everyone understand this, but they even accept it—or so it seems to me—as something done in the interests of their own safety. Back home a policeman—fifteen years after the fall of the totalitarian system and the end of the police state—is still unconsciously seen as an enemy of the citizen; here people see him far more as their defender.

As a dissident you wrote about the skepticism that the very word "peace" aroused in people of the Soviet bloc, not to mention the phrase "the struggle for peace." That was a very provocative idea in the West, and yet you were given the prestigious Olof Palme Peace Prize. Did not that seem to you a little odd?

On the contrary: I was glad that my thoughts at the time were understood very precisely. A criticism of the stupid totalitarian misuse of the word "peace" is not an expression of distaste for peace itself but merely a distaste for lies and deception.

Washington, April 11, 2005

The center of this city reminds me in some ways of ancient Egypt: just as they built enormous pyramids to memorialize their pharaohs, some of the most important American presidents also have great memorials here. To a Central European, with his traditional indifference or even distaste for the grandiose, it can seem rather comic, but in essence it's endearing: society lets it be known that it has a history, that it knows about it, and that it respects it and that it remembers those who helped create that history. Part of the traditional American sense of democracy (most people once arrived here with the same-sized bundle, that is, with no prior privileges or advantages) is clearly a certain respect for political authority, be it the office or the person in it. Although even here, as we know, you can really go after someone politically, even the president. But the neoclassical architecture of some of the government buildings gets less of my respect. They are uninventive replicas of antique architecture appropriately inflated (they remind me of Fellini's enlarging eye) and appropriately soulless. There's a broad range of modern architecture here. You can see beautiful buildings alongside absolutely boring blocks of concrete.

(March 15, 1994)

1) First, some brief information about the state of my health: all day Saturday, Sunday, and Monday I was incapable of doing anything, not even reading. I merely slept, perspired, thrashed about on the bed, or stared at the ceiling. I also had horrific, feverish dreams; for example that S. called on me immediately to resign the presidency because I had insulted six neighboring countries. Today, Tuesday, is the first day I've felt more or less normal, and so I am gradually getting back to my desk. So far I've had a wide-ranging conversation with Mr. S., and we've agreed on certain things. Besides that, I telephoned Honza Ruml to find out what they're doing about Zhirinovsky's visit. I was satisfied with his response. If the press wants to know my opinion, please do not issue a statement without consulting me.

2) During the time that I was unable to do anything, not even read, I occasionally thought things over, that is in my better moments. I thought about several specific things, but mainly about something that might be called the conception of my presidency over the next few months, or rather for this year, and I concluded that out of the amorphous mass of my activities certain priorities should regularly, and in various forms, emerge—something like my "presidential themes." That is, it seems to me as though my presidency has been—if I may put it that way—not

"thematic" enough. I have been too much the object of events, reacting to them one way or another, and not enough in control. (. . .) I simply feel the need to create a more specific political profile for myself and to give a more specific profile as well to the mode and style of my presidency. I am satisfied with the first year but only on one assumption: that it be seen not as an example of how I intend to act as president until the end, but rather as a year of preparation. I've settled into the new country, the new position of president, the new political situation. I've looked for my place in the sun, tried to stake out my territory, and, last but not least, I have shaken off the filth with which I was smeared by the press during the period when I was not president. (. . .)

3) (. . .) (b) Therefore I feel the need to foreshadow these themes and regularly—in a variable way!—to return to them. Another possible "presidential theme" from the area of domestic policy: energy. Here I see one great absurdity: we are building the nuclear power station at Temelín to give us more energy—and at the same time we are trying to lower energy consumption in the field of production. We are building Temelín to reduce the mining of brown coal and to get rid of our coal-fired generators—and at the same time, the mining goes merrily on, consumption is not decreasing one bit, the plans to reduce the mining of coal are minimal, and no one is shutting down any of the coal-fired generating plants. This calls for an objective analysis not only from the sources provided by the minister, Mr. Dlouhý, but also from the various green movements.

We want to enter NATO, and we emphasize how important it is to offer the world an army that is ready to go into action—and at the same time the army is psychologically pushed back to the peripheries of life (the oath-taking is allowed to take place only in fields outside the city, as though we were actually ashamed of the army). In other words: we shouldn't visit just the general headquarters but arrange brief, unannounced visits to individual units as well. Right now, we have a company based a short distance from Sarajevo. Doesn't that provide an opportunity for me to visit them for half a day, before Zieleniec or Baudyš swing into action?

The "presidential themes" naturally exist in foreign policy as well. I will list them in brief: since 1989 I've been consistently concerned with what is called the architecture of Europe, or the new European order.

I've given dozens of important speeches on this theme, most recently in the European Parliament. But it has always been to a large degree the work of happenstance: on one occasion I was invited to the NATO headquarters; on another I was invited to the American Congress; at yet another time, to speak to the parliamentary assembly of the Council of Europe or at its summit; I've been at two summits of the CSCE; I spoke at a Prague meeting of the Council of Ministers of the CSCE and at a conference on a European confederation, etc., etc., etc. I've always spoken on the same theme, but in fact it's always been only because the country sent me somewhere or I was invited somewhere (even my appearance in the European Parliament was the idea of the Ministry of Foreign Affairs). Shouldn't we take more active control of this "presidential theme" and devise for me the kind of program that would systematically develop it, as it were, over time, conceived in dramatic terms, not just in the time that flows around us and offers occasional opportunities? (. . .)

4) I have been speaking of civic society from time immemorial and about the nonprofit sector, and about decentralization; I have been talking about the possibility of bombing Serbian positions for more than a year. Everyone was against it and now everyone's for it. It even appears that this attack might produce a genuine cessation of hostilities, but no one will remember that there was someone here who predicted that that would happen. (. . .)

(April 17, 1994)

(. . .)

4) Sometime in the next little while (before the grand duke's visit) I would like to have a meeting with Mr. D. (possibly with other interested parties, and with Olga) about the food, the dishes, the cutlery, the style of service, and so on at the Castle. After several years of domestic and foreign experience I believe I have some germane remarks to make on the subject. Just one example: the more exotic and unusual the food with which they intend to honor us, the more tasteless it is, so you have no idea what you're eating. Or another thing: there is apparently a stash of beautiful silver cutlery that some old crone is hoarding in a cupboard somewhere in the Castle, and she refuses to allow it to be used, so that

during our banquets we are compelled to eat with whatever the catering service in question provides us with, tasteful or not.

(May 9, 1994)

(. . .)

6) Why does my computer make the space between every line a different width? (. . .) Why does it often become so fond of a certain piece of text that it prints it over and over again and can't be stopped? (. . .)

8) I want to discuss, in detail, the final composition of our delegation and entourage to Romania, Bratislava, for D-Day, to the USA in July, and to the USA in September and lock it in at our very next program meeting, so that it will be clear to everyone well into the future where they're going and where they're not going. I have my own questions about this. (. . .)

(June 7, 1994)

(. . .)

3) (. . .) I would ask the DFP to write a thank-you letter to the English queen and the French president. It's appropriate to remind the queen and, in a separate letter, Major, that both of them promised me they will do everything they can to ensure that the queen comes next year, that I am reminding them of this in this way, and that I am hoping that it will work out well.

(. . .)

5) I would ask Mr. Řechtáček to please repair and refill my lighter and send it back. (. . .)

(September 11, 1994)

(. . .)

8) Kalvoda promised that his office would write various support documents (arguments) for a speech in parliament that would touch on the importance of reforms to the civil service. Kalvoda is not always the most

reliable person, and therefore it will be necessary to gently remind him. (. . .)

9) More on the question of the composition of our entourage to the USA: (a) at one time T. told me, though he wasn't happy about it, that only one pistoleer could travel with me. Now he says that there must be at least two. Fine. Let there be two. If he could be one of them, I would welcome that. But there can't be an extra one, for a total of three. That would contradict the whole concept of minimalizing the entourage. (. . .)

(October 23, 1994)

1) It's noon on Sunday and I have spent some time gathering my strength to write a speech for November 17. I'm reading the notes that I've received. I'm thinking about how to conceive it, and it's becoming more and more clear to me that this has to be a meeting specifically with students, and not with young people in general. Not only because it smells of the communist cliché (our youth, our young people, the future of the nation, the Czechoslovak Union of Youth, the Union of the Young, Youth Leads Brno, etc., etc.), but above all it makes it impossible for me to address a specific community and to speak about the importance of getting an education, about the traditions of student rebellions, the traditions of November 17, etc., etc. I'd have to always be putting in phrases like "our working youth," and ultimately it would collapse into banality. I can address apprentices at another time. I'm writing about this now mainly because invitations will probably be going out soon. Let there be a couple of Boy Scouts, a couple of Sokols, maybe even a couple of students from 1939. Even so the main public should be university students (and perhaps a smaller group of high school students). I don't want to set up a Youth Day: I don't know how we would invite young people as a whole and why we would make November 17 a day for youth when it's a day for students.

2) Over the weekend some of you will have received a new version of the speeches for October 28 to the mayors and to the Congress of the Pen Club. Monday afternoon is the last chance for you to make or suggest small changes, either stylistic or otherwise. Twelve o'clock should be the final deadline for all three of these speeches. We can't play around with

them anymore after that. Something will certainly be found; I myself know already of at least one word that I would strike out (in the October 28 speech) and about two sentences that seem to me unclear. Please make this your top priority. (. . .)

(October 30, 1994)

1) I am sending the speech for November 17. I'm not entirely happy with it. It seems to me to be a little rough and does not have a strong enough message. (. . .) The deadline for remarks is noon on Friday, because I intend to do the final edit on Saturday. (. . .)

(November 27, 1994)

1) If Dr. Kalvoda keeps his word, I will get a letter from him by courier on Monday informing me of the proposal by the foreign minister, Zieleniec, to grant the government, once and for all, general powers to negotiate international agreements, and he will ask me for my position. It's already arranged that I will give him, by return of courier, a negative response. (He agrees with this.) It would have caused constitutional problems because by permanently delegating to the government a power that now lies within the presidential competency, I would be posing the question as to why the constitution had not already given this power directly to the government. I would like someone to start preparing this letter right away. It's enough to consult with me on the text by telephone before it's sent, and then it can be printed out on my presigned letterhead, which I include now, and then it can be sent by courier to Kalvoda.

2) (. . .) (e) From Friday, December 9, until Tuesday, December 13, I want to be closeted in Lány and to be disturbed by absolutely nothing so that I can, in peace and quiet, concentrate on writing the New Year's speech. I have, practically speaking, no other time to do it. I would appreciate it if, during that period, one of my colleagues could be available in Prague so that I could send him separate versions for immediate consultation. A couple of people outside the Castle could read it as well. It has to be, for the time being, the culmination of all my recent

speeches—and that requires an extended period of focused time. In other words, I must not be disturbed by anything during this time. (. . .)

3) (. . .) (c) I should meet unofficially before Christmas with Kalvoda and Lux in the Little House: we haven't seen each other for a long time, and I've spoken with Kalvoda about it and he's very keen to do it. It would be a meeting analogous to last year's (again we met before the New Year's speech and I attempted to lay the ground for its favorable reception). It seems that the frequency of my contacts with Klaus is growing, and it's not balanced with contacts with his coalition partners. (d) Miloš Zeman is constantly inviting me for a beer. Sooner or later I'm going to have to give in, but perhaps we could arrange it for sometime in January. (. . .)

(December 11, 1994)

I am sending the first draft of the New Year's speech, which I managed to sweat out of myself, though the birth pangs were extremely difficult. (. . .) I welcome specific edits in the text, cuts, changes in formulation, additions. My advisers need not torture me by including essays and justifications for their remarks. I would likewise welcome it if it were possible to coordinate, if not all, then at least some of the remarks. It would greatly simplify my work because the worst thing is to have to deal in parallel with incompatible remarks. I know that the style is occasionally awkward, and therefore I would welcome any tidying up of the language. The deadline should be Friday so that I can do my final edit on Saturday. (. . .)

(December 25, 1994)

(. . .)

4) In March I'm due to make an important speech in parliament, and it would be good if the office would start now to assemble the materials for it. (. . .) In general my concern is that just as the New Year's speech went a step beyond the speech for October 28, so the speech in parliament should go a step beyond the New Year's speech. (. . .)

7) (. . .) More about those laws: if parliament passes them in their original form, it will be necessary to say that I don't take this as a personal defeat because I don't see my right to return the laws for reconsideration as in a tennis match. I'm behaving in harmony with my conscience and with my sense of justice, and the point for me is to express, through my actions, my opinion as head of state. If this opinion is overruled, I bow to the collective wisdom of parliament, which reflects the collective wisdom of the public. Should it appear necessary to me, my responsibility, however, is to go against even this collective wisdom, with the proviso that if the collective wisdom prevails, I will, as a democrat, fully respect that decision. (. . .)

(December 29, 1994)

(. . .)

4) As far as the Conversations are concerned (. . .) I would like to talk about the theme of urbanism, preserving the character of our towns and cities, about methodological approaches to architectural competitions for the designing of prominent buildings and similar matters. I'd also like to get in a final word about the Four Seasons (all the more so because Koukal has quite misrepresented the content of our conversation) and let my presidential themes come back dramatically, alternate and intertwine. (. . .)

Washington, April 11, 2005

I've just realized that on my laptop, which I don't even know how to operate properly, there are stashed away, unbelievably, several thousand pages of instructions that I wrote—mostly on weekends—to my staff from 1993 until the end of my presidency in 2003. It was a little bit like a diary. I've decided to splice some excerpts from these ancient memos into this book; perhaps they will reveal more about the life of a president in the Czech Republic than many a reflection after the fact. It will be a very difficult choice, because it will be hard to judge which are more important and which less, which are still lively, and which are simply endlessly and incomprehensibly boring, which of these confidential instructions to a few of my colleagues the book will sustain, and which not. And so, in the end, I will choose them more or less randomly; at the same time—for the sake of clarity—I will make tiny corrections where necessary. Perhaps I might have found passages that were more interesting, more historically important, more suspenseful, I don't know; I can't really judge.

But I must admit to two fundamental impressions from reading those ancient, hastily written instructions, intended to be read only by my most immediate staff. 1) I realize—and this is encouraging—that in fact I have always thought more or less the same way and worked—how successfully is another matter—to achieve the same things. 2) I now better understand, after the fact, one of Mr. Hvížďala's first questions, the one about ingratitude. When I think of all those thousands of meetings I held as president, of how many worries and preparations were necessary for every one of them and how many things I had to, and wanted to, think through, and how many questions I had to answer—from the very basic ones concerning the future organization of the world to the most petty ones concerning, for instance, the placement of cutlery or the seating arrangements for some official dinner—it occurs to me that not only will no one ever be able to fully appreciate all that but that today, practically no one knows about it anymore.

How wonderful it is, by comparison, to be a writer! You write something in a couple of weeks, and it's here for the ages. What will remain when presidents and prime ministers are gone? Some references to them in textbooks, most likely inaccurate.

What a pity I don't have those memos from the very beginning, that is, from 1989. I wrote them when I was Czechoslovak president as well, and most likely they are scattered somewhere among my colleagues at the time. I haven't gone looking for them; perhaps they'll surface somewhere, sometime.

Politics works with personification: for the breakdown of the totalitarian Soviet empire, the West already had a pope from the East, a worker from Poland, and now it needed a "third king" for the game, an intellectual who had suffered five years in prison for his beliefs.

This story was fascinating for the West, where something like that is impossible. You must have known and sensed all of that, and yet you accepted the role that was offered to you even though it held many hidden dangers. Weren't you tempted to play the role of the rebel for the West as well, that is, to reject the role that someone else had begun to write for you?

I have always done what I believed to be right and not what someone else prescribed for me. In any case I know of no one having prescribed anything for me. I only know what we've talked about already: that my "story" had some of the features of a fairy tale with a moral, and as such it attracted more attention than I might have desired or than was appropriate. As for being critical of the West, I have no need to criticize the West to show some kind of "balance," in other words to demonstrate my independence: I'm secure in my independence and therefore feel no need to demonstrate it. I have been trying to subject the West, and in fact modern civilization in general, to critical reflections for a very long time now, but I'm not led to do so for any other reason than an attempt to speak the truth and a sincere concern about where humanity is headed.

Washington, April 12, 2005

That reminds me of one of my recent experiences: I gave a speech in Paris for the representatives of the largest multinational corporations, the actual rulers of our current global world. I wrote a pointed speech that was highly critical of the behavior of global corporations, of their unscrupulousness, of the growing uniformity of the world, of the omnipresent dictatorship of advertisements, of profit, and so on. I was extremely nervous before the speech, which I read in English, because I was afraid that they would boo me off the stage or walk out in protest. Just the opposite happened: they listened to me very attentively, and when the speech was over I was given an enormous round of applause that ended with a standing ovation. There are three ways to explain this: 1) they weren't applauding what I said but me personally, or more precisely the "icon" that Mr. Hvížďala is talking about, that is, my "story," with its touch of the fairy tale about it and the remarkable happy ending; 2) they were applauding themselves, that is, their limitless power and their broad-mindedness in hiring such a sharp critic of their own activities to whom they could, at the same time, pay their respects and thus, in fact, in the most elegant way imaginable, undermine his ideas; 3) I don't discount the possibility that they simply agreed with me and were glad that someone had said it for them. Many of them, in what they do, may not be expressing their true feelings about the world and about how it ought to flourish but are merely being dragged along by the gigantic "automatism" of modern civilization, which they dare not say anything against, because in doing so they might risk their own livelihoods, the ambivalence of which they are very well aware.

Let's move on to some of the specific events in the second half of the 1980s: on September 4, 1988, in Lipnice, you publicly appeared before your fellow citizens for the first time since August 1968, when you spoke to the workers in Ostrava. You were invited to the podium of the Lipnice folk festival by the moderator, Jan Rejžek. How do you recall that event?

It was a very brave idea. It came from Jarmila Poláková and Jan Rejžek, and in the dressing room I first made sure that none of the performers would mind. At the time they might very easily have been handed out some rather severe punishments—for example, there might have been a ban on any more such public performances. But they all agreed, which in itself testified to a shift in the social climate. At that time people probably didn't know what I looked like, but they obviously knew my voice well enough from the foreign radio broadcasts, and they were no doubt familiar with my story and my opinions. I can't otherwise explain the huge applause that followed my arrival on the stage. Part of that applause belonged to the festival organizers for their courageous idea.

On October 21, 1988, in the framework of a theatrical "magazine" called *Rozrazil No. 1*, the Brno-based Theater on a String performed your hour-long play *Tomorrow*, naturally without mentioning the author. What was that experience like?

Rozrazil No. 1 was a special journalistic show that Theater on a String prepared for the approaching seventieth anniversary of the founding of Czechoslovakia. Petr Oslzlý, a friend of mine and the theater's dramaturge, asked me at the time to write something for the show. I decided that I would write a kind of theatrical reconstruction of what one of the founders of Czechoslovakia, Alois Rašín, might have experienced on the night before the declaration of independence. The theater rehearsed the play without anyone discovering that I had written it. They staged it, and shortly after the premiere, on October 28, that is, on the very day of the big anniversary, it played in Prague. I was supposed to attend the Prague performance, but I didn't make it because I was in police custody for the whole two days. I only heard that the performance was a success and that outside the windows of the theater during the performance you could hear the rumbling of armored vehicles going into action against the unofficial and more or less spontaneous demonstration by which some citizens were commemorating the anniversary. I saw the play for the first time after the Velvet Revolution, an event whose preparation, in some ways, turned out to be reminiscent of the play itself. The October 28 performance, too, took great courage, and it, too, was a sign that the ice would soon begin to break.

(January 22, 1995)

I've written the first draft of the German speech. Please see that it is quickly distributed to all the usual Castle vetters and other experts (including Gruša) so that as far as possible all the remarks can be coordinated by next weekend. As usual I would welcome it if there were no voluminous commentaries, explanations of the meaning of remarks, and microessays on the margins of the theme, but rather concrete suggestions about the text itself—how to make it more precise, what to add, how to balance it, how to enrich it, and how to give it greater stylistic elegance. (*Bons mots* are welcome.) In my opinion it needs more zip, impact, a certain loftiness of style (like my speech on the occasion of Weizsäcker's visit to Prague, for example). I simply haven't been able to pull it off myself. It's another time, and I'm utterly fed up with the fact that various illiterates criticize me for everything. I'm losing confidence, and given the excessive volume of speeches I have to write it's also possible that the ink in my pen is drying out. All the more work, then, for my consultants. If many incompatible remarks or notes come in, I would ask someone, for example Mr. K., to sift through them and attempt to amalgamate them. (. . .)

(January 29, 1995)

1) I thank Mr. K. for his meticulous preparation of the comments on my speech. At first sight this new version, which I attach, will seem almost the same as the previous version. It is, however, a misleading impression. I worked for sixteen whole hours incorporating the remarks!!! It was incomparably more difficult than writing the speech itself. I tried to take everything into account. Even so, a lot of remarks remained unincorporated and many now appear in the text in a modified form. I would be able to explain at length why I did not incorporate individual notes, but perhaps that won't be necessary. If I had slavishly used all the suggested changes the result would be—among other things—an absurd hybrid with no sense of structure, style, or melody. But to some degree or other I have taken account of everything essential. (. . .)

2) A letter to Herzog: Dear Mr. President, As we agreed, I am sending you the text of my lecture on Czech-German relations. I will deliver it on February 17 in the Great Hall of the Charles University in Prague, which is organizing my appearance together with the Bertelsmann Foundation. It is intended to be part of both a lecture series sponsored occasionally by the university and the Bertelsmann's Series of talks on Germany. Czech Television will broadcast my speech live, and it can be expected to attract considerable attention both in the Czech and possibly also in the German media. The speech is to be a major statement intended to

initiate a new phase of Czech-German dialogue and cooperation, which in recent times has somewhat languished. It seems to me an appropriate time for such a revitalization because election year is over in Germany and the fiftieth anniversary of the end of World War II is approaching. I—like many other Czech officials—have plans for other activities as well (visits, invitations, and so on) that are aimed at reviving our relations. It may be that my speech will, in several places, seem somewhat harsh or pointed (particularly in the matter of Sudeten German claims), but I would ask that you understand the situation in which I find myself: the politicians and the public in this country hold me accountable for awakening Sudeten German revisionism by my apology for the expulsion, and they say that my apology was a grave political error. I naturally disagree, but I feel that since I have said unambiguously (and against the thinking of the majority of our society) what I think about the expulsion, I must at least, with the same emphatic tone, reject Sudeten German claims, which are being closely followed here with increasing uneasiness. (And some parties are even trying, through expressions of anti–Sudeten German sentiments, to gain voter support.) By the way: I think I've already told you that in 1991 I set in motion a daring initiative aimed at a partial rectification of the damage caused by the expulsions and that it was the German government that did not react to this initiative. Now something like that would be impossible, so greatly has the situation changed. (Mainly as a result of the increasing and ever-louder demands from the leadership of the Landsmannschaft, but for other reasons as well.) I would be very grateful if you would read my speech carefully, think about it, and, if appropriate, inform me in some way of what you think of it before I deliver it. As you will certainly understand, all of this is completely confidential between the two of us. If you were to decide to somehow publicly respond to my speech once it's delivered, even polemically, I would welcome it because it would be a clear signal that a concrete dialogue has been renewed. I look forward to your coming unofficial visit to our country, and I send you my best wishes. Yours, Václav Havel.

3) When Mr. S. speaks with S., have him slip him my report on Auschwitz—as a gesture of my good intentions to cooperate with the ministry. The DFP will probably have to edit the text a little and give it the necessary packaging (I don't know what kind). Report on talks in

Auschwitz (secret!). On his own initiative Mr. Holbrooke, whom I had not known before this, sought me out and had a half-hour confidential conversation with me. He assured me of his regard for me; he said that he knows my speeches and articles and apologized that he wasn't at the dinner with Kissinger and he told me the following: the USA has a serious interest in our quickly becoming a member of NATO and they understand that it's a strategic necessity. Halfway through the year they will start talking about this inside NATO, and by the end of the year they could start negotiations with us. Apparently they have the unqualified support of GB (that corresponds to what Major told me). They have qualified support from France, and they see Germany as the main stumbling block. I asked him whether he felt that the Germans were supporting our membership in the EU because they play the dominant role in it and that they do not support our membership in NATO because there the main role is played by the USA and the Germans would rather deal with security issues in Central Europe themselves, or rather in cooperation with the Russians, without the assistance of the USA. He told me that that is precisely how it appears to him, and he asked whether I had any proof. I said that I have no direct evidence, that Kohl had even confirmed his support for our entry into NATO before our entry into the EU, but that various signs, the way certain German politicians have behaved, etc., create such an impression. He said that a great deal now depends on us, and specifically on me: we ought, apparently, to put some concerted pressure on the Germans, for it is now more or less up to them. He sees our entry into the EU as a long-term matter and strategically perhaps somewhat less important; he considers our joining NATO one of the fundamental tasks of this period. (. . .)

(February 25, 1995)

Dear Colleagues, I have read your comments on the first (incomplete) version of my parliamentary speech. I thank you for them but at the same time I wish to tell you quite frankly that if I have suffered over the writing of this speech for three days, then—if I wanted to comply with all your comments—I would have to suffer over it for another ten days. I would love to, but where would I find the time? A few things that you suggested to me I have incorporated; the majority, however, unfortunately not. For various reasons. For example: your comments contradicted one another. You all recommended a more personal and more essaylike tone at the expense of a survey of the ministerial resorts; yet almost all of you at the same time have drawn attention to ministries or themes of which I have not spoken and should speak about. Many of your comments, if taken into account, would expand the text, although all of you have recommended shortening it. Many of them would disrupt the style, the tone, and the kind of intellectual architecture or the way the ideas are structured or arranged in the speech. Anything more personal, more literary, more gently provocative you have cut. At the same time, however, you recommended a lighter, more personal, and more vigorous (more provocative) tone. Etc., etc., etc. In short: I took into account what I could, given the limitations of time and what I have just said; the speech is now written and, for the time being, edited; it's not going to get radically better. (Whose idea was it anyway that I should be writing a "state of the union" address? Was it me, for heaven's sake?)

(March 6, 1995)

(. . .)

3) My plan is that on Monday, while I'm in Holland, the speech will be delivered to the prime minister. That won't leave him time to publicly respond to it, but at the same time it will be a gesture that could perhaps result in his being mentally prepared for it, so that when I read it, he won't make too many faces at the cameras. If my speech upsets him slightly in advance, it won't be such a shock for him when I read it. If he doesn't have a chance to read it on Monday evening before my Tuesday appearance, it won't make a bit of difference. The very act of sending it to him ahead of time might just soften his response, even a little. (. . .)

5) More on those orders: I would ask the DDP to begin to prepare our list of those who should be decorated on October 28. I don't precisely know who already received an order during the federation and who did not. We have to have our list ready in time so that we will be more prepared than Tollner, who will come to us sooner or later with a (preliminary) list of suggestions from parliament. We mustn't forget to include

various fields of science, resistance against the Nazis and communism (Čermín, etc.), journalism (Tigrid!, Ducháček in memoriam, Medek, if he hasn't already been decorated, etc.). And of course, artists: Kundera, Škvorecký, Hrabal, Forman, Chytilová, Boštík, Bauch, Pištěk, Šimotová, Juráček, Voskovec, and Werich in memoriam?, Čestmír Kafka, Mikuláš Medek, Kohout, ? ? ? etc., etc., etc. And athletes: Navrátilová, Lendl, and such. Those who live abroad will have to be invited in time! (There will be problems, mainly with those who were at one time communists, but I'm prepared to go somewhat against the prevailing political opinion.) (. . .)

(April 16, 1995)

1) First some brief news about myself: I spent the first two days of Easter (Friday and Saturday) in a rather poor state. I was angry at the whole world; either because I have no Easter and I have to work (along with emergency room nurses and train drivers), or because I have to write so many speeches at once, or because I have such a thick file of documents and altogether so much weekend reading from you (circa three hundred pages), or because my printer isn't working and without it it's practically impossible to write speeches, or because I can't find anyone to repair it because everyone's away somewhere for the holidays. I felt as if I were out on a limb, a man betrayed by history, which has burdened him with endless tasks and now mocks him for his inability to master them, and I've paced back and forth like a lion in its cage consumed by anger at an unspecified perpetrator (even though the lightning rod that drew my ire was my staff). In the end, however, the situation took a turn for the better: on Saturday evening people were found who could at least make temporary repairs to my printer, and on Sunday morning, that is, today, I finally began to work. I am sending you the results: 1. the edited speech for May 5; all you have to do is decipher my notes and rewrite them in nice big letters; 2. my speech to the rural mayors. It's nothing special, and I'd welcome any improvements (why aren't the city mayors going to be there? Shouldn't it be called instead a Congress of Villages?); 3. a speech for NATO. This seems fairly good to me, and therefore I would only ask for a subtle retouching to improve its con-

tent and style. I will look the results over on Wednesday, and then it must be sent for immediate translation so that next weekend I'll be able to practice reading it in English!!! If I manage to write a speech for May 8 as well, I will attach it to this package; if I don't finish it, I will bring it with me, I hope, on Wednesday. I very much doubt that I will manage to write the Barcelona speech given that I've had this stupid loss of two days. (. . .)

6) In planning my program it will be necessary to include the fact that here and there I'll need time to prepare for meetings and visits. (Kuchma, the Swedish king, etc.). I must have the documentation in time and not just a few minutes before the event, when I generally have no time even to look at it. (. . .)

11) Sometime soon we must have a meeting about the state orders! I have various suggestions of my own. Parliament has already closed off its list of suggestions. I want to somehow clarify it and harmonize my own notions with those of parliament. (Voskovec, Werich, Vančura, Valenta, Josef Čapek, Bass, Kundera, Forman, Zenkl, Feierabend, Navrátilová, Lendl, Cáslavská, Tigrid, Medek, Ripka, Stránský, Kilián, Haken, Beňačková, Suk, Trnka, Hrabal, Škvorecký, Chytilová, Juráček, Boštík, Kafka, Šimotová, Bauch, Cardinal Tomášek, Cardinal Trochta, Wichterle, Hejdánek, Váchal, Zrzavý, Tichý, Halas, Holan, Kolář, etc., etc. Some may already have received the order; I can't remember.) (. . .)

14) I would ask Mr. M. to find out why the pope's visit has not yet gone to the cabinet and when they'll deal with it, and then I would ask him to call the cardinal with the results of his investigation. The thing is, the cardinal called me and asked me for an explanation. He's afraid that the Church is going to have to pay all the expenses. (. . .)

(April 23, 1995)

(. . .)

6) I learned from Mr. D. about the preliminary composition of the delegation to Moscow. I am very happy that the delegation is small. Of course it's lacking a "political" colleague who could advise me if a politically delicate situation should arise, but in any case the ambassador will

play that role. I would like as soon as possible to receive for my approval the composition of my delegations to Mons, to London, to the Litomyšl meeting in Hungary, and to Harvard. (Including reporters.) I usually don't find out about such things until it's too late to change anything.

(May 13, 1995)

1) (. . .) On Friday I found our house beautifully decorated with flowers. Nevertheless, all that beauty suddenly ceased to please me, for I was compelled to pose the question: Did the kind Castle flower ladies decorate my home illegally? Or will I receive a bill on Monday morning from the PCA for ten thousand crowns? If I had to pay that much each week for such a wealth of floral decoration, I would sooner give the money to some badly needed shelters for the homeless and buy myself a couple of ordinary bouquets from a flower shop now and then. Or: B. and J. keep telling me how difficult it is for Mrs. Oušková to launder my shirts, how much work she has, and how little money she gets for it, and how everyone is trying to solve this huge problem. For God's sake, give Mrs. Oušková what she deserves for her flawless ironing! Give it to her from my money, from the state's money, from the general budget, from sponsors, or however you want, but don't continually ask me about something or blame me for something. And if this problem is truly insoluble, then tell me and I'll find another laundress, even though no laundress in the world is, understandably, as flawless as Mrs. Oušková. Or: Olga lives in some sort of symbiosis with the gardeners in the greenhouses. She provides them with exotic seedlings and they cultivate some kind of plants for her, and then I suddenly learn that this symbiosis is illegal! Or: it was explained to me that any papers I have written on or thrown away, full of state secrets, I must shred, but the Castle cannot lend me the shredder and therefore I must carefully gather together all these papers in a secret place and every once in a while secretly transport them to the Castle shredder. But really, I'm not here to play the fool for anyone. Etc., etc., etc. You will certainly understand that when I spend far more time with these pseudoproblems than with, for example, the historic question of Czech-German reconciliation, I have a right to get upset. In short, sort this out any way you like, and please don't drag me into it anymore. And

one more thing: if the PCA interprets the law to mean that they don't have to look after me if I don't live in their residence, then I would ask the PCA whether it has any responsibility for me when I do stay in their residence. If the answer is "yes," then I would ask the PCA when it is going to compensate me for everything that was stolen from me from the residence which they administer (ninety thousand crowns in cash, a television set, a radio, a Dictaphone, a tape recorder, a new iron, etc.). And with that I will put this subject behind me forever. (. . .)

2) I would remind you of what I have already tentatively arranged with L.: I will ask him on Monday morning to invite the Russian ambassador to see him in the afternoon and then immediately afterward to call the MFA and inform them that he is going to be speaking with the ambassador in the afternoon and to demand the most recent and precise information about the proposed march-past of the Russian heroes of the genocidal Chechen war in front of my eyes. On the basis of the information obtained (and after any eventual consultation with the MFA) let him formulate my position (a question? an expression of bewilderment? protest? indignation?); he can consult with me about it by telephone and ultimately pass it on to the ambassador and immediately afterward give it to the ČTK. (. . .)

10) From the news I've just seen it follows that immediately after the cease-fire, called because of the anniversary, the Russians mounted an enormous offensive in Chechnya. It's an obscenity, and therefore I propose that L. add, to what he will say to Lebedev, my own urgent appeal to Yeltsin to immediately stop this military operation. Should that appeal take the form of a letter? Should I hand over the letter personally?

11) I spoke with Queen Sofia about the Spanish visit. They're both very much looking forward to it, but they want to see the historical and cultural sites, the teeming streets, and they want to go to a pub with me. Juan Carlos is not just your garden-variety king for whom the throne is a lounge chair. Therefore I'm recommending a nonstandard scenario: second day, by plane or helicopter, to Telč, a tour of the castle and a walk around the square: then by plane or helicopter to Krumlov, lunch there (the Rose Hotel is disgustingly decorated!), a tour of the city and the castle, and then return to Prague; dinner in the Rudolf Gallery, but full of small round tables, candles, intimate lighting, full of people. Some short performance or concert before or after the dinner in the Rudolf Gallery?

in the Spanish Hall? in the House of Children? A tour of the Castle.
Wouldn't it be possible to give him the Order of the White Lion? Naturally Nerudová Street and the Charles Bridge. They were here under
Husák, and it gave them the shivers. They want to see the changes that
have taken place here. After dinner, a pub, something teeming with life,
for example that pub where we went with Andulka. Full of normal cus-
tomers! Juan Carlos invited me into just such a pub on Majorca. In other
words, I ask that early and particular attention be given to this visit. I'll
be happy to attend any short meetings on this subject.

(June 24, 1995)

(. . .)

8) (. . .) (c) Institutional changes in the U.N. and the EU. Both of
these will become current issues in the fall, and therefore I would like
some suggestions and documentation. (My thoughts on the institutions of
the EU: a president as a symbolic embodiment of the ideas behind them,
without broad powers. A two-chamber parliament, a "people's assembly"—i.e., that which exists today, with a direct vote, representatives
based on the size of the population, etc.—and an assembly of nations
with equal representation from each country just as in the U.S. Senate,
every state represented by two senior members of its parliament, in other
words, not chosen by direct vote. The commission as a purely specialized
executive organ, without broad political powers, representation to which
does not depend on state citizenship but only on profession. The European Council: three kinds of voting: unanimous voting on fundamental
matters, majority voting (the number of votes according to the size of the
country) on matters of average importance (with the result binding on
everyone), and then voting, the result of which is binding for those members who so wish, that is, with the possibility of opting out. Further:
something like a charter embodying the fundamental ideas of the EU.
And then something like a constitution that would merge all the documents under which it is governed from the Treaty of Rome all the way to
Maastricht One and Maastricht Two into a single new and comprehensible text. The charter that applies today is understandable only to a
small group of experts.) (. . .)

(July 24, 1995)

(. . .)

17) Foreign Minister Zieleniec ceremoniously announced to me that he would be accompanying me on my trip to the U.N. This is obviously the result of a great internal struggle as well as pressure from the people around him. (We know how loath he is to travel somewhere with me so that he doesn't have to be in my shadow.) I would ask Mr. D. to ensure in time that we have the large aircraft, but the good one, not the crummy one. (. . .)

(August 10, 1995)

(. . .)

1) On the basis of documentation from S. I sketched in, for his private use, a draft of a Czech-German declaration. This is not so much a presidential intervention in this whole matter as it is literary assistance to a friend. He requested that I not give anyone anything of this to read and that I mention it to no one. I am just beginning to understand his caution. I did as he asked, and my little text was hand-delivered to him by special courier. (. . .) But I would ask that this whole matter not be spoken of anywhere. If anyone inappropriate were to learn that I had participated in this, the whole thing could fall through. We merely have to look at the speculation in the newspapers about who the negotiator is going to be, etc., etc. (. . .)

(November 3, 1995)

(. . .)

7) I agree that October 28 turned out well and that everyone who helped out deserves recognition. Once again I thank them. But at the same time I agree with all the small critical comments of V. and Š. I particularly regret that there were empty rows in the hall (I did not see

them). As always, this time too I warned several times that this could happen and I asked Mr. D. to arrange with a number of friendly guests at the reception, and with employees of the OPR, to kindly wait in reserve and, if need be, fill the empty seats in the hall. I don't know why this didn't happen. (. . .)

(November 26, 1995)

(. . .)

5) More specifically on the subject of Japan. I don't know what to take with me; I have no idea whether it's a hundred degrees below zero or a hundred degrees above; I don't know how I should dress for the emperor and for the speech, and whether I will have to change during the day or have anywhere to do it, whether I should wear only black suits everywhere, or whether gray or another color would be more suitable, or whether I should take something more sporty, which coat I should take, if coats are necessary at all, whether I need a tuxedo even in places where dark suits are called for. (I don't know a lot of other things as well—for example, how big the dinner with the speaker of the parliament will be, who will be there, and whether the dinner is being held only because of me and whether I have to propose a toast or not, what my various interviews should be about, what Wiesel's foundation is doing and what it is appropriate to say after the prize has been granted, what the prize is really for, etc., etc. These concrete details are more important for me than most of the information I get from the ministry, like how many square kilometers there are in Japan.) (. . .) I'd hate to discover once I get to Japan that I can approach the emperor only in tails, which I happen to have although I've never worn them. (. . .)

(December 17, 1995)

(. . .)

10) On Friday evening I saw the new illumination of the Castle. I hope that it's not final! There were two serious problems with it: (1) the

illumination was still (especially in comparison with St. Nicholas) not warm enough even though it was somewhat better than the "neon" that we've had so far. (2) A far more serious problem was with something else: green and yellow together, as is well known, produce purple. Therefore the green palace of the aristocrats became a revolting purple, almost like sugar candy, as though it were part of an incredibly tacky cake. It can't remain like that. We'd be a laughingstock!

(December 17, 1995)

To my great surprise, on Saturday evening (in four hours) I managed to write the unwritable, that is, the New Year's speech! (. . .)

Washington, April 12, 2005

Last night I was suddenly overcome by a fit of shivering. I had a temperature and I felt truly awful. I was quite frightened; it wouldn't be a good thing to fall ill here just a few days after our arrival. The thing is that every garden-variety virus is potentially fatal to me because it immediately turns into pneumonia and given that part of one of my lungs is gone and that I have some slightly tangled breathing tubes, it can turn into almost anything. Several times I have been on the point of dying, but somehow it's been Dáša, mainly, who has always managed to pull me out of it. This state before the virus or the flu or angina sets in is always extremely unpleasant. It is marked by a complete lack of energy and vigor. In normal circumstances, I have very little energy in the morning as it is, but if this particular state is added to it—as it was today— it's very bad. I didn't want to get out of bed at all, and I had to mobilize all my will to do so. I think a lot about my general state of health, and I have very mixed feelings about it. On the one hand I know that I am a rather tired, older man who should have the right to rest, but on the other hand I'm always for- getting and behaving as though there were nothing wrong with me and I fling myself into everything.

This evening we have a dinner at the embassy for some of the former American ambassadors to Prague who did wonderful work there and who even now wish to contribute to a good cause.

On February 21, 1989, you were sentenced once again, this time to nine months in prison. Did the course of the investigation and your imprisonment differ in any way from your previous experiences with the repressive institutions of communist power?

I think that this prison term merits particular notice because it reveals a lot about the events that preceded our revolution. In January of 1989 there was the twentieth anniversary of Jan Palach's suicide. The spokesmen of Charter 77 at the time were to lay flowers at the statue of St. Wenceslas, not far from where Palach set himself on fire in 1969 to protest the Soviet occupation. I decided to stand on the sidewalk and observe the ceremony on the sidelines so that if the police intervened I would be able to deliver a timely report to friends and the foreign media. The police actually did intervene, but so clumsily that it aroused the interest of passers-by and immediately mushroomed into a large spontaneous demonstration. I watched the whole thing from a distance, fascinated, although I knew that sooner or later they could arrest me. And then I walked away from Wenceslas Square to prepare my report. They arrested me on my way home and then, absurdly, found me guilty on the basis of false testimony and, as a result, the whole affair contributed considerably to the changing conditions, almost as though it had been a deliberate act of sabotage. It immediately created a huge wave of protests, not just from abroad this time, but at home as well. Petitions for my release were signed on a massive scale, even by the so-called official artists, above all by people from the theater community. The regime clearly hadn't been expecting this and did not know how to respond. It's not a problem to lock up individual dissidents, but locking up all the famous actors in the country? That was something that they no longer dared do.

And by the way, I probably wouldn't have enjoyed such widespread support at the time if I'd been some sort of fundamentalist dissident who held in contempt anyone who had ever made any kind of compromise with the regime or who was somehow just riding it out. I wasn't like that at all; I kept in touch with officially permitted theater people, to an extent that didn't place them in too much danger, and thus my absurd arrest and sentencing just for having watched someone lay a bouquet of violets somewhere was something to which these people could not remain indifferent.

Then in prison I really was a rather special prisoner, strictly isolated from the others and under strict surveillance, but nonetheless enjoying very circumspect treatment. Compared with my previous stints in prison, this was almost like a holiday. Among other things, I was in a cell with two hand-picked communists who had been locked up for many years for economic crimes and were afraid to speak with me at all for fear of making their own situation worse. In the end they were happy when, after I was elected president, they went home on an amnesty.

You got out of prison on May 17, 1989. How did the atmosphere before your imprisonment and after it differ? What had changed in Czech society?

I think that more had changed in those four months than during the years of my previous incarcerations. It wasn't just because a lot had changed in the neighboring countries—in Poland, Solidarity was already having a huge influence on the communists, and in the Soviet Union there was perestroika—but mainly because Czechoslovak society had begun to awaken from the anesthesia into which it had been plunged in 1968 by the Soviet occupation. It seemed to me that just as we had once built on the solidarity for the imprisoned musicians of the Plastic People of the Universe, and created Charter 77, we should now try to transform the solidarity I had enjoyed during that obscure incident into something more general and lasting. And so, after consulting with chartist friends and along with those "official" colleagues from the theater, Saša Vondra and Jiří Křižan and I organized a petition called "Several Sentences," which was then signed by tens of thousands of people. The Czech services of the Voice of America and Radio Free Europe would broadcast the list of new signatories at least twice a week, which made these programs the most popular on the air. The regime couldn't think of any other way to respond than to publish a long article expressing the views of a handful of artists who condemned "Several Sentences." They soon came to regret it, because, unlike the notorious Anti-Charter of 1977, this statement was really only an occasion for ridicule. "Several Sentences," in a nutshell, demanded the renewal of fundamental civic freedoms. It was completely straightforward, something every civilized person could agree with, though of course granting it would have meant, essentially, a change of regime.

Washington, April 13, 2005

The former ambassadors are prepared to continue to work for us. In other words, the evening turned out well. But to return to my narrative: as I respond to Mr. Hvížďala's questions I'm aware of how many important things I've forgotten. In some cases, I remember the atmosphere, the smells, the insignificant details, and I forget about incredibly important events such as my conversations with world statesmen about the future organization of the world. After a quiet study of various sources, I would certainly be able to recall and freshen my memory and then gradually write about it. So why am I in such a rush? Where am I going in such a hurry? Perhaps it's only an excuse not to do the research, perhaps not. But I simply cannot shake the feeling that I don't have much time left.

In the early days of November 1989, things were already changing: Evžen Erban, a high-ranking official with the communist regime, invited you to his home; the musician Michael Kocáb and the journalist Michal Horáček set in motion an initiative called *"Most,"* and they tried to mediate between representatives of the opposition and Prime Minister Adamec; you were planning a demonstration for December

10, on the International Day of Human Rights. You were intending to summon the signatories of "Several Sentences" to Palacký Square in Prague. The program for that event even appeared in the official party daily, *Rudé právo*. You were in Hrádeček, at your cottage, when the Berlin Wall fell on November 9. Even so, did you not suspect that the Czechs might simply wait and see how everything would turn out once again? And why in fact did you hide away in Hrádeček? It really could have appeared, as someone wrote, that the Prague opposition "had burrowed into the mud."

There were quite a few in our country who "had burrowed into the mud" at the time. And I would say that the opposition was the least offender. After all, developments were beginning to prove it right, more and more people were joining in, and it was being taken increasingly seriously. I don't remember that period at all as one of pessimism or of "burrowing into the mud" but, on the contrary, as a period of unusually hectic work. It was a kind of curtain-raiser for our revolution, when we began to realize the value of everything we'd done for the last twenty years or longer, something we were never sure we'd ever be able to do.

The invitation to see Mr. Erban was, on the one hand, a marginal curiosity. But even that testified to the fact that things were in motion. The other initiative you mentioned—"*Most*"—would have seemed like pure madness a year before. Whether I was in Hrádeček on November 9, I don't remember; at the time I was moving a lot between Hrádeček and Prague; in Prague I was arranging things, and in Hrádeček I was either writing or having meetings, though in a smaller circle of people and in a more focused way. In any case I was certainly not hiding away in Hrádeček, neither then nor at any other time; it would have been the worst possible place to hide. Whenever I felt the need to hide, either from the state police or from the whole world, the first thing I did was to get out of Hrádeček, which in the general mind was connected with me far more intimately than my Prague flat.

That conditions in Czechoslovakia were changing essentially more slowly than in other countries of the Soviet bloc was of course true. There were many reasons for that. Above all, the occupation of our country by the Warsaw Pact in 1968 had given birth to one of the most repressive and most conservative communist regimes, so that whereas elsewhere various reforms had long since taken place and a freer wind was blowing, in our country they were still locking people up. Society was demoralized; no one believed in anything any longer; everyone was afraid—but of course, against this background, everything that happened in 1989 before the revolution must have seemed like a great awakening of society. But that's not the only thing; every country or community has certain models of behavior determined by its history, and these are passed down from generation to generation. Part of the Czech "national character" is, traditionally, a heightened caution, a mistrust of change, a reluctance to move quickly, an unwillingness to make sacrifices, a tendency to wait and see, and a certain skepticism. Perhaps it has something to do with the persecution and elimination of the Czech aristocracy in the seventeenth century and the plebeian background against which the modern Czech nation was formed. Czechs simply hesitate a long time before acting. They wait for the right moment, but what they do next—as much as possible without great sacrifice—is worth the wait. To a certain extent this is true as well of the period that we are now dealing with: our revolution was one of the last to come, but on the other hand it went ahead more rapidly than others, and, in its own way, it was more radical. After all, we had no entr'acte of perestroika or reform communism, but we started directly, after a few days of revolution, to build a normal democratic society. Czechoslovakia was also the first country in the entire Soviet bloc where a genuine and lifelong noncommunist, who moreover had only a few days before been a leading dissident, a "star in the theater of opposition," became the head of state.

CHAPTER TWO

Washington, April 13, 2005

This year didn't begin well, either for the world or for me. Its beginning was foreshadowed by the waves of a tsunami. You had to ask yourself: was the planet trying to tell us something, warn us of something, challenge us to take some action? In other words: was this just another one of the billions of cosmic events that create the history of the world, or was it something more? Coincidentally, at that time or shortly before it, Dáša and I were to have been in that part of the world on our "grand Asian tour," but we had to cut it short almost as soon as it began. This was caused by my tumble. The very first day of our trip I fell so awkwardly that I broke a small but important bone—the collum femoris—that joins the femur to the pelvis, and I had to resort to using a wheelchair. It happened in Taiwan, and, as a result, we stayed only two days, long enough to get through the official part of my program; then we returned home. We were to have visited several countries, where, along with my public responsibilities, I was to have had private time for leisure and exploration.

I've been falling a lot recently (for example, I fell last night in our town house in Georgetown, but fortunately I wasn't injured). It seems to happen most often in Asia. I fell in the royal palace in Bangkok (three broken ribs), in a luxury hotel in Seoul, and a year ago in a hotel in Delhi (again, three broken ribs). The Indian tumble ruined our first attempt at a "grand Asian tour"; the repeat effort less than a year later was spoiled by my Taiwan fall. Will we ever try it a third time? I don't know.

My Asian falls have followed a pattern. I complete a flight lasting many hours, halfway around the globe, luckily without suffocating. I check into my quarters, unpack everything, prepare my things for the next day, read through my briefing notes, have a good dinner with an excellent wine, and then lie down for a long and deep sleep, after which I hope to begin the new day truly refreshed. Naturally, I take a sleeping pill. The time difference, the change of climate, the wine, the pill, and the relief that the long flight is over combine to create a certain kind of discombobulation—and later, when I'm groping about in the middle of the night searching for the relevant room in an unfamiliar and usually vast presidential apartment, it happens: I bite the dust. Mostly, the blame for these falls, which always complicate the lives of many people, and of Dáša above all, lies entirely with me; I feel too responsible for everything, I experience everything too intensely, and ultimately, I overdo it (using a combination of incompatible substances) in my effort to drive away all cares and thoroughly clear my head. So for me, the year 2005 began with a broken collum femoris, a wheelchair, and stints in the hospital. But mainly, it began under the shadow of my generally miserable mood, my inability to concentrate on any proper work, an alarming degree of forgetfulness, and a deepening feeling of general inadequacy and doubts about the significance of what I do and the way I do it.

To be a dissident meant to criticize, to point out contradictions between what was said and what was real, to analyze the falsehoods of language, to chart offenses against human and civic rights, or to organize protests. All these activities meant more or less taking things apart. A politician must of course continually take things apart, but at the same time, he must build something new; he must have a goal, a notion of where he wants to take society. When did you first become aware of this?

I don't think my public activities before I accepted political office were merely about taking things apart. On the contrary, I felt that I could and did criticize purely because I saw how distant the world around me was from my ideas about how things ought to be. Particularly in childhood and youth, my ideas were undoubtedly naive, but I had them all the same. I'm naturally a very constructive person, and I wouldn't know how to go about tearing something down for no reason, without knowing why it ought to be torn down. So when I suddenly found myself in a political office, I certainly didn't have to invent any political ideals or goals; I merely had to draw on what I'd been thinking all my life.

How one achieves or approaches one's goals in the real world, of course, is another question. Life is beautiful because, among other things, it is unpredictable and you can never be completely prepared for what comes along. I have to laugh when we are sometimes rebuked for being unprepared for our revolution, for not having a new democratic constitution and all the other essential legislation already written, and even for having no idea who would be minister of what, and so on. I find people who are completely prepared for history rather suspect. They have a lot in common with the communists, who so arrogantly believe they have completely understood the world and therefore know perfectly how everything should be. And then, when everything turns out to be slightly different, they try to squeeze the world to fit their notion of it.

When you accepted political office, you must certainly have thought about whom you were doing this for. Did you, from the outset, take into account that in the preceding twenty years of communism, people had turned their backs on politics, that they had entirely lost interest in it, and that once the revolutionary euphoria had died down, the situation would more or less return to what it had been before?

I don't think I ever had any great illusions. It's true that in the 1970s and 1980s, society became morally crippled, and this was the source of people blatantly turning their backs on everything public, but the massive epidemic of looking out for Number One and indifference to others was hardly new or surprising. There is plenty of evidence to show how opportunistically a large part of society behaved in the 1950s, when it was common to sign petitions demanding the death penalty for various "enemies of socialism," or how little support from society our domestic resistance against the Nazi occupation received during the Second World War. Only a fool could believe that the nation, or the whole of humanity for that matter, would change overnight and that everyone would start to behave wisely, unselfishly, altruistically, ready to make sacrifices for a good cause. Naturally, I knew this to be true, even during the "Velvet Revolution."

On the other hand, however, I know that from time to time the cup of patience runs over, people come to their senses, and things happen that would have been scarcely imaginable a short time before. Such an upwelling—and in our country it happens about once every twenty years—does not last for long, of course, and in a way it would be unnatural if it did. The point is to seize the moment and use it to bring about certain irreversible systemic and other changes to ensure that everything will be at least somewhat better than before.

I think that even during the revolution, I was sober, down to earth, and cautious, and did not try to achieve the impossible. That does not mean that I never succumbed to the heady atmosphere of the time. But when I did, it was fortunately not in any basic political decision-making, but only in my rhetoric, or in my "unconventional" presidential behavior. In short, I may sometimes have done things that a year later I would not have done and could not—and rightly so—have gotten away with. Mainly, though, despite all the things that so upset us today, conditions now are incomparably better than they were under communism. Moreover, the country is part of such a solid system of international relationships and guarantees that any form of subjugation coming from outside now seems virtually out of the question. I think that we have never, in our entire dramatic history, enjoyed this kind of certainty before.

I recall how, during the Velvet Revolution, Professor Milan Machovec said in the wings of the Realistic Theater: you are greater than God! How did you resist the growing adulation of yourself, which so often clouds one's judgment?

I don't know that he actually said it, but if he did, he certainly meant it partly as a joke and partly as a metaphor. He probably meant to say that—in those days, at least—I had an influence on events that was not only improbably large but also obvious to everyone at first sight. God, if he exists, has a greater influence than any earthling, of course, but let's face it, that influence isn't as clearly visible, because it is strangely connected to our free will, which is probably one of God's most mysterious creations. In other words, I don't think that what Machovec said was an expression of pure adulation.

On the other hand, I admit that for a time I really was the object of adulation, but I think that anyone in my position would have been: after all, I was seen as someone who had led the citizens to a successful and generally painless victory over an infinitely more powerful political machine, as someone who had come out of their own ranks and not out of the womb of the hated regime. Later on I had to pay a high price for that adulation. Uncritical respect is always punished, but it is the object of that respect who is punished, not those who confer it.

The psychological aspect of this matter—that is, anger at one's own former servility—was not the only reason for the disfavor into which I later fell. A no less serious, and perhaps even more significant, reason was the fact that I often embodied the minority position and thus didn't entirely fit the generally received notion of the politician as a mirror of prevailing moods or opinions or tendencies or mentalities. Though it was certainly not my intention, many saw me as their own bad conscience, not only in the period of dissent but also when I was president. And that kind of thing cannot be forgiven.

But you asked about whether all of this clouded my judgment. That's really for others to decide. But if it had, I would certainly be incapable of observing my own confusion and talking to you about it.

At the beginning of the Velvet Revolution, the Civic Forum, as the first supraparty revolutionary grouping of critically thinking people, rejected the idea of taking power. The historian Jiří Suk, in his book *Through the Labyrinth of Revolution*, writes that perhaps for the first time in history people came to the fore who did not consider politics to be their métier. At the time, you—the Civic Forum—claimed that the Communist Party of Czechoslovakia had created the mess and that therefore it should bear responsibility for it. But you did not mean by that that you were going to put the party on trial. So how did you understand this at that time?

It's true that the Civic Forum was created not to take power in the country but to articulate the public will and the longing for a change. None of us was a professional politician—where would a democratic political class have come from in a totalitarian system? None of us knew, or could have known, that the system would start collapsing so quickly and that the regime would practically offer us power on a silver platter. But even if we had known that, the declared intention to take over power in the country would clearly, at that moment, have been the occasion for general ridicule and the public might easily have turned their backs on us rather than supporting us. What they wanted to hear was "The emperor is naked," not "I want to be the emperor in his place." So it wasn't just that we weren't ready to assume power, but that the situation wasn't ripe for it. A few days later it was completely different. History, you might say, was rushing forward so quickly that we could barely keep pace with it.

By way of illustrating the speed and the improvisation that prevailed at the time: I recall trying to persuade Professor Valtr Komárek to accept the position of vice premier, in the backseat of a car that was driving us to a meeting with state officials where that very matter was to be decided. Clearly, there'd been no time for such a conversation before that. That was what it was like. I wouldn't be surprised if we were not the only group who got into power without thinking about it beforehand. In many communist countries at the time, academics and artists and journalists were accepting political office, because a fully prepared and fully formed alternative political class did not exist anywhere.

As far as the Communist Party is concerned: we had always said that crimes had to be punished. I said it myself in my first New Year's speech, delivered two days after I was elected president. As a political party, the Communist Party of Czechoslovakia was given a chance to reform itself. Not because it had surrendered power so quickly, without a struggle, but because it was the logical thing to do. After all, most of the communist parties in Eastern Europe had successfully transformed themselves into various kinds of social democratic parties. They were absolutely clear about repudiating their past and all those associated with it, and all of that turned out to be for the general good. Why should our communists not have been given the same chance? That they did not use this opportunity, or rather that party conservatives repressed all such efforts, is another matter. That they got away with it was probably a mistake, but it was certainly not mine alone. If the will to take more radical steps had prevailed in society and in the newly forming political representative bodies, it would certainly have happened.

I was certainly no dictator with unlimited power to decide which political parties would or would not be banned. Perhaps I can be blamed for not repeating that idea often enough and loudly enough at the time. But it does not seem to me that at the beginning of the 1990s the atmosphere was conducive to banning the party outright; just think of how many people, including those who later became famous anti-communist politicians, had themselves been members of the party, and how many people might therefore have feared that such a ban could have dire consequences for them.

The Mafia-like way in which the communists exploited privatization was a different matter: from the very beginning I came out sharply against it. You might remember, for example, my rabble-rousing speech on Wenceslas Square in August 1990. But mine was a voice crying in the wilderness. The government's position was that you can't make an omelette without breaking some eggs. We talked a lot at the time about setting up a kind of "ethical tribunal" to render a verdict on the moral and political responsibility for conditions under the previous regime, but there obviously wasn't the appetite, or even the energy, for that.

The saddest thing of all is our miserable record in successfully prosecuting actual crimes. The state of our judiciary was clearly a factor here. Don't forget, after the country was occupied by Warsaw Pact troops in 1968, the process of identifying and weeding out the politically unreliable was far more rigorous than in other communist countries. That's why, after the Velvet Revolution, personnel changes were more difficult and took a longer time. You can't produce a thousand brand-new judges overnight.

Washington, April 15, 2005

I'm finding Americans more and more likable. I am bothered less and less by things I once found hard to accept, or even ridiculous. Nevertheless, to be fair, I will mention several such annoyances. They love to chew gum, which makes them look like ruminants. This bothers me particularly in the case of women. They love putting their feet on the table, or at least the men do. They eat incomprehensibly thick buns that they stuff with everything possible, including lettuce. Eating these requires special skills. I'm always afraid that if I tried to eat such a bun (I've never eaten one in my life) I would either tear my mouth because it was too big, or I'd squeeze it and everything inside it would fall out onto the ground. They wash this bun down, at best with water, at worst with Coca-Cola or milk, either from a bottle or a can, or a plastic container or cup. I wouldn't call myself an alcoholic, but the thought of not drinking beer or wine with a meal is hard to contemplate. In any case, drinking water with meals reminds me of my years in prison. And regarding those cups: as a Central European, America appears to me as a land of wrappers and refuse. I don't know exactly why this is; after all, we have wrappers and refuse in our country. I will investigate this further.

Americans place great store in white teeth, something I find generally agreeable; they have dozens of ways of achieving dental perfection and whiteness, and I don't think it's unusual for people here to have a relatively healthy set of teeth replaced with one that is artificial but more beautiful.

One big change, compared with earlier visits, is the increasing predominance of European and Japanese cars. They are smaller and more economical than American cars, which, for unknown reasons, have herds of useless horses under their hoods and are capable of speeds many times greater than is allowed anywhere here.

At a demonstration on Letná on November 26, 1989, the Civic Forum did not demand the resignation of Prime Minister Ladislav Adamec, but rather gave him a free hand to form a new government. Why the hesitation to force him out?

The Czechoslovak revolution, as I've already indicated, was a drama in several acts. But more than that, the situation was changing and evolving by the hour. At first the Civic Forum did not demand the resignation of the government, it merely demanded the same thing as the students were demanding: the departure of some of the most compromised figures from the state leadership; a proper investigation into the brutal suppression of the demonstration on November 17, 1989; the release of all political prisoners; freedom of expression. Later, as the situation developed and the public became more mobilized, these demands begat further demands, including an appeal for the fundamental reconstruction of all three governments and parliaments—Czech, Slovak, and federal—the abolition of the leading role of the Communist Party, and so on. I no longer remember all the details about the course of the various negotiations, but there is already a well-founded scholarly literature about it all, such as the book by Jiří Suk that we've already mentioned.

If I remember accurately, not only did we not demand the prime minister's resignation on the day you mention, we never specifically demanded it at all. But our demands clearly escalated beyond his ability to fulfill them, so he resigned on his own initiative. At the same time it appears that he would have liked to have become president and wait out the storm in the relative shelter of the Prague Castle, from which he would then, as it were, sail forth into altered circumstances. But even if such a thing were possible, it became unacceptable after a few days, both to the increasingly radical public and to the Civic Forum and the Public Against Violence, each of which essentially articulated prevailing public opinion. Perhaps Mr. Adamec believed in a compromise of the Polish type, where the opposition applied the principle "You have the president (Jaruzelski), we have the prime minister (Mazowiecki)." The somewhat special position that Adamec enjoyed— a certain regard for his person—derived, among other things, from the fact that he was the first and the only one in the entire communist leadership who, without the permission of his politburo, was willing to negotiate with the opposition. In doing so, he risked a lot, since he couldn't be certain that the secret police might not try to crush him somehow; the upper echelons of the party knew better than ordinary citizens that things could be made to happen. But when no one moved against him, it immunized the opposition to a certain extent as well: it would have been hard for the police to lock up people who were officially negotiating with the prime minister in a government office. The demonstration on Letná you refer to came after one of the many negotiation sessions with Prime Minister Adamec, when I invited him to speak. I announced his appearance in a somewhat vaudevillian manner ("and now may I present the one and only representative of the state who has the time of day for us—Prime Minister . . . Ladislav . . . ADAMEC!"). He received a huge ovation, and he might well have had a chance, at that moment, to be fully accepted by the public and thus to continue having a career in politics. Instead he read a boring and evasive perestroika-like speech, and people more or less booed him off the platform. It wasn't just that he was pushed into retirement by the accelerated course of events; he himself deserves a lot of the blame for his own demise.

Washington, April 19, 2005

Yesterday I went to dinner at Zbigniew Brzezinski's. Madeleine was there and perhaps another fifteen important people—diplomats and journalists. A long and intensive political discussion took place in which I participated at some length. Everyone praised my English, which surprised me a lot. It depends a great deal on my mood, on the momentary state of body and soul, on a thousand tiny circumstances. Sometimes I can't manage to utter a single decent sentence. At other times I'm bold enough to engage in a grand discourse. Essentially, however, I belong to a generation who were not encouraged, in their youth, to learn languages: I had no time for it nor, in truth, much opportunity. And though I've been trying to learn some languages all my life, essentially I don't know any very well. Besides, I obviously have a negative talent for languages. If I can't remember who visited us on a state visit and when, or which

countries I've been to, how am I supposed to remember how to say "horserad-
ish" in English?

Mr. Hvížďala occasionally asks me some very strange questions and it
annoys me somewhat, either because the questions focus on marginal matters
or because they are based on long since discredited media canards. But perhaps
that's what's so good about them: they may provoke me to a more lively
response, making this conversation more animated. That, at least, was how it
worked in Disturbing the Peace, *a conversation between the two of us that*
took place almost exactly twenty years ago.

Judging by the accessible materials, it seems as though you were
aware of your responsibility and your broad influence only because of
the people in the public squares and in the factories on December 8,
during the first negotiations of the so-called decision-making political
forces. Today it seems that the communists knew sooner than the
members of the Civic Forum did that their hold on power was coming to an end and that you came to realize this only gradually. Is that
how it was?

You could feel that something was changing from the very beginning. I recall, for example, that I went to an improvised meeting in the
Činoherní Klub, the theater where the Civic Forum was created, several
hours before it was to begin, to lessen the risk of being arrested on the
way; it turned out to be an absolutely pointless precaution. From the
earliest moments the state police almost ostentatiously ignored me and
the rest of us, even though previously they would have arrested us for
something absolutely trivial. It could have meant they were merely trying to lull us into dropping our guard while they gathered their forces to
mount a sudden and massive attack. But it could also have simply
meant that they were totally abandoning the battlefield. We had no idea
which it was, and I don't think the regime was clear about it at first
either. It was only after major conflicts inside the top leadership that
they finally decided on the second alternative, that is, abandoning the
field. Or so I've heard. In other words, the regime came only by degrees
to the decision to surrender power, and we began to realize this only by

degrees as well. I don't think that the meeting you refer to, on December 8, had any special significance. It was pretty much like all the others, except perhaps that it concluded one phase in the conversations, and therefore, for reasons that were more ceremonial or formal, many representatives of the Czech and Slovak puppet parties and the other organizations in the National Front were present.

(January 29, 1996)

1) For the time being I'm not capable of writing the speech to parliament, partly for obvious reasons, partly out of a dislike of repeating things I've already said a thousand times before. I will try to write it next weekend (it may be possible after the funeral). For the time being I have merely read through all the assembled briefing notes and come to the conclusion that the speech should be short but firm, not long-winded, each word a pearl of wisdom (nice aim, hard to realize), and that it should fall naturally into three parts: (. . .)

3) (. . .) and then there would be a series of questions: How do they envision the Senate? How do they see bringing about a decrease in the influence of party politics on political life? What about the constitution? Shouldn't we be planning to pass a new one in ten years, one that would have what the current one lacks—national emergency measures, for example, or the territorial divisions—but above all, one in which, in the light of our collective experience, we would fine-tune everything that has not yet been fine-tuned (because of the haste in which the present constitution was written); there would be a more exact definition of the relationship among the state institutions, improvements in the charter of fundamental rights and freedoms, which should be an integral part of the constitution; an ombudsman, should we decide to have one; the possibility of delegating certain aspects of state sovereignty to the EU, etc., etc., etc.? And more questions: the defense laws, reform of the public administration, the cultivation of a civil service and the laws relating to it, the creation of a nonprofit sector, reform of the budgetary and contributory sectors, etc., etc. Social funds not part of the budget. A simplifica-

tion of the entire legal code. Economic strategy. Can the market really solve everything? The creation of a civil society. How well the politicians will do in the elections, and how the country will develop from this point on, will depend on how convincingly and intelligently they respond to these questions.

4) The third part should be more philosophical, and its basic theme would be that democracy is not just systems, institutions, and their interrelations; in other words, it's not just a technique but above all it is a relationship to the world and to society, a way of thinking, the spirit of public life. People feel this—I refuse to believe they don't—and they require clear words and clear behavior; they need to hear something about the nature of the state, about its position, its program. The technology of democracy is unthinkable without a democratic culture. An appeal to remember this in the upcoming elections as well.

(February 4, 1996)

(. . .)

7) I'm sending a parcel of shirts for Mrs. Oušková. (. . .)

(March 10, 1996)

(. . .)

6) Please make copies of my speech to parliament—for all the members and for the press—and make sure it is well presented, in that folder with the state coat of arms on it. As last year, the members will all want me to autograph it, more so than last time, since there is an election coming and many of them won't be reelected. The only change from last year—and this has already been arranged with the parliamentary leadership—is that my speech will be followed immediately by the debate, in my presence, of a brief, noncontroversial item, after which there will be a recess. The speech will be handed out to members only then, and for two reasons: first, so the members will listen to me and not read the speech, and second, so that the autograph session will not disrupt the debate immediately following my speech, as it did last year. That was very distasteful.

7) I'm sending the toast to the Canadian governor-general with some slight stylistic changes. It's a rather conventional toast—a "standard" toast—which in this case doesn't matter very much. But it's not possible in the case of the English queen! (. . .)

(March 17, 1996)

(. . .)

3) The same source tells me that Klestil is annoyed, if not angry, with me for going to Sarajevo without him. Apparently he will need to be stroked somehow. Please think about how to do that. (. . .)

(March 31, 1996)

(. . .)

5) Couldn't Mr. M. mediate a meeting between Dr. Ch. and the cardinal's lawyers about the cathedral? The cardinal did not call as he promised. He's risking the possibility that a future parliament (and there will be a rare agreement on this between the ODS and the opposition) will completely nationalize the cathedral. I'm open to any compromises; he, clearly, is open to none. I remembered this because last night, for incomprehensible reasons, I dreamt that Zdeněk Mahler forced me to sleep in his bed. (. . .)

Whose idea was it not to dismantle the communist government institutions, but rather to make them part of the transitional power structures? Was it the democrats—that is, the dissidents—who decided that, or was it the former or current communists, who saw in that "constitutional" solution their only chance of remaining, at least partially, in power?

By far, most of the people active in the Civic Forum or the Public Against Violence were of one mind in thinking that the state, with all its constitutional institutions and the entire civil service, could not be dismantled and a new state built entirely from scratch. That would have been utter nonsense. We tried to fill existing posts with new, uncompromised people and then as rapidly as possible, by democratic means—that is, by passing constitutional and ordinary laws—to carry out the systemic changes we were able to agree on as the most necessary and the most important. There was a serious shortage of appropriate people for the various posts, so we had to persuade rock musicians, translators, television hosts, scientists, writers, maybe even our friends from the pubs, to accept positions. There were tens of thousands of civil servants, and there were certainly not that many dissidents. But even if there had been, I don't know how they could have taken over the running of the country from one day to the next without causing many catastrophic disruptions. And then add to that human resources whirlwind a fundamental transformation of the state institutions? I can't imagine a greater chaos, or a better opportunity for the disciplined machinery of communist power to intervene. After all, the basic idea of putschists everywhere is national salvation through the restoration of order. The new countries that came into being after the two world wars were not created by sweeping away everything that constituted the old order: in the early stages, they all took over institutions and public servants from the previous period. In the law on the creation of Czechoslovakia drafted by Rašín on the night my play was about, the very second sentence was an appeal to preserve all the existing institutions.

And there's something else that relates to all this: life under communism was based on lip service. And so the Civic Forum was suddenly inundated with offers of help from countless communists, police officers, soldiers, civil servants, and so on. Such people were very necessary because, as I've said, it was impossible to fill all the posts with dissidents alone or our friends from the underground; but how were we to distinguish those who were sincere, those who with genuine relief wanted to work for the success of the new democracy, from those who were simply impostors trying to rapidly insinuate themselves into important positions? Just one small example: when I first arrived at the Prague Castle as president I was greeted, flowers in hand, by the local chapter of the Civic Forum established by the employees in President Husák's office. It was a while before my friends and I were able to determine

which of those could go on working with us, and which we would have
to let go.

**Wasn't this the main reason why so many communists remained in
power at various levels of government?**

Who, in fact, is a communist? Someone who was once in the Communist Party? But everybody and his uncle was in the party; in recent
decades alone seven million people had passed through its ranks. Naturally they weren't all faithful, enthusiastic communists, genuine servants of the regime, but you couldn't just separate the good from the
bad by waving a wand. It would be a long and difficult process, particularly since we wanted to be both just and pragmatic. Suppose we had
wanted to demote or fire everyone who was a member of the Communist Party? We'd have had to dissolve the entire Academy of Sciences
and strip most of the universities of their faculties. We wouldn't have
had a single higher-ranking officer in the armed forces, nor a single
criminal investigator, a single CEO, a single diplomat, and maybe not
even a single air traffic controller.

**Why did Adamec's right-hand man, Marián Čalfa, become the first
prime minister? For the longest time you couldn't get his name right
and you called him Šalfa, or Štolfa, or Štalfa. Why did the prime minister have to be someone who understood the communist technology
of power? Wouldn't it have been purer to completely separate your-
selves from the former regime and to govern, for instance, by decree
with the support of a revolutionary parliament until elections could
be held?**

I don't recall getting Čalfa's name wrong in that way, but if you say
so you must have gotten it from somewhere. When Adamec refused to
form a new government—as a matter of fact, he did form one, but it
was whistled down in the streets before it took office—Čalfa became
our main negotiating partner. He was a young Slovak lawyer who had
lived in Prague for a long time and who was in charge of legislation in

the office of the communist government, and later he became deputy prime minister. We knew nothing about him, and, if I did get his name wrong at first, that may have been why. As soon as we started dealing with him, however, everything began happening as smooth as butter. No tricks. No intrigues. No smoke screens. He was absolutely down to earth, and he never talked about trivialities. He told me quite clearly that the Communist Party had lost power, that there was no point in even talking to it, and that he, as the top negotiator for the state, would make the decisions with us, Civic Forum and the Public Against Violence, on the mechanics of the transition of power.

And that's what happened. He came up with a way to get rid of the worst members of parliament and to co-opt new ones; we decided with him on the composition of a "government of national understanding," and it was he who later explained to the Federal Assembly why they should elect me as president, and he held them to a deadline that allowed me to deliver the traditional New Year's speech on January 1, 1990, as president. We couldn't possibly have managed such technical matters by ourselves, even if they had occurred to us.

Ultimately, it was Čalfa who taught the new government how to govern. There was not a lot that was specifically communistic in what you call "the technology of power" once the leading role of the Communist Party no longer applied, and things were no longer decided first in the politburo. The government simply meets on certain days; there's an agenda, there are procedural rules, the ministers have to receive their briefing materials in time, and so on; there were hundreds of "technical" or "technological" details that we had no idea about, nor could we have.

But there was more at stake than purely administrative matters. Čalfa had a decisive share in the first and the most important of the new transformational laws. Moreover, no prime minister after him was able to create within the government such a hardworking and constructive atmosphere, or to broker agreements so quickly between people who had been at loggerheads. I was criticized for reappointing Čalfa as prime minister after the first free elections, which meant that he wasn't merely an "inherited," transitional prime minister. Yet only someone profoundly opposed to democracy could hold that against me. In the first place, Čalfa won the election outright in his electoral district in Slovakia, and he proved to be the most popular Slovak politician. In the second place since the president was Czech, custom dictated that the prime minister be Slovak. In the third place, the leadership of the Civic Forum—which received more than 50 percent of the votes in that election—and the Public Against Violence immediately and unabashedly urged me to appoint Čalfa prime minister again. Even if I had thought someone else should be prime minister, how could I have ignored the will of those who had won the election?

Sometime after announcing your official candidacy for president, you and Čalfa had a private meeting in which he apparently offered you certain services. What did he promise you then, and what did you promise him? Some claim you promised the communists immunity from punishment in exchange for your election. Is that true?

Not long ago Petr Pithart, who was an eyewitness, told me something I had completely forgotten about: that I had been opposed to that meeting and did not wish to go to it. We felt it was important to do everything publicly—our revolution was probably the first and the last in history to be completely recorded on tape, even quite internal discussions—and an invitation to an off-the-record meeting was entirely against that spirit. Nevertheless, on the recommendation of friends, I went to it. It was held in a room in the cabinet office that Čalfa had determined was not bugged. There he told me, straight out, with no sentimentality or evasions, that he felt communism was over in our country and that now everything had to be done to ensure the smooth transition of power into democratic hands and the renewal of a market economy. He offered me nothing more than his help in transforming the system, and he asked nothing of me in return, certainly not any favors. After that, we really did speak only about the "technical" details. He came up with an idea that at the time seemed very radical to me, that I should be elected president as early as December 29. He had everything very well thought out. I also understood why he wanted to speak to me one-on-one. It wasn't just because the Civic Forum was a huge gossip mill that could easily have gotten the elements in this scenario mixed up, but I suspect mainly because he didn't want anything to reach the ears of the other camp, be it only through our own indiscretions; above all, he didn't want the members of parliament to get wind of it because they could begin to organize various counteroffensives against my candidacy. His plan was to quickly present them with a fait accompli before they could prepare to oppose it.

Today it occurs to me that he perhaps knew more than I did about secret police collaborators among us and he didn't want any details to travel through them to those I called at the time "friends of the old order." It's funny, but it was Čalfa, not I, who behaved like a real revolutionary. I promised him nothing, of course. Any promise of the kind you have in mind I could not, on principle, have given him and even less so with no mandate to do so and no witnesses. I understand why, after all these years, there remains such an interest in this meeting: the notion of history as a permanent conspiracy full of secret talks and deals is very sexy.

Washington, April 19, 2005

It may be that Mr. Hvížďala's questions have taken us too precipitously into the middle of the revolution and that perhaps I should say something about what happened immediately before it. I had been well aware for a long time that the students were planning a large rally at Vyšehrad, in Prague, for November 17, 1989, which is International Students Day and at the same time the fiftieth anniversary of the Nazi execution of Czech students. I also knew that the rally was meant to be independent, that is, not manipulated by the organs of state power. But it was organized by an official student organization, not by some dissident group, and by that time I was so well known as a dissident that had I taken part, I would have attracted major attention not only from the state police but also from the public and the Western media. I was afraid this might create the impression among the students that I was trying to expropriate—or, to use current language, to hijack—an event they had planned and organized entirely by themselves, and that I would inadvertently create the impression that the rally had been organized by Charter 77 or that these students were merely an adjunct of the Charter. I've had a lot to do with several generations of students, and I well know how sensitive they are to things like that.

My wife and my brother went to the rally, but I decided to retreat to Hráde-ček, where I followed everything on Radio Free Europe. When I heard what had happened—that the police had brutally suppressed it—I understood immediately that the regime would not get away with it so easily. The atmosphere was charged with a kind of electrical energy, and I felt that any snowball could start an avalanche. Besides, we weren't living in a complete vacuum; we knew that in Poland, Solidarity was already half in; we had witnessed the exodus of East German refugees from Prague; we knew about the reform activities in Hungary; and of course we knew about Gorbachev's perestroika. The explosion would have to happen sooner or later. It was only waiting for the appropriate spark.

The next day I hastily returned to Prague, met with various friends, and within two days we had founded the Civic Forum. At the same time—or perhaps a minute or so sooner—the Public Against Violence was created in Bratislava. I wrote the Civic Forum's first declaration. Almost immediately Civic Forums—loose, informal antitotalitarian associations—began to spring up throughout the country, in companies, factories, cities, towns, and villages, and inside organizations. We had to coordinate our activities with the students while fully respecting their independence, so that they would not feel the revolution had been "stolen" from them, though here and there, some did feel that.

On the other hand, it would have been immensely irresponsible to leave it all up to the students, given that a structured opposition already existed, consisting of people who were known at home and abroad and who offered the prospect of taking it all further, and not letting the momentum die once the students had gone back to school. And the dissidents would have betrayed themselves and their long years of struggle if, at precisely the moment when this struggle might have led to something, and when their strengths were needed more than ever before, they had suddenly walked away from it and said: this is a student matter—let them handle it as they see fit.

Of course, theater people played a very important role at the time. They went on strike and began traveling around the country, holding meetings with the public, explaining what was happening and what our aims were. Their cooperation with the Civic Forum and the Public Against Violence, as far as I *can remember, went smoothly. These extremely important activities were a direct outcome of the solidarity they had expressed to me—for the first time in such a direct and extensive way—earlier that year, during my last imprisonment. And so, as it turned out, the regime's pointless attack on me the previous January came back to haunt it several times over. But possibly—albeit subconsciously—some people from the theater world might still also have been trying, through their activities, to make amends for their unfortunate signatures on the Anti-Charter of 1977.*

On December 10, 1989, you withdrew from actively leading the Civic Forum and sequestered yourself to focus on the power struggle for the presidency. You were criticized for doing so at the time and accused of having left your successors—Petr Pithart and Jan Urban— a confused and murky legacy. How would you respond to those critics today?

It was my mildly dramatic idea that we would have all the basic changes in place by December 10, that is, the International Day of Human Rights. There was a certain symbolism in that deadline that appealed to me, and we succeeded: on that day, we had a new federal government—Čalfa's "government of national understanding"—and President Husák, who embodied the dark era of "normalization," resigned. After the high tension of the preceding days—the general strike, the enormous demonstrations, and the fundamental political changes that followed—a moment arrived that seemed to offer a certain breathing space, so I took advantage of it. I retreated for about a week to the studio of my friend, the painter Joska Skalník, because I was so tired and exhausted that there was a danger of making mistakes. After all, people had been talking at me all day long, day after day, and from all sides, and as a result I wasn't feeling well at all. Of course, I kept on having the most important negotiations and meetings there, but it was quieter than at home, not to mention at the Civic Forum headquarters. In short, I had to get some sleep, order my thoughts, and find the peace and quiet to write the first television speech of my life, a speech on which the future of the country greatly depended.

It had nothing to do with a power struggle, and I don't know exactly with whom or against whom—at that particular moment, and in that studio—I would have struggled, and mainly I don't know what kind of power I'm meant to have struggled for. The broad campaign for my election took place without any guidance from me; the government was already in our hands, so I simply don't know what they mean.

Occasionally I had to leave the studio, and one of these excursions is worth describing. One day, highly placed emissaries from Gorbachev himself approached me in a very conspiratorial fashion. I don't know whether they were from the Central Committee of the Communist Party of the Soviet Union, or from the Ministry of Foreign Affairs, but they were probably colonels in the KGB. I went with a tiny entourage to an unfamiliar flat where the meeting was to take place. On the whole, it was an innocent encounter; these gentlemen simply wanted to take a look at me, an exotic breed, to judge whether I was an enemy of the Soviet Union or its friend, and whether I was a dangerous zealot or merely a simpleminded poet. That in itself would not have been so interesting. But the cameraman Stanislav Milota, my friend, revolutionary sidekick, secretary, and bodyguard all in one, accompanied me to this meeting, and, hidden in his jacket, he had a small state-of-the-art tape recorder that Zdeněk Mlynář had brought us from Vienna. Stanislav, of course, wanted to secretly record everything. But what Mlynář had neglected to tell us was that this little machine had a special feature: when the tape ran out it began wailing like a siren, and of course this happened right in the middle of the conversation. The colonels shot out of their seats and almost pulled out their guns, but they relaxed when they realized that it was only a minor oversight on our part. They themselves must certainly have had their own recording device, a better one than ours, one that didn't wail.

I would not, however, connect my stay in Skalník's studio with my alienation from the Civic Forum. That happened, as far as I know, much later, at a time when I was already president. At that time I had the fond illusion that I would go on sitting around as I had before, in my sweater, in the Civic Forum, taking part in various debates and discussions, making some decisions; in short, I thought that after becoming president, we would carry on as we had during the revolution and that once a week I would pop into the Prague Castle in a tie and carry out the duties required by protocol.

It was, of course, an absolute pipe dream. The Castle swallowed me up whole, and I had to represent an independent Czechoslovakia in lightning visits to every possible country, receive state visitors, speak to parliament, travel about the country, and hold a thousand and one meetings. I had almost no time for the Civic Forum. And it felt slighted. Moreover, we started to have certain conflicts, or at least there was occasional tension between us. It couldn't have been otherwise: several of the central figures in the Civic Forum had left with me to the Castle, and thus there automatically arose two power centers side by side—state and "the party." That could not help but cause bad blood, even if we'd all been angels.

As for the murky legacy I was meant to have left my successors, the Civic Forum was a body created for a single purpose: to peacefully push aside the previous regime and mediate the transition to democracy. It was meant to exist for a couple of weeks and then dissolve into normal political parties. I fought strenuously for this, and I spoke about it at a January congress of the Civic Forum. I felt that were it to exist even a day longer than necessary, the problem of its identity would arise: that is, the question of what exactly it was. A party? A trade union council? An association? A federation of many individual associations? Could something so amorphous, something that played a role that in normal circumstances would be played by hundreds of institutions of civil society, have a meaningful role to play?

I wasn't able to push this notion through. Everyone wanted to hold on until the free elections in June 1990 and to run in them as an organization. I admit that new parties could probably not have formed, or older parties reformed themselves, so quickly, and that the overwhelming, though entirely predictable, electoral victory of the Civic Forum and the Public Against Violence made many things happen more quickly, at least for a time. The problem was that, once members were elected on the Civic Forum ticket, they couldn't suddenly just dissolve it, because it would have been a betrayal of voters' confidence. In other words, the fact that it didn't dissolve itself voluntarily and in a timely manner condemned it to a later demise that was unplanned, involuntary, and decidedly strange. But that is truly another chapter.

Still on the subject of that "murky legacy": I am, believe me, someone who loves order, who is almost pedantic about it. I have an actual physical aversion to disorder. So that if anyone suffered from this legendary chaos inside the Civic Forum it was I, and if anyone attempted, here and there, to at least clarify and consolidate a few things, it was I as well. The Civic Forum was chaotic through no fault of mine or anyone else's but by its very nature. It was a nationwide, spontaneous movement, which came into being over the course of two or three days, and it should have, the moment it had achieved its objective, just as quickly dissolved itself. With slight exaggeration, you could say it most resembled a street demonstration or a large public rally. Such an institution can play an intermediary role during historical turning points, but it cannot very well be a fixture in normal political life. Similar movements in other countries have had problems with their identity as well: they did not know precisely what to be in the new situation, and at the same time they lacked the resolve to disband themselves voluntarily.

Washington, April 19, 2005

It's no easy matter to set up house in America, drive into the country several times a day to walk the dogs, decline or accept all the invitations, learn how to speak American English (Dáša), look after the house, and go to work every day to write something. Today, for the first time without a great to-do and checking by telephone, they let me into the Library of Congress parking lot, where a space is reserved for my car. It has always involved endless dickering that usually climaxes with a telephone call to the miraculous Mr. Edler, who is some kind of chief custodian of this Castle, a Barnabas whom we have never seen but whose name has magical powers. At the end of all those unsuccessful arguments with the parking lot attendant, the police, and the gatekeeper, it's enough to mention Mr. Edler's name—and with a single phone call from the booth everything is suddenly possible. I don't know, however, what would happen if Mr. Edler were to fall ill or be transferred somewhere else. Otherwise, I have already filled out many forms and gone through many procedures, at the end of which one is always delighted by the fact that everything turned out well but at the same time upset because everything was more expensive than they had originally suggested. I am very surprised that the traffic rule of right of way on the right does not apply and that on hundreds of Georgetown intersections everyone is always stopping and politely giving the other person the right of way. In such a situation in Bohemia there would be a multicar pile-up at every intersection every couple of minutes. Ah well, I suppose that where there is a proper culture of relationships it may not be necessary to have so many regulations. So far I don't think I've seen a single damaged automobile. Or are they just able to repair them very quickly?

(April 6, 1996)

1) Today (Saturday) I dashed off the first draft of my speech for Latvia. I'm saying the same things I've said many times before, but there's probably no other way to do it. I would ask for comments from all the usual commentators. (. . .) I must have them by Tuesday around 3:00 P.M. if I am to finish editing it on Tuesday afternoon, so the translation can be started and the speech copied and printed, etc. on Wednesday morning. (. . .)

3) (. . .) In our comments on the legislation on heritage sites I'm missing a more elaborate formulation of the interrelationship between heritage maintenance and the rest of the activities in the Castle. I'm in favor of writing something directly into the law to make roughly this point, that the daily and daylong cooperation of the Heritage Department with the Maintenance and Development division of the Castle Administration, with the Protocol Office, with the other departments of the OPR and with the president himself is essential to the daily business and development of the Castle; without that it is simply unthinkable; the state, political, social, representative, cultural, tourist functions of the Castle are so closely linked with the aesthetics of the Castle, and therefore with the stewardship of its heritage, that the Castle could not function without its own heritage department coming under the jurisdiction of the OPR.

Moreover, the president is traditionally responsible to the public for everything that goes on in the Castle, from state visits to tourism and development projects, and if he were to lose that connection between the aesthetic and the other activities in the Castle, which he now exercises through the Heritage Department of the OPR, he would not be capable of shouldering this responsibility. (. . .) State holidays, the visits of kings and queens, tours for ambassadors, the various kinds of social activities, etc., etc.—none of this can happen without the constant heritage oversight of those who know the Castle and have lived with it for decades. The aesthetic and political functions in this case are two dimensions of the same thing, which has no parallel anywhere else. And therefore to make this anomaly part of the system is entirely systemic.

(April 28, 1996)

(. . .)

2) Mr. S. did as I wished and had a confidential meeting with his highly placed Iranian friends about the shot-down Israeli pilot. He was told in confidence that the man is alive. For the time being Iran is not telling anyone where he is, but they are preparing to pull him out as a trump card at the right moment. I would like to send a private and coded message to that effect to President Weizmann. (. . .)

5) Lunch with the Iron Lady. I've a table at home for six people. That means her, Saša Brabcová, Rudd Lubbers, Hanička Suchocká, myself, plus one more to be decided; perhaps it could be reserved for Henry if he happens to come. A light lunch? (. . .)

10) I looked at the comments on the Aachen speech. There aren't as many as usual. They are more detailed. Some are nitpicking, and others, though they aim at a greater exactitude, destroy the whole conception of the speech, above all the disquisition on time and history in various cultures. But I genuinely believe that the absolutely fundamental difference between the European tradition and other cultures lies in the different notions of time and that it is the most fundamental source of the European idea of development and progress. Other cultures, on the contrary, honor the status quo, quietude, leaving things in place, etc., etc. (. . .)

(June 23, 1996)

1) On Monday evening the coalition negotiations will continue. Perhaps they will result in an accord and a signature on the coalition agreement, perhaps not. However it turns out, I would ask that all three coalition chairs be invited to the Castle for Tuesday at 10:00 A.M. The inaugural session of parliament begins that afternoon, and thus it's an appropriate moment for them to tell me how far they've gotten, to acquaint me with the coalition agreement, with their plan for the probable composition of the government, with their strategy for the inaugural session of parliament, if there are outstanding problems, and with how they intend to communicate with the Social Democrats. They should probably be officially summoned by our office, to avoid, as far as possible, any discussion about whether it is appropriate or not. (. . .)

2) If we should happen to get into the final of the European football championship, which I'm not counting on, we would have to stop off in England on our way home from Ireland and watch the match. Kohl will be there as well as the queen. It fits into our time schedule perfectly. It's probably also necessary as an alternative to let Klaus know; he will certainly want to go there as well, and the question is, is it appropriate for us both to be there? (. . .)

4) Apparently there was some embarrassment at the Castle at Šípek's Saturday event. There was no reason for it. Unconventional artistic expression is part of my own personality (just remember the dances and the rock concerts in the Castle courtyards after I was first elected president), and ultimately—in the spirit of Bakhtin's teaching—jokers, jugglers, fools, etc., that is, elements that deflate pomposity, belong in the court of a ruler. Our best artists played at Šípek's reception, and the point of the event was an unconventional and entertaining critique of the boorishness of most Czech receptions, where the diners rush into the hall, fling themselves at the tables groaning with delicacies, bolt everything down, and then go home. The leisurely preparation and the slow and ritualistic presentation of the delicacies in small portions were a very good trick. (. . .)

9) But now back to Hillary: I hear that her program is gradually

changing and becoming more concrete and that everyone and his uncle has something to say about it, from the embassy to the MFA, from the White House to Mrs. R. Nevertheless, in my program so far there is nothing about what I am supposed to be doing with her and when. I have to know this. If only because the government could resign at any moment, a new government might have to be named, there would be political negotiations, etc. I would therefore ask that everything, as far as possible, be made absolutely clear and included in my program. I would ask E. to begin her role as supervisor of the dinner at my home and of the subsequent lunch with the Germans. (. . .)

Washington, April 20, 2005

Today I won't write very much. I'm meant to have lunch with Mr. Billington, the director of the Library of Congress, whose guest I am, and for dinner we've been invited to the White House. It's awful for me to have to eat twice a day: I barely eat once, but both invitations are important. I'm entering a strange time. Either I'm always sweating and there's a risk that some virus could get hold of me and my illnesses will be off and running, or some air-conditioning blowing on me and the same thing threatens, perhaps in an even worse form. Add to that occasional heart troubles. But the main thing is, I am permanently tired. I'm curious about how all this will turn out.

I've just come back from lunch. It wasn't a lunch with Mr. Billington alone. There were perhaps a hundred to a hundred and fifty people there. They were all terribly pleasant, and I was able to have decent conversations about many things with many of them. The main drawback was that the strange, tasteless American food was unsalted. I asked, to no avail, for salt, until finally Mrs. Kluge, the wife of the man who established the foundation that is paying for my stay here, went to get salt herself, but she too was unsuccessful. It was unpleasant, and I experienced directly the meaning of that ancient folktale about salt, whose worth is greater than gold.

When you went to the Castle, you parted company with the then leader of the Civic Forum, Jan Urban, on bad terms. Why was that?

I don't have the feeling that we parted on bad terms. Perhaps there was a certain tension between us at the time when he was leading the Civic Forum to victory in the elections and I was going through my first months in the Castle. It would have been a miracle if there had been no tension between us in that situation. The Civic Forum had sent me to the Castle, and they felt I should bow to its will more frequently; I, on the contrary, felt I should do what I myself thought proper. At the time my influence was enormous, and I was seen a little bit as the savior of the nation—as your questions have made reference to—but the influence of the Civic Forum was just as great. I could not surrender my own judgment and point of view, but neither could the people who were leading the Civic Forum at the time. There's nothing shocking in that. After all, in stable democracies, which we were certainly not, discord between loyalty to the state and to the party often exists. I no longer know specifically what Jan Urban and I argued about—perhaps it had something to do with the Ministry of the Interior. It could not have been a very serious falling-out, for after all, like others, I was involved in the Civic Forum election campaign, where Jan Urban and I must have worked side by side and been in agreement. Whatever it was, it's long since forgotten. Urban and I occasionally see each other, and we talk about everything except such ancient matters.

Can you be successful in politics without a hunger for power? Sometimes I have the feeling that Czechs believe one should become a politician almost by default. Even you write, in the conclusion to *Summer Meditations,* that you've never struggled for power. Your colleagues see it differently: they claim that from a certain moment on, you fought for the presidency. How do you see it today?

In democratic conditions with their own tradition, their own continuity, and their own culture, it's obvious that anyone who wants to be successful in politics has to work for it. That means he must have a program, a vision, convictions, political goals he believes will contribute to the common good. At the same time, though, he must take that pro-gram into a political competition and push it through, as a real person standing behind the program. In other words, he must, as you put it, struggle for power. This is neither disgraceful nor immoral. What's important is that power be not an end in itself but rather the true expression of a desire to serve a good cause. The problem is that every-one who runs for office talks about serving the nation and it's up to the voters to distinguish between those who mean it seriously and those who are only saying it to claw their way up the ladder.

I was a special and completely atypical phenomenon, one that could probably have happened only in a revolutionary situation. I genuinely did not want the position of president and for a long time resisted the pressures on me to accept it. When I finally realized that I had no other choice, I certainly didn't begin to struggle for the position. The cam-paign was conducted by others, and in any case, it quickly became the general will that I be president, which at the time was astonishing. After all, people didn't know me very well, and if they did it was not as some-one who desired political office.

The truth is, however, that when I do something I try to do it prop-erly, so that when I accepted the candidacy, I also accepted the various obligations that flowed from it. It would have been absurd, at that point, to have kept reconsidering, hesitating, expressing embarrassment, or being coy. Perhaps that's where the impression that I was fighting for the office comes from. It's nonsense. I wasn't fighting for anything.

But I was, I hope, the last of my kind. Politicians who hold office out of necessity and by default, as it were, if not merely out of politeness or because they can't bring themselves to disappoint people by turning them down, ought not to be part of normal politics.

Washington, April 21, 2005

Yesterday's dinner in the White House was for about sixty people, and it was to honor Shakespeare. It was followed by a short performance. There were many important people there, and the Bushes were very pleasant: they introduced us as the guests of honor. Many of the guests told me I was their hero, that they had read my speeches and essays and seen my plays. I never know exactly how to respond to this. Yesterday I tried to explain to several of the guests that if I seem to be a hero it's certainly not because I ever set out to be one. It was only a long series of events, circumstances, or dilemmas that provided the setting in which I had to make certain decisions, and that every decision—while remaining faithful to certain values—inevitably determined the next, although of course one never knew in advance what that would be.

I used that explanation to mask my embarrassment. America is fond of stories with heroes and happy endings. I find that endearing. But perhaps Mr. Hvížďala is right to suggest that I was pushed hard into this positive role. Yet who among us has never, from time to time, been forced into playing some role? The important thing is to be conscious of that role and to be able to reflect upon it and one's relationship to it.

I must add one more thing: not only was there salt on the table in the White House, but the food was excellent. It bore no resemblance to the tasteless American cuisine that one finds everywhere here. It was a pleasant evening, but later when we got home I was afflicted by coronary fibrillations or arrhythmia. It was quite unpleasant and Dáša subjected me to various treatments. I feel better today but I'm terribly tired. This evening I will be present at the Czech embassy for the awarding of medals to veterans of the Second World War.

Your main rival for the presidency of Czechoslovakia was Alexander Dubček, who, in the eyes of the rest of the world, was a symbol of reform in communist countries. What kind of an impression did he make on you?

As far as I can I remember, I was the only official candidate for president. No political movement or party ever formally declared Alexander Dubček as its candidate. Nevertheless, there was much talk of him as a possible president, mainly among reform communists and in Slovakia. I think that he himself really wanted to be president, although he never said so directly. The Public Against Violence and the Civic Forum, however, vigorously opposed Dubček's candidacy, on the one hand because he was too closely connected to reform communism, which the public no longer had any appetite for, and on the other hand because people still held his ambiguous behavior after the Soviet occupation against him.

I recall that no one was able, or dared, to persuade him to abandon his ambition, or rather his undeclared candidacy. And so in the end it fell to me. It was one of the most absurd tasks I've ever had to perform: being myself a candidate for the presidency, and moreover having been dragooned into it, my task was to explain to someone else that he shouldn't run for the same office.

I had several confidential conversations with Dubček on that subject, and I must say I felt very sorry for him and that my mission was excruciatingly unpleasant. On the other hand, I came to realize that Dubček, in his own way, was not very resolute; he was someone who, if confronted with a fateful dilemma—as presidents in our country often are—might once again fail to deliver. I think that he was an honorable person, decent, pleasant, modest, but hopelessly mired in communist ideology and phraseology: he always spoke at great length, and it was difficult to discern what he was actually trying to say.

Wasn't Ivan Dejmal right when he wrote to you on December 19, 1989, and suggested that by supporting an empty symbol, Alexander Dubček, for the position of chair of the Federal Assembly and bumping Stanislav Kukrál, the democratically elected incumbent, you had betrayed yourself and your slogan about "living in truth," and in that moment you lost a part of your credibility and honor, at least in the eyes of some people?

It was clear that if Dubček weren't to be president he should have the second highest office in the land; if he had been completely bypassed and pushed aside, the Slovaks would probably have raised a ruckus, including all those Slovaks who had opposed him. That would have caused a very profound crisis. After Alois Indra, the living symbol of high treason, surrendered his post, Mr. Kukrál was quickly appointed the speaker of the Federal Assembly in his place, and he probably knew better than anyone that it was just an interim position. He fully understood Dubček's claim to the position and was happy to step aside and assume the post of first vice chair. That was how things were at the time; there were people who occupied a given position for perhaps only a few days.

But again, I'd like to remind you that while I might have had enormous influence in those days, I was certainly no dictator. Both of the main political entities at the time, the Public Against Violence and the Civic Forum, agreed that Dubček would be proposed as the chairman of the Federal Assembly. I felt that it was the way it ought to be, that Dubček should return to the position from which the occupiers had once driven him, a position that was near the top of the hierarchy but of more prestige than substance, and that it was in the interest of harmony between the Czechs and Slovaks. At the time I simply couldn't imagine carrying out my duties as head of state without having Dubček somewhere beside me. That's all true. But it's not true that it was my decision. The political forces proposed Dubček and parliament elected him. It was no more and no less democratic than the election of Mr. Kukrál.

How did you feel when you were elected president by a communist parliament? Did you understand it as humiliating for them or for you?

I don't think it was humiliating for anyone. But it was certainly very odd. When I watched the proceedings immediately before the election of the president on television, for example, and I saw the members of parliament endorse my election in the name of every possible organization that, to this point, had been run by the state, from the Union of Women to the Czechoslovak People's Army, I was overwhelmed by a sense of absurdity. After all, only a few days or weeks before, these same people had loudly approved my prosecution and imprisonment. It really did seem like something out of *Ubu Roi*.

But once again, it wouldn't be fair if I were merely to ridicule it; it would be like ridiculing the police for not arresting us or the army for not having the gumption to carry out a putsch. Certainly, fear played a role in parliament's behavior, but at the same time there was something in it—perhaps only a trace of something—that bespoke a kind of responsibility for the country. My name, my photograph, my portrait were everywhere. No centrally run or government-financed campaign could have achieved anything like that. Parliament was surrounded by students who offered the members of parliament bread and salt to indicate their desire that power change hands peacefully, and my election became a kind of climax to the revolution, or the ultimate test of its validity. The members of parliament merely looked around at the true state of affairs, and—perhaps through clenched teeth—respected the general will. None of us knew at the time what would have happened had they not elected me. To the extent that they possessed even a modicum of good judgment, there was nothing else they could have done.

What does one lose and what does one gain when one steps across the threshold of the Castle?

Naturally, I can speak only for myself. I took on a job that demanded everything of me, that consumed me entirely and made it almost impossible for me to pay attention to anything else. I lost a large piece of my freedom because I sometimes had to express myself more diplomatically than I would have wanted, behave somewhat differently than I would have behaved had I not been in that position, dress differently, and so on. I also missed out on many developments, something I realized only when I stepped down and was confronted not only by a new generation of cell phones, cars, computers, and other devices whose evolution I had not followed closely, but above all by a different kind of civic life than the one I had stepped out of years before. True, during that entire period I tried to live as ordinary a life as possible, to occasionally go shopping, to wander through the streets, to look around me, and not allow myself to be hoodwinked by anything. But it couldn't be helped; it was not an entirely normal life. That was simply impossible.

What did I gain? One thing, in fact: I became a direct participant in great changes in our world, and I could have an immediate influence on those changes. I consider that a tremendous gift of destiny.

Washington, April 22, 2005

To tell you the truth, it's not just Americans and other foreigners who think of me as a kind of fairy-tale prince or at least as the main character in a fairy tale; I too am often aware of something utterly unbelievable in my own destiny. And I'm less and less able to understand that destiny; at times I even see myself as a minor freak of history. How could this ever have happened to me— and to me in particular—to be in the very center of events so momentous that they determined the fate of many nations and millions of people? Why did I, the author of absurd plays, experience hundreds of absurd situations such as the one that happened on my first visit to the Kremlin? (I will come back to that later.) Sometimes I think my life is just a dream and that one day, very soon, I will wake up in 1958 as a soldier in the barracks in České Budějovice; the alarm will have sounded, and I—someone with no sense of balance—will have to go down a busy street in the morning rush hour on a bicycle with no rubber tires, wearing a helmet and full battle gear, carrying a machine gun, a gas mask, and a cardboard box full of live ammunition, in order to wake up an officer in his flat so that he can lead our entire sapper regiment to the western borders on an exercise to defend the communist world against NATO troops (the same organization whose summit I will inaugurate in Prague forty-four years later). But in fact, even my two years in the army, and even more so my five years in prison, seem to me an unreal and indescribable dream, albeit in this case a very dark one. And so I must ultimately pose the question as to whether all of this—the fact that such a peaceable man ended up living such an adventurous life—isn't a result of the fact that life itself, even the most ordinary and the most inconspicuous life, is an unbelievable miracle. A fairy tale at times beautiful, at times suspenseful, at times terrifying.

(July 7, 1996)

(. . .)

4) The German lunch. The food was average by international standards, as in any hotel, not a disaster but nothing special. The dessert was the best; it was truly marvelous. They served pointlessly large portions; that's something that happens only in the Czech Republic now. The guests left 90 percent of it on their plates. It also wasn't good that the waiter remained standing in the room observing us; he was clearly waiting in case someone wanted a top-up, but it wasn't appropriate because the conversation was about very delicate matters and the waiter almost certainly hasn't taken an oath of silence. (. . .)

(August 23, 1996)

(. . .)

4) Latin America is my great trauma. S. supplied me flawlessly: I have a suitcase full of detailed briefing materials and books. It frightens me; the sheer amount of it is blocking me, and so far I've only been able to study a tiny amount, about 3 percent of it. I'm absolutely terrified of that suitcase. Not because there might be something uninteresting in it, but just the contrary; a casual sifting through it all has merely revealed to me how little I know and that I will never be able to acquire any thorough knowledge of the subject. I admit that I've essentially been avoiding the suitcase. That's how much I fear it. Oh well, I'll get over it: as the trip gets closer, I will read more of the material and separate the important and the memorizable from the less important and the unmemorizable. What's worse is that this trauma has affected my ability to write the most important speech, that is, the Brazilian speech. And the more I'm reminded of its importance and of the nearness of the day when I have to deliver it, the more blocked I am. So far I don't even have a single line. Today is Friday; theoretically it's possible that on Saturday or Sunday I will write something. But I consider that highly unlikely. (. . .)

(September 1, 1996)

1) On Saturday I was able, after all, to write the Brazilian speech. (. . .)

(November 3, 1996)

1) It's Sunday morning and I'm gathering my strength for the Ukraine speech. It is, as usual, a nightmare. If I succeed in writing it, it will be included with these memos and it should be quickly assessed so that I could start the final editing as soon as possible. If it's not included with these notes, that's a bad sign because it will leave me only Monday, a day when I have a harder time writing than on other days.

2) This point is secret. (. . .) It's about several transactions that the cardinal and I have agreed upon. (a) In the next few days the cardinal's secretary will hand-deliver the cardinal's letter in which he will inform me that the Church surrenders its claims to the ownership of the cathedral and offers it to the country. He will, of course, ask for the fulfillment of certain (easily fulfilled) conditions allowing the Church a say in the day-to-day running of the cathedral. He is concerned that this be seen as a generous gesture on the part of the Church and not as a precedent that in any way recognizes the expropriation legislation as valid, which would mean that the state could retain for itself everything that is currently in state hands with no further negotiations. (. . .) (d) A return favor for this gesture by the Church would be an executive order handing over all of the other ecclesiastical buildings within the Castle precincts to the Church. I talked to Lux about this, and he said it's not a problem to include them in the list of real estate to be handed over and that it would be passed by the government. (. . .) (e) In a certain phase, when both these matters are well on their way to a successful conclusion, we (the Church and us) would withdraw our lawsuits. (. . .)

3) I had a rather thorough discussion with Zieleniec and Vollmerová about Czech-German matters and the ideal timetable for the next steps. I will inform any colleagues involved in the matter orally, for example over

soup, where Mr. Š. might be invited as well and which would also be a preparation for Berlin on Thursday. (. . .)

What were your first days in the Prague Castle like?

They were obviously affected by the atmosphere prevailing in the country at the time. I know that we laughed a lot, though I can hardly remember what we laughed at or why. We were a group of friends from various branches of the arts who had suddenly found ourselves in a world we had known only from a distance, and which up till then had been merely a target of our criticism and ridicule, and who had to decide very quickly what we were going to do with this world. My colleagues could certainly recall dozens of unbelievably absurd or humorous incidents from that time. I like to remember one that was somewhat symbolic: it seemed to me that on the same floor where my office was located, there were fewer rooms than you would expect, given the size of that part of the Castle. So one day we got hold of top secret architectural plans of the Castle and we saw what the situation was and began to demand access to rooms which, up to that point, apparently did not exist. And what did we find there? An enormous, clumsy, and incredibly secret Warsaw Pact teletype that only top officials could use. We got hold of the cryptologist, and I used the teletype to send greetings to Mikhail Gorbachev. Later I learned that the Soviets were impressed that we'd found it so quickly. It's possible that—like many other things—it was supposed to have remained hidden from us, as though someone somewhere had said, We don't know yet how everything's going to turn out and perhaps a couple of these things might still come in handy. Or perhaps someone had said, maliciously, let them look. Or perhaps they'd simply forgotten about it, and it was another of the thousands of examples of Czech slackness on the job.

But one has to be careful: memory can be deceptive and has a tendency to retain mainly the pleasant things. Both during the revolution and during my first months in office, I also experienced some very tense moments. It's easy, for example, for someone who wasn't responsible for making fundamental decisions to say, in hindsight, that we shouldn't have been so lenient with the communists. But when you're dealing with an opponent who has every imaginable instrument of power in his hands, you have to be pretty damned careful how you act if you don't want to feel guilty for the rest of your life for pointless bloodshed. Just deciding how to lead a demonstration with almost a million people taking part is no easy matter: think of how little it would take to trigger a mob response, for someone to fall for an act of provocation, for a squadron of fighter planes, for instance, to fly low over the demonstrators and cause a bloody panic. This last example is not something I've pulled out of my head: the minister of defense later told me that it wouldn't have been a problem to do this. In other words, someone in the high command had obviously broached the idea. In any case, I understand that far more dangerous ideas had cropped up in such meetings, including the occupation of Prague by an armored division. We had to proceed carefully. But just because we were circumspect in our behavior when confronting such an all-powerful regime, it certainly did not mean that we were committed to doing so in the future, as some people think.

You are very often criticized for the generous amnesty you granted on January 1, 1990, and also for your later acts of clemency. How do you evaluate these activities of yours today?

The amnesty of January 1990 has been held against me for fifteen years without anyone explaining to me why it was bad. Was it supposed to have increased the crime rate? The crime rate did go up, but for entirely different reasons; if I remember correctly, the release of prisoners in 1990 accounted for only a 9 percent increase in the general crime rate in the Czech Republic and 7 percent in Slovakia; in other words a slightly larger percentage than freed prisoners contribute to it every year. In any case, a large number of those released would have been released anyway that year, or a year later; after all, part of the amnesty was meant to reduce sentences for more serious offenses by one year. The amnesty, of course, was prepared by experts, among whom were well-known people like the current ombudsman, Otakar Motejl, and the current chief justice of the Constitutional Court, Pavel Rychetský, the then minister of justice, Dagmar Burešová, and others. I read subsequent statistics and penological analyses of that amnesty, and nothing alarming came out of them. Yes, it was truly generous. But it was necessary to make it absolutely clear that conditions were changing fundamentally and that we wanted to part company with everything that was degrading about the communist justice system.

As far as the criticism of my presidential pardons is concerned, that is also a terrible cliché, part of the national mythology that had its beginnings in the criticisms of that first amnesty. In any case, there is a detailed book coming out about those acts of clemency by a former employee of the relevant department in the Office of the President, in which every case is described and justified in detail. I granted between seventy and a hundred pardons annually, which wasn't a lot. In rare cases, it was a question of righting a miscarriage of justice, but most of the cases were decided on the basis of compassion. Every pardon is in essence controversial because you are granting it to someone who has committed a crime. Precedence was always given to people who were old or sick or who were mothers. Those who prepared the documentation studied each case on its individual merits. They visited the prisoners, either in jail or on parole. They studied their files. They looked into their family circumstances.

Naturally it would have been easiest to grant pardons to no one. I would have been immensely more popular. But I wasn't the president in order to be popular. Paradoxically, the same judges who sent someone to prison would occasionally request that I grant that person a pardon. They had acted according to the law in sentencing them, but they knew the person didn't belong in prison.

What was it like, in the first months of your presidency, dealing with former communists or reform communists in the new government? You once complained to me quite forcefully about Zdeněk Jičínský.

Some of them really caused us a lot of problems, but not all of them. They don't all belong in the same basket. Nevertheless, quite a few former communists seemed genetically inclined to indulge in what I would call "collective cabinet politics." They attended all our joint meetings in that period, so they knew everything that went on and had a say in everything, but we knew very little about the meetings or private consultations they held among themselves, somewhat in the way the party "inner circles" would meet in the old days. Likewise, we knew very little about the separate meetings they held with government representatives.

On the whole, they probably had no ulterior motives; it was just how they were trained, and not even those twenty years away from the party and practical politics, those years spent within the dissident opposition, had cured them entirely. Sometimes they appeared to get along better with those in power than with those of us who were noncommunists, mainly because they shared a common language. Many of them would like to have instituted some kind of new "socialism with a human face," or perestroika communism, but such notions scarcely stood a chance, mainly because most people had no desire for any such thing. People were allergic to that kind of language, even in its more enlightened form.

Perhaps the most trouble for me, personally, was caused by Zdeněk Jičínský, a tireless lawyer and chartist, and a leading proponent of reform communism in the 1960s. I'll give two examples: during the Velvet Revolution we were negotiating with the government delegation about striking the article on the leading role of the Communist Party from the constitution. Čalfa and the members of his delegation conceded to our demand. The matter was settled. And at that moment, Zdeněk— who was in the Civic Forum delegation—asked to speak and said that in its place we could entrench the leading role of the working class, or of working people. Objectively, it was nonsense, merely an expression of nostalgia for communist ideological language. We kicked him under the table, and he dropped the matter. In any case, even Čalfa thought it was nonsense; he more or less said, if we're going to do it, let's do it. We have to do the best we can and not make any phraseological compromises, especially if no one is asking us to.

We had a more serious clash with Jičínský in the spring of 1990, when the new electoral law was being prepared for the first free elections. Petr Pithart and others, including me, were fighting for a majority, first-past-the-post electoral system that promised that future members of parliament would be trustworthy people, elected directly in small constituencies, and not servile products of party apparatuses. Zdeněk Jičínský led a dogged battle for a proportional system, and in the end he won. I didn't know at the time why he fought so strongly not just for a proportional electoral system, but against the voluntary dissolution of the Civic Forum. Later, I began to understand it: had the reform communists contested the election as an independent group, their chances of getting into parliament would have been slim. Their only hope was to remain a part of the Civic Forum, but for that to happen the Civic Forum had to exist, and the electoral system had to be proportional because, had they stood as individuals in a first-past-the-post, single-member constituency system—given the general coolness toward reform communism—they would have lost. In short, with the proportional system, and as part of a Civic Forum list, they were assured of seats in parliament.

And by the way, later, when the new parties were already taking shape, I tried to push through a change in the electoral system, but I came up against absolutely adamant resistance from the Civic Democratic Party (ODS). They clearly had the same fears that Jičínský had had earlier: that a majority electoral system could deprive them of the positions they had already achieved. Today, on the contrary, the Civic Democratic Party is campaigning for a majority single-round electoral system, because with that it has the chance to win an absolute majority of the seats. I think it's a sad thing that the parties, rather than thinking about which system is best for the country, always think first of all about which system is best for them at a particular time. Consequently their positions on referenda, the direct election of the president, the electoral system, and similar themes are constantly changing, or rather, being passed from party to party like a relay baton.

Would you say the greatest defeat in that period was allowing the nationalist card to be played to the extent that it was in Slovakia?

I'm sorry, but we were really trying to move—in a stumbling fashion, to be sure—from a totalitarian system to a democracy, and not to some kind of new dictatorship. It would have been against all my principles had I tried to determine for the Slovak people a way in which they might or might not express themselves as a nation. It's true that I had taken an oath on the federal constitution and had sworn to defend the integrity of the state, which, in fact, I did, but at the same time I couldn't simply ignore the emancipation movement in Slovakia, let alone attempt somehow to suppress it. Nations have the right—if it is the will of the majority—to go through a phase of independent statehood.

The majority of Czechs, who were brought up on the idea of a Czechoslovak nation and who automatically connected the notion of Slovak independence with fascism, had little grasp of Slovak sensitivities and ambitions. I think I had a stronger grasp than many others, but I too may not have been entirely free of certain historical prejudices and misconceptions. It's true that the Slovak nationalists were somewhat ridiculous and annoying, but that does not mean that something fundamental in the relationship of our two nations did not have to change. At the time, I supported the idea of an "authentic federation," which means not a federalized totalitarian state as we had under communism, but a federation based on the genuine equality of both subject states and both subject nations that comprise it. In this the Civic Forum and our friends in the Public Against Violence saw eye to eye. In 1990 and 1991 we spent thousands of hours in various political meetings looking for the optimal model of coexistence between our two peoples in a common state. We didn't come up with it and we probably couldn't have: not only the Czechs but also many Slovaks at the time clearly did not fully understand the Slovak state of mind. After all, if the Slovaks had really wanted to live with the Czechs in one country, they would have revolted somehow against the breakup of the country or simply not have allowed it to happen. Yes, there was a petition supporting the idea of a common state that was signed by tens of thousands of Slovaks, but the fact that no one paid attention to it, nor did they have to, makes it all pretty clear.

Nevertheless, all those meetings weren't simply a waste of time. On the contrary, without that immensely interesting and constructive attempt, we would probably never have come to understand what exactly happened and why.

On the "organizational" side of things, I had only two major objections. In the first place, the breakup of the country was not decided by a referendum. I suggested one be held. My legislative initiative to that effect was tabled in parliament, but no one supported it; they were probably all afraid that the Slovaks would vote for a common country. Today I'm not sure that a referendum would, in fact, have been a good thing: if the Slovaks had voted for a common state, everything would have started all over again and would probably have ended the same way. It would only have been a further waste of time. In hindsight, it seems to me that while most Slovaks did not consciously want separation, they were drawn to it subconsciously.

My second objection is that the country was divided not by its governing bodies but by political parties. Every night during the summer of 1992, representatives of the Czech Civic Democratic Party and the Movement for a Democratic Slovakia, two parties that had a lot in common, stood at the microphones and informed their publics about how one country would be divided into two. In systemic terms this seems to me to be quite wrong. It is merely the old principle of "the leading role of the party" in a new guise. The leading parties, which after all are civic associations with no right to negotiate on behalf of a state, decide something and announce it, leaving the government—this time without microphones—to carry it out.

I myself resigned, in July 1992, more for symbolic than practical reasons, and in any case my mandate was going to be up in three months anyway. My point was to show that someone who had taken an oath to defend the constitution of a particular country cannot then sign into law an act dissolving that country. That is simply not done. And in our country it does not evoke pleasant memories. Just recall our weeping presidents, or presidents obsessed with explaining the meaning of their capitulations.

To stay with Slovakia for a moment: at the time, the Slovaks criticized you for not going to Slovakia first after your election, for not following the Slovak newspapers, and for not keeping your promise to appoint Milan Kňažko as your vice president. Are such criticisms valid?

I was in Slovakia a few days before I was first elected president; I had enormous rallies in the public squares. I visited factories and so on, so I felt I didn't have to return right away. Perhaps it was a mistake; I was clearly not aware enough of Slovak sensitivities. But it seemed to me far more important to communicate immediately to Europe, to the world, and to our neighbor Germany the essence of what had actually happened in our country and to begin to consolidate our international position as an independent country. So, shortly after my election, I made a brief trip to Germany. It was only in relation to this journey that the question arose as to why I didn't go first to Slovakia. But for me Slovakia was not a foreign country, and I went to Germany to promote the interests of both our peoples.

Regarding the newspapers: Czechs tend to read Czech newspapers, and Slovaks tend to read Slovak papers. I've never played at being a Slovak, and it would have seemed terribly hypocritical of me. When something important appeared in the Slovak papers, of course I read it.

Regarding Milan Kňažko: he could not have been vice president because our constitution doesn't recognize such a position. I wouldn't have been against it, and I even think that in the proposal for a new federal constitution that I presented to the Federal Assembly, that position was included. Kňažko was my friend and adviser, and once, in public, I jokingly referred to him as my vice president. In time I stopped making jokes in public—they always come back to haunt you.

Washington, April 25, 2005

Before the weekend began I was at another "political dinner," this time at Madeleine's. The arrangement was wonderful. The important people who were present—for example Jim Lehrer from PBS and General Ralston, the former commander in chief of NATO—were engaging. Madeleine moderated the discussion skillfully and wittily, but nevertheless I had, once again, to respond, in American English, to many political questions, and it left me completely exhausted. The more of these discussions I have (and they keep seriously multiplying even though I turn down most invitations), the more I realize one important difference between America, or rather Washington, and the Czech

Republic, or rather Prague. Here people enjoy politics; in our country they don't. Here they really enjoy talking about politics; in our country they merely complain about it. Here politicians, scientists and academics, journalists, and other important people appear to stay fresh the whole day, and perhaps they say the cleverest things in the evening. In our country, by the evening, such people are either tired or desperately trying to catch up on work, or they're drunk or just glad to be home watching television with no need to talk to anyone.

Perhaps this isn't entirely accurate, but so far I have the impression that political Washington is populated mainly by gentlemen who wear a tie all day, who work politically in the morning, then have a political lunch, then work again politically in the afternoon, only to go from work to some kind of political dinner. And throughout all this they remain good-natured, calm, handsome, and charming. This is also true of their wives and the political women. Why is it that we Czechs are always so harried? Always so irritated? Why are we always complaining about something instead of doing a decent day's work?

(April 13, 1997)

(. . .)

7) I've noticed that the Czech papers are full of reports or speculations on the disagreements over the protocol status of state officials, and that in some cases they involve me and the fact that I have allegedly decided this or that in such and such a way. I will attempt, therefore, to put things in the proper perspective, with the request that in any further statements, you hold to this "proper perspective." There is no law that says anything about an order of protocol. The whole business is merely a matter of interpreting the law, in this case the constitution. The protocol offices and the legislative departments of the Chamber of Deputies, the Senate, and the OPR—as they interpret the constitution—disagree about the protocol status of the chairs of the legislature and the Senate but have, however, agreed that the officials of the legislature rank higher than the prime minister. I have taken this interpretation on advisement.

That's all there is to it. I would ask that I not be involved in this any further. As far as the dinner with Chirac is concerned, it is true that over soup, Mr. S. mentioned that Pithart would have a better place than Klaus, and it's also true that I took that into consideration. But I did not know that Mrs. Muchová was going to be seated between Pithart and Klaus, just as I did not know other things which then stirred up such a ruckus that the cabinet may even have discussed it. Of course, I disapprove of the pettiness of those who concern themselves with such matters, but at the same time I don't want to bear any more responsibility for it than is appropriate and just. (. . .)

(July 20, 1997)

(. . .)

3) (. . .) (d) I question whether my trip to England in December makes any sense. Wouldn't it be better for me to go there as newly reelected president, should I in fact be reelected? It would provide a nice symmetry with the year 1990, when I went on a state visit to England as the freshly elected Czechoslovak president. Why should I go there to say farewell? I'd rather go there to remind people that I represent a future member of NATO and the EU, that is, as a valid partner and not as a sentimental reminder of the fall of communism and an eternally self-promoting fairy-tale prince (dissident to president—a traditional Anglo-Saxon fairy-tale cliché). And moreover, before Christmas and before the new presidential election the public will be particularly sensitive to my presence at home; they'll want to see me at all those Christmas programs for children, participating in whatever domestic political discussions take place; they'll want me to be with them and not somewhere else.

(August 2, 1997)

(. . .)

4) I will recapitulate, again, various matters that have come out of my conversations with the DFP or from our correspondence. (a) I will expect the Japanese minister on August 21 at Hrádeček. (b) I will receive the

Luxembourg prime minister (the morning of August 26). (c) We (Dáša and myself) will be with Charles at the opening of the art show, and then at a small dinner in some nice little pub (Nebozízek?); Dáša will accompany him to the Botanical Gardens. (d) I'm counting on a visit from the Philippine president. (e) The trip to the Middle East has been canceled. (f) On October 1, Dáša and I are flying to Paris, and that day we are there strictly privately. (. . .) October 2 is the receiving of the prize and other official events. October 3 we fly to New York to receive the American prize and then two or three days of rest with Forman or in New York, and then we return. Then two days at home and after that, Strasbourg. (. . .) (g) Concerning the German prize, we are waiting for Mandela. (h) For the Spanish prize, I will make a video clip. (i) I must probably also accept the Lange Prize. But going to Italy to before Christmas would seem impossible. (j) How about the trip to GB? Can't it be shifted?

(August 17, 1997)

(. . .)

2) I have one idea related to the floods. Many ugly buildings, badly and expensively constructed and in the wrong place, were destroyed. A flood is an opportunity for us to give our country a slightly improved appearance here and there. But the danger is that exactly the opposite will happen; that people will be in a hurry and build something even uglier than they had before. Therefore I would consider it a very good thing if this fall, in Olomouc or in Kroměříž, there could be a three-day symposium that would be attended by, let's say, twenty of the best European architects who have experience in urban design and modern municipal or public housing, plus ten of the best Czech architects. They would explain, using photographs or film, to the mayors and the chairmen of district councils, the ways in which it is possible to construct buildings that are economical, well built, and pleasing. At the same time, people from building firms should be invited. Bořek Šípek was here, and he was enthusiastic about my idea and offered to take care of the foreign participation (with the possible assistance of Mr. Koch). The mayors and the chairpersons will certainly be glad to support this and to take part. The only issue is who would run it and who would pay for it.

Perhaps the EU would provide funds. I don't know. However it works, it will only be a small step, but it could be an important one; at least it would show a few people what can be done today and what makes sense. Otherwise how would these people know? I would like to be the patron of this event and possibly even go there for the opening. I would thus ask the DDP to think about this project and then to get in touch with the appropriate people or institutions.

4) As far as my nightmares are concerned—I mean my speeches: I will possibly write the Forum 2000 speech here. It doesn't make sense to write the Jordan speech before the return of the advance team. I would like it to be a short improvised speech, off-the-cuff, expressing my thanks, and S. has been given the job of arguing for that. The greatest nut to crack will be my speech for the USA. I ask that ideas and research be assembled. A possible subject: the arrogance of power (Fulbright's book), versus the responsibility the U.S. has to the world. The speech at the summit of the Council of Europe will obviously be brief and conventional. The speech for October 28: I will ask for suggestions on a theme. This year's floods suggest the theme of solidarity and the meaning of the state as a way of mediating it. The speech to both legislative houses: an accounting and future projections. It should be a major speech and should enrich my old themes with new ones. It would really help to have a few free days to write it. The New Year's speech could then be short and personal; it worked well last year (even though, understandably, it's impossible to repeat that). (. . .)

(October 25, 1997)

(. . .)

4) The Spanish king has, once again, cordially invited Dáša and me to his cottage on the Canary Islands. (. . .) One way or the other, from my personal point of view, I would consider it a very good thing to go on a recuperative trip just before the presidential election, at the time when all the campaigns against me will come to a climax, especially if I could go (. . .) without taking along any briefing papers whatsoever. But how politically viable is this? Isn't it the assumption that if I am to become president again I will have to drain the cup of bitterness to the very

dregs? But why should I have to do that? After all, I'm serving my country, not the other way around, so why should I be punished for it? I put this out for consideration with the proviso that we have to decide within the week. (. . .)

8) Would somebody please, immediately, write a brief appellative letter to Václav Klaus which would have the appearance of an order and which could, in extreme circumstances, be publishable, and which would urgently request him to finally deal with Bratinka's Roma material and with that entire situation, at his Wednesday cabinet meeting. (Before sending it by courier please consult confidentially with Bratinka.) Have the Ministry of Foreign Affairs write its own report on the immediate state of affairs with England for this meeting. Consider also the possibility of a brief, demonstrative visit by me, to the cabinet meeting. I can't read Bratinka's reports because they are at the office on my table and in any case I have no time to read them (it's like a whole book) so I would ask someone to assemble a one-page précis for me. Further, I need to know any other initiatives that I could come up with. The thing is, everyone is saying something different and—what is even worse—I have the impression that on the whole the government and parliament don't really care. I must do something but I have to know what. Likewise, if I am to call Blair, I have to know what I want to say to him. So far I don't know. He is clearly avoiding the conversation because he really wants to impose visa restrictions.

Washington, April 25, 2005

And one more thing fascinates me here: people are fond of their country. You can tell this not only because the American flag is flying from every third house, but from many other less obvious indications. Yesterday, for example, I watched a conversation on television with the sister of a criminal, perhaps a pedophile condemned to death for murder. They asked her what she wanted to do, whether she intended in some way to make amends for what her brother had done. Very calmly, with a smile, and very matter-of-factly, she said that she wanted to serve the United States by performing some difficult task, for example, in a war. It was persuasive and, in its own way, moving. I can't imagine something like this happening at home. Some people would laugh, but others would start casting stones at that person and at Czech Television.

Another large problem: the state security forces—the StB, the secret police. Why did it take a month to disband it? Why didn't you occupy the headquarters of this important organization right away, as befits a revolution—and paralyze it? This gave it the chance to destroy the files of its most important informers and collaborators.

The secret police had countless buildings, both known and unknown, all over the country. We didn't occupy them most probably because we had no army or police division that was both loyal to us and well informed. Naturally we gave no one permission to burn those files; it's just that we probably didn't know where they were and where they were being burned. I doubt that anything of exceptional interest was burned. As far as I know, no records were kept on the most important collaborators of the StB, nor were they registered anywhere. It's said that a lot of files on dissidents were burned. I don't know why that should have happened. I would rather have expected someone to have hidden them somewhere, so they could then be pulled out at the appropriate moment to blackmail or create scandals.

At the time I pushed hard to have all the archives sealed at once. But there were clearly no forces that could have done that either; after all, they kept everything secret, even from one another. You can seal something only if you know where it is and what it is you're meant to be sealing.

Just before the elections in June 1990 it was announced that Mr. Josef Bartončík, one of the important candidates, had been a longtime collaborator with the StB. This was made public by the deputy minister of the interior, Jan Ruml, in the period when the legal moratorium on any further electioneering was in effect. Don't you think it was one of the fundamentally erroneous steps that you took at the time?

About a week before the elections, I learned about the long-term work that Mr. Bartončík, who was then—in fact he'd just been elected—chairman of the Christian Democratic Union–Czechoslovak People's Party coalition and the deputy chairman of the Federal Assembly, had long been in the pay of the StB. I immediately called him in, and, with no one else present, I told him that we knew, and suggested that he resign his position and his candidacy for reasons of health. He agreed, for he probably didn't want a scandal either. He immediately went into the hospital, then called me to confirm that he had done what we'd agreed upon. Relieved, I left for Moscow—perhaps for a meeting about the Warsaw Pact, I no longer recall—but when I was still there I learned that Mr. Bartončík had not resigned from any of his posts and was still running for election. Ruml, who had promised me he wouldn't do anything before my return, was waiting for me at the airport and told me that he and Jiří Křižan had decided to release the truth about Bartončík. I wasn't very happy about it; I don't like these public executions; but I couldn't stop them from doing it.

The whole thing needn't have happened if Bartončík had kept his word instead of relying on our goodwill. In my opinion, releasing that information wasn't breaking the law. True, for two days before the election it was forbidden to campaign for parties or candidates, or to advertise, but it wasn't forbidden to speak the truth. If that were the case, then during those two days, all the newspapers would have had to cease publication, and there could be no television or radio broadcasts.

But there is something more important here: thousands of years in prison sentences, executions, tens of thousands of lives ruined—that is the work of the StB. I completely understand Honza Ruml and Jiří Křižan, whose father they executed, wanting to tell people about someone who had the gall to ask for their support during our first free elections. On the one hand you are surprised that we didn't deal with the communists more decisively during the revolutionary period, and, at the same time, you would keep secret from the public the fact that an informer was about to be elected? In any case, I think that if our reform communist friends had told us everything, the matter could have been sorted out long before the elections. Dubček had clearly known about Bartončík for a long time, for he warned me about him several times.

(March 2, 1998)

1) This weekend I had one of my deepest depressions for a long time. Perhaps you could tell from our meeting, or rather from my introductory words. If I spoiled anyone's mood, I apologize. On the other hand, I say to myself that it's not a bad thing at all if my colleagues occasionally get a glimpse into the dark side of their boss's soul.

2) Being in a depression, I could not, of course, write anything. It wasn't until this afternoon (Monday) that I forced myself, through a persistent effort of will, to write a speech for Poland. I'm sending it for comment. I will look at the speech for Geneva as soon as I have a little time and my mood improves. I won't get to it today.

3) (. . .) (f) I don't know how to do this, but I feel that somehow my rest time must be separated from my speechwriting time. For many years now, my weekends have more or less all been occupied with the writing of speeches. It's awful. You're afraid to go for a walk or anywhere because you are haunted by unfinished work, and so you allow yourself to be terrorized the whole weekend, only to write it desperately on Sunday evening, or on Monday. That is not good. Speechwriting is also work, and it ought to be scheduled for me just like any other work and not mixed up with the weekend, or stuck into my rest time. Someone wrote an essay in *MFD* about how I am becoming another "run-of-the-mill politician." I don't know whether I am or not, but if I am it's because my speeches are no longer punchy and written with verve. (. . .)

(May 30, 1998)

(. . .)

10) The honor rolls. The proposed list is, as usual, a dog's breakfast. There are many people on it who are less deserving of the honor than

others who are not on it. There's a preponderance of the dead; you can tell that some of the suggestions are various friends, acquaintances, or political fellow travelers of the suggesters, etc., etc. In short, there are thousands of possible objections. Nevertheless, I will endorse it and agree with it. I have no intention of making trouble; consider it a collegial compromise. However, not as a mere proposal, but as a final decision, I will add these names to be recipients of the Order of Merit: Jiří Kuběna, the Brno poet, for his lifetime literary work and his unshakable civic convictions; Věra Chytilová, the filmmaker, for lifetime achievement; Václav Benda and Petr Uhl, for their services in resisting the totalitarian regime. If he hasn't gotten it already, Otomar Krejča should definitely receive one for his lifetime artistic achievements. In all seriousness I would propose further Jan Kačer and Marta Kubišová. I propose for consideration Josef Suk (the violinist), Dominic Hašek (the goalie), Jiří Pelikán, who is seriously ill, and the very aged Jaroslav Foglar. (Josef Šafařík, Jiří Kolář, and Jindřich Chalupecký have already, I hope, received the order; if not, all three of them should be given the Order of Tomáš Garrigue Masaryk.) (. . .)

18) For many weeks now the politicians and journalists have been annoying the public with a strange form of amusement: speculating about whom I will appoint to form a government, who will be the prime minister, and whether the largest party has or does not have a claim to that, etc., etc. The whole thing is silly, unqualified, hysterical, and humiliating for me because within it lurks the suspicion that I intend to ignore the results of the election and I will entrust the formation of the new government to the gardener in the local park. I would ask Mr. Š., Mr. P., and all the others to not allow themselves to be dragged into this game any longer. (. . .)

(Undated, 1998)

(. . .)

I very much regret what happened, that is, that TV Nova broadcast my lament that the OPR had grown somewhat lax in my absence. I deeply apologize to all of you for that, and above all, to those of you who, in my absence, work hard for very little money and purely for the cause, and I would ask that you try not to be too fed up about this. By way of explanation:

1) It was recorded without my knowledge, when the microphones were meant to be turned off. I didn't notice until it was too late that the camera from Nova—i.e., a station that honors no agreements—was very close to me.

2) My lament was influenced by the atmosphere created by what came immediately beforehand: I had had several enervating telephone conversations with the OPR about the lack of coordination in my program. I was mildly agitated, and my lament was clearly the fading echo of my agitation.

3) In general I am on edge and I often get upset and more than once I have wronged someone unintentionally. It is caused by a confluence of many circumstances, including my annoying and chronic health problems and the fact that I can't smoke. I have warned your bosses and told them that if I speak in an irritated or exaggerated way they mustn't always take me too seriously.

4) On the whole there wouldn't have been any uproar about my incriminating statement (after all, I've said such things and worse to many of you straight to your faces) had it not come out in public. That's the bad thing about it, I admit, and I leave it to Mr. Š. to attempt to somehow set it right, if that's possible. Perhaps we might all be reassured by the known fact that today's sensation will be completely forgotten by the day after tomorrow and that everyone is already looking forward to the day after tomorrow's sensations.

In conclusion, a word of praise: thanks to the workers in the OPR, a missing piece of paper was found, the definitive loss of which I would have considered the greatest disaster of my presidency.

(July 4, 1998)

(. . .)

3) And now at last to the crises: I had a very long and open telephone conversation with Honza Ruml, as well as with a member of the leadership of the ČSSD. It seems to me that, somewhat thanks to my various negotiations but mainly thanks to the evolution of events itself, the pos-

sibility of a coalition between the ČSSD and the KDÚ-ČSL [Christian Democratic Union–Czech People's Party Coalition] tolerated by the ÚS has not yet been definitively buried. I am not very optimistic, but there is some percentage of hope here. Whether it is large or small we will learn gradually. One way or the other, I will have to name a prime minister by the end of the week. In the less probable, and better, case, it will be Lux; in the more likely, and worse, case, it will be Zeman, supported by an agreement with Klaus. (. . .)

(July 12, 1998)

(. . .)

3) (b) (. . .) On Friday 17, (. . .) Tošovský should come to me at 2:00 P.M. We should have a half an hour for conversation in my office or elsewhere, and then there would be the ceremonial act of handing over the resignation of the government. I ask that all the necessary papers be prepared. I would ask the government to remain in office until a new one is named. I would speak off-the-cuff, thanking Tošovský's government. At 3:00 P.M. Zeman would come. We would chat for half an hour, then there would be the ceremonial naming of him as prime minister. Once again, I will speak off-the-cuff. An opening for questions I assume that he will, in confidence, tell me the proposed composition of his government. If not, I will be very cool and pretend that I don't know when the new government will be named. (c) In reality, I'm counting on the naming of the new government on the 22nd at 2:00 P.M. Any speeches, once again, will be off-the-cuff. The full ceremony, flags, fanfares. In the evening there will be a farewell to the old government in Lány, at night return to Prague, and the following day admission to the hospital and then let God's will be done. (. . .)

(August 29, 1998)

(. . .)

2) My condition: with the move to Lány, it has rapidly improved; the nonhospital environment is having a beneficial influence on me.

3) I thank the OPR for their work during the long period without me. It seemed that everything functioned as it should have. (. . .)

8) (. . .) I have to consult privately about the highlights of the visit, what to say where, and what should rather not be said. I must seek advice on the answer I have prepared for a question about Lewinsky. (I will be his first state visit, and thus his first big official press conference, after the affair. Monica will be the heroine.) And again about the USA: I soon expect to have a perfectly translated speech for the garden of the White House (. . .) —it is, as I know from an earlier state visit (1991), the most important speech. (To satisfy my whims: please find out where Martin Luther King is buried and whether it's realistic for me to pay my respects to his memory. Have we managed to arrange for Lou to play in the White House? That would be sensational! He's counting on it, but I don't know whether he's living with an illusion. (. . .)

(September 20, 1998)

1) I am announcing that I have returned from the USA. I thank all of those who worked in the domestic resistance. Likewise I thank all of us who worked in the foreign resistance.

2) It appears that the visit to the USA turned out well. At least I have fond memories of it. The most demanding moment was the last evening, when I learned at the very last second that I had to speak in English on the most popular television channel about jazz. So I did it, and all the Americans in the White House indicated to me that they understood what I was saying. (. . .)

(Undated, 1998)

(. . .) I come back from the United States utterly bewitched, and just before I fall asleep several people tell me that I was viewed on various TV networks by a billion people and that I was "magnificent." I thank them for the compliment. I'm about to go to sleep, and at that moment Mrs. Havránková asks me when I want the water turned off at our house. I reply that at the moment I don't have a clear opinion about that. I think about it for a while and decide to call Mrs. Havránková, and I discover that my telephone doesn't work. Mr. Siemens comes. He looks at it. He says it works. I try the telephone again, and once again I find that it doesn't work. (. . .)

To this day it's held against you that on your first trip on January 2, 1990, you went to both German states, and that journey was perceived as an excessively accommodating gesture to our second most recent occupiers. Why did you not first go to the United States, which probably everyone would have recognized as a clear signal of change?

It was impossible to prepare a trip to the United States in the course of three days—that didn't happen until six weeks later—and, moreover, it would have looked rather embarrassing: previous Czechoslovak presidents had always gone to present themselves first to Moscow, and I was meant to demonstrate that we were different by traveling to Washington? You must see that that would have been somewhat laughable. But there are other reasons why I wanted to visit some of our neighboring countries first. In Poland the president was General Jaruzelski, and understandably I didn't want to start with him: in Hungary, there was also a communist president serving out his term. In Austria there was Waldheim, so that even if Germany had not been our largest neighbor with the longest border, it was really the only place I could have visited. I certainly didn't go to visit our second most recent occupier or even our most recent one (i.e., the GDR), but rather to democratic West Germany, and liberated East Germany, and the two reuniting Germanys. I considered this unification, which I had long supported, to be an essential precondition for the integration of all of Europe that I believed must follow the collapse of the Iron Curtain. It was thus a trip to an important democratic neighbor with a wonderful president, a journey to a dramatically transforming GDR, intended to support their roundtable discussions, and—symbolically—a trip to a unifying Europe. It was mainly the communists who criticized me at the time, because an anti-German stance, supported by a militant anti-Sudetenism, is a fundamental plank in their platform. And of course, with a public they had massaged with propaganda for years, this always works. But my aim was—among other things—to start breaking down these prejudices from the outset.

When did you abandon your utopian vision of a "new" politics? On your trip to Germany you apparently raised with Kohl the idea of disbanding all political parties and forming a single European party. What were you thinking about at the time?

If you think that something as foolish as that is "a utopian vision of a new politics," then I certainly never had to abandon that vision because I never had it. Why, in God's name, would someone who had struggled for political pluralism all his whole life want to disband all political parties?

Later you also suggested the dissolution of NATO along with the Warsaw Pact.

The question of whether, with the end of communism, the fall of the Iron Curtain and the dissolution of the Warsaw Pact, NATO would lose its raison d'être was discussed before the revolution, among both left- and right-wing politicians and political scientists in the West, but also within our own opposition. Thought was given to the creation of a new Euro-Atlantic security community, one that would include all of Europe and not just half of it and that would have a completely different mission from protecting the world from the spread of communism or from Soviet missiles. Soon, however, the day was won by the reasonable suggestion that instead of creating something new from scratch, the North Atlantic Alliance would simply be transformed.

And this is in fact the way NATO has been going for the last fifteen years, and it's really only today, after its most recent expansion, and after a thorough transformation of its entire doctrine, and mainly through its actions, that the vision of those days has become a reality. We did a lot to promote this development, and it was quite appropriate, therefore, that perhaps the most important NATO summit on expansion—the one held in 2002—took place here in Prague, the very city where the Warsaw Pact had been dissolved earlier. When I was in the United States in February 1990, I spoke at length on that subject with President Bush and other politicians and I even referred to it in my speech to Congress. And if you look at that speech you will see that I said more or less the same thing as I'm saying now.

Washington, April 26, 2005

The idea that I wanted to dissolve NATO is something I've been hearing for the past fifteen years. I don't know where it comes from. Perhaps the so-called Prague Appeal (from 1985) or another dissident document that I signed contained the idea of replacing both these opposing pacts in the future with a unified democratic security structure. In any case, I don't see anything shameful about that idea.

Far more interesting than the actual origin of that idea, however, is the persistence of the claim that I wanted to dissolve NATO and its broader context. That tells us a lot about current Czech circumstances. Shortly after the revolution and the arrival of freedom, a very special kind of anticommunist obsession established itself in public life. It was as though some people—people who had been silent for years, who had voted obediently in communist elections, who had thought only of themselves and had been careful not to get into trouble—now felt the sudden need to compensate in some aggressive way for their earlier humiliation, or for the feeling or suspicion that they might have been found wanting. And so they took aim at the people who least held it against them, that is, the dissidents. They still felt, unconsciously, that the dissidents were the voice of their bad conscience, living proof that you didn't have to completely knuckle under if you didn't want to.

It's interesting that, at a time when dissidents appeared to be a tiny group of crazy Don Quixotes, the aversion to them was not as intense as it was later, when history, as it were, had proven them right. That was too much; that was unforgivable. And paradoxically, the clearer it became that the dissidents themselves blamed no one for anything, nor even less did they hold themselves up as an example to others, the greater the antagonism against them grew. Ultimately, many a new anticommunist vented more anger against the dissidents than against the representatives of the old regime.

Out of this was born the strange legend that dissidents were "left-wing," that they were "elitists" (how can someone who spent ten years in a boiler room or in prison and has never turned his nose up at anyone be considered an elitist?), or that they were insufficiently respectful of tried-and-true Western institutions, and so on. For instance, the claim that I was not sufficiently enamored of NATO from my youth belongs to this psychological-ideological mind-set.

By the way, this ideology revealed a lot about itself in a recent article claiming that the dissidents played no special role in the fall of communism because communism was brought down by "normal" citizens behaving conventionally, that is, by putting their own private interests first, which means that they may have stolen the occasional brick from a building site. That kind of thinking obviously resonates with a large part of the public, which sees it as a confirmation that they made the right choices in life: now, when it's permissible, we praise capitalism to the skies and condemn everyone who thinks critically about it; earlier, when it was not possible, we marched obediently to the polls to vote for the communists so that we could, in peace and quiet, look after ourselves. And who is constantly stirring things up? The left-wing dissident! I'm glad that Mr. Hvížďala has inadvertently touched on a theme that I have long been preparing to say something about. I'm only somewhat surprised that when we're talking about dissolving military pacts, he doesn't ask me how we dissolved the Warsaw Pact, for that was no simple matter. Perhaps we will still get to that topic.

It is also said that you offered yourself as a mediator between the Arabs and the Jews. Jiří Suk writes that your thinking at the time was not ideological but utopian. Evil tongues have since declared that you were becoming alarmingly cocky. How do you see those efforts today, after almost fifteen years?

In 1990, things were moving toward confidential negotiations between the Palestinians and the Israelis about a truce and a road to peace in the Middle East. I did not offer myself as a mediator, but in private conversations with both sides I summarized the reasons why I felt that Prague would be an appropriate place for such negotiations to take place. If I remember correctly, both sides were very much in favor of this. In the end, those negotiations took place in Oslo. Unlike their Norwegian counterparts, Czech politicians didn't want to bother themselves with someone else's peace process; they decided that we shouldn't get mixed up in it, and that it would cost too much money. (For what? Hotels?) I think that was a pity.

If it's true that I had more self-confidence than I do today, it was a very good thing I did. I managed to do hundreds of things I'd never dare to try now. Many of my initiatives failed, of course, but I don't know of anything I bungled because of my allegedly overinflated self-confidence. I am glad to hear that my policies were not ideological. I don't know what to make of the claim that they were utopian. If it's utopian to offer someone a place to negotiate peace, then I'll happily admit to being utopian.

Washington, April 26, 2005

And here we are once more, on the subject of Czech small-mindedness. Look after Number One, don't get mixed up in other people's business, keep your head down, don't look up—we're surrounded by mountains and those whirlwinds from the outside world will blow over our heads and we can go on burrowing away in our own little backyard.

How many wise essays or books have been written about this domestic self-absorption of ours! My late friend the literary critic Jan Lopatka, who had a chronic illness, collapsed one afternoon on a busy Prague square. He apparently lay there for two hours before someone helped him and called an ambulance. Indifference to others is frequently offered to us as a national program, and many people subscribe to it. Not everyone, of course, and not always; even in the darkest times there have been honorable expressions of solidarity. But that doesn't change the fact that Czech small-mindedness—čecháčkovství, as

Professor Václav Černý called it—is an important phenomenon in public life, and again and again, in some form or another, it keeps popping up in our political life as well. I would claim that it's not part of the national character, in the sense of something genetically imprinted on our nature, but rather a complex of certain historically formed ways of behavior. I don't know when it first appeared; most likely it was sometime after the Battle of the White Mountain or during the time of Maria Theresa, when the center of empire gradually shifted from Prague to Vienna and when Prague ceased to be an important European city and became a provincial town. The "plebeian" nature of our national awakening probably played a role as well. After all, one of the most important events in the life of the main heroine of Božena Němcová's novel Granny, our national bible, was the moment, in a field, when she meets the emperor, that embodiment of "foreign domination," and he gives her a thaler.

In modern Czech history, a situation repeatedly comes up in which society rises to some great occasion but then its top leaders execute a retreating maneuver, a side step, a compromise; here they capitulate, there they give something up or sacrifice something, and they do it all, naturally, to save the nation's very existence. And society, traumatized at first, quickly backs down, "understands" its leaders, and ultimately sinks into apathy or goes straight into a coma. Then a tide of mud inundates public life, the media is taken over by the dregs of society, and only a handful of dissenters or resisters struggle to maintain the continuity of the free spirit and human dignity, and for their pains they are perceived by the majority of the population as provocateurs who are pointlessly dragging the rest of them into danger.

It was that way in the post-Munich period, then between 1939 and 1945 during the Protectorate, then in the 1950s, and finally in 1968 after the Soviet occupation. First you hear sentences like "They betrayed us," "They sold us out," "They conspired against us." Next you hear things like "There's nothing to be done," and it ends in the shouting of nationalistic slogans, and speeches about "national interests," and silent consent to the persecution of some minority. It's the triumph of Czech small-mindedness in the worst possible sense of the word.

Unfortunately, I caught a whiff of this atmosphere in our country after it split up. It seems that an eruption of this bitter provincialism, this indifference to others, and this hatred of everyone who thinks differently often precedes a diminution of the state. After Munich, they took the Sudetenland from us; with the breakup of the country, we lost Slovakia. When such events happen, *there is inevitably a call for the further homogenization of society: we get rid of Jews, then Germans, then the bourgeoisie, then dissidents, then Slovaks—and who will be next in line? The Roma? Homosexuals? All foreigners? And who will be left? Pure-blooded little Czechs in their own little garden.*

It's not just that such a position or, ultimately, such a policy is immoral, it's also suicidal. Today, in a completely different and much more sophisticated ideological cocktail, these positions are appearing once more. Their most visible expression is anti-Europeanism. It's essentially an expression of the same relationship to the world. Why should we have to consult with anyone? Why should we have to listen to anyone? Why should we have to share power with anyone? Why should we have to help someone else? What do we care about their technical norms (of course, a distaste for "their" technical norms conceals a distaste for "their" moral norms as well). "We are quite sufficient unto ourselves." This is merely the new face of the old familiar Czech small-mindedness. But a word of caution: the small-minded Czech will have the nerve to shout out valiant slogans only if there's no danger to him; on the contrary, if he's facing a powerful and cruel opponent he withdraws and ultimately becomes servile. Just like that member of the Council for the Defense of the State who did not want to support Yeltsin after the Moscow putsch because, he said, "We don't know how it's going to turn out."

Are you still as suspicious as you once were of the role that political parties play in a democracy?

I think more or less the same as I've always thought. It's just that over the years, and particularly during my presidency, I have refined and moderated my opinions a little. I think that political parties are an important instrument of democratic politics, but they are not its most highly evolved form, nor its ultimate meaning. They should provide a place where people can come together, refine their opinions, encounter the views of experts in public policy; where political personalities are formed and aspects of the political will are articulated. They should not, however, be more important than the key institutions of the state, like the government or parliament. They should not be superior to them but, rather, serve them. They should not be places where brotherhoods aimed at seizing power are born, quasi-legal metastructures of the state; instead, they should be the icing on the cake of a richly structured civil society, a place that draws nourishment from that society and gives it a political expression that can then be used in political competition. Only a living civil society can provide spirit to political parties as well, or rather can provide the roots from which they receive their vital nourishment. When civil society languishes, when the life of organizations and voluntary associations is curtailed, then sooner or later political parties will begin to languish as well, until, ultimately, they become degenerate ghettos whose only purpose is to elevate their members into positions of power.

Parties must not be more important than the public interest. They must, on the contrary, serve it. Loyalty to the country, or to the civil service, or to the interests of society, or to one's personal conscience must always be more important than loyalty to the party, otherwise the parties will produce only nonentities who speak only their own anti-language that people will ultimately find repugnant. Partyocracy—that is, government by party secretariats and politburos—has had a great tradition in this country since the nineteenth century, and unfortunately it threatens us today as well. After all, we are close to a situation now in which people are beginning to feel ashamed that they voted for a certain party, or even that they belong to it. This can only lead to the decline of democracy.

And by the way, notice that the more fanatical the party member, the more they suspect that I have nothing good to say about parties or that I don't want them around at all. At the same time, all I want is for parties to play the creative but modest role that they ought to play, within the bounds of parliamentary democracy. If they do, the public will not ridicule them but, on the contrary, respect them.

CHAPTER THREE

Washington, April 29, 2005

I have been to two more "political dinners" at Madeleine's; many important people were there, such as the former secretary of defense William Cohen; the director of PBS, Mrs. Pat Mitchell; Senator Barbara Mikulski; the Democratic leader in the House of Representatives, Mrs. Nancy Pelosi; the deputy secretary of state, Mr. Nicholas Burns; and many others. Many of them I had met on earlier occasions, others I had once been introduced to, but I had forgotten those earlier encounters. Madeleine, once again, moderated the discussion wonderfully; it was lively and spontaneous and exhausting, naturally. I had the constant feeling that I was speaking of things about which these people knew more than I did, and moreover I was doing so in a language I don't know very well. Now that it's over I'm glad I did it, and I'm grateful to Madeleine.

It's paradoxical: every evening I meet with the most important people here, and then, during the day, I run afoul of banal American red tape. Yesterday, for example, we had to return our rental car and then turn right around and rent it again, even though we'd already paid for another month. I understand the thing itself—it's an accounting matter. What I don't understand is why the transaction consumed almost an entire, valuable American day. Standing at the window where all this took place, and where more and more complications kept surfacing, I found it hard not to lose my temper. My Czech pistoleer often uses a trick I don't much like: he reveals who I am—if I'm not recognized, that is. But in this democratic country, favoritism is out of favor, and so the results are always the same: great delight that they've met me, great astonishment that I, of all people, have turned up here, of all places—and then an immediate return to the original situation. It doesn't speed things up by even a minute. That was yesterday. I barely had time to change for dinner at Madeleine's.

But that wasn't the end of it; two unpleasant things happened this morning. The first was something I knew was bound to happen, that is, our Barnabas, Mr. Edler, was nowhere to be found, and so they wouldn't let us into our parking spot. (Later the director of the Kluge Center had to sort things out himself at the entrance.) And the second thing was something I could not have known would happen, and which says something about the state of my memory. At the entrance to the library, where they put my bag through a scanner, they discovered a metal kitchen knife in it, which is not allowed. I expressed surprise and denied it, of course, because I'd completely forgotten that I'd put the knife in my bag that morning so I could spread jam on my roll. They searched the bag and I was caught red-handed. There was nothing to do but hope I wouldn't be arrested, then go outside and toss the knife in the garbage. (Fortunately it was not made of silver.) I felt very silly.

I often can't understand Americans when they speak, especially black Americans, and this is the source of many other embarrassing moments. Yesterday, for example, a young black man who was with me in the elevator told me how much he admired me and asked me for my autograph. Then he mumbled something I didn't catch, though it was evidently a question. For the sake of simplicity, I replied, "Yes." As soon as I'd spoken, I realized that he was asking me if I had written The Unbearable Lightness of Being. *I couldn't very well change my answer, and there was no escaping, so I had to remain in a state of embarrassment until the moment of liberation when our elevator arrived at the right floor. A truly Kunderian situation.*

Let's return to some of the half-forgotten events in your "federal" presidency. What can you tell us about the so-called hyphen war over the renaming of the country?

As a matter of fact, I remember precisely how it began. In February 1990 I was in the White House to sign some agreement or other. Under my signature were the words "President of the Czechoslovak Socialist Republic," and the ceremonial folder displayed the heraldic two-tailed

Czech lion with a red star above its head, the kind they used to hang over the entrance to communist concentration camps. I must have reddened slightly as I was signing, and I remember deciding in no uncertain terms to do what I'd been wanting to do for some time, that is, to present parliament with a proposal to change the name of the country. I didn't think anyone else would do it, and, moreover, it seemed exactly the kind of thing a president ought to propose. The constitution in force at the time gave me the right to present bills to the Federal Assembly, which it would then be required to consider. And so when I returned home from the USA, I drafted a constitutional law that would drop the word "Socialist" from the country's name. Since parliament was still largely made up of communist delegates, I didn't want to offend those for whom the word "Socialist" was holy, so my main argument was that a word describing an economic system has no place in a country's name and that to refer to our country as the Czechoslovak Socialist Republic was just as absurd as calling it the Czechoslovak Capitalist Republic. At the same time I proposed that our army no longer be called the Czechoslovak People's Army because it was likewise absurd. After all we don't have more than one army—a people's army, and another one that is not a people's army. Finally, I proposed a new coat of arms that would eliminate the red star and more accurately reflect its historical form and would, in general, be in better taste. At the same time I wanted the Slovak elements, and the historical symbols of Moravia and Silesia, to be made more prominent. I consulted our most famous expert on heraldry, Mr. Louda, and the coat of arms was given a final design—as was the new presidential standard—by Joska Skalník. Similar changes had been ceremonially passed in a matter of hours by parliaments in neighboring countries, and I had hoped the same thing would happen here. It almost did; my speech in parliament, including the presentation of the new coat of arms, was broadcast on television and was well received; one member of parliament moved for an immediate debate on the issue.

But in the end it all went off the rails. The lion's share of the responsibility for this falls to Zdeněk Jičínský, who argued, successfully, that it had to be debated by the national councils and their committees, by both governments, by federal parliamentary committees, by special commissions, and so on. This might have made sense for the coat of arms, but I could not understand why such a simple and obvious matter like dropping a single word from the names of the country and the army had to go through such a complicated process. That is how it all began.

Among the Slovaks, the opinion arose that if the name of the country was to be changed, then they should be more clearly represented in that name as a separate nation; the word "Czechoslovakia" may have conjured up too vividly the long-abandoned Masarykian idea of a single Czechoslovak nation. They recalled that during the First World War, the Pittsburgh Agreement talked about the will of our two nations to live in a single independent country, and it spelled the name of the country with a hyphen, with each element capitalized—Czecho-Slovakia. They also recalled that this abandoned tradition was revived several months after Munich. The Czechs, among other things, didn't like the fact that using the hyphen would mean calling the lands of the Czech crown by a new name: "Czecho."

Suddenly, every politician was a linguist, a historian, and an expert in heraldry. There were endless meetings of all the highest officials in the land. The final one was held in the presidential château at Lány, where, as a joke, I had the meeting room locked as if this were a conclave of cardinals at the Vatican, and I said we wouldn't unlock it until they had chosen a new name for the country. Another time, perhaps it was before then, I was in the hospital for a hernia operation, watching the televised debate in parliament, and I couldn't stand it any longer, so against the doctors' orders I got dressed and went off to the parliament, where I handed Dubček my letter of resignation. Very wisely, he didn't read my letter at that session. In the end, to general sighs of relief, the name Czech and Slovak Federative Republic was chosen. It was wrong both orthographically and semantically: rather than expressing the idea of a common country for Czechs and Slovaks, it suggested that there were two federal republics. The whole rather absurd process lasted several weeks, and it was incomprehensible to outsiders. Historically, it's interesting for only a single reason: it was a testament to how sensitive the Slovaks were to anything touching on their integrity as a people, and to how little this peculiar sensitivity—often relating to things that were apparently quite superficial—was understood by the Czechs.

That happened about three months after the revolution. Had you noticed before then that something wasn't right between the two nations?

To tell you the truth, I had thought there was something wrong with that relationship ever since my youth. I had always had a heightened understanding for those who lived in the shadow of others, who were in the minority, or had in some way been shunted aside. I simply felt that Slovakia was a different country and that the Slovaks were right to feel put out when Czechs essentially treated them as a more backward version of themselves. I recall, for example, that in the early 1960s as a freshly inaugurated member with a reputation for rebelliousness, I proposed that the Union of Czechoslovak Writers be federalized, that is, decentralized. Since language and literature are the chief attributes of nationhood, then if any institution should have a separate branch for each of our nations, the Union of Writers should. At that time the union was organized, like all state institutions, according to the asymmetrical model. Naturally all the executive members of the union ridiculed my suggestion, including the Slovak members, who, much later, in the early 1990s, fought for Slovak independence when there was no longer any personal risk in doing so. In 1968, during the first serious political thaw, the question of making the country a proper federation naturally came up for discussion, but then foreign armies marched in and what eventually came out of that was merely a formed, federalized totalitarianism. Then, during the revolution in 1989, it was clear to me that something would have to happen in this matter as well, even though I had no idea what specifically we were in for. I became keenly aware of this when a large delegation of leaders from the Public Against Violence came to Prague to meet with the Civic Forum. We were all good friends, and I thought it would simply be a normal, freewheeling discussion. But when it began, I suddenly had the strange feeling that I was taking part in bilateral negotiations between two separate delegations. Even our most lighthearted friends appeared to have suddenly turned serious, and it was as though they had agreed beforehand on the order in which they would speak. There was no real conflict or disharmony among us; what took me by surprise was the atmosphere. The Czechs tended simply not to notice such "minor details," to their own detriment. Had they been more observant, they might have avoided more than one disappointment and many a trauma.

Was the breakup of the country a traumatic event, then?

I think it was, especially for the Czechs. Clearly they had the deep-rooted idea that the Czechs and the Slovaks were two branches of a single nation, that we belonged together, and that anyone in Slovakia who did not think this was either mad or a fascist. The existence of a few obscure Slovak nationalists only confirmed what the Czechs felt about this. There was probably a fair amount of paternalism on the Czech side. Unintentionally, we considered Bratislava as no more than a branch plant of Prague.

I'm not fond of remembering the period shortly after the breakup. The bile that flowed from the newspapers! "Let them go!" was the slogan of the day. "We won't support them!" "We won't let them hold us back!" "We existed before they did; we'll exist after them!" " A great burden has been lifted from us!" And so on. Such moods existed in the Czech lands in parts of the media and the public. Even more intense than the attacks on the ungrateful Slovaks were the attacks on those who had fought to preserve the common state and lost. They were labeled "left-wing intellectual dreamers." I had the honor of being included among such people. It was very similar to the hue and cry against Masaryk, Beneš, and Čapek after Munich. But what is most interesting and most important is that the trauma was very quickly healed and today relations between the Czechs and Slovaks are perhaps better than they have ever been in history.

Washington, May 4, 2005

I haven't written for several days, and it's made me anxious. But we've had a full program. For example, we were in one of those consumer paradises a con-

siderable distance from Washington where everything is five times cheaper than in the city. The Palouses looked after us very well and we bought a few new things. Then I videotaped greetings to various important conferences to which I had been invited but couldn't go. I dealt with my correspondence. We went to the National Gallery. I wrote a speech that I will give at the end of my stay. I'd like to support Chinese dissidents, the Cubans, the Tibetans, the Belorussians, and others who are struggling against dictatorships; they invited me to speak to them, and I simply do not have the time. So we have invited them all here, along with various congressmen. And the day before yesterday I had a large meeting at Georgetown University. Madeleine and the students asked me questions; there were several hundred of them jammed into the room. Once again, I spoke American English! Apparently it went very well, although I had a terrible hangover from it, even a feeling of hopelessness. I must have drunk a lot very quickly, and I felt miserable the next day. One of the local television stations filmed the entire discussion and then broadcast it several times. I was shocked when I discovered this. They must have heard something about this in Prague, judging from the fact that Lidové noviny published a sardonic commentary directed at me.

You mentioned earlier that you had written a proposal for the new federal constitution. This has, I think, been completely forgotten.

It probably has. Right after the revolution I argued successfully that after the first free elections there should follow a two-year transitional period for all official institutions, during which time the constitutional structure of Czechoslovakia would be clarified, a new constitution would be drawn up, and political parties would take shape. And after that, more or less fully formed political parties would be elected to the representative bodies, which would, by then, be clearly defined in a new federal constitution, and in new constitutions for the two republics that would be harmonized with the federal one. I felt the country couldn't exist for four years in this uncertain state, with mass movements like the Civic Forum operating alongside the noncommunist parties that had survived communism, the unreformed Communist Party, and dozens of new parties, large and small. Moreover, the existing constitution had about ten quickly approved additions or changes tacked onto it, and the very nature of the federal state was constantly being debated. Sooner or later there would have had to have been premature elections anyway. Naturally the presidential mandate was limited to two years as well. That's how it is in other countries that are going through a transition to democracy, the most recent example being Iraq: a constitutional assembly usually precedes the formation of a regular parliament, and that's how it was done both after the creation of Czechoslovakia after World War I and after its renewal after World War II.

And so you tackled this job yourself.

To this day it's not clear to me why experts and other politicians didn't come to grips with this job immediately after the revolution. It would have taken at least six months to prepare the first draft and another year to discuss it calmly. Nothing of the sort happened; instead there were constant negotiations about the relationship between the two parts of the federation. Clearly everyone thought that as long as this relationship was not thoroughly thrashed out on the political level it made no sense to wrestle with the wording of a new constitution. Only the Charter of Fundamental Rights and Freedoms was passed. That was very important, of course, but in my opinion it should have been the preamble to the constitution, not a stand-alone constitutional law, as it remains in both republics to this day.

When no one else appeared ready to do it, I took on the job myself. It's a testament to my nature, and it may help to explain why some people think I'm after power, and have an inflated sense of my own worth, and that I push myself into the forefront and so on: but I'm just someone who loves order and who often takes charge of a cause because he knows how important it is and can't stand around and watch other people doing nothing about it. That's how I've gotten involved in many matters in my life, perhaps most frequently in the early days of my presidency. Now I'm more settled and I let many things take their own course, even when I may think it's a disastrous course, because I know that I can't sort everything out myself.

I invited an old colleague from the opposition days, Pavel Rychetský, to help work on the constitution. I think it took us two or three week-ends. Then I held a press conference at which I explained the entire constitution in detail; it lasted over an hour and was broadcast on television. Of course, I also presented it to the Federal Assembly, but as far as I know they never discussed it, and in fact, that was the last I heard of it. I think that Dubček, who at that time was greatly influenced by Zdeněk Jičínský, let the whole matter die quietly in some parliamentary committee. I don't think my version of the constitution would have been able, in itself, to prevent the country from breaking up, but discussions about the country's constitutional shape might have been more germane had they taken place with reference to a specific text.

I'm speaking about this now only to complete the picture and to illustrate what the somewhat anarchic postrevolutionary period was like, when the country hardly knew what its name was and didn't mind living with a constitution that was glued together from so many changes, additions, and additions to additions that no one—apart from Pavel Rychetský—could understand it. He had a special copy into which he would cut and paste changes as needed. I also mention this to illustrate my accursed need to intervene in everything that cries out for intervention.

How did your proposal deal with the relationship between the Czech Republic and the Slovak Republic as two members of a common federation?

I recall one principle that seemed to me quite important. The system of a bicameral federal assembly, with two chambers—the Assembly of the People and the Assembly of Nations—that existed in the communist constitution was not a good one and did not work in practice. The Slovaks who were sent to Prague to take up federal positions, either in the government, parliament, or elsewhere, were not taken very seriously back in Slovakia, where the Bratislava-based Slovak representatives were always considered the more authentic. The approach that has worked in the United States—that is, that the equality of the states is expressed by each state sending two senators to Washington—did not work in our circumstances. The voice of a Slovak from

Bratislava always had greater weight than a voice of a Slovak based in Prague, and in any case the Slovak in Prague was bound by discipline to the leadership of his party, which was in Bratislava. That is why some of the negotiations on constitutional arrangements—those that were accorded the greatest political weight and importance—were not conducted on the floor of any of the federal bodies, but between the top official in each of the national parliaments, the Czech National Council and the Slovak National Council. These national representative bodies were understood to be the only ones competent to negotiate these matters. Therefore the principle of indirect elections, which is familiar in constitutional systems like Germany's and Austria's, was entrenched in my proposed constitution: in the upper chamber of the federal parliament, where the principle of the equality of both nations was to apply, members would be elected not directly but indirectly; that is, the seats would be automatically filled by the executive officers of each national parliament. One consequence of this would be that representatives of each republic at the federal level could not be considered less authentic than the representatives of the republics at the national level because they would in fact be the same people. The Council of the Federation, as this upper chamber was to have been called, would have had the right to approve, return for more discussion, or veto any decision made by the lower chamber of the federal parliament. The drawn-out and ineffective process by which federal legislation was discussed in the national parliaments would be eliminated because the republican parliaments, represented by their executives, would have a direct share in decision-making at the federal level. It would strengthen the federal bodies and significantly simplify their decision-making. This proposal of mine was not a purely theoretical fantasy but grew out of very specific experience. I mention it here in such detail because I tried twice after that—in other circumstances—to propose a similar principle.

Do you remember any concrete situation that was connected with the breakup of the country? What in fact was your role at the time?

In the first place, what happened was what I expected to happen, and it was why I pushed for such a short transitional period between elections: both the revolutionary civic movements which had won decisively in the first free elections—the Civic Forum and the Public Against Violence—began to fragment. It was a necessary and inevitable process, but all the same, it took place in a rather strange way. The Public Against Violence made a big mistake when they proposed Vladimír Mečiar as Slovak prime minister after the first elections. By then, it was already clear that there was a lot of tension between them and Mečiar, but none of the Slovak intellectuals who led the movement wanted the job and Mečiar was the only one to lobby vigorously for it. So he became prime minister. But after several crises, he left the movement and founded a new party, the Movement for a Democratic Slovakia, the HZDS, with people who were faithful to him or close to him, or who were hungry for power, and, in Slovakia, that movement won the next election, which took place in 1992. That, I think, was what sealed the fate of the federation. Mečiar never said that he wanted an independent Slovakia, but he did everything he could to divide the federation: for example, he kept inventing new demands for the transfer of various powers from the federal to Slovakia, demands which, had they been met, would have completely hobbled the federal state. The more obvious this became, and the more intransigent Mečiar's position became, the more Czech politicians began to realize how intractable the situation was, and many of them saw separation as the only possible way out, and began, quietly or aloud, to wish for such an outcome.

In the Czech lands a similar thing happened but in quite a different way. The assembly of the Civic Forum was supposed to elect a chairman. Václav Klaus, a hardworking and ambitious man, mounted a vigorous but well-concealed campaign to become chairman himself. He traveled around to the regional branches of the Civic Forum, presenting himself everywhere as the only man who knew what he wanted and what had to be done with the country, and, without actually declaring his candidacy openly, he created circles of supporters everywhere to whom he made various promises and whom he flattered in various ways. Meanwhile, the other leaders of the movement were sitting around, mainly in Prague, talking about constitutional arrangements, laws, reforms, and so on, and conducting profound political analyses, while at the same time serving in the various positions they had taken on after the first elections. Clearly, they paid little attention to the life of their movement and to the question of who would lead it. Then suddenly, like a bolt of lightning out of the blue, came the news that Václav Klaus was the newly elected chairman of the Civic Forum. No one had expected this, and it came as something of a shock to everyone.

Of course it was also a great paradox: Václav Klaus has never made much of this entr'acte in his career, because he always considered the Civic Forum—and still does to this day—as something concocted and ultimately run by left-wing elitists and former dissidents, a group to which he has never belonged and that he despises. His chairmanship of the Civic Forum was merely a prelude to transforming the Civic Forum as quickly as possible into a regular political party—his own, naturally. And that was how the Civic Democratic Party, the ODS, came into existence. In its ethos, the ODS, or at least its leadership, was quite different from the Civic Forum, and Klaus's merciless critics have described his method as that of hijacking the Civic Forum's assets.

I wouldn't go that far. I would merely say that Václav Klaus did precisely what any smart politician who is not overly burdened by scruples would have done in his place: he grasped the chance that was offered. To build a party on the foundation already laid down by a mass movement is more practical, after all, than creating it from scratch. The split was carried out correctly; a majority of those to whom the spirit of the ODS was alien formed their own party called the Civic Movement. Others left to enter other political parties. The assets were properly divided; the ODS demanded no more than what was appropriate under the agreement. Perhaps they already felt, or knew, that in time they could find far more abundant sources of funding.

And so in the elections of 1992—that is, two years after the first free elections and at the end of the transitional period—these two new powerful political parties emerged as the strongest in their own republics. Klaus's ODS in the Czech lands and Mečiar's HZDS in Slovakia. Both leaders became prime ministers of their respective republican governments knowing full well that the position of federal prime minister was by now only a temporary, and mostly administrative, relic of earlier times and that the real power would be in the hands of the republics, or rather in the hands of their prime ministers and the winning parties. The position of federal prime minister was assumed by Mr. Stráský, a decent man, an economist, and at the time a member of the ODS.

And so the evolution from amorphous, broadly based popular revolutionary movements to regular political parties took place less elegantly than I had imagined it would. But that's the way things are in politics. Shortly after that election in 1992, those two parties began to negotiate the breakup of the country. I, who until recently had been the main organizer and host of all those endless negotiations about the constitutional shape of the country, was immediately shut out of the process, and it was a good thing too, because I would only have gotten in the way.

Washington, May 9, 2005

The weather here is beautiful now; we paid various visits over the weekend, went on walks, and dealt with different housekeeping matters—Dáša with matters pertaining to Vize '97 and I with matters to do with my public activities. I became quite out of sorts because my writing is at a standstill. Yesterday was the sixtieth anniversary of the end of the Second World War. I signed several open letters on the subject but mainly followed it on television. It seems that Putin is treating this anniversary as somewhat of a celebration of himself and his way of governing, which understandably causes some awkwardness. At a discussion at Georgetown University—in response to someone's question—I criticized his remark that the collapse of the Soviet Union had been a great misfortune. My comment got a favorable response here.

In the news from home I learn that no sooner was our president, Václav Klaus, offended on behalf of the whole country by the response of some members of the European Parliament to his comments on the European constitution than he was offended once again, this time because foreigners are mucking about in our Czech pigsty. Yes, that is literally what's happening. For those not in the know, some background: during World War II a concentration camp for the Roma was built near the small village of Lety in South Bohemia. Czech prison guards worked there, and many Roma died or were killed, including many women and children, but otherwise—like Terezín—it was mainly a holding camp for prisoners on the way to Auschwitz or other death camps. The

Roma, rightly, see this place as a memorial site, and they find it intoler-
able that a mega pig farm is standing on the spot today. For years there has
been a discussion in our country about whether or not the government should
pay the owner of this pig farm to move his animal concentration camp down
the road so that in the appropriate place a burial mound, or some other
reminder of the fact that there was a human concentration camp here once,
might be built. Naturally the mega pig farm still occupies the spot. The Euro-
pean Parliament passed a resolution on the Roma and the solving of their
problems that makes reference to the Czech pig farm and recommends that it
be relocated.

And that is what offended Václav Klaus: such gross interference into our
purely Czech affairs! We'll look after our own little Czech pigsty ourselves, and
we're not remotely interested in any assistance from outsiders! And in any
case—that Czech concentration camp wasn't really much of a concentration
camp; it was only a place to put those who didn't want to work!

When one hears this, one is overcome with a secret longing that demo-
cratic, educated, and cultured Europe will meddle as much as possible in our
Czech affairs. It is demonstrably in our own interests.

(January 6, 1999)

(. . .)

4) About the speeches: (. . .) February 25 in Berlin: I will speak off-the-cuff on a given topic. The beginning of March in Paris: the things you mention that I should say, I can easily say extempore at a press confer-ence. At least then the press conference will have some substance. It's not necessary, therefore, to seek an occasion for me to deliver a special speech. All the more so because I have already given a speech when I was in Paris, on a stage with the highest profile, the Academy of Human-ities and Political Sciences, during my induction as a new member. On the other hand, I must give myself plenty of time to prepare for a speech at the NATO summit. It will be written; it will be delivered in English. We must make advance preparations for its publication. It should be a major speech. We'll need to be familiar with the new written version of

the current NATO strategy! I would ask that the program in Canada, Minnesota, and Michigan be kept to a minimum! About the speech in Warsaw, we'll have to consult with Adam M. As far as Budapest is concerned, it is apparently meant to be a kind of homage to Soros, who of course would like to be recognized as a thinker and not merely as a stock market speculator. Perhaps in that case the theme could be the open society, and above all how an open society can be created with open people, that is, that the struggle for it is the struggle against the enclosure of people inside doctrines, ideologies, and prejudices, etc. (. . .)

8) I would like to see suggestions for letters about decorations and invitations to the tenth anniversary of November 17 (Bush, Thatcher, Kohl, Weizsäcker, Gorbachev, Wałęsa), Palme, Kreisky, and others (in memoriam) could receive decorations on October 28. It's been agreed with Zeman and it's urgent. (. . .)

(January 10, 1999)

(. . .)

5) If there is going to be a meeting with the party chairmen after the meeting with Klaus, then it would be a good idea if it were to have its own—confidentially prearranged—agenda. For example, the five basic points on which there is general agreement and which say what must be done in a given situation (the privatization of the banks, amendments to the laws governing the capital market, including the law on bankruptcy, unity in foreign policy, a transformation of the civil service, the budgetary and fiscal spheres, and the reform of the tax and social security systems). Without an agenda that meeting would be a little like whistling in the wind. (. . .)

6) As the state of my health is rapidly improving—during the second part of my stay—the state of my nerves is improving as well. My comments on the domestic campaign against me contained in my previous memos were probably marked by a certain irritation. I think that has subsided and I have now managed to step back from that kafuffle; in other words, I'm no longer troubled or bothered by it, and in fact, it doesn't really interest me much anymore.

(. . .)

(January 17, 1999)

(. . .)

10) (. . .) Apart from information about the army, I will need to know about preparations for the NATO summit in the USA. As far as Zeman's possible participation is concerned: I would probably not speak to him about it for the time being; it would be better if Mr. P. were to meet privately with Lánský and explain to him that if Zeman were to come, he would get into a rather awkward situation: I would be the head of the delegation and he would be a part of my entourage? All the attention would be focused on me and he would suffer from being in my shadow, just as Zieleniec and Kavan once did. Moreover, his presence would certainly revive memories of how he pushed for a referendum, nonnuclear status, etc. Of course it would be possible for him to arrange a couple of bilateral meetings (if there's any time at all for that!), but otherwise he'd essentially be toiling in the underbrush. (. . .) And would we fly in two huge aircraft? Or would Zeman fly with us as well to Canada, Minnesota, etc.? That whole idea (undoubtedly born in Lánský's head) is even more absurd in that Zeman is going to appear at the NATO headquarters in Brussels on March 1. Clearly he'd like to harvest all the fruit of something that he has no claim to. (. . .)

(April 11, 1999)

(. . .)

8) We need a longer hose for watering. (. . .)

(June 6, 1999)

(. . .)

8) I was somewhat taken aback to learn that the final planning for the state visit to Turkey has already begun. (. . .) A noncommittal roundtable discussion with intellectuals does not seem to me to be an adequate response to my requirement that I have talks with some authentic, and

therefore persecuted, representatives of the Kurds, as far as possible on Kurdish territory. Please understand: I have to conserve my strength, and I cannot wear myself out doing something that will clearly be used against me.

(August 21, 1999)

(. . .)

6) In the closet where the vacuum cleaner is kept, there also lives a bat. How to get rid of it? The lightbulb has been unscrewed so as not to wake it up and upset it. (. . .)

(September 12, 1999)

(. . .)

3) Constitutional changes. The discussions in Amálie (Klokočka) confirmed my deep conviction that the proposed changes put forward by the commission of the ODS and the ČSSD are utter nonsense. The entire matter has become quite urgent after what the leadership of the ČSSD approved. They have even begun to campaign for these changes. What are we to do? (. . .)

(September 26, 1999)

(. . .)

8) I promised Schuster that I will write a proposal for the Smokovec Declaration. I would ask you to take a look at it, evaluate it, and if there are no more serious objections to fax it immediately as a highly confidential document to Schuster. If he agrees, the next phase will be a round of confidential consultations with the presidential offices of Árpád Göncz and Aleksander Kwaśniewski. For the time being I would leave the MFA completely out of it. (Kavan also kept his Greek initiative secret from me.) Only after they've all approved it or amended it would I send it to the attention of the MFA and the relevant ambassadors (but not until the

eve of that meeting). I also don't want Kavan to take ownership of this and to start announcing it to the world before the meeting in Smokovec, which he is quite capable of doing. If everyone approves it in this form— that is, as a broader and more fundamental declaration about Visegrad— then the best arrangement would be for us, at 6:00 P.M. (after the meeting and at the beginning of the press conference), to all ceremonially sign it and then for some of us to read passages from it. Of course copies of it will be distributed as well, but our hope that texts of such fundamental importance might get proper coverage is, as we know, faint. We might improve our chances, therefore, by reading from it. (. . .)

12) Regarding my schedule: you can erase the time allotted for writing speeches for October 28 and November 17. Only on October 2, before roasting the pig, you insert "editing speeches for October 28 and November 17." I will go to the roasting at 1:00 P.M. at the earliest, that is, after working on the speeches.

(. . .)

13) Please ask the nuncio how long a speech is expected in the Vatican, where it is to be delivered, in what language, and what other parameters it should have. Then please ask Tomáš Halík for a one-page treatment, suggesting some formulations I might use. I would like to touch upon three matters: a) the proposed new relationship of the Church to Hus as an act of confessional reconciliation: b) the related idea of the ecumenical future of the world as a way of saving civilization: c) the meaning of the Christmas holidays and the Christmas tree. (. . .)

(October 30, 1999)

(. . .)

2) I welcome the good news about the participation of all opposition Serbian leaders, including Djukanović, as members of my delegation in Istanbul. The OSCE must understand what I'm doing and somehow organize it. At the same time, with regard to my delegation, please ask for permission to give a longer speech. It's necessary to work intensively on this. We should also argue that there's a chance to meet with Madeleine, and, who knows, Clinton as well may make time for this. He's already received them before, though never all at once. I'd like some brief infor-

mation about how preparations for my holiday are coming along, as well as about development of matters around November 17. I consider it important to make the hall look good, different from October 28. I would like to look in on the dress rehearsal on November 15. Be prepared for some changes. (. . .)

5) I welcome any advice or thoughts for the New Year's speech. (. . .) and of course for my speeches in the Vatican. I already have some things, but it's more just for the sake of information and interest. The suggestions provided by the Church dignitaries are unusable because they are written in the language of their sermons. (. . .)

Looking at what you were criticized for most as president, I see that high on the list is your apology, at the very beginning of your presidency in 1990, to the Sudeten Germans for their expulsion after World War II. Shouldn't such an apology have come later, after a wider public discussion and after receiving assurances that Germany would respond appropriately?

Reams of paper have already been written about this, and what interests me is that no one has noticed an important detail: in none of my presidential speeches is there an apology to the Sudeten Germans. In the fall of 1989, when I was still a dissident, I wrote a letter to President Weizsäcker (perhaps to thank him for his part in awarding me the German Booksellers' Prize, presented in my absence in Frankfurt) in which I said that I thought Czechoslovakia should apologize in some way for that "resettlement," or at least subject it to some critical reflection—I obviously don't recall the exact wording. The president quoted from my letter in his Christmas speech—again, before I was elected president. I referred to it once more in a television interview, but that too was before I took office. In other words, I was speaking as a private citizen, and I didn't offer an apology, either on my own behalf or on the state's behalf. I merely said that a Czechoslovak apology would be a good thing.

I don't mean to say that I later changed my mind on the postwar "transfer," as we so euphemistically refer to it to avoid the expression "expulsion." On the contrary, when the expulsion of the Sudeten Germans was subjected to critical examination, thanks to the new atmosphere of freedom, I became even more convinced that I had been right to condemn it. In my speeches, however, I used far more diplomatic language and did not directly apologize for anything, one reason being that I had no clear mandate to do so.

But frankly, I'm not very fond of ritual apologies. What is more important is matter-of-fact and utterly unbiased reflection, or possibly even action, to alleviate the consequences of a wretched event. In my presidential speeches, the point I made was that evil begets evil and that we too had become infected with that disease: we too had begun to resettle our nationalities, to ethnically cleanse our country. We may even have paid a higher price for it than the Germans who were expelled; not only morally—if it hadn't been for the expulsion, communism would not have found a foothold here so easily—but materially as well: it would be enough to do a little research into what happened in the border regions as a result of the expulsions. The consequences of liquidating thousands of farms, workshops, factories, and cultivated farmland, as well as the extreme social destabilization that took place when new populations were moved in, are obvious to this day, more than half a century later. I've talked about these things on many occasions, for example in a speech in the Vladislav Hall during the first visit of the German president, or later in the Carolinum, and oddly enough that didn't evoke a storm of protest. The storm came later, and it was a reaction to something that never happened, that is, to a presidential apology.

By the way, at the time we had a generous plan for certain ways to alleviate the consequences of the expulsion that would disadvantage no one and help everyone, but the German side, unfortunately, did not accept the plan. It clearly seemed too audacious for them, and so I suspect that Chancellor Kohl let the whole matter subside rather than sweeping it off the table once and for all. Sometimes it's advantageous to keep certain problems alive by doing nothing about them, because you never know when they might prove useful. However it was, I certainly feel proud of the good relations we have enjoyed with Germany since 1990, relations that are unprecedented in our history. And should it sometimes appear that we are a colony of Germany, or of anyone else, then we have no one but ourselves to blame: we are destroying our countryside to set aside absurdly huge, sprawling industrial zones in the hopes that a rich foreigner will drive by and decide to build a factory there, one that, five years later, he will relocate to Pakistan—but that will be in five years. It reminds me somewhat of the girls who wait to be picked up by Germans on the E55 highway.

Let's return to your early trips abroad. You went to the United States in February 1990, a few weeks after your election. Apparently you took an unexpectedly large delegation with you and had to use two aircraft instead of one. Is that true? And, if so, why did that happen?

I have no idea how I managed to do so much at the time. I undertook large tours around the country, and I probably made a trip abroad every week. I hosted state visits in Prague. And in addition to that I had to worry about new political conditions, about a new constitutional system, about the economic transformation, about the Prague Castle, about the setting up of my office, and about many other things. Today I couldn't manage even a tenth of that, but I was younger and healthier then, and above all, in a strange way, something was pulling me forward: not just the atmosphere of the time but mainly, perhaps, a subconscious feeling that I was, for a short time, at the center of great changes in our country and in the world and that it would have been almost criminal of me not to make the most of such an opportunity and pour my entire being into it.

This feeling of responsibility—together with my total lack of experience—obviously made me arrogant enough to talk to the most influential people on the planet with no sense of shyness, hesitation, or embarrassment, to present them with daring ideas or opportunities, to deliver speeches on fundamental matters in parliaments, and so on, and in all this to maintain a smiling face and a certain ease. Today I find that hard to imagine: I tremble before every meeting, but it was probably a good thing for the country at the time.

As far as the trip to America is concerned: it was full of improvisation; professionals plan such journeys months in advance, and we amateurs had about two weeks to do it. But it succeeded beyond our expectations. I had important meetings with President Bush; he invited us to lunch and took me on a tour of the White House and even showed me his own private quarters. My speech at a joint session of Congress met with unprecedented success. They still remember it there today, and some say that it was the best speech they ever heard in Congress.

I take such praise with a grain of salt because I know that the success was the result of something more than myself or my writing: it was the absolutely unprecedented situation in which I found myself. I was the first top representative of the countries of the communist bloc to bring to Congress the unambiguous news that communism had collapsed, that the Iron Curtain had fallen, that it was the end of the bipolar division of the world and the Cold War, and that it was necessary to create an entirely new political order on this planet. News of that magnitude isn't heard in Congress every day. That was probably the source of what, for me, was an incomprehensibly overwhelming response. I watched the speech later on Czechoslovak television, and what impressed me most was that Martina Navrátilová, who was in the balcony and is probably a pretty tough woman, was crying. Very few know, however, that I had to write that speech in a single afternoon—I had no more time for it then, and I did not seriously consult anyone about it; I think only my closest colleagues read it. I read it in Czech because there was so little time to translate it, which gave me no time to practice reading it, and I couldn't do it without some coaching; all it takes is a skewed phrasing, or bad pronunciation, or the wrong intonation to completely turn the meaning of a sentence upside down.

We flew first to Iceland, where I saw my play *Slum Clearance* in their National Theater. It was the first time I had ever seen that play onstage and the first time in twenty-one years that I had seen any of my plays performed in a professional theater. Then we went to Canada, where, unfamiliar with the impact of time differences, we found ourselves nodding off at a state dinner, and then we were in the United States.

Yes, there were a lot of us, and under normal circumstances such a large delegation would not have been appropriate, but I wanted to demonstrate the unity of the new leadership, so I brought the prime minister, Marián Čalfa, along with me, and probably three government ministers as well, each of whom had his own important agenda;

after all, this was a time when various embargoes were annulled and new agreements signed. We also had to make sure there was an appropriate balance between Czechs and Slovaks. I don't think the delegation was excessively large; there was enough room for us everywhere, and we all had our opposite numbers on the American side. Many came with us so that they could meet their counterparts in the United States. We had, for example, to include some of the student leaders, representatives of the academic community, and the CEOs of important enterprises. I don't think we flew in two aircraft; you could get at least eighty people into those enormous Soviet aircraft in the government fleet at the time, and there were certainly not that many of us, not even counting reporters. Nevertheless, if we really did use two aircraft, it might have been because at the time there was a regulation—later withdrawn—that the president and the prime minister could not fly in the same aircraft. Under the communists, the fear of aircraft of their own manufacture, and of a possible power vacuum, was obviously very great.

Shortly after that first visit to the United States, you went to Moscow. Not much is known about that visit today. The most familiar memento is a photograph of you standing under an enormous portrait of Lenin delivering a fiery speech. How did you feel there? It must have been a little different from receiving the applause in the United States Congress.

When we returned to Prague from the USA, it was the anniversary of the communist putsch in 1948, the first opportunity to mark the occasion after the fall of communism. I gave a big speech to a crowd that filled the Old Town Square. I don't know when I wrote it; perhaps on the plane returning from the USA. It was a long speech and it was well received, but I made the occasional joke, and that was a mistake. I think it was on this occasion that I inappropriately referred to Milan Kňažko as my vice president, or perhaps it was at the press conference before the speech. What sticks in my memory are the shouts of protest from a crowd otherwise favorably disposed to me when I announced that we were going to abolish the death penalty; for some reason, people are very fond of the death penalty. Immediately after the meeting in the Old Town Square we flew off to Moscow.

From my point of view today, the agenda was practically suicidal. In the plane we talked about how to avoid signing the agreement to prolong the traditional serflike treaty of friendship between our two countries for another few years. The Soviets considered it an automatic part of the visit; they didn't ask us whether we wanted to extend the treaty or not. The Yekaterina Hall in the Kremlin was ceremonially prepared and lit for the signing. It occurred to me that we could simply tell the Soviets that a joint declaration of a new quality in our relations, one that would allow the Soviets to rescind Brezhnev's doctrine of limited sovereignty, to distance themselves from the 1968 occupation, and to recognize that we were now two independent states, would be far more important than a formal treaty no one would read anyway. Jiří Dienstbier, my onetime fellow prisoner and now the minister of foreign affairs, agreed, so I asked Luboš Dobrovský, who was his spokesman, to write the text quickly. I edited it lightly, and we decided to try it out in the Kremlin. Under normal circumstances it was diplomatically unthinkable. But this was certainly not a normal time.

There were large numbers of secret police everywhere in the Kremlin. We finally found ourselves in a huge, gloomy chamber with a set of leather chairs and couches in the corner. We wondered if we'd meet the same fate Dubček had in 1968; would the ubiquitous musclemen suddenly blindfold us, tie our hands and feet, and carry us off to an unknown destination? Our Bohemian presence in these rooms seemed more than absurd to us.

Then Gorbachev arrived, accompanied by an aide. He smiled at us pleasantly and asked us to sit down. He was evidently curious to know what a dissident looked like. Until that moment he'd never seen a live one—and certainly not one who had never been in the party and, moreover, who had become the head of a relatively important Soviet satellite, strategically and economically speaking. I was obviously an exotic species. The process of taking each other's measure lasted for some time. In the end—including dinner—we spent about nine hours altogether in the Kremlin. Gorbachev slowly, but I think genuinely and sincerely and convincingly, warmed up and began to understand that I was a human being like everyone else, that I didn't want war with the Soviet

Union but, on the contrary, sought friendship, though one based henceforth on equality. In the end we understood each other, to the point that today we are—I dare say—good friends.

The greatest surprise, however, was that as soon as we produced from our pockets the declaration we had written on the plane and had hastily translated into Russian, he agreed to it without a word of comment and immediately gave an order to prepare the ceremonial copies for signing in the Yekaterina Hall, which had been set up for something quite different. His staff must have been upset, but we appreciated it as the gesture of a reasonable man who understood that the world—partly thanks to him—was changing, and changing far more rapidly, and in a different direction, than he himself had imagined until quite recently.

There was no smoking in the Kremlin, and after about two hours, when I managed to summon the courage to ask if we could light up, Gorbachev nodded somewhat reluctantly. By the way: I introduced smoking into the White House as well; but now that I've been a nonsmoker for several years, the great powers needn't be afraid of me anymore. Gorbachev had only to nod and ashtrays appeared immediately from different quarters. When I said that we would no longer be a satellite but a partner, Gorbachev had an interesting reaction. He said that "satellite" was a very strong and inaccurate word, but that he would forgive me for using such a colorful expression because I was a literary man. And I said to myself, so this is how history is made! From that moment on, all the theories about secret conspiracies hidden behind visible history seemed to me even more ridiculous.

In the USA a friend of mine had given me a real Indian peace pipe. I thought that since I was going almost directly from the USA to the Soviet Union it might be witty to play the peace envoy and present the pipe to Gorbachev. It was incredibly complicated to get it through all the various checkpoints, but my bodyguards finally managed it. When I presented it to him, Gorbachev said, "I'm sorry, I don't smoke!" I don't know whether it was lack of understanding or an attempt to be witty, but I prefer to believe the latter.

In your first New Year's speech, delivered two days after your election, you spoke about your intention to renew diplomatic relations with Israel and with the Vatican, to invite the pope and the Dalai Lama, and other daring plans. Did you seek anyone's advice about this, or were you just shooting from the hip?

In all honesty, the latter is closer to the truth. There was no time for long consultations; a couple of friends certainly read the speech beforehand, but that was it. The specific promises I made were fulfilled. The pope came within three months, although his journeys are normally planned years ahead. It was the first visit of the pope to our country in its entire history, and it was truly glorious. The first free elections were approaching; the electoral campaign was sometimes a bit like a vaudeville show, and at times it was pretty wretched and the pope was able, for a while at least, to direct the public's attention upward and compel it to think about serious matters. A sentence I greeted him with at the airport became a public watchword: "I'm not sure I know what a miracle is," I said, "but I'm not afraid to say that I'm part of one at this moment." Everywhere nuns would shout out to me, "It's a miracle!" Again, I concluded my opening remarks at a meeting in the Prague Castle between the pope and intellectuals and artists with the sentence "I welcome you, Holy Father, among us sinners!" It was a time when I still enjoyed writing speeches and coming up with unconventional turns of phrase, and our newly liberated society found it amusing as well. Every conversation I had with the pope, no matter what it was about, was like confession. And always, after this confession and the implied absolution that went with it, I felt as though I had been born anew.

The Dalai Lama's first visit was a magnificent occasion as well. I was the first head of state to invite him for an official state visit; our politicians generally disapproved, and the one who protested the most was—who else—Zdeněk Jičínský. But his worries were pointless: behind the scenes the People's Republic of China assured us that, although they would protest loudly, it would have no effect on our mutual trade.

We quickly established diplomatic relations with the Vatican and with Israel; and I have vivid memories of my first trip to Israel in April 1990. But at the time, I had visited not only all our neighbors but most of the European countries as well. I felt that I had to introduce our republic as an independent state as quickly as possible, since for many politicians and societies in the world, Czechoslovakia blended into a single colorless lump with the other countries in the communist bloc. I have wonderful memories of many of those first visits, so full of joyous excitement. For example, on my visit to Poland I was greeted by my old dissident friends. By then they held high positions in the state, and they organized an emotional ovation in the Sejm for me. It was strange to see, at a state dinner, Zbyšek Bujak, the legendary leader of the Warsaw branch of Solidarity, Jacek Kuroň, Adam Michnik, Bronisłav Geremek, and many others sitting beside General Jaruzelski and other former members of his putschist government, including his minister of the interior, Czesław Kiszczak, who reminded Bujak that the state police still had his coat. It's interesting that Jaruzelski apologized to me often and quite sincerely for the occupation of Czechoslovakia in 1968, when he was the Polish minister of defense. He told me how they had recalled him from his holidays when the whole thing was under way; but he never apologized in any way for his 1981 putsch against Solidarity; clearly, he was deeply convinced that by imposing martial law he had saved his country from a bloody Soviet occupation.

Washington, May 11, 2005

Yesterday the director of the United States Archives, under whose aegis all the presidential libraries partly belong, took us on a tour of the main archive and then invited us for a good lunch. We've known him for a long time, and he has now offered to help us in the creation of the Václav Havel Library. After lunch with the archivist, I did not manage to write very much. Lunches always knock me out. In the evening it took me a long time to get out of the library; everything was locked up. Then we spent time with friends in the Georgetown pubs; at night I felt strange. I couldn't catch my breath; I took some oxygen and I also took some more sleeping pills, but I didn't fall down. This morning the alarm rang and hundreds of people had to immediately leave the library. They said it was only a drill, but it soon turned out that Congress and the White

House had also been evacuated. It was all because an amateur pilot had lost his way and was flying in a no-fly zone and didn't respond to radio appeals. One important thing: I've gotten myself some salt and I carry it around in my pocket. Now I'm one step ahead of everyone else.

(February 6, 2000)

(. . .)

2) Regarding the program in the Royal Gardens for the IMF, I would recommend turning not only to Stivín and the Forman brothers, but also to other acts that have proven themselves in the past, like the Spiritual Quintet, Hradišt'an, Iva Bittová, some jazzmen (Koubková). There's a problem with rock musicians: they need a lot of equipment. Certainly some that we ask will not have time. Those who can come could perform in various places throughout the garden or take turns playing on a single stage. Perhaps you could consult with Petr Oslzlý about this. There should be an artistic director; perhaps you should ask Andrej Krob's advice; he knows more people than I do and will recommend someone. I would like to supervise the whole event from a distance. The OPR has the difficult task of drawing up a guest list. I will look after the aesthetic side of things.

(March 12, 2000)

1) On Saturday I saw a televised party press conference at which Zeman announced radical changes in the leadership of the police force that I recently visited and praised, which was shrewdly—and why not!—combined with shots from my visits, including information about the medal presented to the chief of one of those units. Perhaps nothing will come of this, or perhaps it will trigger the most serious crisis so far in my relations with the political elites. What led Zeman to do that? One reason, a less important one: to piss me off and show who's boss in the coun-

try. A far more important reason: one of the units was led, by a series of clues it had turned up, directly to Šlouf, who has in turn been pressuring Zeman, perhaps even blackmailing him in some way, to fire the head of the department in question. This friend of the Soviet Union clearly has his own reasons for not liking the boss of the second unit. Grulich, and I know this for certain, has to go because he resisted those changes. The point is that the chiefs in question are named by the minister of the interior on the recommendation of the president of the police, not the prime minister. Please consider what to do about this. For the time being the only solution that occurs to me is to play dead until Grulich's resignation lands (it could well be this week!), along with the recommendation for his successor, and then immediately invite his successor and tell him clearly that before he is appointed he must declare that he will make no sudden personnel changes in the top ranks of the police for several months regardless of who asks him to, because his first task is to become thoroughly familiar with the terrain and to understand who's who. If he refuses to so declare, I won't appoint him and there will be a real political crisis. (. . .) Zeman mustn't know that I have this weapon in my hands and that I am prepared to use it. Oh God, how this reminds me of Victorious February! (. . .)

3) The State Security Council. There are two possibilities. The first: be sick. It's the simplest, but it's probably not right. The second possibility—to go there—requires that I be impeccably prepared, not only for the meeting itself and my appearance in the media, but also for encounters with Zeman, Klaus, Kavan, Bašta, and Grulich, etc., in a situation where there is high tension among them, and between me and all of them (least of all, now, between me and Grulich). (. . .) I've read the briefing materials carefully again, but even so some things are not clear. In the first place: I need to refresh my memory (using a flow chart and a map) on the current structure and deployment of the units. In the second place I must remind myself as well of future plans for their transformation and of what is contained in the relevant, boring army conceptual documents, including the NATO documents, that I approved at the summit in the USA. In the third place I need to know what is important in all the laws concerning the military that I have signed (there are hundreds of pages). (. . .) (2) Draw the attention of the public and all politicians to

the possibility of a NATO summit in Prague in 2002. Explain its significance, not only for us but for Europe: it will show all doubters that the NATO of today is different from the NATO that existed before the fall of the Iron Curtain. (. . .) (4) After years of embarrassment, which has made us seem ever more ridiculous in the eyes of the public, we must immediately put out a call for tenders for fighter planes and set a deadline for wrapping it up and declaring the results. (5) Commit to finding the means to building a NATO command post in Tábor. (By the way, it's an idea I've had for several years.) At the SSC I will be in an unfriendly environment and everyone will have speeches full of concrete data written by their gigantic staffs. I mustn't embarrass myself in front of them by a display of ignorance about the current state of the officers' and NCOs' ranks: they're all waiting for a chance to ridicule me. (. . .)

(March 26, 2000)

(. . .)

15) I gleaned something from everyone I spoke to, for example even from Müller and Madam Prosecutor. For my own entirely personal and internal overview, I would need a kind of flowchart about the ownership relationships of PPF—the insurance company—Erste (Šlouf's request for a bribe)—the savings bank IPB—Motoinvest—the banks whose assets were stripped by Motoinvest—the various criminal indictments and their "deferral"—Agrobanka, Moravia Banka—money laundering by the Russian-speaking Mafia, which was allegedly the start-up capital for this entire real estate–Mafia jigsaw puzzle. Investigations of ODS bank accounts. The ownership of Prima, TV Nova, Milevsko, etc. Perhaps Mr. J. and Mr. N. could go around to various people (Macháček, the police, Kotrba is offering help). What am I to think of Tomin's inspection? Madam Prosecutor indicated to me that clouds are gathering over my favorite Skoupy. It would be worth finding out more about that (the Moravia Banka is at issue here). I would need all of this only for myself and for my own assurances. Unfortunately I can't make any of this public. If it were possible as well to find out three

figures I would be very happy: the total amount of the asset stripping (the report by PSS talks about six hundred billion crowns, but I don't know what they mean by that concretely); the amount of the nonrecoverable loans of all the banks and the losses of those that went bankrupt; how many hundreds of billions has the state given and will still give to the banks (in the case of the Komerční Banka they are talking about up to a hundred billion). The total sum of unpaid taxes over the last ten years. Can it be said in general that a trillion crowns were in part stolen and, in part, wasted? (. . .)

(April 26, 2000)

(. . .)

4) I suggest writing an official letter to Kavan telling him that I've decided to campaign for holding the NATO summit in Prague and that after a conversation with him (in the plane from Istanbul) I have begun this campaign and that Zeman is in agreement, and that I invite him to cooperate with me and that, above all, I would like him to provide me with a precise estimate of the assumed expenses. We have to expose his mendacious and absurdly inflated estimate of nine billion crowns, which even Zeman laughs at. He has clearly said that he would agree to a budget of three hundred million KČS. We should consider that binding. Please bring the minister Vetchý, Martin Palouš, Kovanda, and others into it. The best outcome would be if the government were to make a secret resolution to that effect. That would give me a mandate to fight for it and I would probably win the fight. The idea greatly appeals to Madeleine, and so the strongest member of the alliance is on our side, despite the risk that Madam Secretary will appear to be a Czech lobbyist. (. . .) The main argument (which ought to be heard by both the left and the ODS) is that this will demonstrate that the NATO of today is different from the NATO of the Cold War. (. . .)

5) I would remind you that (. . .) I wish to continue (. . .) my fight against Mafia capitalism. (. . .) The situation is favorable after Zeman offered a truce in his struggle for control of the police command (. . .).

(May 28, 2000)

(. . .)

1) The fact that I spoke about it on Friday in a slight state of nervous excitement (which by the way happens to me more and more often) doesn't alter the seriousness of the matter in question, that is, the very strange taste and the very strange behavior of the PCA. Bořek's version: that in presenting the specifications for plans for the art gallery the PCA requested that the café remain where it is. Bořek took their specifications into consideration, but along with this he called for a freely accessible vestibule immediately after the main entrance into the gallery, where pictures would be on display but which would not require an admission fee, as is usual in galleries. From this vestibule people could enter the café without having to pay admission to the gallery. Admission would be required only upon entry into the main rooms of the gallery. Under such circumstances people might be encouraged to use the café. But the PCA, without Šípek's knowledge, apparently built some kind of an ugly wooden thing right inside the main entrance where they collect admission, so that no one ever goes into the café. There is now apparently a plan to solve that problem by opening up a direct entrance from the courtyard into the café. Someone drew up the plan, which is naturally not in Šípek's style (although we had recently agreed that the entire courtyard would be maintained in a single style), and I'm told it looks like the entrance to the most ordinary supermarket, and the entire reconstruction is meant to cost a fortune because the ventilation must be changed, etc., etc. That is Šípek's version of things. K. will certainly have a counterversion, but I tend more and more to believe Šípek because what he's telling me fits exactly with everything else. Why did they put up a so-called gardener's shed, a disgusting thing in the most exposed spot (the corner of Jelení and Brusnice), which has no connection with anything and does not anticipate any cohesive solution to the entire northern precinct? It stands out strangely from the facades of the buildings around it; it's lit with neon lights (the favorite form of illumination of the PCA), and how is it no one ever told me anything about it beforehand? It's one of the two new structures in the whole Castle complex that will be a definitive symbol of my era! And I'm ashamed of it. They know very well

that I take a great interest in that whole northern precinct and Jelení Street.

(June 18, 2000)

(. . .)

7) I'm looking forward to taking a walk in the Jelení moat, and a concrete agreement about the planned event. Nevertheless: has anyone been working on it? Have the organizers put it in the general calendar of events? Is a guest list being prepared? Has Wolfensohn sent his proposals as he promised? Can we invite people without securing accommodations, travel expenses, etc.? If so, it would be appropriate to invite Sachs, the liberal economist critical of the IMF; Bauman; Soros; and perhaps other people who deal with globalization. How are we handling representatives of the IMF and the World Bank, the ministers of finance and the governors? Private bankers and entrepreneurs? How about the representatives of NGOs? Czech state officials and other dignitaries? Journalists? Czech intellectuals? Who, and according to what key, and on the basis of what knowledge, will make the choice? I think that the entire event itself, its organization, its course and tone, will be a far lighter and easier task than choosing who is to be invited. (. . .)

11) At any moment a situation could arise that will demand my rapid response in the matter of the electoral law. At the same time I could be hard to reach at such a moment. Therefore will you please, once more, prepare as thoroughly as possible for the different circumstances that might arise, including relevant letters and press releases. The basic scenario: the Senate passes it. In that case, on the same day that it is sent to me, I will send the legislation back to parliament. That is, I won't wait until the last minute. Another scenario: the Senate passes it only with an amendment to the clause on by-elections to the Senate in the case of a candidate's withdrawal; it will then go back to the lower house, which will pass it in its amended form. In that case, once again on the same day that it is delivered to me, I will send it back. In both those cases the Chamber of Deputies would probably quickly call a special sitting and pass it again. If that happens, then, on the same day that it is published in the official gazette, a courier will deliver my request to the Constitu-

tional Court for adjudication, not of the entire law but only of those paragraphs concerning certain basic principles of the 2002 elections to the Chamber of Deputies—in other words, not all the principles and procedures of the elections. As I see it, that means I will be able to issue a writ for fall elections to the Senate according to the new and, by then, valid amendments to the law, and that the Constitutional Court can examine at their leisure the paragraphs that I have challenged. (At least I hope that that is possible.) The general line, then, is this: I will not take into account that technical matters concerning the upcoming elections have been deliberately mixed up with fundamental matters concerning the elections of 2002. That's a typical dirty trick on the part of the ODS. At the same time, however, I will not offer my enemies a single day's delay on my part, which they might then use to blame me for this or that. From the sequence of my steps, and mainly from my justification for them, it must be as clear as day that the last-minute combination of technical matters relating to the fall elections and fundamental matters relating to the elections of 2002 is no more than a trap that they have set for me and for democracy in the Czech Republic. I do not intend to step into that trap.

In that period of enthusiastic hyperactivity in the early days of your presidency, the idea of Visegrad—an informal association of three, and later four, former communist countries, Czechoslovakia, Hungary, and Poland—came into existence. It later became the object of continual and long-term criticism by Václav Klaus. Was Visegrad not a somewhat wild and poorly prepared political project?

Originally it wasn't a project at all, but a meeting that I organized in April 1990 in the Bratislava Castle. It was a time when communism had collapsed everywhere, though in a different way and at a different tempo in each country. And people came to power who were often unknown; they had come from very different backgrounds, and we didn't even know what kind of relationships they might have with one another. Poland, Czechoslovakia, and Hungary make up a single unbroken region in Central Europe, and they are historically and culturally very close to one another. At the same time, however, it was common knowledge that they had seldom had good mutual relations and at times had even been at war. So a question hung over Europe about how these newborn democracies would get along. Would they carry out more or less coordinated policies? Or would each be different? Was there some archetypical mutual animosity that might be reawakened? In short, what did these precipitous changes in the central part of Europe mean for Europe as a whole and what might come out of them?

My concern was that we should examine all these matters in a friendly and substantial fashion and, at the same time, get to know one another. So, from all three countries, I invited not only the top state officials but also other important people in public life, those who form public opinion, to meet for a day. Counting the press and the delegations, perhaps several hundred people met in the Bratislava Castle. It was one big improvisation. No rules of procedure were established in advance, no themes were set, there was no set order of speakers, there were no delegation heads, there were no special salons set aside for individual delegations. It was simply to be a very special forum for discussion at which participants would have the chance to introduce themselves to one another and get to know who was a minister, who the leader of a certain party, and who a historian or a reporter. The day before it was to take place, Luboš Dobrovský suggested canceling the whole thing because we were totally unprepared.

I gave a long introductory speech, but I suffered a great deal during the discussion that followed because I had just been operated on for a hernia and my bowels were behaving strangely and I had a terrible case of diarrhea. However, as the initiator of this whole enterprise, I was the only one who couldn't just get up and leave for a while, and precisely thanks to this intimate discomfort I remember the whole event vividly. Despite all the confusion it was—I do not hesitate to say—one of the most important encounters of that time: we essentially agreed that we wanted to abolish the Warsaw Pact, that we wanted to get the Soviet troops out of our countries as quickly as possible, that we wanted Western organizations like NATO and the European Communities to open up to us, and, above all, that we wanted not only to cooperate in these matters, or coordinate our steps, but to combine forces to achieve certain goals. At the same time we demonstrated to the West that even though the political changes in our countries had taken place in very different ways and sent very different people into the top positions, the period of mutual friction had ended and the time had come for creative cooperation in building a new Europe without the Iron Curtain.

We met frequently after that; everything, of course, was better prepared and organized, and I'm certain that some of the things we achieved in Europe we would never have achieved without this cooperation. Other postcommunist countries, the Balkans and the Baltic states, were able to take their cue from us, to draw on our efforts and at the same time strengthen them. It was the Hungarian journalists who began calling us the Visegrad Group, after a meeting in the Hungarian town of Visegrad, where a joint document was signed that constituted this group *de jure*. The Hungarian premier at the time, Joszef Antall, was a historian, and he chose that place because, many centuries before, the Hungarian, Czech, and Polish kings had met there. It was certainly an appropriate historical reference point, but, for accuracy, I would add that in no document from that period did we officially call ourselves the Visegrad Group.

What did Klaus have against it?

His self-centeredness always projected itself into his politics, and as a proud Czech, or, at the time, a proud Czechoslovak, he couldn't bear the thought that we should join forces with anyone else, or that anyone so clearly less developed than we were could be in the same crowd, or that we could allow ourselves to be held back by them and not go forward as befits the one at the head of the class. He cannot bear the slightest sign of any expropriation of power or any transfer of power from the center of the state: and that's why he struggled to the very last moment against the decentralization of government, why he struggled against the nonprofit sector, against civic society, and why, today, he is still opposing the European Union. So he railed against Visegrad as well; he saw it as some kind of left-wing intellectual expression of false solidarity which might cause us to lose our position as the crème de la crème.

Once, in the course of a casual conversation at a meeting of the

Visegrad Group, I said that our three countries might apply for membership in the European Community all at once, that the application might have greater weight, even though it might not necessarily mean that any of us would be accepted at any particular time. Everyone, including Wałęsa, who was president of Poland by that time, agreed. The one exception was one of my colleagues, a friend who was sitting in on the conversation. He had always been under Klaus's spell, and he began tearing his hair in a fit of horror at what I had just said. Perhaps he thought it would have been better to say nothing and then suddenly be the very first to apply for membership.

It's a bit like politics as basketball. Later, of course, we presented our applications at approximately the same time and were accepted into the European Union together. It was, after all, the logical, wise, and practical thing to do.

In general, then, I am not so sure that the expansion of the European Union and NATO would have proceeded as smoothly as it did had it not been preceded by the cooperation of the Visegrad Group.

Today, how do you view the beginnings of the transformation from socialism to a market economy? Did you have doubts about it from the start? And if you did, why did you not express them at the time?

I once studied for two years at the Faculty of Economics, but I have never thought of myself as an economist, and therefore I tried not to get too involved in the high-level discussions on the economic transformations, though of course I listened intently. But it was impossible to remain completely uninvolved. I convened or chaired many a discussion on economic reform, and so, in one way or another, I was unavoidably drawn in. By the way, one of the most important sessions on the nature and the pace of economic reform took place in Hrádeček, our private country place.

The main impression that remains after all these years is this: I should have relied far more on my own common sense and trusted less that the experts knew what they were doing. I remember that quite a few things struck me as dubious at the time, but I didn't have the confidence to speak up. For example, the real value of large segments of state property was hidden behind a veil of vouchers that were distributed gratis to the citizens; the new ownership was fragmented and anonymous; the privatization funds were given a broad scope in which to maneuver, and many went ahead and expropriated the privatized properties they were merely meant to have administered and placed an exaggerated value on them. But I drove out my doubts and suspicions by arguing that there was probably no better way to do it. And everyone else was telling me the same thing.

In *Summer Meditations,* I wrote about something else: in the so-called small privatization process, when shops or small businesses were auctioned off to the public, I argued very strongly that their employees should have the first right of purchase. It seemed logical and just to me, and I believed it would have created a certain continuity and stability in the goods and services sector. At a joint meeting of our three governments—the federal, the Czech, and the Slovak—they voted on this, and the opposing position won by a narrow margin. And so suddenly laundries became bars, bars became casinos, and milk stores became fashion boutiques. But it wasn't a catastrophe. On the contrary: the market itself ultimately showed where certain things were needed, and what was more needed and what less, and the whole retail network began to respond to the general demand better than the rigid, unchanging, and artificial network that had existed under communism had ever done. In this case, the economists were right and my own rustic common sense was not. Today, once again, everything is somewhat different, and that network is being tragically disrupted by the supermarkets. But that's another story.

Many years later I began, for the second time, to change my mind. It happened when I observed that the majority of our most dubious new capitalists, mafiosi, and entrepreneurial con men had emerged from the small privatization process, that is to say, from the auctioning off of small businesses. At the time, anyone could borrow money, buy any property at an auction, and then either sell it off again at a profit or strip the assets and file for bankruptcy. Then all they had to do was keep on investing borrowed money, without, of course, ever returning the loan. This led to the collapse of banks or to enormous state bailouts in the banking sector. But in the end everyone had to pay for the fact that so many speculators were given so much room to operate—like the money changers from the communist era. I'm not saying that giving employees first purchasing rights would have radically altered the situation or could have prevented what happened in any significant way; it merely seems to me that the fundamentalist solution that was chosen led to a certain public cynicism. If, for example, a baker loved by the whole street or neighborhood didn't stand a chance against someone who excelled only in cunning, this could not contribute to a positive climate in the country. What bothered me most, however, was the fact that I found a lack of conceptual vision, not only in the economy, but in our very understanding of what the state should be. "The invisible hand of the market" was supposed to take care of everything, but there are things it simply can't take care of, and I would even say that this glorious "invisible hand" is occasionally capable of committing some highly visible crimes.

A country that finds itself at a historical crossroads must have an idea of what it is, of its possibilities, of what it wishes to be, of what role it wants to play, of what it will put its money on, and, on the contrary, what it will try to avoid. This view must be partly the outcome of a very broad and practical discussion that draws on a variety of expert analyses, and it must reach beyond the limits of individual political programs or electoral mandates. But at that time, any kind of conceptual thinking was almost taboo, or at least it was the subject of organized ridicule, and now, tragically, we're paying the price for it. I must say, however, that in this matter my conscience is clear. From the very beginning I spoke about it countless times—in parliament, in public, on television, everywhere. Ridicule or not.

Can you be more specific? In what sense should the country have had a clearer notion of itself, and what should it have done to that end?

I'll give you an example. At the very beginning of the 1990s the Americans made a generous proposal: on a empty piece of land near Mladá Boleslav, not far from Prague, where there had once been a Soviet military zone (the troops had by then departed), they would build an enormous modern airport that would be one of the main European transport hubs of the coming century. Had such a project been realized, it would of course have had far-reaching consequences, from a rapid transit connection to Prague, to the development of a road and rail network, to the flourishing of all related services. Was it a good idea that we ought to have pursued? Or would it have been a catastrophe for our country? That is something that I don't dare to judge; I incline to the latter opinion, but that's not the point. My point is that such a fundamental and far-reaching decision, one that would have a long-term, if not permanent, impact on the nature and importance of the whole country, is not something to be discussed as one of thirty points on the agenda of a single cabinet meeting; it must follow from a principled consideration about what we wish to be as a country. Do we want to be an important world hub, like Singapore, for example, which has based its economic development and prosperity, as well as its strategic importance (which includes the security aspect of it), on the fact that everyone travels through it and everything is transported through it? Or do we wish to go a different route, for instance the route of fundamental resistance to the destructive influences of globalization on the landscape and its patterns of settlement, influences that could lead to a situation in which, in fifty years, our country would no longer be our country and would become a single, gigantic, and unattractive agglomeration in which many things flourish but most of all crime?

I'm deliberately exaggerating, but for a reason: I want to stress that even minor decisions are better made within a framework of ideas; without such a framework, it's all random groping and an opportunity for lobbyists and con men. What's the point of this story? I was present at a cabinet meeting that took place a week after the American proposal was discussed, and I made a point of asking some of the ministers what the government had decided. They couldn't even remember! It was simply one more item on the agenda.

Let me give one more example: energy. After the fall of communism we had to decide whether we would finish building a nuclear power plant and expand and modernize an older one, that is to say whether—like France after the Second World War—we would put our money on nuclear energy, which would enable us to save the country-side in northern Bohemia from both open-pit and underground mining, or renounce nuclear energy and come up with something else. No fundamental decision was ever made; obviously they were waiting for the invisible hand of the market to decide. It did, but in the worst possible way: now we are developing atomic energy and even considering the construction of more nuclear power plants, but at the same time we go on merrily strip-mining coal in northern Bohemia. Of course we don't need that much energy—we are a major energy exporter to the rest of Europe, despite lacking the resources to do so. We are merely destroying our land and selling the fruits of that destruction, blindly led by the law of profit. Naturally, the profit is small and short-term, and God knows what it's being used for. The long-term effect, though, would make you weep.

Washington, May 12, 2005

This morning at 8:30, I was at the Clintons', who live not far from us. Clinton looked very good after his operations. He was calm, not too overweight, had a smooth complexion, and he exuded an expansive equanimity. I've always somewhat envied that in him. We talked for about an hour about everything imaginable—Russia, Ukraine, common experiences, his visits to Prague. We also discussed whether Hillary should run for president. He was in favor. Hillary once asked me if I thought she should run for the Senate and I said that she certainly should, and she won! When I see Hillary again, I'll remind her, as a joke, that it's worth listening to my advice and that I'm naturally in favor of her running for president. I was struck by one thing that Clinton touched on, but which I had heard as well from other leading American Democrats, that while the Republicans can always position themselves as strong supporters of certain basic values, such as the family or the right to life, the Democrats are at a certain disadvantage: they refuse to make their lives simpler by holding to simple and traditional dogmas without qualification and without regard for the current state of the world, and for that very reason it can appear as if they are not defending clear values. I think that the Democratic Party has at its disposal a great fund of intellectual and political capital but that it's waiting for the right person to bring the two together and articu-

late a clear, comprehensible, yet modern hierarchy of values. Perhaps Hillary will be the one to do that, who knows? Naturally I have no great insight into the real background of politics here, but I must mention at least one impression. Everyone I've met so far seems outstanding for their competence, their matter-of-factness, and their generosity. In this regard Czech politics still has a long way to go and a lot to learn.

(July 14, 2000)

(. . .)

3) I am confirming once more, and in no uncertain terms, that my submission to the Constitutional Court stands. I will submit it on Saturday morning, at which time the complete text can be provided to the media. If the Constitutional Court does not sit on Saturday, they will receive it by Monday morning at the very latest. From my point of view, however, it has been submitted on Saturday. (. . .)

(August 27, 2000)

1) I am sending my second attempt at a speech for the IMF. It's nothing earth-shattering, but I have tried to improve it and make it more subtle. (. . .) Perhaps it no longer has that irritated, anticapitalist tone. But I don't want to retreat any further from my "antiglobalism." (. . .)

9) (. . .) I have too much work: a speech for the Vize Prize and for the October 28 anniversary. (Provincialism and the absurd talk about losing our identity to the EU are good themes for October 28. I would develop the idea that it is we ourselves who are undermining our own identity— by the terrible way we speak, the appalling architecture we put up, our lack of respect for the landscape and historical buildings, our dubious urbanization, the way we've given up on the plurality of trades and small businesses, the depopulation of the countryside, the construction of ever greater monuments to consumption without increasing the productivity and efficiency of our own industries or making a sophisticated attempt to

market our own products, etc., etc.) We are becoming just another glob-
alized country. (. . .)

(September 17, 2000)

(. . .)

5) (a) Your Royal Highness, my dear friend, (. . .) And something else
about how the market economy is devastating the cultivated face of our
countryside; a group of top Czech ecologists, architects, and sociologists
is, at my suggestion, preparing a large three-day conference for next January to be called "The Face of Our Land" (. . .). The ceremonial opening
will be on (. . .) in the Spanish Hall of the Prague Castle. The organizers
would be immensely honored if you could fly to Prague for at least a few
hours and bring greetings to the conference during the opening ceremonies. They are convinced that your presence would greatly enhance
their good cause, which I too fully support. (. . .)

(Undated, 2000)

I am sending my heartfelt thanks to the employees of the OPR, to the
PCA, and to the Castle police, who contributed to the success of the
risky event in the Míčovna, where the IMF and the World Bank met for
the first time with the main "antiglobalists." Everyone agrees that the
event came off well and that it was utterly unique; indeed, it may be that
nothing like it has ever happened anywhere before. Therefore everyone
who helped make it a success deserves praise. Please convey this in
some way to Mr. Kratochvil and all the participants. (. . .)

Dear I., I am surprised and disappointed to learn that the _____ company belongs to you. Why am I surprised and disappointed? Because I
have known you for many years as a professional in your field and therefore I find it hard to understand how your firm could, yesterday, have
committed the abomination of which I was not only a witness and a participant, but for which I am ultimately responsible before the whole
world. I am speaking of the dinner for the participants in the anniversary
session of the IMF and the World Bank in the Spanish Hall, of which,

although it was paid for by the Ministry of Finance, I was the formal host. 1) There were no salt or pepper shakers on the tables. But that was the least of it. 2) The food that was served was different from the food that was approved at the tasting; the dumplings were cold, dry, and made from ready mix; there was not enough gravy, and it was merely dribbled on the meat as though it were some kind of rare aromatic condiment, the meat being just as dry as the dumplings. Everyone was waiting for someone to come around later with the gravy, which didn't happen, so that most of the guests didn't eat their dumplings, if they were served them at all. 3) The worst thing of all: there were unbelievably few waiters, and they were unbelievably slow. Several times in the afternoon and during the dinner, I asked them to make sure that it was done briskly. It was not done briskly. Everything took forever, and I finished my dinner before the last guests had been served their food. These people were in session all day; they were exhausted and tired after complicated discussions about how to help this miserable earth. They are ashamed to eat lest it be said they are stuffing themselves instead of talking about poverty. And then, finally, they are invited to dine with the president in a splendid castle in a magnificent hall—and what do they get when they arrive? Nothing! I simply ended it all after two and a half hours without even being able to call it a dinner. That the whole thing was a colossal disaster was confirmed to me by Messrs. Mertlík, Zeman, Klaus, and others. So far it's the biggest disgrace that I've ever experienced in the Castle, and it was a disgrace that took place before the entire world—and I mean that literally and to the letter. The day before, a dinner was held, in the same place, catered by the same firm, for the commercial banks, billionaires, and millionaires. It apparently came off without a hitch. If your firm is capable of giving decent service only to billionaires but not to mere ministers of finance or governors of national banks, then it truly has no business in the Castle. One receives better service in any fifth-class pub. I wanted you to know this even though I would have much preferred it if the owner of the firm in question was someone unknown to me and not an old friend. But what is to be done: after all the slogan "If the shoe fits, wear it" still applies today (or, more precisely, should apply).

(September 30, 2000)

(. . .)

6) (. . .) (a) About half a year ago Motejl gave me his resignation. It was in my safe. At that time they talked him out of it. He withdrew his resignation somewhat uncertainly, though it remained in my safe. (b) Not quite two weeks ago he came to tell me that this time he was really submitting it. He asked me to pressure Zeman not to try to dissuade him. He let me know that he would accept the position of ombudsman. I welcomed the idea not only because he would make a good ombudsman but because he could be a common candidate both of mine and of the Senate, which would be a disarming gesture, demonstrating the ability of state officials to occasionally agree on something and not always play their stupid games of one-upmanship. (c) The same day at dinner with the Zemans I informed Zeman that Motejl would submit his resignation and I advised him not to try to dissuade him and suggested that Motejl be the common candidate of the Social Democrats (or rather the Senate) and mine for the post of ombudsman. All this was new to Zeman, but he agreed to everything—whether he was happy with it or not I don't know—and he promised to discuss the matter with the party leadership (which was clearly only a formality). He was supposed to let me know the outcome, and we were to agree on a date to make the resignation public, the naming of a new minister, and a declaration of our common candidate for the position of ombudsman. (d) He did not get back to me. He informed me of nothing until yesterday evening, when I learned from Mr. F., and then this morning from the newspapers, that the Social Democrats were declaring Mr. Motejl as their candidate for ombudsman, and that if he is elected, he will have to leave the government. In other words: another petty betrayal.

8) It seems to me that I have to come up with some objective and wise response to the session of the IMF and the World Bank and somehow evaluate the whole thing and bring an end to the matter. Scarcely two days have passed since that event, and the media is full of new myths and superficialities and distortions. Železný and Zuna (speaking for international capital?) are leading a campaign against me to the effect

that I underestimated the security preparations (a deliberate and cynical lie). Some are inventing stories of police brutality, which they need like a fish needs water, and others (Macek) would have preferred to shoot them all; virtually all of them agree that the session was pointless and brought us no benefit (two more lies); almost no one has attempted to analyze either the reasons for the mood of antiglobalization or the errors of the INPEG, or the source of the aggressiveness of the aggressors, or the rather sad role played by the media in all this. (. . .)

(October 1, 2000)

(. . .)

The reasons for my ill temper:

1) This computer is not only wailing at me with an increasingly sharp and annoying voice, but it is behaving more and more willfully (for example, it suddenly begins to write in English and then in a different alphabet, and then it digs in its heels like a mule). Etc., etc.

2) Czech Television broadcast a strange and garbled account of how Mr. Š. said that I wanted Motejl for ombudsman and for that reason didn't want to hold back his resignation and so on. It's no surprise that Mr. Š. was the first to feel my wrath. I was angry that he commented on such an important matter without consulting me first. (. . .)

5) The telephones are not working, and if I've been able to call anywhere it's only because my kind pistoleer, Mr. Slavíček, has lent me his cell phone. The Castle telephone repairman refused to interrupt his weekend at the cottage until Dáša persuaded him, through the director of the PCA. And even then he didn't fix it.

6) (. . .) Everyone burdens me with work, assuming that I am healthy and that I will do the work, while they themselves hide behind their answering machines or at their cottages. (. . .)

Washington, May 12, 2005

According to many people, the war in Iraq has divided America in two, which is not a good thing. People talk about this war a lot here, and whenever there's a conversation on politics it sooner or later turns to Iraq. It seems to me, however, that the conversation is pertinent and calm, not hysterical. I am often asked my opinion, and I always say the same thing. It's not possible— particularly in today's interconnected world—for us to remain entirely and permanently indifferent when massive and cruel crimes are committed against people somewhere. You can't forever tiptoe around a regime that wipes out its own citizens or throws them into swimming pools filled with acid, the way people walked around Jan Lopatka lying helpless on the sidewalk. Therefore it's a good thing that Saddam's regime is gone.

But the whole thing was not done in the best way. First of all, the justification for it was questionable: it is very hard to believe that Iraq was threatening America or the world with secret long-range missiles hidden in the desert, armed with bacteria or poison warheads. Moreover, the existence of such weapons was never proven. Why didn't they just tell the truth, which was that a decent people in the world could no longer sit by and watch someone committing genocide? Of course, it's not so that whenever and wherever someone commits a crime, America or the democratic world must immediately invade that country militarily. Each case must be judged on its own merits and in a highly responsible way.

In principle, however, I believe that there are cases when it is possible and proper to go to the aid of innocent people, even at the cost of violating state sovereignty. In one of my speeches I said: a state is the work of humans, a human being is the work of God. What I meant was that defending human beings is a higher responsibility than respecting the inviolability of a state. One must, however, constantly and carefully scrutinize such humanistic arguments to determine that it is not just a pretty facade concealing far less respectable interests, be they strategic, economic, or other. The world should never automatically approve the intervention of one state against another state that is justified by a defense of humanity.

We're very sensitive about this in our country: after all, our sovereignty was violated twice in the twentieth century—once by Hitler and once by Brezhnev—precisely in the name of an alleged defense of people or human values. In other words, whether to intervene or not, and how to intervene, is something that must be decided case by case and with immense caution, taking into consideration every possible circumstance.

I'm not so sure this happened in the case of Iraq. Why should the attack have come at that time and not, for instance, five years earlier or five years later? The thousand and fifth unfulfilled U.N. resolution, or whatever the number was, is not a sufficient argument to persuade the broad public. I recall the Gulf War: at the time the reason for it was absolutely understandable to everyone. A large and powerful country, Iraq, had invaded a small and weak country, Kuwait, and stolen its wealth. That such a thing is unacceptable and that it is appropriate to go to the aid of the weaker party should have been clear to everybody. And yet even so, the American administration at the time made a great effort to persuade the world, and particularly the U.N., of the need to intervene. I remember how Secretary of State Baker visited all the permanent and temporary members of the Security Council and explained the whole matter to them. Also, there were no huge public protests against the invasion, and the international coalition might well have gotten away with it had the troops gone all the way to Baghdad and toppled Saddam.

This time, however, not enough was done to gain international support, although the invasion cried out for a far more persuasive argument than the invasion of Kuwait did. It's equally unclear to me what all those thousands of government and nongovernmental political analysts were doing if they couldn't draw the coalition governments' attention to what could happen: that a liberated Iraq might become the main battleground for terrorists. Nor does the American notion of "exporting democracy" to the Arab world strike me as the most auspicious of ideas. Perhaps they might have talked about solidarity with suffering people. I don't know. However it was, it was not done well.

I am not just speaking as an armchair general. I remember at least twice before the intervention in Iraq—once in the USA and once in Prague—I warned President Bush about this danger, though I certainly used a more diplomatic language than I'm using today. But my tact did not derive from the fact that I was unaware of what might happen. On the contrary: I felt, perhaps uncertainly but very powerfully, that it could provoke great indignation in the whole world and rebound against America and many of its friends.

In July 1992 you resigned from office and thus became the last president of Czechoslovakia, which ceased to exist a few months later. Then the following January you became president again, this time of the Czech Republic. After the revolution you didn't want to run for that office, and then you accepted the position, allegedly for only a brief transitional period, and then you were elected again, and then two more times as Czech president, so that you spent almost thirteen years in the Prague Castle. Isn't there something very odd about that?

It's very odd. I often have the recurring thought—why hide it?—that it might all have been a mistake, or rather a single, extended blunder. But how hard it is to predict everything that might happen to one and what the consequences might be! After the first free elections—that is, half a year after I first assumed the position to which I was elected by a parliament that was still packed mostly with communist appointees—I had no choice but to seek the approval of the freely elected parliament. The point was to confirm the legitimacy of everything that had happened, and of everything I had done so far. No one would admit any other possibility. I had started something at the Prague Castle, and my departure at that point would perhaps have been perceived as an even greater betrayal than if I had never stood for office in the first place. It was only for a two-year period, however, and I hoped, in that time, to be able to groom a successor—or even better, a female successor.

But again everything turned out differently. After the breakup of the country everyone told me that I couldn't just walk away, that I was obliged to put the recognition I had gained on the international and the domestic scenes to the service of the new Czech Republic, and that it would be hard enough even without that for people to get used to the new country. By refusing to run for president, my gift to the new state would in fact have been a kind of diminished legitimacy.

When I say that now, I suddenly realize how unconvincing my explanation may seem to someone who hadn't been following the course of events here, or who can't remember them, or who didn't experience them. But I know how it was, and I know that I have to accept the fact that it will always be hard to explain this to some people. The prospect of becoming president of the newly created Czech state for five years was not a very pleasant one. The main role at that time was played by the coauthor of the breakup of Czechoslovakia, the victor in the Czech elections and the Czech prime minister, Václav Klaus. Without wishing to pass judgment now on his incumbency, I simply had no appetite for continual dealings with him, for a constant tug-of-war with him over this or that, or for enduring his constant hectoring. By that time I knew him well enough to be able to imagine what it would be like. I had played my role, no catastrophes loomed, so let Klaus do things his way, and let me have some peace and quiet at last. I wanted to write, to travel and broaden my horizons, to read, to enjoy my freedom without the state police at my back all the time, to live in my own way. I may have a thousand bad qualities, but one thing I know for sure: a flashing light on the roof of my car cannot cast a strong enough spell on me to make all those trials and tribulations worth it.

And yet I ran for president again. As in the previous election, and as it would also be in the one to follow, the appeal to my sense of responsibility won out over the pull of my private interests. Today I ask myself if I might not also have been slightly exploited: they wanted to have some other measure of values than Klaus's standard measure, and so they said, that's what Havel's for! And so I occasionally had to pull the chestnuts out of the fire for other people.

You were the last president of one state and the first president of another. Was it hard to shift gears?

You may be surprised to know that, on the whole, it wasn't. I believed, and I still believe, in certain values that I tried to honor in both countries. The nature of that country—whether a federation or a unitary state—was not, from that point of view, the most important factor.

What did you do in the interregnum—those few months between the two presidencies?

I had an extensive agenda and a large staff: the Office of the President of the Republic had no problem seconding that staff to me, something that today would no longer be possible. I was treated not as a former player but as someone who was still in the game, and so once again I became—this time far more so than in the period of dissent—a very special kind of institution. One of the interesting things I realized in that period was how deeply people in our country need to have a head of state and how uneasy they are when the presidential standard is not flying above the Prague Castle. The breakup of the state was, of course, traumatizing, but at times it seemed to me that people were even more upset because there was no president. It was as if the presence of someone in the Castle was a guarantee of a certain stability, a sign that things were in order, that they were just as they ought to be, and as though the absence of such a person was a reason in itself to be uneasy. It has nothing to do with the actual powers the president may have, or with his real influence. It's a slightly mystical thing. Even if the president did nothing, I think people would still be more at ease than if he simply did not exist at all.

But there's more: it would even seem that people expect their head of state to declare the importance of certain moral norms. It doesn't automatically mean that these norms will be more respected by anyone. It only means that that's how people think it ought to be: the standard should fly, and someone should set the standard.

Everyone, even those who constantly violate the standards, clearly needs to know that there is someone here who will stand up for them, and thus, that there is something to be violated. The absence of standards creates unease even among the most notorious violators. I experienced that in prison. Even the worst criminals would have been very upset if the head of state were to clearly approve of something criminal. Everyone has to play his own role: it's up to the president to say you shouldn't steal, and it's up to the thief to steal. If the president were to say that stealing was okay, the thief would be very put out. It would call into question his whole identity. And so people would visit me in Hrádeček, little delegations of them, and plead with me to come back to the Castle. They knew that there was nothing I could do to prevent the breakup of the country, and many other things for that matter, but that seemed less important to them than that some kind of ruler be in place.

Washington, May 13, 2005

When I recall that period at my leisure, I realize what an utterly strange time it was. One small example: in the fall of 1992, the Federal Assembly was debating a constitutional law according to which, on January 1 of the following year, it would dissolve the country of which it was the representative body, transferring all the former functions of that state, as well as all its contractual relations, to two as yet nonexistent independent countries.

I was no longer president at the time, and I followed the discussion and the voting from the public gallery. The act itself was nothing that remarkable: countries come and countries go, and it was a good thing that in our case it happened in a peaceful and lawful way. What was strange, however, was that when the law passed, all the members, Czech and Slovak, began to clap, they sang their respective national anthems, they embraced each other, they rejoiced. Clearly, they had all had enough of the endless negotiations on the legal organization of the state, and, at the same time, they were afraid that the law would not pass and that the arguments would continue, or even that someone might actually remember to hold a referendum, thus posing the risk that Czechoslovakia would go on existing. They were almost literally dancing for joy over something that, two years before, not a single one of them could have imagined happening. It's not often that the parliament of a country would celebrate the dissolution of that country and thus the dissolution of itself.

I repeat what I've already said: it was probably a good thing in the end that it happened, and it probably had to happen, but still the separation did have a slightly slapstick quality to it. If there is a loss here, then of course it's cultural: today Czechs and Slovaks have a much reduced opportunity to enjoy each other's cultural achievements. They are even gradually losing the ability to understand each other's language. In the spiritual and cultural sense, our country has become undeniably smaller and poorer.

(October 13, 2000)

(. . .)

10) Of course, those people from the PD who say that my speech ought to be "balanced" and that I can't just criticize, but have to praise as well, are right. But that's the hardest thing of all!!! For ten years now I've been forced on New Year's Day, and on all other occasions as well, to write in a balanced way about the successes and shortcomings, and for a writer that's an awful thing to have to do. At least for me. (. . .)

(October 22, 2000)

(. . .)

4) I've written a new version of my speech for October 28. Please comment, but at this stage I can only accept minor and technical notes, and moreover they would have to arrive by Monday afternoon. I regret that I was unable to put various suggestions by the PD into it, but it was simply impossible. I try to write speeches as if they were short poems. They have to have a beginning, a structure, an end, their own melody, energy, and drama. Otherwise it's impossible. The formulations you suggested would be politically more precise and perhaps even more appropriate, but somehow I wasn't able to incorporate them. Please accept this as a fact and try to judge the speech in the framework of its specific genre and try to catch any material, linguistic, or stylistic errors, etc., etc. (. . .)

6) A very private request for S. Many people have already told me something that I have silently thought myself, that the inscriptions on our family grave are hard to read. Perhaps it was my fault for choosing bronze lettering (wanting to avoid gold) and not realizing that it could not be seen against gray marble; perhaps someone should have warned me that this would be the case and didn't. Be that as it may, I have decided to fix it. Do you think that you could get hold of the company that made the inscriptions or any other that would be able to redo the inscriptions in black by All Saints' Day? That apparently is how it's usually done on gray marble. I would think it could be done in one afternoon. If they can't do that they could, at least, do the inscription on the front of the head-

stone and leave the sides for another time. My layman's brain tells me there's nothing to it. They would simply take a small brush with the appropriate color and paint over the bronze inscriptions to make them black. If they claim that they would have to take down the headstone and move it to a workshop to do it, and that it's going to cost a million crowns, just laugh at them. In that case I would go there myself to paint it with black enamel because I don't like people taking me for a fool.

(November 2, 2000)

(. . .)

3) Dear V., all my documents, old and new, are printing out in some strange English Cyrillic. Your instructions for fixing it didn't work. After half an hour of this I was ready to write by hand, but then, essentially by accident, the normal letters came back. Please never exchange my old computer for a new one or put new programs on it. This always involves more work, and there are always more and more things to remember. I'm not the kind of person who can endlessly play with a machine and take pleasure in how complex it is. Fortunately, the complexity of my computer—unlike the complexity of the Temelín nuclear reactor—is not a danger to anyone. By the way, the more advanced my computer is, the more easy it is for me to wipe everything out. I'm not saying it's a great loss, but the old computers were incomparably more practical. (. . .)

Don't you sometimes have the feeling that whereas democratic Czechoslovakia was based on a certain founding idea, the Czech Republic doesn't have its own founding idea and that it's just a kind of a leftover country? Isn't there a certain danger in that?

The founding idea of democratic Czechoslovakia is generally considered to be Masaryk's humanism. It's true that our political elite today declares allegiance to that, but only formally and ritualistically. They have not internalized it. I would not say, however, that that's a direct result of the breakup of the country. The policies of the government would still be just as technocratic, just as unintellectual, just as materialistic if we had not separated, though perhaps—thanks to the religiosity of the Slovaks—it might have been in a more subtle form. On the other hand, it is a fact that immediately after the breakup of the country there was a strangely stifling atmosphere in our public life, marked, among other things, by a considerable antipathy toward the intellectual and the spiritual. By far the highest ideal was conforming to "norms"—essentially the ideal of mediocrity, banality, and a kind of middle-class philistinism. Anything outstanding, in no matter what way, was shouted down. Hostility to the former dissidents at that point was in its heyday, and it was hostility to anything that was not usual, that stood out, that went beyond the majority model of behavior. Concern for oneself and one's material possessions, economic growth, even if it meant an unprecedented destruction of the land, a kind of strange antipathy toward ideas of all kinds—all of this was part of that time. It seemed hopeless, and it appeared that it was going to go on forever.

Do you see this as one of your personal defeats?

It depends on how you look at it. In my first New Year's speech I described, in the rather high-flown terms that were appropriate at the time, the kind of country I dreamed about, and among other things I said I dreamed of a spiritual country. If we were to see that as a specific promise, then we would have to say that I did not fulfill that promise. It is true that—internally and emotionally—I really do experience that as my greatest defeat, and again and again I ask myself a question that is difficult to answer: Did it make any sense at all to go into this thing, and was I really suitable for the job? This country has a spiritual and moral potential at least as great as any other. It's just that this potential has found very little expression in the form and behavior of the state. Sometimes I have the impression that the main ideal of our state is to exploit and disfigure our country to the hilt in the interests of a somewhat problematic consumer paradise for the present generation, and to slap the face or kick the shins of anyone who resists this. If anything has been alien to me, and if I have systematically come out against anything, it has always been this material vision of the world, or rather its banal Czech version. Rationally, however, it doesn't make much sense for a single person operating in democratic circumstances, no matter how long he may have held office and however exalted that office may have been, to take personal responsibility for the fact that his country is going in the same dangerous direction as the civilization of the entire planet.

In any case, ideals are something we strive for; they are somewhere on the horizon of our efforts; they provide meaning and direction; they are not, however, static quotas that we either fulfill or do not. The notion that we could, for example, tick off "decency," as though it were something on a list of goals that we had already achieved, making it no longer necessary to strive for, is utterly absurd. It would be just as absurd to claim that I, or anyone else, is to blame because we haven't yet ticked off "spirituality" on the list of things to be accomplished. That doesn't mean, of course, that I couldn't have done more to see that things moved closer to my ideals than they are today. But how do we know if that would even have been possible? And where is it written that someone who espouses a minority opinion can, in free conditions, necessarily persuade the majority that it is harming itself? Yes, I might have done so, but only under certain very special conditions. Did such conditions exist in this country, or did they not? And was there someone who could have achieved more in my place or not? Certainly there was. But what can we do about it, since destiny placed me and not someone else in that role?

CHAPTER FOUR

Washington, May 16, 2005

Yesterday at the embassy, together with many of the local Czechs, we watched the final match in the World Hockey Championship, which the Czech Republic won. As usual, it seems that the whole nation was caught up in it. I shared in the general excitement, the admiration of the players' skills, and the joy of victory, but I couldn't help thinking again about something that has bothered me for a long time: these marvelous players are like billboards on skates. Anyone who didn't know what the Czech coat of arms looked like, which probably means most of the people in the world, would have no idea that these boys were playing for the Czech Republic. It looked more as though they were playing for the Škoda automobile works and a cooking pot called Zepter. (Sometimes I've seen them play for a cell phone company, at other times for a brewery, which has also lent its name to the top football league in our country.) The name "Škoda" was emblazoned on the uniforms, the helmets, the boards, the ice, and in the corner over the boards there was even a real Škoda car blocking people's view. The agency that does the Škoda advertising must have no taste. Otherwise they would surely know this merely turns people off the Škoda. At least, that's the way it affects me. All these companies simply spoil the joy of watching hockey for me. The paradox in yesterday's game was that the Canadians were wearing the same ad for a pot, so it looked as though it was Zepter vs. Zepter.

The worst thing is of course that our time in Washington is drawing to a close. We've barely settled in, and now we have to get ready to leave. We haven't managed to get to most of the museums and galleries. We've had to turn down most of the invitations we received, and a side trip to New York or anywhere else was out of the question. I will clearly not finish this book here. But when will I write the rest of it? My schedule, when I return, is full. I can't, unfortunately, do what my friend and colleague Pavel Kohout does: slip out of a party and write the scene of a play, or the chapter of a novel. I have to gather all my strength, concentrate, work myself into a good mood, have nothing else ahead of me, and so on.

It's almost beyond my understanding how I was able, for almost fifteen years, to write a speech every weekend, a speech that had to be finished by a certain day, and to which I allotted a precise amount of time. No one cared whether I was inspired to write, or had a good idea, or was in the proper mood. Perhaps it's because of all this hard labor that I now find writing so difficult. And it's not made any easier by the urgent feeling I have that it's getting too late, and the obsessive worry that I won't finish what I set out to do. It's almost as though I were stricken with fear that I'll be called to account and won't be properly, bureaucratically, prepared, with flawless documents in my hands. It doesn't bother me at all that I'm coming to the end: I'm happy to write plainly about that, and it doesn't seem tasteless to do so. But what does bother me, terribly, is the thought of leaving disorder in my wake, and that I will never have the chance to come back, even for a few minutes, to put everything in order and properly explain everything.

In the hiatus between your Czechoslovak and your Czech presidencies in 1992, a new constitution for the Czech state was drawn up. At the time, though, you were a mere citizen with no public office, although you certainly had a special standing. Did you take part in the writing of this constitution? Was anyone interested in your opinion? Am I right to think your nature did not allow you to simply stand aside?

You're right. For the first working draft of the new Czech constitution, I wrote one or two commentaries that were at least thirty pages long; some of that was addressed to Václav Klaus and some of it was intended as a kind of internal briefing for the meetings of the Czech National Council's constitutional committee, who had been put up in the château at Lány while they were preparing the constitution, using material provided by specialists. They didn't say so publicly, and I certainly didn't mention it myself, but I know that they dealt with my suggestions in all seriousness and incorporated many of them into the constitution. The preamble is from my pen, although my colleague Milan Uhde, who was then chairman of the Czech National Council, added something later. I don't know if the "green reference" to preserving our national heritage and the mention of civil society would have been included without my suggestion. The atmosphere at the time was really quite strange. The environment, civil society, and the nonprofit sector were practically treasonous issues, and many were afraid to mention them. A kind of subconscious feeling of uncertainty, or even of danger, connected with the demise of Czechoslovakia led, though I don't know how this could have happened, to a widespread intoxication with the simplistic and dated dogmas of the free market economy, and to a general intimidation by the "snide brigade," as I called that odd species of journalists who sneered ironically at everything they felt was not capitalistic enough for them.

What part of the constitution provoked the most disagreement?

I think the Senate. In fact, no one much wanted a Senate; it seemed to everyone that, in our case, two parliamentary chambers was a luxury that had no compelling reason to exist, and no strong tradition behind it. We are not a federal state, where a second chamber, in which each member of the federation is represented by an equal number of seats to protect the interests of the less populous members, is necessary. In the First Republic—between 1918 and 1938—the Senate had no influence whatever; it was merely a dumping ground for retired politicians, and after the war it wasn't revived. This time around, the original reason for considering a Senate was rather silly: the members of the final Federal Assembly—Czechs and Slovaks—made their support for the law dividing the country contingent upon a promise that after the split, the Federal Assembly would become a second chamber in each of the new parliaments, which meant that the members would not lose their positions when Czechoslovakia ceased to exist. Jan Kalvoda, who was chairman of the ODA, the Civic Democratic Alliance party, called this planned "transformation" of one parliament into another "changing troughs." Nevertheless, more noble reasons for the creation of a Senate emerged, and they were, coincidentally, proposed by the ODA and based on Friedrich Hayek's idea of the division of functions: one chamber would deal mainly with private law, and the other with public law. It's a lovely idea, but it's purely theoretical and utopian; at least I've never heard of that principle ever being tried anywhere and I'm not certain that it ever could be.

The constitution, of course, had to be accepted by a constitutional majority and there was no time for endless discussion: the new independent country was to come into being on January 1, and it would have been truly unpleasant if it was to be a country without a constitution. So one side met the other halfway; there was some horse-trading and everyone made compromises until the constitution was finally passed—including a Senate. Fortunately, the constitution also enshrined the idea that the Senate be elected using the majority system, not by proportional representation, as the lower house was. This proposal, which came from a single representative, went almost unnoticed, and it passed if not actually by mistake, then definitely when the members were in a state of exhaustion. In systemic terms it wasn't very logical, but the Good Lord took pity on us and let it pass, and today it is only because of this proviso that the Senate makes sense and is quite significant, because the senators are not dependent for their mandate primarily on their party, but on the electorate, to whom they must appeal directly, in person. The Senate contains more responsible and independently thinking people than the Chamber of Deputies, and it actually works as a kind of safety measure against any eventual excesses on the part of the legislature. It's only a pity that the lower house can so easily overrule amendments sent back to them by the Senate, and pass laws virtually unchanged that have been rejected by the Senate.

What position did you take on the Senate?

When it appeared that there was going to be a Senate and that it made no sense to resist it, I felt that it would be good to oppose the threatening danger of a state that was too unitarian, too centralized, and too centripetal, by having the Senate slightly overlap with the various federal councils: all the regional governors would automatically become members, along with one or two additional representatives from each region, or two more members of the regional council. At the time, the regions had not yet been created, but that was in the plan. And it seemed to me that if the principle of indirect election, similar to what I had already suggested for the federation, were to be applied in this case, it would have several advantages: the regions would thus have a direct institutional role in the central government, thanks to which their interests would not have to come to the attention of the central authorities by strange, indirect byways, or through a two-track system of representation, but directly and authentically.

The majority electoral system may give the present Senate the appearance of a body that can defend regional interests, because each senator must be elected in a particular district, but that's precisely what seems wrong to me, because it raises the question of the Senate's identity. Is it a "chamber of the wise" that deliberates on the basis of a complex overview, providing us with a check against any eventual arbitrary actions by the political parties and their momentary whims, or is it a stage on which regional interests can contend? If the regions or districts are to be represented somehow in the center, let them be represented there directly and authentically by representatives directly elected by the regions.

It's interesting that the ODS, which has always opposed reform of the public administration (which means that they have also opposed the decentralization of the state—allegedly to avoid its disintegration), recently supported this view of the Senate, probably because they so clearly dominate most of the regional assemblies, and because most of the governors come from that party. Meanwhile, nothing has persuaded me that such an arrangement would not be simple, cheap, practical, and logical. The outcome would not be a federal state; it would mean only that the regional governors would not have to go to Prague to lobby, but would legally take part in the decision-making. Of course, a lot would depend on what powers would be accorded to such a Senate, and how its relationship to the Chamber of Deputies would be defined. I no longer remember in what written form and at what stage of the negotiations I proffered this conception, but I'm not surprised it wasn't approved, because it would have required precisely that reform of the public administration that so many deputies resisted at the time, and which wasn't passed and implemented until many years later, when the political forces were aligned differently.

Let's say the Senate had turned out the way you wanted. How do you think the Chamber of Deputies should have been elected?

I've always favored a two-round majority electoral system, and I blame myself for not fighting for it more doggedly in the first weeks after our revolution. But we've already talked about what happened then. Later I occasionally mentioned the possibility of a formula that would combine a majority system with proportional representation, but I hadn't thought through how that would work in practice. On second thought, I did think it through. Professor Klokočka, a distinguished expert in electoral law, came up with a very elegant solution after discussions with me, and I completely endorsed his idea. I think this was at a time when the subject of the electoral law appeared again in public debate, which happens periodically.

The proportional system naturally has some advantages of its own, above all that it makes a greater plurality, diversity, and the representation of various minorities possible. Today I would probably suggest a fairly simple solution: we have two hundred members of parliament, so let one hundred be elected by one principle and the other hundred by the other. Perhaps that would bring us the advantages of both systems and limit their disadvantages: it would lessen the danger of ongoing political and government crises which pure proportional representation encourages, and also prevent the constant, endless, and unchanging rule by the largest majority which a pure—and particularly a single-round—majority system would lead to.

Of course, it depends an awful lot on the concrete provisions of the electoral law: there are many degrees of proportionality, and it's a very special field of expertise in which even mathematics plays a role. I was persuaded of this when, at one point, I asked the Constitutional Court to annul a dubious and newly passed electoral law on which the ODS and the ČSSD had agreed, and which would have meant, in practical terms, that these two parties alone would have been able to govern forever. You wouldn't have known this by simply perusing the law. You would only realize this after it was explained to you that small parties need one hundred thousand votes to gain a seat and large parties need only fifteen thousand—I'm not sure I have the numbers exact, so don't hold me to them. I looked into this at the time because I had to defend my submission to the Constitutional Court against a truly well-prepared opponent, the head of the government legislative department and the vice chairman of the government, Pavel Rychetský. I was the only layman who took part in that debate and therefore I take considerable pride in my victory at the time. Nevertheless, we don't know what the future will bring in this sphere, and that is a reason for continual vigilance.

(January 21, 2001)

(. . .)

4) Naturally, once again, I won't get a chance to write my speech for JAMU this week. But I will next weekend, particularly if I don't receive thousands of pages to study, which will probably happen (Paris, the Middle East, and so on). A question: should I keep to my original philosophical, introspective "meta-theme" of longing, and the impossibility of expressing oneself (*The Chairs*), or should I write a purely political, major speech evaluating the broader context of the whole affair around Czech Television and mainly of the situation that it bears witness to? (A typical postcommunist conflict between two notions of politics: politics as something that lends proper support to an open society—Popper—or politics as a technocratic technology of power, legislative formalism as an instrument of cynicism, political arrogance, direct or indirect support for the interest of the Mafia-like capitalists.) Please talk it over and give me your collective recommendations. If I went the latter route I would be establishing a solid tradition, that of making major speeches, like my Rudolfinum speech, in various places in the country, and before different forums, like the American president.

5) (. . .) (c) After the Senate I am going straight home to study a mountain of papers on the electoral law so that I will be prepared for Brno.

(January 28, 2001)

(. . .) It would seem to be a good idea to make changes in the leadership of the PCA right away, that is, by February 1. The atmosphere there is clearly oppressive, which doesn't help matters. I might have contributed a little to that oppressive atmosphere myself when I rashly said, at a meeting of Vize, that I had indications that the PCA might reconsider its objections to the tunnel and that work on the tunnel might begin in the spring after all. (. . .)

4) (. . .) all the more so because a large part of the money that I will now bring back from Paris and which I will give to Vize, I could put into the tunnel.

I don't know how many crowns five hundred thousand francs represent but if we add to that the two million that the PCA has in its account from me, and the fifteen million that Vize has, it could amount to about twenty million crowns, which could be quite adequate for this year. It's important because that would fulfill one of the first and most important ideas that—as far as the Castle is concerned—we had from the very start: that is, unbroken public access to the whole Castle area from the Chotková road all the way to Pohořelec. (My ancient wish to integrate the Royal Gardens with the Chotkovy Gardens can also be one of the subjects of our discussions.) (. . .)

7) It's impossible to stop the reconstruction of the Institute of Gentlewomen, and it wouldn't make any sense anyway (I believe it was necessary); that insane doghouse can't be torn down either, nor can the architect be taken off the job. The PCA must watch him closely so that from the functional point of view (heating, wiring, etc.) he does not commit the same abominations that made him notorious in the case of Dělostřelecká Street. And furthermore it's vital for me to be able to have an influence on aesthetic matters that can still be influenced. For example: the selection of lighting fixtures or the color of facades (sooner or later the whole palace will be painted on the outside, and not only the appearance of the Castle but the whole of Prague depends on its color—

just notice how awful the present green color looks from Charles Bridge).
I bear responsibility for this in the eyes of the world, therefore I want to
have a say in it.

(. . .)

(February 4, 2001)

1) Yesterday I wrote the speech for JAMU. I don't know yet what I
think of it. The intention was interesting but I have no opinion on its
execution. (. . .)

2) Dear V., I don't know if you overlooked my last message concerning the computer. My computer is still driving me crazy. The main thing
it does is that every time I leave it for a moment, or don't write something, it goes to sleep and then it doesn't want to wake up. It plays dead.
After a dozen attempts—I talk to it, I hit it, I tickle it, etc.—it usually
comes back to life. Can't this be fixed? Why can't the screen stay on
unless I deliberately shut it off? This is a typical example of an improve-
ment that makes my life immensely more difficult. (. . .)

(. . .) (a) The project—the so-called laying of paving stones on the
approach road to the barns at Lány, and the paving of the yard (something that otherwise is very necessary!)—conceals a shocking consequence. For some utterly incomprehensible aesthetic and architectonic
reasons (which clearly conceal business for a friend and his company)
the road is to be lowered by half a meter, which means lengthy heavy-
duty bulldozing, carrying away the fill, etc., etc. The consequences: it
concerns all the underground pipes and wiring that have to be redone
because of this. It will probably kill that ancient linden tree that's standing in the middle of it. A hideous fence has already been built around the
construction site and it will be sitting there in all its ugliness for a year
(!!!). In other words in Lány, for which there is no money for more important things, they will be spending a whole year doing work that, according to Mr. Š., and according to me, is totally pointless and which will cost
us many millions. They will be putting down red asphalt at the very end.
That's probably not a problem. At the very most we can change the color
(the intention is to pave the approach road halfway in red, and then it is
to continue normally, that is, in black!). I'm afraid there are more such

pseudo-improvement projects in the Castle. (For example, no one can understand why they require three years to lay paving stones down in Jirské Square.) (. . .)

(March 7, 2001)

(. . .)

In the Ministry of the Interior and in the presidium of the police there are dark forces, tightly ranked, that are manipulating the minister and aiming to take over the Castle police force, which is for the moment a relatively free and independent enclave (but where in any case they have their points of connection). We have to send these forces packing. (. . .)

I tried an experiment: I concocted a fictitious date and place for the alleged and naturally secret wedding of our Nina, and I told it to only one other person in the world. At the time and place that I had concocted, a group of reporters was standing around. (. . .) A goat cannot be a gardener. (. . .)

(March 25, 2001)

(. . .)

I don't understand why we have so many production greenhouses (including a new one from Jiřičná) in such prominent places. Productive gardens once had to be part of the royal seat. I understand that. But that was at a time when the northern sides of the Castle area were not surrounded by the city. Now you can rent space and put up greenhouses anywhere outside the city. In any case, not even that is necessary because we have more than we need in the Castle already. (They have been trying to sell produce from them, which is somewhat laughable at a time when tulips flown in from Holland are cheaper than our local ones.) Nevertheless, with some sensitive adjustments the greenhouse or the gardener's shed or whatever it is could be incorporated into the rearrangement of the whole area that I have long dreamed and talked about.

(May 13, 2001)

(. . .)

4) I am sending several notes on the specific arrangements for the NATO summit. I think that as far as suggestions for its political content or outcome is concerned I have already done that sufficiently in my Bratislava speech (I hear only praise from the outside world, but so far no response from here), so perhaps I don't have to say anything more before September—let it be inferred from what I've already said. But before September I should, theoretically, have time to make concrete arrangements for the Prague summit as well: everything that I know or think at this point I have put into written notes, which I append both on paper and on diskette. Please send them to all interested parties: i.e., to Saša Vondra, to Mrs. Hlavsová, Michael Kocáb, etc. (. . .)

(May 15, 2001)

(. . .)

5) In spite of everything I am prepared to recommend (should anyone ask for a recommendation) that Kavan be appointed ambassador to the U.N. A shirt is closer to the body than a coat, and the farther that person is from this country, the better it will be for this country. (. . .)

(May 27, 2001)

(. . .)

4) I'm gathering together suggestions for decorations and medals because it's coming up. I'm recapitulating the names that I have already heard, or which have occurred to me, and I'm adding some new ones (I don't know who has already been decorated): For literature: Hauková (I highly recommend her), Hiršal, Stránský (with regard to his *A Land Gone Wild*). Sport: Železný, Loprais. Human rights: Šilhánová, Uhl (hasn't he got one already?). Miloš Hájek (Špidla asked for it; I concur). Theater:

Josef Somr? Vlastimil Brodský? Bolek Polívka? Beňačková? Film: Jan Němec, Stanislav Milota. They argue for Kratochvil (he died recently). On Czech TV they (just) recommended a gentleman who was the king of Šumava; there's apparently an interesting movie about him by K. Vlachová. What about Šverma? Probably not, but there'll be a scandal around it, just like there was around Zilk.

(June 10, 2001)

1) Thank you for the briefing note for Brussels. The next time I would welcome it if they were a bit more comprehensible. A small example: "There already exist channels of communication ... NEEA/PSC, NEEA/MS and a new suggestion, NEEA/MC. The consultations have made it possible for the NEEA to contribute to the development of the CESDP as well as the CFSP." Such sentences, if there are a lot of them, fill me with terror and awaken a desire to simply get sick and go nowhere. (. . .)

3) I am a little depressed at the continual objections made by our heritage department against the creative plans of Bořek Šípek. Why are they so attached to wooden gates, like a barn door, in the second courtyard, making it impossible for the various entranceways in this courtyard to reflect the same signature style, to create the effect of a conversation between the gates, and will mean that after my time in the Castle is over, something will remain that is not only beautiful but that has rhyme and reason? Or are those gates protected heritage sites? It seems to me that the issue is not saving the gates but some kind of jealous resistance to Šípek's artistry, (. . .) which I can only explain as a scarcely understandable but fatal preference for a totally soulless clumsiness as opposed to anything that is happy, light, decorative, and truly creative. (That's probably why the inventive plans by Kurt Gebauer to relandscape the Deer Moat were once, with no explanation or apology, tossed into the wastebasket.) I guess there's no disputing taste, but an aversion to any kind of ornamentation, inventiveness, or fantasy should not wrap itself in the noble garb of protecting our heritage. (. . .)

(June 17, 2001)

(. . .)

7) I thank you for the briefing notes on the Constitutional Court; there are a lot of them and I am studying them thoroughly. Perhaps I will understand everything. I will deliver a short and suggestive speech there. I will write the points on a card beforehand as is my wont. I have not been able to find among my papers our submission to the Constitutional Court in the case of the Czech National Bank and the submission on behalf of parliament. I should be familiar with that as well. (. . .)

10) I hear there will be a meeting on the granting of decorations. Petr Pithart has made a strong submission in favor of an order for that gentleman from Ležáky. There is talk of Brodský; I would remind you of Stránský, whom I mentioned for consideration (*A Land Gone Wild*, his coming to terms with the past, his time in prison, approaching seventy), and Milota. He's a kind of original conscience of the nation and no cinematographer has ever received it. The director Krejčík. Did the Wahls receive it? I knew them both. The father was executed by the Nazis, the son by the communists, and it would be a nice symbol if both of them should receive it in memoriam, if not the order then at least a medal. (. . .)

(July 26, 2001)

(. . .)

3) I thought a little about the composition of my speeches toward the end of my presidency. For now it appears there will be six major speeches: (a) October 28, 2001. Coming to terms with the past. (b) January 1, 2002. Mainly the approaching membership in the EU, which should be signed off in the year 2002. (c) The preelection speech. I have thought through a rather strong preelection address in which I would reflect on the fate and the future of the country. We should already be negotiating this with the television network now that it's returning to normal. About fifteen minutes long, read in my office. (d) October 28, 2002. The new world order, the meaning of NATO for us, the approaching

summit. Point out its key historical significance as a turning point for the world. (e) January 1, 2003. A brief inspiring New Year's greeting. (f) About a month after that, on my last day in office, or shortly before that, a farewell. What I would wish for this country, what I would struggle for if I were the young and healthy leader of a political party. A short evaluation of the good and the bad things that happened during my presidency. (. . .)

Washington, May 17, 2005

It's terrible how time flies here! Yesterday I came to my "workplace," that is, into my tiny rooms in the Library of Congress. I read my diplomatic news briefs about what was happening at home and in the world. I read letters from Prague. I made telephone calls. I arranged various things. I approved the wording of greetings. I refined my schedule. And then I began to reply to Mr. Hvížďala's questions. Before I knew it, it was almost six o'clock and I had to get ready to leave, otherwise I'd be locked in. Yesterday we went to dinner at Madeleine's with Hillary. Hillary made a marvelous impression on me. She looked good. She listened carefully, which not all politicians do. Everything interested her. She spoke concisely and clearly and I understood her American English very well, which gave me the courage to talk on American subjects myself. I think that she would make a wonderful president. I put considerable pressure on her to that end and she merely laughed. Next year, in the fall, she will run again for the Senate, and according to our plans at the moment we will be there at the same time, and if it's possible, or appropriate, or useful, I will support her somehow. The important thing is that her candidacy for the Senate not overlap with her later run for the presidency. But it needn't. After dinner, to my surprise, John Kerry showed up with his wife. As the Democratic candidate for president he got more votes than any other Democrat in history, yet it was not enough to win. I think he still hasn't come to terms with that. But he's a very sympathetic person, more so in person than on television. Both he and his wife knew a lot about us. They had both been to Prague. He even spoke again, and very nicely, about my speech in Congress fifteen years ago (he's been a senator for twenty years), and about my indirect presence in the political life of the USA. I was embarrassed. I blushed and changed the subject. It's too bad that our snide brigade didn't hear that. All—or almost all—politicians here are very suave, particularly the senators. They must have first-class barbers who trim their elegant gray hair; they certainly exercise every day, and somebody must give them facials, or—another possibility—they're made of different stuff than we are. But they are not merely suave, they are also, and this is more important, very charming, well mannered, and erudite. They all complain about the decline in the political culture of the United States, but I don't exactly understand what they're complaining about. I have to finish. Perhaps I will continue tomorrow.

What do you think of the Czech constitution as a whole? Has it proven its worth?

I think it's essentially good. As long as the structure of the representative bodies or the electoral system doesn't significantly change, I think a few small adjustments would be enough. For example, it should be easier to recall the government or to declare early elections; the procedures around how ministers resign, are recalled, or appointed should be made clearer. Whenever anything happens in these areas, there are furious debates about what is, or is not, in compliance with the constitution, what the constitution intended, or what a given formulation actually means. Lawyers have their own vocabulary, and I think I understand most of what is said or written on these matters, but it's not just about me. The language of the constitution should be as clear as spring water, and it should be immediately and fully understandable to every student. It should, in short, be the real property of the people, as it is in the United States. I am no friend of an overly formal, positivistic notion of the law, because I know how much injustice can flow from a mindless and literal cleaving to the letter of the law. I incline more to the concept of "natural law," in which the letter of the law is subordinate to its meaning, its spirit, its aim—which is justice. But that doesn't mean that the text of the constitution should be vague. The clearer everything is, the better.

What do you think in general about changes to the constitution? Many experts think that we should be much more cautious in such matters.

In our country, for very good reasons, quite a few additional constitutional laws have been passed over the course of time, which essentially do no more than make the constitution more precise in places where something was left incomplete or where a new situation demanded changes. This concerns, for example, defense, threats to the country, and the State Security Council. It concerns the relationship between our constitution and the laws of the European Union, and several other matters as well. At the same time, the Charter of Fundamental Rights and Freedoms should, in my opinion, have been modernized in some ways; it was simply transferred mechanically from Czechoslovakia to the Czech Republic, so that the first three words are "The Federal Assembly." Therefore, I would consider it a very good thing if someone, somewhere out of the public eye, could prepare a new version of the constitution that might, one of these years, be adopted. It would be nice if the permanent constitutional laws that concern the very form of the state itself—as opposed to, for example, constitutional laws on individual referenda or early elections—could be incorporated into the constitution in the appropriate places and become an integral part of it. The Charter of Fundamental Rights and Freedoms would naturally be a candidate for inclusion; in fact, it belongs at the very beginning of a constitution. On that occasion dozens of minor amendments in the language could be made: the terminology could be made more consistent in places, or more concise, or broader, so that the constitution as a whole would not be thrown out of whack by having a minor item described in excessive detail, whereas other important matters, such as the electoral system, are given only very cursory treatment. Such a constitution created in an atmosphere of calm, beyond all political pressure, might then exist for a long time without further changes. It might even become a popular text, one that, within the education system, would become a natural part of our general understanding of the country in which we live.

Wouldn't you change the president's powers? What about the veto? In your ten years as Czech president, you exercised your power to veto legislation twenty-seven times.

Yes, the power of the president to return laws to parliament for reconsideration is a good thing. Even though one wonders if it isn't a bit odd that we have a system of double veto—that is, both the president and the Senate can return laws to parliament for reconsideration—while at the same time, either veto can easily be overridden. The presidential veto has one undeniable advantage: responsibility for it is borne by a single individual, who makes his decision based on his own good sense, and his conscience, and who then bears a clear, personal responsibility for that decision. The collective, and therefore less personal, will of parliament can—thanks to the many "deals" struck between the members and the parties, and also as a result of many often contradictory amendments—result in something that parliament itself is unhappy with and that almost no one can personally endorse. This provides an opportunity for the president to examine the whole matter again. But I didn't limit the exercise of my veto to such cases. I vetoed bills when I thought they contained evident nonsense, obvious injustices, or when it seemed to me that they might contradict our constitutional order and the values it's based on. I didn't veto legislation very often; the number you cite is quite low. If, during those ten years, I had vetoed every bill that contained something I didn't like, I would have had to veto most of them.

Regarding presidential powers: on the whole, some details might be improved, but I wouldn't change anything fundamental. It seems to me that the position of the head of state in our country is commensurate with our conception of parliamentary democracy.

Do you think the president should be elected directly, by the electorate?

That's one of those Czech farces. They've been talking about it since November 1989—that's almost two decades—and every time the subject is reintroduced by the political party for whom a direct presidential election would be advantageous at that moment, it is quashed by the party for whom the opposite is true. It seems to me that almost all our parties have played either one role or the other several times. How can one then respect their positions?

But to answer your question: I am in favor of the direct election of the president. It needn't lead to significant changes in the president's powers, it would merely give him a different kind of legitimacy than the other political leaders have, and it would thus enrich representative democracy as a whole. The more ways in which people are elected into various positions, the richer a democracy is, and at the same time the more stable it is, the more resistant to dangerous fluctuations. If the government is derived from parliament and the parliamentary elections, then it wouldn't hurt to have the president's mandate derive from a different source, so that the president would not be bound by political conditions in the same way as the government is. I know from my former presidential colleagues that wherever the president is directly elected, the system of checks and balances is enriched, and to a considerable degree it emancipates the president by separating him from the political organizations from which he came, or that supported him. This can only be a good thing. The issue is not merely the president's formal powers, but the actual legitimacy and authority of the one in whom they are invested.

There's one other thing that's something of a farce, and that is the arguments over the use of referenda, which some parties always support, and others always reject, depending on which position is most to their advantage in a given moment.

I've been following the debates on referenda for almost fifteen years. I think that the option of holding referenda should be enshrined in the constitution in a very precise way, and not merely as a general reference to the possibility of direct decision-making as it is today. The referendum option should be a permanent part of our constitutional order, and it should not require a new constitutional law every time we want to hold one. A situation could arise in which a referendum is needed but could not get the constitutional majority required in parliament. That doesn't mean, of course, that a referendum should be held very often, or for any reason at all. In the First Republic that possibility also existed and at the same time not a single referendum was held. It should merely be a kind of insurance policy that we know is available to us in extreme circumstances but which is not in any way overused.

(September 9, 2001)

1) As promised, I have written up a draft declaration from the meeting on the reform of the army. Please see that it passes quickly through the usual approval process inside the OPR and the MOPR and then that it be discreetly shown to all participants in that meeting for their comments. It seems to me that Pithart and Zeman should be invited so that all the highest state officials would be present. Please focus mainly on providing concrete remarks and less on stylistic comments. I would like a certain elevated tone to be preserved. It's in the interests of success and it increases the hope that some newspapers will publish it. The biggest problem, as always, will be with Klaus, who will immediately sense my hand in it, become jealous, and try to torpedo it. What to do about this? Perhaps it would be best to go over the matter first with Nečas, and when you get his agreement ask him to negotiate it with Klaus himself. (. . .)

(December 16, 2001)

(. . .)

5) I have looked at various briefing notes about the law on the judiciary. Please draft a short critical letter to parliament that I will append to the law when I sign it. The letter could contain the information that I am considering submitting the law to the Constitutional Court. You may start work on that presentation. It has to be flawless if we are going to win. It must be persuasive to the public. (. . .)

(January 1, 2002)

1) I greet all my staff in this New Year (the last full year of my presidency) and I wish them all the best!

2) It seems that I am well again.

3) On Wednesday 2, according to my schedule, I will expect the cardinal, and after him a meeting on Forum 2000. (. . .)

12) An important matter: the more politics disgusts me the more I cling to aesthetic matters concerning the Castle which I have neglected for years, and, in which in many respects I have allowed myself to be deceived. (. . .) I have never met a single person who likes the Wide Corridor in its present form. Regardless of how well intentioned the changes were, I can't help but feel that it still looks like a district House of Culture from the era of normalization. That ultimately contributes to the grubby, undistinguished ambience that that corridor has during gala events. (. . .) For those who don't want to touch anything because everything is a heritage site: if our predecessors had thought that way, there wouldn't have been a Castle, we'd only have some kind of pagan fire pit. Everything new in one way or another violates the old. In the case of Šípek's humanizing of the Wide Corridor, what was violated was totalitarian boredom, and it was done only in a way that allows it to be restored to its original appearance, which I hope that none of my successors will ever attempt. (. . .)

(February 2, 2002)

(. . .)

9) Could S. ask around the Castle to see if a modern bed could not be found, a kind of studio couch (in other words a mattress on legs without a headboard) for my little room. I can never stretch out for a while, take some air or gather my thoughts, because it's impossible in that beautiful country bedstead, with its duvet and its headboard and footboard, the kind that the great-grandmothers of those who were poorer among us used to have in the village (at that time people either slept in these beds, or died in them, but they were certainly not designed for a fifteen-minute catnap). (. . .)

(February 24, 2002)

1) The minister of justice, Mr. Bureš, is continuing his attack; he gave a major interview and won over many commentators. I would ask for further information or briefing notes for our planned encounter. I would need something like an analysis of his interview and information about the people that he names in it as better candidates. (. . .) I think that the submission to the Constitutional Court should remain under wraps for the time being; it should be sent to them on the morning before the minister's arrival and I would then give him a copy for his information. (. . .) The issue is a defense of constitutionality, the independence of the judiciary, and a nonformalistic approach to law. (. . .)

5) The Saudi prince who visited me wrote to Dáša and arranged to meet her in Paris on March 6, when Dáša is there. Please prepare a letter, which Dáša would give to him, to say approximately the following (the text might get longer): Your Highness, I have fond memories of our brief meeting at the Prague Castle. I am most grateful for your promise of a generous gift to our foundation. As soon as the money arrives, our board will meet and decide how best to allocate it. Immediately afterward I will inform you and ask for your approval. You might have heard of several absurd statements made by the Czech prime minister. He explains them by claiming that his English is bad and that he was misunderstood. However it was, please be assured of my continuing interest in the Middle East peace process, in the talks between the Palestinians and Israel (we've organized some of those in Prague within the framework of Forum 2000), of my respect for the Muslim world, and of my continuing intention to organize a multireligious meditation, a gathering and a conference, which is also to be one of the projects undertaken by our foundation. These activities of mine fully conform to the foreign policy of the Czech Republic, as it has often declared and demonstrated by its actions.

(March 24, 2002)

(. . .)

2) I put to you for your consideration the question of whether I should send, on Monday, a request to the Security and Information Service to investigate the activities of representatives of the firm that is offering Gripens. (They are running around Prague, lobbying wherever they can, and probably handing out bribes.) (. . .)

(April 28, 2002)

(. . .)

3) (. . .) I've written a proposal for a law on the cathedral. I took into account the outcome of the meeting with the cardinal, and the written documentation. I would ask your department to evaluate my proposal. So far, it's the work of an amateur. At the same time I'm sending it to the cardinal, and he too will have it evaluated. My concern is to exclude the cathedral from all the other ecclesiastical property restitutions, which could easily drag on for another fifteen years, to treat it separately and in such a way that it would not create any precedent for the future. It should have a merely symbolic meaning. (. . .)

(May 13, 2002)

(. . .)

14) It doesn't make sense to go to Lány on election weekend. On Sunday I will obviously be meeting in the morning with the "winners" of the election, in the Little House. On Monday the Indonesian woman will be here.

(June 19, 2002)

(. . .)

3) (. . .) On Saturday 29 I am to see the Dalai Lama. It's not in the schedule and there's no indication of where I am to see him. In the schedule it says that I will be in Lány, but I can't be there, because Lány will be occupied by the Dalai Lama and I would naturally want him to have the place to himself. There is a possibility then that I might visit him there on Saturday afternoon. It would be a nice way of closing the circle because it was in Lány that we had our first common meditation twelve years ago. (. . .)

6) Please tell Špidla, or his aides, by word of mouth, that more facts are piling up that argue against the candidacy of a certain minister whose name had dropped from speculation but has suddenly, and surprisingly, returned. It's not just a matter of the result in Brno but also about what some of the women told us during a conversation on the grantings of clemency (that he is an arrogant and unbearable tormentor of all his direct and indirect subordinates). (. . .)

(July 6, 2002)

I would ask Mr. M., and through him other selected departmental directors and other members of the staff of the OPR, to provide me, by the end of July, with a written report on what they think the Czech president should have at his disposal, or rather, what should be provided to him when he ceases to be president. That means answering the following questions: (1) What is it like in other comparable countries, from Germany to Hungary? (2) Should he have a kind of mini-secretariat and how large should it be? Under whose aegis should it fall? Or should it be completely independent? (3) If it were to be independent—which would naturally be better (having an office with two masters does not make for good blood)—then what kind of legal entity would it be? Or should it just be physical persons employed by the physical person of the former president? And where would such an office be located? And naturally the fundamental question from which everything else follows: would the state contribute to it or pay for it? Or would the state, on the contrary, have no interest in it, present or future, and should the former president simply carry out his agenda in any way he is able? (4) What, on the one hand, is the ideal understanding of my staff on the solution to this problem, and what, on the other, is genuinely realistic? (5) Would it be possible for some sensible understanding of this to be included in the law as it now stands, or would the law on public officers have to be amended, or would some special government order have to be issued? (6) Is anyone else thinking about this or looking after this? I'm sorry, but there is now some urgency in the matter and I would like to know where I stand, and what my present employees think about this, and whether I myself should do something about it.

(. . .)

It's impossible to consider the last fifteen years of political life in this country and not talk about your successor as president, Václav Klaus. I understand that you don't wish to comment on his performance as president, but he wasn't always in that position, and there are subjects we can't seriously broach without saying something about this undeniably forceful figure in our postrevolutionary history. Where do you know each other from? What are your personal relations like? How did Václav Klaus get into politics?

In the 1960s we were both members of the editorial board of a noncommunist literary magazine called *Tvář*. I don't remember much about him from that time, but I do remember his articles on economics, which were interesting in that they almost made no use of the reform communist economic jargon, or if they did, they did not strike one that way in the given context. Then I heard nothing of him for twenty years, though he did cross my mind several times, and I wondered what he was up to. I thought that he'd probably emigrated long ago and was a professor in America.

And then, as the Velvet revolution was getting under way, he suddenly appeared in the Civic Forum. Rita Klímová, who was spokeswoman for the Civic Forum, brought him in because we were looking for economists to help us, and because she knew him well from certain private economic discussions that took place in people's flats in the 1980s, and later perhaps in certain research institutes about which I knew almost nothing. There were even some articles in the samizdat version of *Lidové noviny* by him, but Rita submitted them as her own, even though they were signed by a pseudonym.

He worked with us in the Civic Forum for several days before I had an inkling that this was the same Václav Klaus that I knew from *Tvář*. He was hardworking and at times quite pleasant, but at other times utterly unbearable. We quickly got used to his presence. He became part of the Civic Forum team and, as an expert in economics, he was invited along with me to press conferences. At one of them I introduced him to reporters. I had forgotten about that, and then recently, to my surprise, I saw it one night when Czech Television was broadcasting some newly discovered video footage from the revolution. We got used to Klaus's occasional offensiveness, to his capacity for radiating a negative energy, to his brand of irony, to his narcissism, and to his aversion—which he mostly kept well hidden—to the rest of us, whom he had clearly consigned to the same Dumpster, with a sign on it saying "left-wing intellectuals."

In the first government, that is, the one led by Marian Čalfa that was put together at your roundtable discussions during the revolution, Václav Klaus was put forward as minister of finance on the recommendation of the Civic Forum. If you already knew him so well, weren't you wary of giving him such an important ministry?

I remember quite vividly my private conversation in the cloakroom of the Magic Lantern with Václav Valeš, my longtime friend and fellow prisoner, an economist with a lot of practical knowledge. He had worked since his youth in the management of various enterprises and during the Prague Spring he had even been a minister. I asked him if he thought this annoying fellow Klaus could be minister of finance. He said that he could, because his job would be to look after the state treasury and he wouldn't get mixed up in politics. That type of person, he said, was ideal for minding the till.

After the first free elections in June 1990, he again became minister of finance.

That had several aspects to it: in the first place, all the members of the first postrevolutionary government became big stars overnight. Suddenly, for the first time in forty years, the country saw normal, candid people in the highest positions, not party bureaucrats, and in the atmosphere of general euphoria they quickly made them their darlings. Klaus, naturally, was among them, and like Jiří Dienstbier (who became foreign minister), he always knew where to stand so that the cameras would pick him up. As someone who is remarkably hardworking, he took a very active part in the preelection campaign and I think that he was also at the top of one of the regional candidate lists. And when the Civic Forum got more than 50 percent of the vote, he was naturally one of the big winners, and consequently he had dibs on some cabinet position.

In the second place, Klaus inconspicuously but systematically worked at being perceived, at home and abroad, as the father of the radical Czech economic reforms. He was not entirely the direct author of these reforms—they were created rather by people like Tomáš Ježek, Dušan Tříska, Václav Valeš, and several others—but he really was their most energetic defender, and I would say that it was Klaus who most aggressively pushed them through. And that was certainly to his great credit, which in my opinion is in no way diminished by the various mistakes, flaws, or shortcomings of those reforms. He was simply someone who could push anything through, though often his partners agreed with him only so they wouldn't have to go on listening to him. It would have been very difficult at the time not to include in the government someone with the reputation of being the "father of the economic reforms."

In the third place, in spite of everything, the leadership of the Civic Forum—which, along with the leadership of the Public Against Violence, was meant to recommend a new government—decided not to include Václav Klaus in the cabinet. By this time everyone knew that he was only using the Civic Forum for his own ends, and moreover, the need for balance between Czechs and Slovaks in the government gave the Slovaks the right to a "power" ministry like Finance, since the Czechs held Foreign Affairs and Defense. I think at the time they were thinking about naming Ivan Mikloš, a young Slovak economist, who later as the Slovak finance minister, both under the federation and then when they were independent, helped to push the Slovak reforms perhaps even further than the Czechs. And so the Civic Forum gave me, as president, the unpleasant task of telling Václav Klaus he wasn't going to be minister of finance, but rather chairman of the Czechoslovak State Bank.

I failed shamefully. When I informed Klaus of this, he shot back that it was out of the question, that the entire world knew him as the Czechoslovak minister of finance, that he could hold no other position, and that his departure from the government would be catastrophic. And I, rather than telling him that that was the decision of the winning party, and if he didn't want to head the state bank, then he could do whatever he pleased, I politely backed down and said something like, "All right, then!" The Civic Forum was very upset with me for not doing the job, and Klaus's antipathy toward me grew into hatred. I had behaved like a typical bad politician: I hadn't done what I'd promised to do and, in the process, managed to make everyone mad at me.

How did the two of you get along during the next two years (1990–92), when the country was still a federation of Czechs and Slovaks?

Moderately well. Our relations were, on the whole, correct. He had to overcome his antipathy toward me—because, at the time, to come out sharply against me in public would have harmed him—and I tried to respect him. Naturally, some sparks flew here and there. He never liked any of my speeches, above all my New Year's speeches, and he always chided me for them. The snide brigade, as I called the pro-Klaus press, took potshots at me as well; later I became their main target, and the notion of "nonpolitical politics" became a popular sneer. Klaus's Civic Democratic Party emerged from the Civic Forum and I didn't get involved much in that, nor could I have; the breakup of the Civic Forum was a result not only of Klaus's capacity for hard work, his cunning, his discreet lack of scruples, and his ability to attract various lackeys and supporters, but also, in equal measure, of the inability of his opponents to maneuver skillfully in the sphere of power.

Do you think that if Václav Klaus had not become the first minister of finance right after the revolution, and if he had not continued in that post after the first elections, he really would have stayed out of politics?

I don't think so. On the contrary, I have the feeling that sooner or later, regardless of circumstances, he would have risen to the top, and perhaps even become the head of state. He knows how to promote himself and he's ambitious. If it hadn't been for his meteoric rise in the first federal government, when, as I've said, every minister was a television star, everything would have been harder for him, but he would have moved in the same direction—upward. But please understand me: I don't mean to say that one should not strive for power or that anyone who does so should not act pragmatically and deliberately. It has to be that way, and in that regard, Václav Klaus is remarkable. But sometimes he pushed it to the very limit of what was ethically acceptable.

How did you and Klaus get along after the breakup of Czechoslovakia in 1993?

Not very well. It is true that both he and his party supported my candidacy for the presidency, certainly not out of any love for me, but simply because it was generally expected, perhaps even demanded, of them. Klaus tried to stay one step ahead, so he used all kinds of techniques to undermine me just before the election so that I would enter the job appropriately humbled. That was his method, and I've observed it many times. For instance, he didn't want to present the law on the Office of the President of the Republic to parliament, although it was ready and prepared and I could scarcely have carried out my job without it. He imposed various conditions, to the point where I would almost call it polite blackmail. He saw me as his main antagonist and he tried all kinds of ways to express this. Because of my innate sense of courtesy and my distaste for confrontation, I was often the loser, but fortunately never in anything of fundamental importance. For example, at a meeting of all the political parties at the Castle, he kept withholding his agreement to our entry into NATO; he had various excuses, but I ultimately managed to get it from him by gently manipulating events. He was always shaking his head over something in the Castle, not because he was really concerned about whatever petty thing it happened to be, but just on principle. Every year there was a huge struggle over the budget. He railed against the meetings of Central European presidents that I had begun to organize, and he refused to come to the first one in Litomyšl. He condemned my positions on reform in the U.N. and other matters, and he would have been happiest had I submitted everything to him in advance for his approval.

I have a bitter memory of Salman Rushdie's visit to Prague. Klaus didn't know Rushdie was there or that I had invited him to the Castle, and when Klaus found out, he came to see me at night and began accusing me of putting the country at risk. To give his visit greater clout, he brought the ministers of the interior and foreign affairs along with him. Both claimed to be equally surprised and upset, though of course they knew very well about the visit—the minister of the interior had even provided a bodyguard for Salman—but they counted on my not exposing them in front of their boss, which of course I did not do. My spokesman, Ladislav Špaček, had to pay a small price for this because I put some distance between myself and something he said to the media. What he said was unfortunate, but that was not the point; the point was that if this confrontation was ever to end, a small sacrifice was required. I could not stand the midnight tension any longer, so I sacrificed Špaček.

I suffered many such defeats. But my worst memories of all are the Wednesday meetings. Klaus came up with an idea that was, on the face of it, quite all right: he suggested that just as the British prime minister visits the queen every Wednesday afternoon to report to her on cabinet meetings and the situation in the country, he would come to the Castle every Wednesday afternoon for an hour. I couldn't refuse. Nevertheless, those Wednesday afternoons very soon became my biggest nightmare, and from Tuesday evening on I was out of commission. The meeting always unfolded in exactly the same way: there would be fifteen or twenty minutes of friendly conversation about everything under the sun, and then the moment of truth would come, the reason why all this was taking place, some complaint about my recent behavior. It was always complete nonsense, but making sense was not the point; the point was to put me on the defensive. If he landed the first blow, I could offer any explanation at all, and he would even agree with everything I said, but I could not erase the beauty of that first blow, nor could I find a way to move out of a defensive position.

I remember a typical instance: at a certain moment, he reached into his breast pocket and pulled out a well-thumbed newspaper clipping, apologized several times for even bothering to bring it up, and then read from it a report that I had expressed my regrets at the death of Frank Zappa. Then, very politely, he suggested that it was inappropriate for a head of state to express regret at the death of a foreign rock musician, when so many of our domestic giants had passed away without a word of commiseration from me appearing in the papers.

What was I to do in such an absurd situation? The proper response would have been to stand up and say, "Václav, this meeting is over." But I can almost never carry anything like that off, maybe once in two hundred years. Instead, I said something about how Zappa had taken an interest, right after the revolution, in what was happening in our country, how he had helped us, and how ungratefully we had behaved toward him, and I explained that Agence France-Presse had come to me for a comment and it would have been absurd to refuse them, and that it's not my fault that of all my many comments on the deaths of various people, the newspapers chose to run this one. I could have been right a thousand times over, but what good was being right when, simply by stooping to an explanation, I had slowly but surely made a fool of myself. Everyone knows that in a country that is still working hard for its place in the sun, I'm not going to risk a war between the president and the prime minister over a press clipping about an expression of regret.

I don't think there was any deliberate, cold-blooded strategy behind Klaus's behavior. It's simply a matter of character and instinct. He doesn't know any other way to behave. Either he's afraid of someone, or he's out to humiliate them.

One day, however, I'd finally had enough and I sent the government a letter announcing I was canceling the Wednesday meetings with the prime minister, and I explained why. Klaus and his minister of foreign affairs, Josef Zieleniec, who, at the time, was still a mediator between us, asked for an appointment that same evening in the Castle. He seemed beaten down and his main concern was not to have to show that letter to the government. In the end I agreed, but there were no more Wednesday meetings.

I don't think that modern, postrevolutionary Czech history ought to be seen as the history of the personal relationship between me and Václav Klaus. It's a journalistic cliché and it still upsets me after all these years. On the other hand, I recognize that I have to say something about that subject, otherwise our conversation would have unforgivable holes in it. More important than whether two people get on each other's nerves, of course, is what their views of the world are, their political actions, their speeches and writings, their influence, and perhaps their legacy. And that is something that others must judge.

Why did you wait to criticize Václav Klaus publicly until the so-called Rudolfinum speech in 1997, after his government had fallen? Some observers found it unconvincing, and above all, too late.

In the first place, as president I gave between twenty and thirty major speeches every year. They all appeared later in book form and they are in my collected works. Anyone who reads them through will notice that they were not occasional shouts provoked by a particular situation and that together they make up a single unified whole, continuing and developing my view of the world, of politics, of the position of our country, and so on. In fact, I deliberately tried to write my speeches that way: more than once I started one speech where the previous speech left off, without anyone's noticing.

Excuse me for interrupting, but while we're on the subject of your speeches, you must have had to repeat yourself often. As a creative person, didn't that bother you?

It bothered me a lot. When I had to express something again that I had already expressed, it was painful. But unfortunately there was no other way. Ivan Medek, who at one time was my chief of staff, always tried to ease my mind by pointing out that Masaryk had in fact said the same thing all his life. The Rudolfinum speech was simply one of the many dozens, or perhaps hundreds, of speeches in which I said—perhaps in other words and in different circumstances—essentially the same as I had said many times before or after. . . . Perhaps it became famous because accident placed it at a time when Klaus's government had resigned, but the speech was in no way connected with the resignation. It had been planned and written long before that. For the most part, the issues I raised were meant for future consideration, or were tasks that I felt we had to confront. Only the introductory part was critical and it wasn't a critique of Václav Klaus himself, but of Czech politics. That those politics were inextricably linked with Václav Klaus, his opinions, and his behavior, is another matter. That's not the speech's doing.

But something else played a role here: the new presidential election was approaching in early 1998, and, knowing that I would probably be in the game again, I wanted to lay all my cards out on the table and avoid any suspicion that I was cozying up to parliament and not telling them straight out what I thought. For that reason, the speech to both the houses was perhaps a little harsher than others.

And now to the notorious so-called Sarajevo assassination. What actually happened concerning Klaus's resignation [in 1997], and how did you perceive it and experience it?

There wasn't anything especially complicated about it. The government was facing economic problems. The reforms were dragging, and the solutions proposed kept getting put off, or else they were only half measures. Conflicts within the governing coalition were growing. Then came the affair involving the uncertain sources of funding belonging to the governing ODS party, complete with secret bank accounts and unpaid taxes. Many people had suddenly had enough. And so it began: the minister of foreign affairs, Josef Zieleniec, who up to that point had been Klaus's closest ally and the cofounder of his party, resigned; next, both smaller coalition parties—the Christian Democratic Union–Czech People's Party and the Civic Democratic Alliance—withdrew from the government coalition; it came to a head with the resignation of several more ministers from the ODS itself, above all the minister of the interior, my longtime friend from Charter 77 days, Jan Ruml, and the minister of finance, Ivan Pilip. If I am not mistaken barely half the cabinet remained, perhaps less. In such a situation, the government had to dissolve itself. It was only logical, and I publicly appealed to Václav Klaus to do it. My impression at the time was that none of those who resigned was capable of saying publicly what his real and most profound reasons for resigning were. All indications were that they had resigned not over specific conceptual disagreements, nor over the affair involving ODS financing and the subsequent attempt by the ODS to deny, obfuscate, and disprove everything, but something far more trivial: Klaus's way of running the government. He was capable of humiliating his ministers in all kinds of ways, ridiculing the proposals they brought to cabinet meetings, and arbitrarily changing their order on the agenda. The atmosphere in cabinet meetings was often incredibly tense and it was his fault. I had seen this behavior a couple of times with my own eyes but in a less extreme form; after all, he toned down his behavior somewhat in front of me. But from various ministers I know how those cabinet meetings often played out. When the material problems began to accumulate as well, regardless of what they were caused by, most of the cabinet ministers had had enough and walked away.

Why was it called the Sarajevo assassination?

I remember that one day Jan Ruml phoned me when I was in Lány to report that he and Ivan Pilip were going to announce their resignation at a press conference that afternoon, but that Václav Klaus had just gone to Sarajevo for a summit of the Central European Initiative, which they said they hadn't known when they called the press conference. When they learned that Klaus was out of town they didn't want to change their plans and create further speculation. That is, at least, how

Ruml described it to me. It was Klaus who called it "the Sarajevo assassination," and he succeeded, as he had in many other instances, in popularizing the notion to the point that he was able to impose his own inverted interpretation of events on almost everyone—and mainly, of course, on the snide brigade—and he did it subtly, by playing on this cliché. The government had collapsed and he presented it as an "assassination" attempt on himself.

Washington, May 18, 2005

One ought never to come to premature conclusions. During the first days of my stay in Washington, my impression was that Americans can't drive. They don't always use their turn indicators, which can be quite dangerous. They sometimes pass each other on the wrong side. At some intersections, it's impossible to tell who has the right of way, and because they don't have the right-hand rule here, which favors the driver on the right, everyone stops and nods at each other. And sometimes they make right turns off multi-lane streets from the middle lane—without signaling it, of course—veering across traffic and blocking everyone's way. But you have to be careful; it's not as chaotic as it seems. This is only what an outsider thinks. More and more, I began to see that it had a firm order of its own; it's just that I didn't know what it was. It's like an anthill: it looks like a lot of meaningless and random swarming, but it seems that way only because we don't know and don't understand—if we're not biologists—the sophisticated systems of ant behavior. In reality, the activity in an anthill is governed by a kind of collective reason in which every individual ant knows precisely what it's doing and why it's behaving in a certain way, and why it must not behave otherwise if everything is not to fall apart. Perhaps that's true not just of anthills and Washington traffic, but of the whole world: everything that exists has its own purpose and system. We just don't know, and we never will know, how to understand it. But there's probably a reason for that too.

(July 24, 2002)

(. . .)

7) It seems that the question of lunch in Lány for the presidents' wives is still open. I don't think the lunch can be held in that vast, ugly room that looks like a factory canteen; it somehow must be made to fit into the blue dining room, or the blue and yellow dining room. In my opinion it can't be handled by a catering firm. The Lány staff should do it and give it a kind of homey quality. At the same time the entire preparation and the lunch itself should be supervised by professionals, so there will be no embarrassing lapses, such as serving the wrong kind of wine, or putting the dessert on the table during the soup course, etc. (. . .)

(August 31, 2002)

(. . .)

4) I thank Mr. M. for the paper on my postpresidential existence. It's very good, although maximalist, and it covers many aspects of the matter that had not occurred to me. Only the legal status remains a problem. It can't come under the OPR. I'd constantly be under surveillance and control, and there would be the continual annoyance of two masters. (We had an indication of what that might be like when my office on the Embankment was partly answerable to me and partly to the Castle.) (. . .) As far as the location is concerned; it certainly can't be in the Castle precincts. That would create a precedent whereby all presidents would remain there until the end of their days.

(September 7, 2002)

1) I have shortened my speech for the White House and adjusted it so that it might be delivered before the meetings. I can imagine delivering it half off-the-cuff, and half from paper. The first day of the visit, i.e., the White House and Congress, seems to me on the whole fairly straight-forward. (. . .)

5) I'll take another look at the speech for the Florida International University, but there probably won't be many changes to it. As far as the dinner in Florida is concerned, here is where various secrets will be revealed. (. . .)

7) Before our departure for the USA, that is next week, the minister of defense, Tvrdík (. . .), wants to know whom I would like to see as army chief of staff. (. . .) I wish to keep my word in this matter and tell it to the minister in time.

8) I have a meeting with Rychetský. We'll be discussing sensitive subjects, like the future presidency, the postpresidential status, the referendum, the Constitutional Court, Bureš, etc. I need an opinion on Baxa as chair of the Supreme Administrative Court. I myself think that it might be he. (. . .)

(September 26, 2002)

1) Since my return I feel miserable, I'm extinguished, burned out, deflated: I only eat or sleep. (. . .)

5) Once again, when it was quiet, I listened to Pavlíček's music. I like it more and more. If I might, as a layman, comment on something, then let me say only what I've said before; in the final mix the "Marseillaise" should be heard one more time, and all the quotations, if it can be done, should be a bar or two longer so that when these motifs recur, even a tone-deaf person such as myself will recognize it in the background noise of the Vladislav Hall. (. . .)

6) I remind you again that I would like to have in hand some kind of approximation of my schedule until the end of my presidency. I know that it may be changed many times, but a kind of overview will help me. That means among other things: the final trip to Brno and Bratislava, the election of the new president (the first and second rounds), the presidential oath-taking, farewell to parliament, farewell to the government, farewell to the staff, farewell to the press (?), moving out of Lány, moving out of my office in the Castle, its preparation by Bořek, moving it to Hrádeček, and so on and so forth. At the same time there are some appointments I still have to make: for example to the CSC, the Constitutional Court, the Supreme Administrative Court and so on. (. . .)

8) I would also welcome a slightly more detailed program of the summit, the number of speeches to be made that are off the cuff, to be read, Czech, English, etc. I need suggestions. A parallel summit. I would also like to approve the arrangements for the first dinner at the Castle; so far I don't know anything about it, as it has remained in the shadow of the second dinner, but that first one will be our calling card, therefore it's more important. Has anyone met with Duo Goelan? If they could, and would like to, they should play somewhere near Bedřich Dlouhý's painting as people arrive for the second dinner. You have to explain to George Bush's advance team that it's utter nonsense to have their boss be the only one who comes through the back door and doesn't walk along the same route as everyone else, including Kilián's ballet. It would make the USA look bad and it would also be risky: it would not save him from having to shake hands; on the contrary it would make the situation a lot worse because people would try to shake his hand at inappropriate places, people would bunch up around him and create traffic jams, etc. Ultimately, his security detail would shoot us all (that is, the other presidents and their delegations) in desperation. (. . .)

10) Are the decorations countersigned? If not, it means an urgent and scolding telephone call to Špidla.

11) I thank you all for helping to make my American visit leave a better impression (perhaps) on the outside, than it made on me personally.

Washington, May 19, 2005

You can feel everywhere how September 11 impacted America and left its mark, certainly more than such a thing would have affected Europe had it happened there. There are many reasons for this, one of which would obviously be the fact that, unless we count the attack on Pearl Harbor, no enemy has ever attacked America on its own soil from the outside, therefore the USA has never experienced the horrors of modern wars, with their slaughter of civilians, their concentration camps, and everything else that goes with them. It's an enormous, powerful, and proud country that is trying to defend the freedom of people and its own security in various places in the world, but so far it has not had to face a military attack directly on its soil. It was really like a bolt of lightning out of a clear sky. No one could have imagined anything like it. For that very reason I am slightly worried about what is about to happen. I have to admit to something I don't know whether I can actually say here: I absolutely hated those two skyscrapers. They were a typical kind of architecture that has no ideas behind it. Moreover, they disrupted the skyline of the city; they towered absurdly over the beautiful crystalline topography of Manhattan. They were two monuments to the cult of profit at any cost: regardless of what it looked like, the place had to have the greatest imaginable number of square meters of office space. I was once on the top floor of one of those buildings for dinner, and I discovered that the whole thing was constantly swaying slightly. I took it as a sign that something was not right and that something was going on here that was, in a sense, against nature. A boat may sway, but a building should not. The view down was dull; it was no longer the view from a skyscraper and it wasn't yet the view from an aircraft.

And here's what I fear: that for reasons of prestige they will build something even higher on the same spot, something that will spoil New York even more, that they will enter into some kind of absurd competition with the terrorists; and who will win in the end, the suicidal fanatics or an even higher Tower of Babel? You have to fight against terrorists with armies, the police, the intelligence services; their sympathizers have to be dealt with by politicians, political scientists, sociologists, and psychologists. Buildings, however, should be erected to enrich human settlements, not to make them duller. Why couldn't new buildings be put up on that spot proportional to the buildings already there, and that would simply blend into the existing skyline? Likewise, I don't think that some bombastic monument should be erected at Ground Zero. What happened there must be commemorated, but tastefully, as the fallen from the Vietnam or the Korean wars are commemorated in Washington, or simply with a single large space or room that would evoke the catastrophe and its context.

What is your view now of the caretaker government led by the banker Josef Tošovský that took charge after the fall of Klaus's government? It was your idea, after all, to appoint Tošovský prime minis-

ter. Why did you do so? Some analysts refer to that time as an era of
disintegration, because the government had its hands tied and was
subject to the whims of a directionless parliamentary majority.

A few minutes after Václav Klaus officially handed me the government's resignation in Lány, I had a meeting there with the chairmen of
the three parties that had been in the governing coalition—that is, with
Václav Klaus, Josef Lux, and Jiří Skalický—and I asked them how they
saw things unfolding. Václav Klaus said that he would propose to a convention of the ODS that they go into opposition. Shortly after our
meeting he actually did this in the form of an open letter to all members of his party. But he said we should wait until after the convention
before doing anything. Without a government in place, however, it
made no sense to wait several weeks for the ODS to decide what we
already knew would happen. In any case, my position was a logical one:
no one from the coalition parties, and in fact, no one from the break-
away faction of the ODS, wanted to join a government led by Václav
Klaus, and the ODS could not afford to make itself look ridiculous by
jettisoning Klaus and then becoming part of a government led by someone else. There was general agreement that there should be an election
as soon as possible. The only question was, who would govern until
then?

With Skalický, Lux, and others, we decided that it should be something like a "caretaker" government, even though our constitution did
not recognize the concept. It would be a government made up partly of
politicians from the former coalition who were willing to serve in it,
and partly of experts. I asked Josef Lux, as chairman of the second
largest coalition party, to negotiate with his political partners with that
in mind. He then came to me with the names of three people who
would be acceptable in the post of prime minister. Two of them, as it
later turned out, fell out of the running for various reasons; the only
one remaining, and the only one willing to accept the position, was
Josef Tošovský.

Tošovský appointed his own cabinet, but he first consulted with me
about all the candidates. He is a good diplomat and a gentleman, so that
there were no further problems, and his government enjoyed greater
confidence in parliament than any government had so far. It was a hard-

working government. The working atmosphere was positive, and as I recall, it did many good things. Perhaps the awareness that it was only temporary had an influence on that. What did these people have to lose? Those who wished to remain in politics could only have profited, because they could appear the saviors of the country in crisis; those who had no political ambitions had no reason to be particularly cautious. That government also enjoyed the highest popularity in public opinion polls. Your analysts, it would seem, have memories that are completely at odds with mine.

In the elections in the spring of 1998, the Social Democrats, who had so far been in opposition, won as expected. Of course they couldn't govern alone, because they didn't have enough seats. What kind of negotiations took place afterward?

Miloš Zeman, who was chairman of the Social Democratic Party at the time and the chairman of the Chamber of Deputies, was willing to form a coalition government with Lux's Christian Democratic Union–Czech People's Party, and the new Union of Freedom Party, consisting of those who had left the ODS during the government crisis. It seemed a good solution to me, if not the only one that made sense. The liberals (the Union of Freedom) and the Social Democrats would act as a brake on each other and the result would be a centrist government. Something like that was created later, and has been in existence now for three years. Zeman was very generous, offering his partners many ministries, and he even considered asking Josef Lux, who is an honorable man and a good politician, to be prime minister. That didn't work out. The Union of Freedom, led by Jan Ruml, dug in its heels. That was a mistake and I think Jan Ruml knows this today. Zeman felt rebuffed, and he's not someone who forgets and forgives easily. He began to sincerely hate the liberals, and especially the Union of Freedom, who had so humiliated him, and he was willing to make a pact with the devil himself in order to crush these ungrateful insects.

And so the "opposition agreement" came into being, which is another product of Klaus's conceptual sleight of hand: it meant nothing other than that the ODS and the Czech Social Democratic Party, the two largest parties, would go on sharing positions of power, compromising with each other, supporting each other here and there, thus allowing the Czech Social Democratic Party to form a minority government, just as the ODS might do another time, and together they would crush those other dwarfs, just as they had tried to do with their changes to the electoral law. It was an absolutely clear basis for creating a closed political system. The leading role of a single party, which we had had under communism, would be replaced with the leading role of two parties. It might have appeared as a victory for the Social Democratic Party, but I would say rather, from the historical point of view, that party simply took the bait and paid for it; the chaos that it subsequently experienced was in my opinion a belated result of the amorality it acceded to when it sacrificed its principles for power and lucrative positions.

After the previous regular elections in 1996, in which the governing coalition got two fewer seats than it needed to gain the confidence of parliament, it was apparently you who suggested that Zeman, as the leader of the largest opposition party, be made chairman of the Chamber of Deputies. Wasn't this in fact a foreshadowing of the future opposition agreement?

Yes, I admit that in hindsight it can seem that way. At the time it was a solution that was acceptable to everyone, and this, in its own way, was just as well: why can't one of the four top positions in the country be held by the leader of the second largest party? I've never understood very well why the strongest party, even though they in fact represent a small number of citizens, has to automatically occupy all the top posts. At the time, however, it was merely a verbal agreement about one of the future votes in parliament; in other words, there was no written agreement about the eternal rule of two parties. In any case, verbal agreements about filling various parliamentary positions with representatives of the various parties are standard; in this case, the principle was broadened to include the function of parliamentary chairman, or speaker, which went against convention. I'd rather not think about what might have happened if Zeman and his party had not, at least in this symbolic way, been taken into account. But you're right about one thing: it was a moment when an inappropriate way of dividing power might have been born. It was as though these two powerful politicians had begun to get used to governing together—as the case is in the Republic of San Marino, with its two Captains Regent. In the period of the opposition agreement the situation was reversed. Zeman was prime minister and Klaus was chair of the Chamber of Deputies.

If you believed that the opposition agreement was so dangerous, why didn't you resign or at least threaten to resign?

It would have been laughable had I threatened to resign merely because two parties had concluded an agreement on cooperation. I could have found an equally serious reason every six months. I had already resigned once before, during the federation, and I knew that it wasn't out of the question that I'd be forced to resign for reasons of health, so I saved that option for a truly extreme situation. For example, if there had been another February 1948, or something like it.

Miloš Zeman is undoubtedly the second most outstanding political figure in recent years. How did you meet him and how did you get along with him?

While we were still under communist rule a dissenting article by him appeared in a magazine and attracted a lot of attention. So I knew about him from that time on. Then—and this was still before the Velvet Revolution—we were supposed to meet under somewhat conspiratorial circumstances in someone's flat, but I couldn't go because I fell ill, so I first met him on Letná during one of those large demonstrations in November 1989. At the time, many people wanted to address the crowds, and we knew that it could end badly if the demonstration was to go on for too long: the agents provocateurs were ready; slogans began appearing that could have resulted in police intervention; and there was always the danger of mob psychology taking over. And so, although we weren't happy to do it, we either discouraged most of those who wanted to speak or we directly prevented them from doing so. Zeman pushed everyone aside and without asking anyone stepped up to the microphone and read his speech. It was excellent, by the way.

Nevertheless, I saw then that he was a tough customer. After the revolution, I would see him on television on talk shows, and I found his sharp economic comments very entertaining. I considered him something of a "popular" economist, similar to some "popular" and entertaining psychologists and sexologists in this country. Later, when I heard he'd been elected chairman of the Social Democratic Party, I couldn't believe my ears; it was as if Jiřina Bohdalová were to be appointed chair of the Chamber of Deputies.

For a long time the Social Democrats remained a small party and were the object of much ridicule. It was almost a disgrace to have anything to do with it. I met with their leadership several times, at which the snide brigade naturally took umbrage. Zeman never forgot that, and for a long time he behaved very decently and correctly to me, which wasn't his usual style. In the end, he couldn't sustain it, and he was vulgar to me as well. As a result, Dáša, for the longest time, wouldn't shake hands with him, which naturally gave the media a lot to chew over.

Why did you not speak out against the vulgar ways he expressed himself, and respond to his unjust criticisms of conditions in the country?

In general I was very critical of our standards of political behavior, but I very seldom took issue with specific statements. It seemed inappropriate to me to get mixed up in that kind of thing. A couple of times I got into a verbal battle with Zeman; for example, when I publicly apologized to Josef Zieleniec on his behalf for the gossip about Zieleniec that Zeman got from Jan Kavan. There were more serious conflicts between us toward the end. There wasn't the same kind of stifling atmosphere around Miloš Zeman as there was around Václav Klaus, but he was capable of being very tough, stubborn, and loudmouthed, and even nasty. I had several run-ins with him that I would rather forget, but one thing I cannot deny him: of all Czech politicians, he was the best orator. Sometimes he said things that were banal, superficial, or even untrue, but he always expressed them wittily, extemporaneously, and in proper Czech. He never uttered a sentence that didn't have a subject and predicate.

Washington, May 23, 2005

Our time is becoming unbelievably short: it's Monday and it's possibly the last day that I will have some uninterrupted time to write. The very best I can hope is that I will finish this chapter here. A while ago I came back from lunch—this time an entirely private affair—with Mr. Billington. He is a wonderful older gentleman and he knows Russia very well. He gave me his book and invited me to come back to the library someday for another study period. He said it would be nice if I could read something in the Library of Congress that I had written here. There was salt on the table. Yesterday Dáša and I went for a picnic with the dogs in a nearby park and there we ate cheese and drank red wine. On Friday we met in the embassy with an organization called the American Friends of the Czech Republic. The reception turned into a political discussion, which then developed into a minor drinking session. We later regretted it. Tomorrow I have to deliver a speech here. I've never enjoyed mornings anywhere, and here, for some unknown reason, they are particularly bothersome. It takes a long time each day for me to come to terms with the fact that I am still alive, that life is constantly making demands upon me, that I always have to be somewhere, talk to someone, decide about something. It is in the mornings that I am always most ashamed of my own existence. During the day that sensation gradually subsides and I feel at my most confident in the evening. If I manage to spend some time in Hrádeček this summer, I will write mainly in the evenings and at night.

Now I'm slightly nervous about my speech tomorrow, which I will deliver in English of course, and mainly about the discussion to follow it. Whether I understand Americans and can reply in their language depends utterly and entirely on an impenetrable interplay of internal and external circumstances. But I've met people who've lived here for fifty years and their pronunciation is even worse than mine.

Yesterday I saw my friend Joan Baez on television; she was marvelous and I remembered the amphitheater at Stanford University where I gave a big speech and she sang and then I carried her guitar off the stage just as I had done in the communist era when I was at her concert in Bratislava. The state police had tried to prevent me from taking part, and I escaped their clutches by carrying Joan's guitar for her: they were reluctant to arrest me in her presence because they were afraid that she would speak about it at the concert. Even so, she dedicated a song to me and Charter 77 and they punished her by cutting off the power. A funereal silence fell over the stadium, and then she sang without a microphone. She was clearly audible. It was very moving and, naturally, it was a far more momentous event than it would have been if they'd left her microphone switched on.

But while I'm on the subject of my speeches, I think that every year while I was president I gave at least one speech in this country. The one I remember most proudly was the one at Harvard. The auditorium was full of students and faculty; it was the annual celebration of the end of the school year and convocation, at which several honorary doctorates were awarded. I was among them and I was supposed to give the main speech. It was rather philo-sophical, rather complicated, and rather long. It was raining lightly, and as the day wore on the students were growing increasingly celebratory. I became more and more certain that no one would listen to my speech that afternoon, either because they would all have something better to do, or because of the rain, or because of my mumbling. But something unprecedented happened: no one left; they were silent; they listened to me attentively and clapped or laughed many times during my speech, always in the right places. When it was over they gave me a standing ovation. Vice President Gore was in the audience as well, as a father. My almost hour-long speech didn't change the course of world history, but I still recall it as one of the most successful moments of my presidency. Unfortunately that memory doesn't give me any courage or self-confidence or certainty today. On the contrary, I know that it simply can't be repeated, and so my panic is all the greater before every speech, particularly if I have to give it in a foreign language.

(October 13, 2002)

1) The speech for October 28 is hanging over me like a nightmare. (. . .) So far I've only more or less twiddled my thumbs and I have no desire to write. If I finish it today I will attach it, but I doubt that I'll manage to do that. (. . .)

4) Dáša and I (. . .) have added quite a few names to the guest list for October 28. We're always remembering someone who may or may not be on the list. Most are probably already on it, but many may not be, and they shouldn't be left off. It's not just people who have done something for us and for the Castle, but above all people who have done some public service. Was this year's list based on last year's? Or was an earlier, and therefore out-of-date, list used? In no particular order I would remind you of the following names: Michal Pavlíček, Václav Marhoul, Jiří Kilián, Ilona Csáková, Iveta Bartošová, Daniel Hůlka (they sing for the foundation), Janis Sidovský, Kamil Střihavka, Bára Basiková, Bára Štěpánová, Pavel Kohout, Květa Fialová, Jan Urban, Tomáš Halík (and that "old crowd" from Amálie), Věra Jirousová, Ivan Jirous, Torst, Paseka, Pupi, Trefulka, Jungmann, Bělohradský, Bursík, Čáslavská, Křižan, the best young writers (get some expert advice on this), etc., etc. Many of them won't come, but on the whole I think it won't matter if there are a hundred more or a hundred less. If all of them don't crowd around the beer barrel they'll all fit in—I remember other October 28 celebrations with the rooms half full and even when the Spanish Hall was only half full. (. . .)

7) Thanks for the first draft of my schedule to the end of my presidency. It's a very solid basis for further discussion. At first glance, however, it seems to me a little rich, or overextensive. For example, a whole series of gala farewells on February 2 is a matter for serious discussion. (. . .)

(October 29, 2002)

(. . .)

2) Rothmayer's Hall, Šípek's new cloakroom, and everything that is related to that works exceptionally well, and I have no further comments.

I would only remark that the place felt draftier than usual. Perhaps that was another reason why there were fewer people than usual. Could there be a new air duct in the room? Was a door left open? Or was I just imagining it? But I've never noticed such a breeze there before. (. . .)

4) Bořek's new staircase seems to be working perfectly. I was surprised how many people used it. How did they know that they could go that way?

5) The New Hall. My greatest sore point. It was the very first (!!!) space in the Castle that I wanted to do something with, to humanize a little, and it's the last (!!!) space that has remained unchanged. A great, a gigantic victory for the Prague Castle Administration! (. . .)

(December 15, 2002)

1) I have written the New Year's speech. Please circulate it to the usual closest circle of people for comments, but it is possible, and even may be a good idea, to consult about it with someone outside who doesn't live in this submarine, as long as it's someone of absolute discretion. (. . .)

2) I still have to write my speech to parliament, deal with comments on my speech to the military, the speech for Germany, and the farewell address. Please schedule time for these speeches (underlined and with exclamation marks), on all my holidays or so-called free days with the possible exception of Christmas Eve. (. . .)

4) If Děvana happens to have time on Friday, December 27, I would drop in on her for a checkup and some dental work. If that day isn't good for her, let's leave it for sometime in the future. (. . .)

7) We are not going anywhere on New Year's Eve, but if anyone has any casual and interesting ideas where one might go, please let me know.

8) So far I have no remarks about my schedule, but I would ask that nothing be added to it. I will need a lot of time for setting up a microsecretariat, for moving, and any eventual crisis that might arise around the election of a new president. (. . .)

10) Please ask Mr. Patočka to meet me sometime after work in a pub. My answer to his question: in my New Year's speech last year, I called on the political parties to propose their candidates for president as early as

possible, that means before the parliamentary elections. I know that the public as well must take these names to heart and that it requires a certain time for that to happen. Moreover, at that time the presidential election was still a long way off and there wouldn't be so many intrigues, speculations, ambitions on display, etc., etc. No one listened to my appeal. First they said that the decision had to be made after the parliamentary elections. Then they deferred it until after the senatorial elections. And now we are faced with the result: the search for a president is taking on the qualities of a farce. I deeply regret that, all the more because I know there are dozens of people walking the land who would probably make a better president than I, but who will never be president because no party has spoken to them, or endorsed them, or attempted to popularize them with the electorate. They are people who are more or less "unknown" (which means that they don't try to get themselves on television every day), and are "unelectable" or "unviable," which simply means that the party representatives or the party factions or the party secretariats didn't think of them, didn't approach them, and in one way or another didn't win them over in time. It's not a happy story, but the country will survive it.

In 1998 you ran for the Czech presidency again for a second five-year term. Do you recall the circumstances of that election? Why, in fact, did you run again?

That's a question I often ask myself and I still don't have a clear answer. Above all, however, I'm still not sure if running for president yet again wasn't my greatest mistake. As usual, pressure from those around was a factor. I recall, for example, how Jan Ruml made a special trip to see me at Lány to convince me to run again. If I didn't, he said, this country would move toward a kind of postcommunist quasi-dictatorship as it did in Slovakia under Mečiar, or Ukraine under Kuchma. All the parties, he said, were mixed up in some kind of corruption, and I was the only person who was cut from different cloth, and who stood a chance of being elected. But not only that: he said that if I, with the degree of international confidence I enjoyed, did not complete my work, we would not be accepted into NATO, and even more seriously, perhaps NATO would not even expand, which would mean a new Iron Curtain—although a psychological one this time—and we would forever remain in a sphere of dubious quasi-democracies, teeming with populists and nationalists. I had to finish what I had started. I had to be in office for our acceptance into NATO and into the European Union.

Other people around me were saying the same thing. They were overstating it, of course, and perhaps I'm even overstating it a bit now, but that was the atmosphere around me at the time. It was as though I were expected—symbolically at least—to pull something out of the fire once more. At that time Czech society was no longer feeling the pain of the country's breakup—we had recovered from that relatively quickly—but a certain apprehension about the future did seem to predominate. A caretaker government was in power, there was no other broadly acceptable presidential candidate, there were extremists out there who were shouting very loudly, and it was obvious that either Klaus or Zeman would win the approaching parliamentary elections, and it may have seemed to many people that there should be at least some kind of counterbalance to these two men.

At the same time, however, I quite frankly did not want to spend another five years living a life that was utterly different from the one I would have preferred. In the end I accepted the candidacy. I repeat: I don't know if I did the right thing. To the extent that I helped our country—something I cannot judge for myself—I did the right thing; if I didn't, then I should have turned my attention to other things. There was certainly no personal benefit to be had from running again.

On the day parliament elected you, your wife whistled in protest after a speech by a far-right nationalist deputy. It may have gained her a lot of supporters but it also won her many enemies. What was your response to that?

Naturally, at an event as serious as the election of a head of state, which takes place in the Spanish Hall, in the Prague Castle, one ought not to whistle. At the same time, however, it was the only possible way that the candidate's temperamental, and absolutely loyal, wife could respond to the rubbish uttered about her husband. What was I to say? That I disapproved and, at the same time, that I sympathized? I simply avoided commenting on it. Today I needn't hold my tongue any longer, and can say clearly: not just that particular nationalist speaker, but many more Czech politicians and their practices, deserve no better than to be whistled down.

But back to my candidacy: in some mysterious way, the arguments for and against it canceled each other out within me, with the odd result that I couldn't have cared less whether I was elected or not. If the outcome was positive, I would serve my country again and experience more remarkable things; and if it was negative, I would retire to a life of peace and quiet, write something, read wise books, get back in touch with friends for whom I would otherwise have had no time, rest, travel, think, occasionally criticize, not ruin my health, sleep in the morning until I was good and ready to get up. I wouldn't have to wear a tie all the time, smile all the time, be worried all the time that I might make a huge gaffe. I knew that most of the political parties and their sitting members deeply disliked me, and it was quite possible that in a secret vote I wouldn't be elected. I did everything I could to make sure they knew everything about me: I think it was at this time that I made a full disclosure of my assets, though I was not required to. I provided parliament with a doctor's report on the state of my health, because I didn't want anyone to think I was hiding anything before the election. Even that speech in the Rudolfinum was part of my strategy.

In the first round of voting I was not elected. Then Dáša and I went to a friend's, Petr Weigl the director, for a dinner that had been scheduled long before, and I didn't even watch the vote on television as might have been expected, but simply arranged for them to call us when the result was known. That too tells you something about the strange apathy that gripped me at the time. I was elected on the second round by a single vote. That seemed to me an excellent result: it could be interpreted to mean that I became the unwanted president, which in the given state of affairs was a double honor for me. It was an honor that I was president again and it was an honor that I was unwanted, unwanted, of course, not by everyone; only by a considerable portion of the political elite. But you're either elected, or you're not elected;

there is no third possibility. I paid no attention, therefore, to remarks about my not being a fully fledged president, that I should have resigned at once, withdrawn my candidacy, walked away and let them do whatever they wanted. In my opinion that would have been, on the one hand, an expression of unforgivable pride, like saying I would agree to be head of state only if I were elected by as many members of parliament as I myself thought proper—and on the other hand it would have been spitting on the democratic process itself, because that is how things work in a democracy: the difference between a majority and a minority can be infinitesimal and still be valid, and someone voted into office in those circumstances has as much legitimacy as someone elected unanimously.

I simply took it as a fact that I was president again and that I would continue to lend my support to good things and resist bad things, and that my dream of leaving office for a life of freedom had to be postponed. I was occasionally ridiculed for that outcome, and Miloš Zeman quipped that the single vote that elected me was his, and that therefore I should do as he said.

How did you experience that second five-year period, in the end?

You know, in my memory I don't distinguish much between those years and the preceding five years. I undertook many state visits to all kinds of countries, and hosted innumerable official state visits to our country. I received someone at the Castle almost every day; there were journeys around the country, summits of international organizations, and speeches, speeches, speeches. Governments came and went; there were elections. I met a lot of interesting people whom I would never otherwise have met, as well as a lot of fools. I paid particular attention to improving the Prague Castle, though, in the end, we were able to accomplish only a small percentage of what we had planned. But even so, we did quite a bit.

As far as the political situation in our country goes, I would say that slowly and surely the gulf between politics and society grew deeper. It was a period of petitions like the "Dřevíčká Appeal," or the ones called "Thank You, Now Leave!" "Television: A Public Affair," or

"Impulse '99." It was a time when an alternative to the somewhat stale governments of Miloš Zeman and Václav Klaus appeared in the form of the so-called Quad Coalition, whose voter support grew, miraculously, only to collapse again owing to internal conflicts. In my own heart and mind, I was on the side of the civic initiatives or the attempts to create a slightly different kind of politics, and therefore, those in political circles were not very fond of me. But in the end they got used to me—as a kind of necessary evil. Besides, I had to constantly keep myself in check and express myself rather cautiously. The thing is, you can't hold the highest position in the country and at the same time be an eternal rebel. Of course, it's possible even in that position to criticize everything and anything, from how mankind is treating the earth to the atmosphere of public life and the specific actions of specific people and organizations. In a certain sense, it even follows directly from the presidential oath, for, as you know, the president must carry out his responsibilities to the best of his abilities and conscience, but it must be done with taste and skill, otherwise one might become an object of ridicule, or provoke general hostility, and rightly so. I don't claim that I always got it right. To the extent that I didn't, it was clearly my own fault.

Washington, May 26, 2005

The day before yesterday I gave my speech in the Library of Congress. The large but intimate hall was filled to capacity, and they had to set up television screens outside for the overflow. I was welcomed with a standing ovation, and there was also long applause when I was finished, so perhaps it turned out well. Then representatives of various exile opposition groups from Burma, Belarus, Cuba, and China came onto the stage and they all spoke very nicely about me. Harry Wu, who had spent nineteen years in prison in China, presented me with a book of my texts handwritten in Chinese. With tears in his eyes he told me that people were locked up for possessing this, but even so they are circulated. I answered several questions put to me by these exiled leaders, and by members of the audience; I spoke in English but I always had the pos-

sibility of asking my friend and translator, Paul Wilson, for help. Everyone seemed pleased but I had my usual hangover from it. Then there was a large dinner at the embassy, where various U.S. senators mingled with the warriors for human rights. Yesterday the merry-go-round continued with a press conference, a visit to the Senate, and a visit to George Washington University. We had dinner that evening with the friends who had provided us with a private aircraft so we could bring our dogs to the United States with us. We will be returning with them as well. Our stay here is at an end; today is in fact the last day I'll be able to write anything.

(December 26, 2002)

(. . .)

5) I'm still not certain about that meeting in Lány with those that I have named. Should the people I'm going to meet in Brno be there as well? And their predecessors? Čalfa and people from the period of the federation are missing from that list. I don't like the various efforts being made to erase that period from history. In any case, the most important economic reforms happened during that time, and not under Klaus's government, as is generally claimed. Are there not rather too many of these farewell events? Won't it be grist for the mill for those who claim that I am just erecting my own monument? Do I really have to talk to the member of parliament who claims that I have never done anything in my life for my country because everything I've done has been only for myself? I have to guard every minute of my time and every ounce of my well- or not-so-well-being. The prospect of another farewell event, including the stifling atmosphere that will prevail, and the absurd reports that some of the participants will give of it (just remember the meeting with the Chamber of Deputies!), terrifies me. And what if Zeman doesn't come in from his place in the Highlands, and Klaus too doesn't come? Then it would be completely absurd. Even more so because it's too much to expect Tošovský to come from Basel. Have the participants already been invited? Does it really have to happen? I understand those various farewells and tributes more as a return to normal life than as a way of

constantly paying homage to my person. At the same time I will have enough worries of my own (setting up the mini-secretariat, moving, etc.), and I feel that I'm drawing on my last reserves of strength. (. . .) All of this puts a great deal of stress on my nervous system, and the main thing is that I manage to remain, until the end of my term, alive and out of the hospital.

6) Please give me more information about the farewell party for the Castle staff. Please invite the entire PCA. I've already told Mr. Š. something about the catering firm. Will the Castle orchestra play? Will there be speeches? Where will it be held if the Spanish Hall is still in use for the election of the new president? On the contrary, if the new president is already elected shouldn't he be invited?

(January 18, 2003)

1) I'm sending a new version of the final speech. I will go back over this speech on the last Saturday. (. . .) I really do wish to deliver a very personal farewell, and not a colorless political speech. (. . .)

3) I would ask the directors of the departments to think quickly about how they can help me with the transition to my new life. Opinions about where I should have my office differ. Opinions about the lease differ. And they even differ on the matter of employee contracts. Lots of advice, not much help. They've already been trying to disconnect and take away the telephones. There's nothing wrong with that, when the time comes, but will anyone help us set up our own telephones? If I had two weeks free I would organize it myself. But I have no free time for it. I'm meant to have a new computer, and return my old (government-issue) one. That too is as it should be. But who will transfer everything that's in it to the new one? And where's the guarantee that this information will not remain in the subconscious of the old computer? There are explosive things in it. I want my own newspapers to start in March. When will we have new passports? Is anyone pushing that through? They don't have to be diplomatic passports, but mine can't have "President" on it crossed out by my own hand. The salons in Lány (and in the cottage V Luhu) are filled with our things. (. . .) The PCA has been reminding me for a year about the four

government-issue chairs that I have at home, but regarding the hundreds of my own things which are in the government-issue spaces, the PCA seems—at least in its lower echelons—to take a very lax attitude. (. . .)

(January 26, 2003)

(. . .)

5) I would ask the PCA to draw up an agreement with me about borrowing (perhaps only temporarily) the chairs that I have in my office in Dělostřelecká Street. I have no time to buy new ones. At the same time I would remind the PCA that they owe me that rare and large painting by Kunc which has mysteriously disappeared somewhere in the Castle, and which, of course, is worth more than four worn-out chairs.

Washington, May 26, 2005

My escape to America is coming to an end. I'm not looking forward to going home, but more travel awaits us. I will write whenever I have the slightest opportunity.

CHAPTER FIVE

Hrádeček, July 10, 2005

I've run away. I've run away to Hrádeček. I'm here alone and I feel uneasy. Everything reminds me of the decades I've been through in this place. I like it here. It's my refuge, my existential home, but again and again I realize there's no going back, and that by now I'm not the same person I was when I wrote my plays, prepared my experimental meals, threw lighthearted parties, and organized secret dissident meetings. I'm older, sicker, wearier. I don't quite know why, but it's as though I were more and more afraid of the world and people. I find it hard just to make a telephone call. And now, to make matters worse, the weather is very strange.

We've been back from America for six weeks now, but I wasn't able to continue writing this until I came here. It was out of the question in Prague— there was simply no time. And I'm only here for a couple of days, so that by the time I get back into it again and overcome my reluctance to write, it will be over.

Dáša and I now look back on the time we spent in Washington as a beautiful period in our life. The return was quite shocking. The political atmosphere was stifling. Dubious weekly pronouncements from the president that appear to bother no one but an enlightened minority; oddly enough, they seem to have caused him to rise in the polls. We live in a world of intermediaries, and intermediaries for intermediaries, in a world of lobbyists, consultants, PR agents. People are paid by others to introduce someone to someone else, who will advise them how to make money on something that someone else has created. How is it possible that our population remains constant and yet we have more and more intermediaries? I'm astonished at the ease with which everyone has accepted this mediational cosmos, and especially at how I was able to hold political office in such a cosmos when it's so alien to me, and when I don't know my way around it at all.

An important thing: after returning home, we began, belatedly, to appreciate American drivers and their habits. Here everyone drives like a madman, and at the same time they're not very good drivers so that going anywhere by car is a rather dangerous adventure. When anyone sticks to the speed limit they tap their foreheads or shake their fists at him. All of this is one of the more trivial symptoms of a general demoralization. Indeed, coming back after a long time away, one seems to be coming back to a postcommunist land of nouveaux riches and con men. But all is not lost: a new generation of free people is growing up, people not deformed by communism or the privatization process, and there are many civic initiatives, associations, and small extra-parliamentary parties that are trying to do something about all of this. Not just to criticize conditions and the unbelievable alienation between politics and citizens, but to take part in elections, to enter into practical politics and have an influence on it. I occasionally meet with them, but they expect more from me than they should—for instance, that I will help them reach a consensus (most of them are at loggerheads with each other).

What have I actually done since my return? In Berlin I received a Tibetan prize from the Dalai Lama; in Austria President Fischer and I read some of my old texts (he in German, I in Czech); I opened or closed several conferences; we were at the Karlový Vary Film Festival; I looked after my friend Robert Redford, who was here with Madeleine, and a remarkable phenomenon called Sharon Stone. On the whole, however, I am habitually dissatisfied with myself. I'm haunted by a feeling that I'm performing badly, and that no one has the courage to tell me. It seems to me that whenever I make an improvised speech I frequently stutter, I don't speak wittily or coherently, I forget what I had intended to say and become muddled. Perhaps it's just exhaustion accumulated over a lifetime. At the same time I have postpresidential obligations, which means I have to receive important visitors, write or at least edit all kinds of declarations related to my international activities for human rights, make decisions about hundreds of details, give interviews, and in all of this, pretend that it's really nothing. Dáša is the one who looks after our foundation Vize '97, but occasionally I get involved, particularly when it concerns Prague Crossroads, an old Gothic church in the center of Prague that was used as a storage space for two hundred years and which our foundation has leased for a hundred years. *The foundation has been restoring it for some time now, and recently it was opened to the public as a new spiritual and cultural center.*

In short, I have escaped to Hrádeček in the hope that I would find rest from the world and inner peace. But even that hope, which may have been foolish from the start, was dashed: the bushes I have been cultivating around the house for almost forty years to provide a kind of privacy screen were cut down when we were away—God knows why! It was a serious attack on my identity, as though someone had cut off all my limbs. Paradoxically I was just experiencing that shock as they were broadcasting the final round of the television contest "The Greatest Czech," in which I placed third after Charles IV and Tomáš Garrigue Masaryk. I was the only living person among the top ten. When I looked out the window at the wasteland outside, I said to myself that I deserved instead the title "The Greatest Fool."

Does a president have any privacy? Were you able to draw a line between your private affairs and your public life?

I think that a completely clear line between a politician's private and public life, one respected by everyone, doesn't exist anywhere. By trial and error, politicians and journalists are forever trying to shift it in one direction or the other. I've always respected the fact that citizens have a right to know more about someone they have entrusted with a political office than about someone they haven't. A politician has to take that into account and be aware that when he steps onto the public stage, he will be subject to scrutiny. To a great extent, it's up to the journalists to determine how far they're willing to take it. And that, in turn, depends on the culture of public life and community standards. Unfortunately, I have to say that the very first thing we caught up to the West in, and then surpassed it, was tabloid journalism. It almost makes you think that, for journalists, the arrival of freedom meant, above all, the ability to crawl under politicians' beds with impunity.

You have closely guarded your privacy all your life; for example, you've never published a single love letter, and you waited until the fall

of 1995 to inform the public about the serious, and by that time terminal, illness of your first wife, Olga. How did you arrive at the decision?

Love letters are not intended for publication. Moreover, I couldn't have published any because I don't think I've ever written any. I am essentially—at least in some things—a very shy person. Besides, I have always tried to be cautious in my writing for fear that what I wrote could be misused, either by the secret police during the dissident period, or by sensation-hunters while I was president. I don't remember now when or how I informed the public about Olga's illness, but I had to do it: people loved her—witness the endless line of citizens who spontaneously came to pay their respects after her death. She was publicly active and, in the general view, had always been closely associated with me. Therefore I had to explain why, from a certain time onward, she was no longer appearing by my side, and in fact not appearing in public at all. She had a brain tumor; we had known it for almost two years and she suffered a great deal, both from the illness itself, from its side effects, and from the chemotherapy. But she bore her lot bravely, and she understood her condition as a private matter; she never complained and she never cried and she hated talking about it. It seemed—to the extent that this was possible at all and not just a gambit employed by someone who didn't like talking about herself—she had come to terms with her approaching death. She would say that each of us has our own allotted time. In the final months she never left home, apart from the time she spent in the hospital.

How did you experience the approaching death of the person who was closest to you, and with whom you had lived for more than forty years?

Naturally, they were very difficult weeks for me. I tried to encourage Olga, to say something sweet to her now and then, but she always saw immediately why I was doing it and told me to save my breath. We weren't much in the habit of saying sweet nothings to each other. We were so closely bound together and dependent on each other that any kind of commentary could only have devalued that bond. Naturally, I thought a lot about our life together, about what we had given each other, and about how I would live without her. Olga urged me to get married again soon; she knew I couldn't really be alone. I knew it as well, and that left me with two choices: either to go with her, or to start a new life.

Personally it was very important for me when she told me on her deathbed that I had never betrayed her. She was talking about something that went far deeper than my "relaxed morals," about which she knew more than anyone else and which had naturally bothered her.

Did the circumstances of 1995 force you to think about your own possible death?

I have never attempted suicide, but I have thought about death all my life, and with advancing years I do so even more. Not because I am growing old myself, and not just because I've looked death in the face a couple of times from a hospital bed, but mainly because those closest to me—my wife, family, friends—are gradually departing. It's impossible not to think about death. I'm preparing for my own end in a slightly bureaucratic way: I want to leave order in my wake. An aspect of that, for example, was overseeing a critical edition of my collected writings. It was as though I wanted complete control over what remained after me. This was not just out of my love of order; who, having experienced the death of those closest to him, and with death itself looming over him, will not think of writing a will and leaving his affairs in order? In the past, it went without saying.

I can't rule out the fact that shortly after Olga's death I might have subconsciously wanted to follow her, or that I occasionally felt that she was calling me to her. And by the way, it was then that I had my first awkward fall at night, and it was at home, not in Asia! I spattered blood all over the room, and they carried me off somewhere where they reset my dislocated jaw. I know that when they were tending to me I babbled nonsense; there was something almost euphoric about the experience. In those first days and weeks after Olga's death, Dáša was a great help to me. She tried not to leave me at home alone in the evenings. It was unpleasant, of course, to have to go to work, to smile at all the receptions, to travel on state visits, trying not to let my emotions show. But I think I have a strong will and a fair amount of self-control.

Is it true that when you were feeling at your worst, just before Olga's death, you had secret meetings about your own headstone, about what the inscription should be?

Those discussions were certainly not secret, and they didn't concern my own gravestone but our family grave. The headstone had to be redone so everyone's name would fit. My parents, my uncle, and one of my grandfathers had been squeezed in on the margin, and not only was there no room to put Olga's name, but there would be no room to put me either, or anyone else in our family for that matter. My looking after this simply confirms what I've said about my bureaucratic approach to death. After all, why should I have cared how we would one day be arranged on a headstone! But I wanted it to be done in a way that respected both chronology and family relationships. I don't want any special inscription on my grave; I don't even want a title or a profession—just a name, and the date of birth and death, just like the others.

(May 29, 1994)

1) I'm sending my Philadelphia speech. Please pass it around to the usual consultants. (. . .)

2) They've discovered a tumor in Olga and operated on her. I will occasionally go to visit her in the hospital, and therefore please do not add anything more to my schedule; on the contrary, try to remove something from it. In my free time I must study the government, Normandy, write a speech for Romania, etc., etc.

3) I need a detailed schedule for Charles and briefing notes for a speech and a toast! I am constantly groping about in a mire of ignorance! (. . .)

(October 8, 1995)

1) As a result of various circumstances (the lustration law, family worries, etc.), I'm a week in arrears in my speechwriting; I've only now written my speech for the U.N., which according to plan should have been written last weekend. This will require an increased pace in the work to come. (. . .)

4) I would ask Mr. Š. to get in touch immediately with Iva T. and for both of them to look up Professor Klener. It would be enough to call him, and settle on the precise wording for a press release about the fact that Olga is going into the hospital. She goes in next Tuesday. (. . .)

(. . .) She will be in a hermetically sealed ward and therefore there is no point in having a pistoleer with her. The pistoleer should only be reachable by telephone in case something is needed. They are going to let me in to see Olga from time to time. Therefore it would be a good thing if on Tuesday one of my pistoleers would accompany Olga to the hospital; he could then find out where the ward is and how to get there, etc., so that we would not create needless panic when we go there. At the same time I should know all the relevant telephone numbers: i.e., to Olga's room, to the nurse, to Professor Klener at the clinic and at home. It would also be good to give Professor Klener every possible telephone number where I can be reached. The last time it took him two hours to get through to me. God knows why. It will obviously be necessary to write down instructions for him on how to get from a normal line to the Z line, and then from the Z line to my office and to our home, and to give him the normal telephone numbers and the numbers of the operations officer as well. The officer can always find me. But he must know about Klener so that he won't think some crank is trying to get through to me. (. . .)

(January 21, 1996)

(. . .)
The organizational and other consequences of the approaching death of my wife, which could happen at any minute, or perhaps in a week or more, compel me to write out some instructions in the event of her death.

You will certainly understand how difficult it is for me to write these instructions when she is still alive. But it seems to me that it has to be done, because I don't know what state I will be in when it happens (it will probably be at home) and whether I will be capable at all of making any decisions. I will summarize everything I think will have to be done, from fundamental things to trivial details, but I want to do it all thoroughly. Please understand this as a part of my auto-therapy. (By the way, please ask V. not to continually improve my computer and its programs: with every upgrade my ability to write anything at all on the computer is radically decreased; for example, I've been writing this paragraph for half an hour, and in the computer's previous state I would have had it written in half a minute.) My wishes and instructions, as I have already indicated, are of very different kinds. Some of them are meant for a wide circle of Castle and other people (CGW, FAO). Others concern only individuals, and they are more or less of a discreet nature. I will leave it up to V. what to reproduce for everyone and what he will give only to those whom it immediately concerns. I will write down my instructions, or my wishes, or my pleas, as they come to me; so fundamental things will be mixed up with details, but I believe that you will know how to sort them out. (. . .)

(February 17, 1996)

(. . .)

13) Mr. Š. has sent me the A list and the B list of guests for the dinner with the queen. I can't distinguish between them; perhaps I have received the same list twice by mistake, or I was inattentive and did not see the difference. However it is, I would suggest that Mr. S. go over the whole list again, name by name, quickly with representatives of the DDP and at the same time try to decide who is missing. (. . .) I didn't see Falbr, Dienstbier, and other representatives of public life, but mainly I missed seeing several of the least frequently invited and more unusual guests, different from the ones that we traditionally invited according to existing lists. A few examples at random: Dagmar Pecková, Pavel Bobek, Věra Chytilová, František Pavlíček, Vlasta Průchová, former Charter 77 spokespersons, Marián Čalfa, Michael Kocáb, Petr Weigl, the conductors Bělohlávek and Kulínský, Saša Gedeon, university chancellor Jařab,

Jaroslava Adamová, Josef Topol (he translated Shakespeare!), Pavel Kohout, Jáchym Topol, Otomar Krejča (he directed Shakespeare), Jiří Menzel, Lucie Bílá, Petr Rezek, Zdeněk Neubauer, Petr Pithart (and that whole gang from Amálie), etc., etc. Perhaps some of these people are already on the list. I didn't check it closely. Perhaps some were not considered for various reasons, and certainly many will not have time, and perhaps there will not be room for so many people. I don't know. In any case—and particularly in such a special case—we should not always keep exclusively to the standard lists and the standard criteria, but look around for various interesting people that we might have forgotten about. (. . .)

14) How does one go about thanking people for their condolences? For the conventional condolences from heads of state and world figures the Protocol Office will obviously reply conventionally and merely give it to me for signing. I would ask that any special or any interesting personal condolences that deserve my handwritten personal reply, whether they come from heads of state or from some select friends, be singled out and given to me for a personal response. I would like to finish this during my convalescence. (. . .)

(February 4, 1996)

1) Bad news: I have not written my speech for parliament. Good news: I've started to write it. The hardest part for me is always starting to write, especially now. I feel that I am starting everything from scratch and that I'm learning the alphabet all over again. The fact that I have begun it offers hope that I will move it ahead over Monday. I would ask therefore not to be interrupted by pointless matters. But you can send me important papers for my signature or for reading, including the magazine *Týden*, where there's meant to be something on Olga.

2) I would ask V. to send this letter through the computer network to everyone in the Castle: *From the bottom of my heart, I thank all the employees of the OPR, the Prague Castle Administration, the Castle Police, and the Castle Guard, for all the work that they carried out without any hesitation and with full personal engagement, in organizing the dignified tribute to the memory of my wife. No less—and perhaps even*

more—do I thank them for being with me in spirit and for coming to pay their respect to her memory in such large numbers and with such obvious sincerity. I was moved by all of this and at the same time strengthened in the feeling that I have fellow workers whom I can trust and on whom I can depend in both good and difficult times.—Václav Havel.

3) I would ask L. to cooperate with T. in finding out in time when the Undertaking Service will lay Olga's urn in our family plot, and for this event, which will have to be included in my schedule (as far as possible in daylight hours), invite my brother and the sculptor Olbram Zoubek (he and I have already agreed on this) and, if possible, an architect that he will determine, because I'd like to use this moment (naturally to be kept secret from the public) to hold a small meeting on the very place about how to deal with the headstone, so that not only will Olga fit on it, but there will also be a place for me and other members of our family, for we too, I assume, will die sooner or later, and I don't know of anyone more appropriate than me to decide about all of this in a timely manner. (. . .)

5) In the coming week it's high time for a meeting about the visits of the British queen and the Canadian governor general; both can perhaps be dealt with in the same session.

(February 25, 1996)

(. . .)

6) I've discovered that reading the letters of condolence, although they have been sorted out and picked over many times, still moves me and breaks my heart, making it all the more difficult for me to reply to them individually. Therefore I would ask J. to write (perhaps in a number of variations) thank-you letters and to send them in my name: for example, *The President was moved by your beautiful letter in which you offer your condolences for the death of his wife. He has asked me to thank you on his behalf and to say that he appreciates the fact that he can consider so many good people as friends to whom he can turn in times of trouble.* Wouldn't that be the way to deal with it? As far as the heads of state are concerned, I have written Š. that we should sit down for an hour at the Castle and I will either sign the standard letter of thanks, or I will add a more personal sentence in English on the spot. Please set aside some time for us to do that.

(March 3, 1996)

(. . .)

2) They didn't include it in the law on the OPR because they said it would be more systematic if they included it in the Heritage Law. Now they say it would be more systematic if they put in the law governing the OPR. It's a topsy-turvy land that hides nothing less than an attempt to hurt the president and to castrate his office as well. But I won't give in! It must merely be stated in the law that in the sphere of heritage preservation, the Prague Castle has the status of a district, and that the OPR has the status of a district office. (. . .)

3) On Wednesday evening I have time to study the briefing note on the trip to Žd'ár. I would like short, pithy, and easy-to-follow notes including a map by Wednesday afternoon at the latest.

4) On Friday at noon at the latest I would like a short meeting and briefing notes for the Canadian governor general. Toasts!

6) I am sending various papers that I've read along with all of the signed thank-you notes for the condolences. (. . .)

(June 7, 1994)

(. . .)

5) I would ask Mr. Řechtáček to repair and refill my lighter and send it back. (. . .)

Let's turn the page toward life. When, and under what circumstances, did you meet your second wife, Dagmar Veškrnová?

In September or October 1989 there was the thirtieth anniversary of the Semafor Theater. Its spiritual father and director, Jiří Suchý, invited me—as a colleague from the small theaters of the 1960s—to the celebration in Lucerna. I have to say it was a very brave thing for Suchý to do. You didn't often find one of the main dissidents sitting among official artists in public, where his presence could be noticed by anyone. I think they even wanted me to speak, but—because I knew the kind of danger they were facing—I naturally refused. In the reception that followed, Suchý introduced me to Dáša, whom I had known only from her television and stage performances. In the company of official and semiofficial stars—who were followed by the media and probably by the secret police as well—I felt very uncomfortable, and Dáša noticed that. We grew closer shortly after that, during the revolution, at the onstage discussions between the audiences and the actors that replaced the regular performances during the theater strike; these occasions were the first time actors appeared onstage with dissidents. And after that, mainly in early 1990. We've been together for quite a long time. It'll soon be sixteen years.

When did you send her your first love letter?

I don't think that she ever got a real love letter from me, even though she claims the opposite. It might have been at the most a brief and rather encoded note saying something like, "Someone will be waiting for you at such and such a time at such and such a place—if you can't make it, send a message!" But who knows: she saves everything, so maybe she really does have something a little more heartfelt in her possession. For example, I recently discovered a small suitcase containing letters I had written to Olga at the end of the 1950s when I was in the army. I have even more interesting things somewhere, but God knows where they are.

Do you remember your first date?

That depends on what you mean by a "date." I know for certain that once, in the spring of 1990, I got home late in the evening after a state visit to Israel—it was the first visit by a representative of our country to Israel after all those years of communist nonrecognition, and the purpose was to establish diplomatic relations—and I changed into tuxedo and went to Lucerna (funny how Lucerna, which was once the property of my family, keeps popping up at key moments in my life) for the

Prague-Vienna ball. I danced with Dáša there and ultimately invited myself back to her place for coffee. I gave my bodyguards instructions to drive quietly with their headlights off.

Hrádeček, July 11, 2005

It's interesting how Mr. Hvížďala, the father of serious Czech journalism, automatically leans toward spicy subject matter. But on the whole I'm not surprised. After all, I enjoy answering such questions as well. Now perhaps it's time to say a few words about how this conversation is being conducted. Essentially it's not really a conversation at all. Just as he did for Disturbing the Peace *in 1986, Mr. Hvížďala did his research and then sent me a mountain of questions. I reply to them in writing. I try to maintain a conversational tone, but they are still written responses. It seems far easier to do it this way than to tape my answers, then transcribe them, then edit the transcript so that it works on paper. It takes ten times as long, at least in my case. However, I select only some of Mr. Hvížďala's questions. I rewrite them, and occasionally add some of my own; in short, I treat Mr. Hvížďala a little like a dramatic character in one of my plays. When he reads it, he may resist at first but then he will, I hope, come to terms with it.*

How does a president go on a date?

In the first place, it's been a long time since I've been on a date, if I don't count dates with my wife.

Would your wife be jealous?

She certainly would. She has a special gift for knowing before I do whom I might find attractive, and then she takes forceful action to prevent any eventual contact with such a person. But that's not the main thing. I've settled down now. As far as private encounters are concerned: in the first years of the presidency everything was a lot simpler because the snide brigade didn't try so hard to embarrass me. If my presence was unexpectedly noticed somewhere by the public or the media it was accepted or published with a certain degree of tender affection, if I can put it that way. At the same time I tried to organize my movements about the world as simply as possible: for example, I reduced my presidential bodyguard to a minimum, and I made sure it was composed exclusively of new people, of friends who had come—on their own account—to protect me during the November revolution. They weren't police but phys ed students. They became policemen once we got to the Prague Castle; some of them are my bodyguards to this day, and by now they have all attained the rank of major. Wherever I asked them to go, we went. They didn't need to know anything in advance. They took no interest in whom I was meeting or why, but only in whether or not someone was threatening me. I received quite a few threatening letters, and there was one attempt on the part of a weird quasi-Oriental sect to cast some kind of magic spell on me. My pistoleers, as I call them to this day, concerned themselves with matters like that, not with whom or why I was having a meeting or a date.

The years 1996 and 1997 seem to have been the most difficult years of your life. Is that the case?

It's hard to say. Whenever you go through a difficult period, you say it was the worst time in your life. I thought it was the worst time in my life in the 1950s, when I was enlisted in the very tough sapper corps of the communist army; I thought it even before that, when I studied for two semesters—partly in error—at the Technical University, and I would lie awake at night, haunted by a subject called Machine Parts, the differential equations that were part of it, and the mildly sadistic professor who taught it. And that's not to mention the five years I spent in communist prisons. I say "communist" deliberately because they were quite different from prisons in a democratic country. But yes, the years you mentioned, and 1995 as well, were really difficult for me.

According to records I have seen, on November 16, 1996, your doctor at the time told you that you had pneumonia. The symptoms worsened and you developed a high temperature. It was then that Dagmar Veškrnová intervened and had you secretly examined in the Prague hospital Na Homolce. Your life was saved by a woman's instinct. Was that how it was?

Naturally, I don't remember the details, and I don't treat the records from that time too seriously, but it's clear that Dáša saved me, not once but many times. I remember only that I wasn't feeling well, took some time off work and went to Hrádeček, where I was alone. Yet far from improving, my condition grew worse. But a recent X-ray of my lungs hadn't shown up anything special, and I was told that it was only "the presidential illness," as they referred to my occasional fits of exhaustion, fever, and other symptoms that were mostly a result of stress. This time Dáša thought there was more to it, so she arranged, through an acquaintance, for a secret CT scan at night in the hospital Na Homolce. The result was then taken for examination outside Prague to some skilled CT scan readers. They found a tumor on my lungs. Dáša immediately contacted Professor Pafko, a well-known lung surgeon, and she persuaded him to come in, although it was Sunday. He looked at the scans and said they'd have to operate immediately because in a week it might be too late.

At the time, I had a full schedule, as usual, including a state visit to Ukraine. So I called an urgent meeting at the Castle of my closest associates. I didn't go to the meeting myself, but Dáša went and explained my situation to them. We weren't married at the time, and they looked askance at her as though she were some kind of crazed actress interfering in matters of state. Even my personal doctor at the time didn't behave very well toward her, because of course he took it as a personal snub. Dáša also insisted that Professor Pafko come to the meeting. He was reluctant, because he wanted to avoid a confrontation, but in the end he came and was quickly able to persuade everyone that the situation was serious.

A day or two later I was in his surgical ward in Londýnská Street, being prepped for the operation. The operation itself was marvelous. Pafko really is an internationally recognized master in his field. But my pre-op and post-op care was miserable; the cause of my near death was not the operation itself but what happened afterward, and it clearly needn't have happened at all. That of course was not Pafko's fault. It was a terribly out-of-date hospital that no longer exists, and the rather idiosyncratic care that I got there may merely have been a natural consequence of its obsolescence. Sometime later, after I was back on the job, I made a brief reference to the whole matter in my weekly radio broadcast, *Conversations from Lány*, because the press was buzzing with speculation about it. I thanked all the doctors for the successful operation, and at the same time I said that my gratuitous post-operational difficulties should now be a subject for internal professional discussion only. My intention was to calm the waters, but exactly the opposite happened. It caused an uproar. All the doctors knew that I was right, but the dictates of professional solidarity were stronger than the truth, and so, via the media—mainly through the offices of the snide brigade, of course—they tore into me. The lesson I took away from this was simple: criticizing doctors can be life-threatening.

What was it like being operated on? Were you afraid, for instance, that you might not wake up from the anesthetic?

In recent years I've been put under anesthetic many times and I rather enjoyed it. You lose consciousness in a matter of seconds, and when you wake up you have no idea what has happened. Sometimes, however, either under anesthetic, or perhaps when I was coming out of it, I would have very vivid hallucinations. In themselves, they weren't unpleasant, but they could have rather nasty consequences, because they were incredibly evocative, far more so than the most vivid dream, and despite all attempts to explain them away I found myself believing them. I thought that they were real, and no one was able to dissuade me. Once it almost led to a minor international incident.

Tell me about it!

That was in Austria, a year later. My intestine ruptured, it was connected with my previous illnesses and it was very dangerous. I pulled through only thanks to steps that Dáša took, literally, at the last minute, and then, of course, thanks to the marvelous work of the Austrian Professor Bodner, and Dáša's constant care, which was appreciated, as far as I know, only by King Hussein of Jordan, who awarded her one of Jordan's top medals for it during a state visit. But back to the story: in my hospital room at the time, there was a list of regulations for patients hanging on the wall, and I became obsessed with the idea that it was a set of instructions for Austrians about how to make the Czech Republic a part of the Austro-Hungarian Empire again. I thought it said that the Czech lands couldn't be subjugated militarily anymore, but that economic occupation would be a far more feasible and modern way to do it. There was a list of all the Czech banks whose shares Austrians were to buy up in bulk, along with other specific instructions on how to gradually turn the entire Czech Republic into an Austrian possession. From economic occupation, it would be a short step to political occupation.

No one was able to dissuade me from my hallucination. My stay in the hospital in Innsbruck ended; my friend Thomas Klestil, the Austrian president, came to visit me, and I was prepared to include in our friendly conversation a strong diplomatic protest against displaying such instructions in Austrian hospital rooms. Fortunately, I didn't mention it in the end. It's true that the Austrians own quite a bit in our country, but not because there are instructions hanging in the hospitals about how to subjugate us. Thomas, who is no longer with us, would probably have been flabbergasted if I had brought that up in Innsbruck.

How many times did you actually come close to death, and how many times did Dagmar pull you through?

Only she could answer that precisely. I remember, for example, that one time—shortly after the first operation—I was in a private room in Intensive Care, and I was suffocating because the technician operating the oxygen tank had gone to the pub and forgotten me, and Dáša, almost miraculously, stepped into the room at that very moment and saved my life. As I've mentioned she persuaded me to go to a hospital in Austria. At the time I was reluctant, but it soon turned out to have been in the nick of time. The odd thing was that whenever Dáša entered the hospital my agitated vital signs on the monitor over my bed would settle into a normal pattern.

It was said that your frequent bouts of pneumonia and your bad lungs were a result of smoking.

Forty-four years of heavy smoking probably did nothing to improve my health. Nevertheless, I see the main cause of my difficulties elsewhere—in my first bout of pneumonia, which was never properly cured and which I contracted after my transfer, in January 1980, from the remand prison in Pankrác, Prague, to the regular prison in Heřmanice, where I served my sentence, and where I had to endure temperature differences of more than forty degrees Celsius. In prison I caught pneumonia several times and of course it was never properly treated, and during one particularly difficult bout—in 1983—they released me from prison because they did not wish to make a martyr out of me. I stopped smoking at the request of my doctors at the end of 1996, but I don't promote nonsmoking as an ideology; on the contrary I feel a deep affinity with smokers and I enjoy breathing secondhand smoke in their presence.

When you were convalescing, as president, you had some new experiences with the tabloid press. Before your first operation, TV Nova rented a flat opposite your hospital room and secretly filmed you; there was something in the press every day attacking you both, and a certain Svora even wrote a book about your illness and your future wife.

I think that fifteen or more books like that were published about me or about us. I haven't read any of them. The worst dirt came out in a preelection tabloid daily, published by the ODS, called *Super.* At one time that campaign was very intense and they took aim mainly at Dáša. She managed to irritate them all in some strange way. There were times when not a day would go by without some nasty attack on her on TV Nova, or in the papers. Most journalists behaved exactly the way they behave in many other situations, like a herd of dumb animals. One of them sets off in one direction, and the rest follow blindly. It's something like fashion. Dáša had never experienced anything like it before. Ever since she was young, she had always been an admired and well-loved actress, and I think she found it hard to take. And then, as quickly as it began, a year and a half later it died down. But it left permanent scars on her spirit. I don't know what the reasons for that campaign were. It may have been partly that the boss of Nova was compensating for his strange inferiority complexes; but mainly I think that the ODS, and those who saw that party as their protector, were taking revenge on me by throwing Dáša to the wolves instead.

Given all your experiences in this, how do you think medical care should be provided to future presidents or to top state officials?

I think it should be, as far as possible, exactly like the care provided to every other patient. Here and there, naturally, a perk or two could be put in place, so that one wouldn't have to spend so much time in the waiting room, for example. But too many eminent specialists standing around the hospital bed can make for bad blood. Each of them may have his own way of treating a patient; one of them may not want to take responsibility for the decision of another; there may be some professional jealousy in the air; and now and then one may actually try to subtly pin the blame on another. In short, excessive medical care may be counterproductive. One can then wear oneself out by skating diplomatically between one's caregivers. I don't mean to say that this has been my only experience. I have seen excellent cooperation between several doctors from various clinics, for which I was always grateful. Each one pointed out a different aspect of the matter, and in the end this led to a meaningful compromise. For sixteen years, for example, I have been given considerable help by the physiotherapist Pavel Kolář, a wonderful, modest man. In recent years, my doctor has been Tomáš Bouzek; thanks to him I am now ill less often than before.

Hel, August 21, 2005

Another six weeks have gone by. What have I accomplished? Why haven't I been able to write? There was just too much else to do, including the move. We sold our little house in Portugal, because it was only a source of worry and we seldom went there. It was used mostly by friends. The idea was that once I was no longer in office, I would spend several months there each year, breathing the fabulous ocean air that always puts an immediate stop to all my problems with breathing and pneumonia. That proved to be a pipe dream. But the worst thing was that we'd filled the house with an awful lot of the things we'd accumulated in our lives, from everything that Dáša had from before our marriage, to the many gifts we have received. We had nowhere to put them, so we moved them there. Now it's all back with us, sitting in the courtyard, filling the garage. We managed to give some of it away and some of it is at Hrádeček. (Among other things, there are a hundred and twenty crates of small objects, books, and writing.) On the whole, there are many valuable or interesting things together with a great many silly trifles. Most of them, however, are somewhere halfway between very special and very insignificant. It was impossible to sort through them all; if we had tried, we'd still be at it now. And so two moving vans brought it all back. Dáša cried a lot; she saw in it the liquidation of her identity, because she had devoted a lot of time to furnishing the house in Portugal with those things, believing that we'd have it for the rest of our lives. And thus the theme of the liquidation of identity came back to haunt us twice, once when the "orchard" in Hrádeček was cut down, and once when we moved out of Portugal. The theme of moving, of leave-taking, and of cutting down was something I may have brought upon myself: the play I've long been preparing to write will work with these themes; it will attempt to allude to Chekhov's Cherry Orchard, to Beckett's Endgame, and above all to Shakespeare's King Lear. It will be about a statesman who has lost his position and has to move out of the official residence provided by the state; it's surrounded by an orchard, and he can't come to accept it. The loss of his position and all that pertains to it means the collapse of his world. He goes slightly mad from it all. (The interesting thing is that I started writing this play before the revolution, that is, sixteen years ago, and then I tossed the manuscript *away in the belief that after all the changes taking place, the theme would no longer interest me. And then, having seen so many politicians around me who could not come to terms with the fact that they no longer held office, I began to return to it in my mind, and then the manuscript I thought had been destroyed was discovered somewhere by my colleague Andulka Freimanová. Too many odd coincidences! I still hope that if I ever have a month with nothing else to do, I will still write that play. But it's far more probable that, having thought about it for so long, I'll never get it written, and then someone else—most probably my longtime friend and colleague Tom Stoppard—will write a play about a writer who prepared his whole life to write the most important play of his life and, of course, he never writes it.)*

The long and short of it is that another month has gone by in a hectic rush and today, on the anniversary of the occupation of Czechoslovakia by the Warsaw Pact, I'm sitting in the top floor of a lighthouse-like tower in the Baltic residence of the Polish president, Aleksander Kwaśniewski, who is a good friend, as his guest. He too will soon finish his presidency and will move out of this remarkable complex that he has built up over the years and that is practically a paradise on earth.

By the way, if I try to remember what I've done in the past month, and can recall nothing but the moving, it is further evidence still of how critical my loss of memory is (they say it has something to do with how many times you have been under anesthetic). For instance I talk to someone for two hours and the next day I can't remember what he looks like, and when I meet him again I try in vain to remember who it is and where I know him from. Perhaps it will reflect itself in this book: I'm constantly battling with the fact that I don't know what I've already written or what I have yet to write, and for some obscure reasons—perhaps out of fear that I won't like it—I'm incapable of leafing back over the previous pages, or even reading what I've already written. Mr. Hvížďala rightly said that I can't put everything in the book and that I should focus on a few specific things and use them to demonstrate who I am. So I can't guarantee that I won't be demonstrating who I am by using the same incident several times.

Eight days after returning from your first lung operation, that is, on January 4, 1997, you married Dagmar Veškrnová at the Žižkov town hall, the same place you married Olga many years before. What led you to such a quick decision?

I had proposed marriage to Dáša half a year before that, and when we were thinking about an appropriate place and time we came up with that date. I was planning to spend the Christmas and New Year's holidays in Hrádeček, and so we decided to have a small wedding in the town hall in the nearby village of Mladá Buka, of which, by the way, I am an honorary citizen. Then the operation intervened and everything had to change, but on the appointed day I was already home from the hospital and there was no reason not to keep to the date at least. We had to find a new location, because in my condition a trip to Hrádeček was out of the question. By sheer chance, if anything is by sheer chance, Dáša lived in the Prague district of Žižkov and, moreover, I knew the mayor of Žižkov, Mr. Mikeska. I invited him over and arranged the whole thing with him. It was to be secret, which he honored. He didn't even tell his wife. At the last moment, however, one of the television channels found out about it—probably from one of my pistoleers—and they were waiting outside the town hall. The journalists were probably disappointed that they didn't know anything about it, and so they began to chide me for marrying three weeks before the first anniversary of Olga's death, claiming that it was standard to wait for at least a year before remarrying. No such rule or tradition exists, as Cardinal Vlk assured me, but any stick is good enough to beat a dog with.

The press has often made reference to the conflicts and the tensions that existed between your wives and your staff. How were the relationships of your two wives and your staff similar, and how were they different?

It's true that such tensions existed. It probably sprang from the fact that both Olga and Dáša had dominant personalities; they were hard to bamboozle, didn't play games, always spoke their minds. They were occasionally quite blunt and hated it most of all when someone tried to manipulate me or use their proximity to me to their own advantage.

I'm a peaceable man and I can't stand tension or confrontation, so I swallow a lot of things in silence. Perhaps that's why I am drawn to that type of woman. My excessive and often counterproductive politeness seems to cry out to be counterbalanced by someone who comes right out and speaks their mind, and damn the consequences. But it's also possible that it simply runs in the family. In the great outside world—and, in the case of my brother, the universe—the men are the big operators; at home and close to home, it's the women who rule, no matter how often they may claim the opposite. Both of my wives could intimidate my staff, at least that's my impression.

And the differences?

For many reasons Dáša had a much harder time of it than Olga, and not at all because she was second in line. It was mainly, I think, because Olga had been a part of my life for as long as anyone could remember, and all my staff and, metaphorically, the whole country had, as it were, married into our family. In Dáša's case it was exactly the opposite: it was as though she were the one who had married into this big family, but she was an alien, an interloper from another world who had leap-frogged over them all and suddenly had more influence than they did. Dáša's openness, her occasional forthrightness, her determination and bluntness, her capacity to create tension in others, naturally magnified this feeling. My staff felt that she was interfering in inappropriate and unqualified ways; she on the other hand felt that they weren't taking her seriously enough and that they were even deliberately making things more difficult for her. She resented those around me for not supporting her or advising her during the massive campaign against us that I've already mentioned; she felt alone and defenseless.

Today this is all long past, and it's worth mentioning only because there was nothing particularly strange or exceptional about it; it was just another incident in the history of the endless battles politicians' wives have waged to carve out for themselves a position that is different from what the masculine world expects. For example, shortly after we got married Dáša began to get hundreds of letters. She had long been known to the public and people liked her for her good nature, so when she became the first lady, people began plying her with requests. At the same time she had a full international agenda. She couldn't handle everything herself, even though she often spent days and nights over the weekend working on these things. So she began to campaign for assistants. In the hostile atmosphere that the snide brigade had created around us, my office was afraid to assign her a secretary or an assistant, arguing that there was no provision for it in the law governing the Office of the President of the Republic, and that it might be used against us. At one point Dáša said, in public, let them change the law then. That was grist for the snide brigade's mill: the ditzy first lady wanted to change the constitution! In the end, Dáša won her fight for a small office staff, and today it would never occur to anyone to question such a thing, let alone regard it as a contravention of the law.

In hindsight, how did your wife carry out her role and the various tasks associated with it? Could she have done anything differently or better?

There are a hundred things that one could do better if one knew everything in advance. Fortunately, life is not like that; if it were, it would be quite boring. I was president for the first time; Dáša had married a president for the first time, and I was the first president in our country's history who had married while in office. No tradition, no precedents. So how surprising is it that—as in so many other things— we sometimes had to grope our way? Dáša is a highly responsible person and she is very thorough, so she took her position seriously; she began reading books about other first ladies, to learn about what is appropriate in given situations, how to dress, how to behave diplomatically, and so on. It's sad, but the fact is that today an inappropriately dressed first lady or prime minister's wife can do more harm to the country than anything her husband might say as a statesman. It's not easy to suddenly find oneself in the public eye, particularly in Dáša's case. Times had changed. When Olga was alive, everything we did— because we were the beloved children of the revolution—was tolerated. Now, nothing we did was tolerated. I have to say that in the end Dáša stood the test very well. To this day she is friends with various royal and presidential couples and they are fond of her, and at home she has gained great public respect through her manner of communicating with people and through her work in the foundation. It was a pity she wasn't able to continue acting. Now she's starting to rehearse again, and she will certainly be able to rise above any nonartistic curiosity about her.

(August 18, 2002)

Wherever I go, I'm asked why I refused to come back from Portugal when there were floods at home. Everyone asks me this, from the BBC and Czech Television to the waiter in the pub. If I look for the reason why they ask this question, I discover that it all goes back to a statement made by Mr. Š. Please provide me with this statement. Further, I would ask for the text of the report that the Czech Press Agency, ČTK, published on the basis of that statement. Finally, I would ask that Mr. Š. and the others face up to this, not make any excuses, or try to defend each other in the spirit of some kind of staff solidarity. For clarity, let me recapitulate the sequence of events:

1) On Monday evening Mr. F. advised me, and ultimately arranged a conversation with the prime minister. Among other things I asked him whether he thought I should come home. He said that I need not.

2) Late Tuesday morning I received a memorandum from Mr. F. in which he explained why he was now advising me to return. I immediately asked Mr. M., by telephone, whether that was the opinion of the whole Castle, or at least his. He said it was. After a five-minute meeting with those who were with me, I called back to say that I had decided to return the following day, that is Wednesday, with Fischer Air. Then there were only details to be looked after. (. . .) My wish, repeated several times, to have my return immediately made public was (with a certain reluctance) eventually acted upon. But by that time the Czech ether was already buzzing with the main news, apparently communicated by Mr. Š., that I was not thinking of coming back. Many people called us to ask what that was supposed to mean. I placed no particular importance on it, but now

I'm coming to realize that, at the conclusion of a lifelong public career, the indelible mark of someone who would rather sunbathe, and has abandoned his nation to do so, has been branded on my forehead. You must all realize that this is unjust and that to a considerable degree it's your doing. That's all I ask of the Castle. The one thing that makes me angry is the inane, childish evasiveness and the show of mutual covering-up that you demonstrated when I wanted to have a serious conversation with you about this several days ago.

3) I repeat my request for future reference: every statement that concerns my intentions or my state of mind must be run by me. I alone wish to bear responsibility for my acts, but I will not go on bearing responsibility for the ill-considered acts of others.

4) And the final question: I'm being told that the minister of defense, Mr. Tvrdík, was willing, at a moment's notice, to provide a military aircraft to bring back our whole party. Apparently he would even have welcomed such a request from the OPR, because the squadron that serves the government does not have enough flying time. So my question is: was the aircraft requested? If not, then why not? If it was requested, was the aircraft then refused? What were the reasons? Or, in the opinion of the OPR, was a special flight out of the question for other reasons?

With the approaching end of my presidency, the hysteria in the media, and these unprecedented natural catastrophes, the gloves are off. Therefore I ask again for an explanation. And a thorough one.

(August 21, 2002)

Thank you. I received a detailed and undoubtedly precise description of the sequence of events, and yes, I'm sure that's how it was. Unfortunately, however, this account did not contain the main thing I wanted to hear. That is, something like a critical reflection on how the Castle handled the matter. After all, if the Castle had said to me unanimously and unambiguously: "Come at such and such a time—Monday, Tuesday, Wednesday, or Friday—and come on such and such a plane," of course, I would have done it. But I had no way of knowing what the situation was, and the Castle voices were wavering and not unanimous. The worst, of course, was the statement by Mr. Š. Why did he even issue a statement, and moreover, from his well-deserved vacation! And if he wanted to issue a statement why did he not consult with me, or at least with that part of the Castle that was in touch with me and could discuss the subject of my possible return with me? It was an insensitive statement and entirely pointless, and I am still encountering the consequences of it to this day, and I probably always will. I know that it was not ill-intended, but it was, at the very least, a serious mistake.

If someone opens the question with me publicly, which I in no way wish to happen, I will probably be forced to stop obfuscating and say how it really was. It's more than enough for me to bear the consequences of my own mistakes and the general cantankerousness of the Czech media, and I really do not want to take responsibility for any more. (. . .)

(April 11, 1999)

(. . .)
8) We need a longer hose for watering. (. . .)

You were often criticized because you were, allegedly, unable to bear bad news, because you forbade your people to tell you bad news and wanted to hear only the good things. They say that various members of your staff had a falling-out with you because of that.

I don't know who had a falling-out with me; I don't have the feeling that I ever fell out with anyone, but it is true that there was one form of insensitivity I couldn't stand, and that was when, a minute before an important political meeting, the course and outcome of which completely depended on how briskly and wittily I would moderate it, someone would whisper something upsetting into my ear that had nothing to do with the meeting at hand and could easily have been told me an hour later. Naturally, it would throw me off balance, and as a result I would not perform well as the keynote speaker or moderator because I was preoccupied with something else. The one who committed this act of insensitivity had no meeting to address or moderate, he could merely sit and watch, or go about his business, and so had no reason to worry about bad news affecting his performance. I really hated that kind of thing. But that I would ban bad news as such is obvious nonsense, though I admit I may at times have said something to that effect as a joke.

I would say, though, that whenever things begin to get really serious and dangerous, others might succumb to panic or despair, but I find myself possessed of a strange sangfroid and élan that allows me to make quick decisions and come up with solutions. To put it another way: the worse the news, the more bravely I bear it. I don't like bad news—who does?—but I don't fall apart because of it and I have no reason to wish it be kept from me.

What influence did your presidency have on your contact with your friends? You always had a lot of people around you; you were at the center of different communities of people, and you tried to bring them together, and now, suddenly, many of your old friends and acquaintances complain that they never see you.

It's true. Many of my friends regret that we don't see each other, and some of them may even think it's because I've become high and mighty. That is clearly nonsense. I would rather spend time with many of my old friends than with some of the people that I am compelled to spend time with today. The reasons I don't are purely technical. I don't have as much energy as I had before. My schedule is very full. It's hard to find a free evening. And if I do have one then I'm happiest just to be alone, sitting somewhere in a small pub gathering my thoughts, or reading various position papers that are meant to prepare me for the days to come. For the same reasons, I very seldom get to the theater, to the cinema, or to a concert. Some of my friends completely understand this. Some of them are satisfied if I have a beer with them once in a while. And some of them have never understood it, and I have never been able to explain it to them. They will always be grumpy about it. That may be one of the many dues I've had to pay. The funny thing is that those who chas tise me most for my distance are the same ones who tried hardest to persuade me to take on the presidency. If they were so keen to go with me to the pub every week, they shouldn't have suggested that I take political office in the first place.

In any case, it's not just a question of time but also of my position, and many can't seem to imagine what it's like. One of my good friends was annoyed with me because at an army dance at the Prague Castle I didn't personally come over to invite him to sit at my table, but rather sent one of my staff to do it. But I knew exactly what I was doing; had I gone myself, the dance would have been long over before I made it to his table, because everyone knew who I was and would have accosted me to tell me something. I'm used to people doing this and I don't mind it, but I'm sorry that anyone would refuse to understand what it's like, or would even take this as further evidence that I've become arrogant. The fact that I have perhaps not learned, even yet, to live easily with this is another matter altogether. For instance, if I observe my friend Aleksander Kwaśniewski, or either of the George Bushes and other presidents, I'm somewhat envious: not because they are able to stop, shake hands, and have a friendly conversation with everyone—that in itself is not a great art—but because it doesn't throw them off or distract them in the slightest from what they have to focus on, such as an upcoming improvised speech.

Whom do you most regret not having time for?

Hard to say. Many friends have died, many are living in seclusion or abroad. Apart from my oldest friends—and I include that most rare man, Zdeněk Urbánek, or the actors Jan Tříska or Pavel Landovský—I miss being in touch with the former dissidents, that is, the chartists, all the more so because I get along better with them than I do with most of the new politicians. I also miss the circle of my literary colleagues with whom I went through the difficult years of the 1970s and 1980s; we did many things together in an attempt to preserve at least some kind of continuity of free literary expression in that underground gloom. I keep saying I'm going to make it up to them in some way, but I never manage to get around to it.

Do your colleagues from abroad complain about a certain alienation as well?

Oddly enough they don't, or at least I don't know about it. Arthur Miller, Harold Pinter, Tom Stoppard, Günter Grass, and other marvelous writers with whom I've had the honor of being friends over the years have never complained. On the contrary, even when I was president we managed to see each other now and again, and even do something together. I was quite amused when I was invited by the queen in 1990 for an intimate lunch at Buckingham Palace, and whom do I see sitting at the table but Harold Pinter! I joked at the time about meeting my highly nonconformist colleague at the queen's table. Someone who's never been annoyed with me for not seeing him very often is my longtime publisher and friend, Klaus Juncker, of Rowohlt Verlag.

Hel, August 27, 2005

We've been here on the Baltic Sea for thirteen days. I have done only a minimum of writing. This may be partly due to a kind of holiday relapse (where is the discipline I had in America?), but mostly, I would say, it's due to all the distractions offered by the generous Polish hospitality, by the beauties of this special corner of the world, and by the luxurious amenities of this complex. The weather is magnificent. You can't help but want to be in the sun, swim in the pool, gaze at the sea, and to delight in the small feasts that they tirelessly prepare for us. In the evening we usually watch television. Our dogs are having the time of their life; we take them for walks through the deep woods, where the residence is located. Our idyll was undisturbed until the day before yesterday when Sugar, our old boxer, fell ill. She probably got some infection from the sea. We've been through a very difficult time with her. Her life was hanging by a thread and Dáša looked after her continuously, giving her infusions, etc., and today she has improved.

This wonderful way of ending the summer, which will come to a head on Wednesday when we take part in celebrations marking the twenty-fifth anniversary of the formation of Solidarity in Gdansk, has naturally brought me back once more to that very special Polish ambience which has always fascinated me, and which differs so much from the Czech. (By the way, my first-ever trip abroad, in 1957, brought me, coincidentally, to these very shores: Olga and I were on a student exchange trip and we spent several days by the sea at Sopot. At the time there was a major political thaw in Poland, after that dramatic October of 1956; we devoured the critical and independent texts that were able to be published here at the time; rock and roll, which was of course unthinkable in our country, was pounding out everywhere, and we heard the whole dance hall sing the song about "The Lost Lvov.") For example, when I see every day on television documentaries or dramatic films about the rise of Solidarity (including Wajda's famous film Man of Iron*), or watch various concerts and follow a wide variety of commentaries, I am reminded again and again how deeply the Poles appreciate their own history, how they continue to identify with their many uprisings for independence, how highly they value the sacrifices they have made. Here in the Gdansk region, Wałęsa is practically a saint; they've named an airport after him, and, of course, John Paul II is a complete and utter saint. I don't think that anyone here, from the president on down to the worker in the shipyards, would understand the attacks the current Czech president has made against dissidents, or his claim that the fall of communism was brought about not so much by those who actually opposed it but by all those crafty people who pretended to be loyal, while quietly stealing from the state. (On the other hand it must be said that here in Poland, the former intellectual dissidents too have been pushed out of public life by new and more aggressive younger politicians; still, I don't think anyone here would dare question their contribution to Poland.)*

Poland is in a different situation from the Czech Republic for a least three reasons. In the first place, it is incomparably larger and might even be called a regional superpower that occupies a very important and sensitive geopolitical location between Germany and Russia. Some of those who have been responsible for carving up this country during its turbulent history now feel guilty and have tried to make up for it. Others, on the contrary, would be happy to take another piece of it if they could. For that reason the Poles feel, far more intensely than the Czechs, that membership in NATO and the European Union is an important guarantee against a repetition of all the terrible things they have endured.

In the second place, the existence of the Polish nation has for centuries been linked with the existence of a national elite (it was no coincidence that Stalin tried to eliminate that elite) and the existence of a powerful Catholic Church which never collaborated with a foreign power and which drew its strength from the deep religiosity of the Poles.

And in the third place, it's probably quite important that the Poles have preserved the aristocracy, which was patriotic and was never eliminated as it once was in our country. That is clearly the source of the sincere and unenvious respect Poles show to those in high office, particularly to the public figures who represent the Polish state. Kwaśniewski had, and undoubtedly still has, many political enemies, but as head of state he is generally respected.

All in all, it seems to me that the Poles have a different and far more heartfelt relationship to their own statehood than we do. It's also true, however, that few nations have had to sacrifice so much for their independence and freedom. Almost everyone here knows that freedom and independence occasionally require you to pay a heavy price. You can't say that about the Czechs; what they consider ideal is the capacity to enjoy various blessings—as far as possible with no struggle, no work, and no cost.

By the way, respect for their own heroic history and the sacrifices they have made has given the Poles a kind of enthusiasm for building and reconstruction. It's not just that all of Warsaw's Old Town, the whole of Gdansk, a large part of Łódź, and other places that were totally destroyed by bombs have been completely rebuilt. The most important reconstructed city centers are exact replicas of the original structures. In our country many would turn their noses up at this, but in Poland everyone understood this was the correct thing to do. And they were right: in a hundred years it won't matter a bit whether a particular house in Gdansk was built two hundred years earlier or later. After all, even the Czechs can no longer distinguish between the Gothic and the pseudo-Gothic.

The nation's existence is also identified with Solidarity. It is expected that the celebrations of its twenty-fifth anniversary will be grand and will be watched by everyone in Poland. It will be a strenuous day for us. I myself am held in considerable esteem in Poland, which in the given situation is more of a liability than an advantage to me. We will see.

Let's come back to your staff. Now that you haven't been with them for several years, what would you say about them today? What were your relationships with them like, and how did the public perceive them? I remember that in the first phase of your presidency, that is, in the Czechoslovak period, your staff—they were called advisers then—were frequently the target of criticism and, in many cases, of hostility.

I'll respond in chronological order. In the early, revolutionary days, when I had to decide whether or not I would run for president, I made my "yes" conditional on a clear imperative to my colleagues: you will come to the Castle with me. I didn't want to suddenly find myself alone with a lot of Husák's officials. And so several of my closest fellow warriors from the Civic Forum promised to come with me. Because we couldn't have changed the law governing the Office of the President in a few hours, nor the organizational regulations, we could begin only by working within the law, which did allow us to make appointments to some advisory positions. That is why those friends of mine who came to the Prague Castle with me all became "advisers," though I admit it seems a little ridiculous today.

Shortly thereafter we changed everything, including the organizational regulations, and my colleagues became department heads and so on. It was quite a job, however, to reorganize the Office of the President. For a long time that office had dealt only with matters of protocol; all the political decisions were made in the Central Committee of the Communist Party, and we had to make substantial changes to the institution if it was to fit the new circumstances. So much for the origins of my famous "advisers."

And now about their roles: as I've already said, I had a huge public influence at that time, which, as a democrat, went rather against my grain. In any case, if I did make any relatively serious mistakes, it was probably during that period and would have consisted in not using that influence to bring about more decisive transformations and personnel changes; instead, on the contrary, I was always consulting with someone about everything. My influence was transferred to my advisers, who, in various areas, had to make very quick decisions in my name and as a result became widely feared and encountered a lot of natural resistance. Thus we quickly found ourselves conforming to the classical fairy-tale archetype: "the good king and his evil counselors." It was as though all the popularity for the liberation fell to me, the elected and favored head of state, whereas responsibility for many of the most unpopular measures fell to my unelected advisers. People had their cake and they ate it too. The fact that I am defending my colleagues at the time does not mean there were no instances when the job went to their heads or when they unwittingly abused their power, or, at the very least, behaved like elephants in a china shop. But I behaved that way myself more than once too, and so I can hardly hold it against anyone else.

That was during the federation period. What about later, after the breakup of the country?

After my election as Czech president, I put together a completely new team of people who stayed with me—with the occasional change of personnel, of course—for the whole ten years. I don't think this new team enjoyed much popularity either, particularly not when the "settling of accounts," that is, the punishment for my earlier adoration, began. Part of what landed on my head landed on theirs as well; some of them took it bravely and assumed the risk that when my presidency was over, their career chances could be over as well, since they would then become black sheep; some of them took it less bravely and maneuvered in the situation as best they could.

In this connection, however, I should mention an important matter you haven't asked me about. The Prague Castle is one of the oldest seats of a head of state in the world; with brief interruptions, it has been so for perhaps thirteen centuries. At the same time it is one of the largest seats of a head of state in the world, almost literally a city within a city, consisting of hundreds of buildings and many acres of gardens, and moreover, it's situated on the most prominent height of land in Prague. Besides being the traditional seat of secular power in the country—by which I mean the Czech princes, the Czech kings, the Hapsburg rulers of Austro-Hungary, and the Czechoslovak and Czech presidents—it is also the traditional seat of religious power, to which belongs the main Czech cathedral, St. Vitus, and right next to it is the seat of the archbishop of Prague and the Czech primate. Every century, something has been added to it, and remarkably, it has all remained relatively well preserved, as a kind of embodiment of our history.

Now, if this Castle or palace environment is also the seat of the presidential office, then obviously this fact must somehow be reflected in how that office is run. It's not as if the Office of the President were located on the second floor of some nondescript high-rise out in the housing projects. Just think of those long corridors! They actually seduce one into a kind of life in the corridors of power, invite one to invent and spread rumors, to weave intrigues. Democracy or not, the Prague Castle is a real court, with all that that entails, including court intrigues, court gossip, and court battles. Of course, this was observable as well in our time, and it will be this way—perhaps with small changes for the better or for the worse—always.

(September 9, 1998)

(. . .) Another example: at Lány, my wife (. . .) started planting interesting trees from around the world, which presidents and other state guests have brought her on request. You promised that the head Castle gardener would look after the trees. The result? The trees are growing marvelously even without the head gardener; people admire them; they read the labels that have been affixed to the trees, but in the meantime, I've heard, a whole series of dendrologists were invited to come in and talk about them (. . .) and they finally came to the conclusion that these trees will not grow in this country. You can't blame this on Socialist Planning anymore, it's pure Dada. Or another example: I go for a walk every day in the park at Lány and from a distance, from up close, and from all sides I have to look at the fact that the château and the chapel are painted in five different colors, none of which goes with any of the others. At the same time, I observe daily how quickly and efficiently the reconstruction of the pseudo-Gothic agricultural building is progressing. I have discovered that every Thursday a large group of people meet here for an "oversight day," be they members of the PCA, architects, builders, etc., etc., and among other things they talk about how the building should be painted. So that we won't end up in another aesthetic quagmire, I tell them it wouldn't be a good idea for the agricultural building to add a sixth, seventh, or eighth color to the mix, for if that happened we would truly become a laughingstock. I suggest a simple solution: that there be a gradation of shades of ocher using the same base color (which has been used on an important part of the Lány château) for the whole complex. (For the time being, of course, only the agricultural building is at issue.) On two occasions they expressed general agreement with my opinion, only to turn around and decide the exact opposite. So in the end I showed up in person for an "oversight day," and we had a friendly discussion about it. We completely agreed! I didn't force anything on anyone—I expressed my opinion quietly, and everyone agreed, in great relief. And the result? It was definitively decided that it would be painted a disgusting bright yellow color, which, in my opinion in the given situation, is worse than if it were purple, with brown window frames on top of it! Just like in any old motel! Disgusting! But so what, window frames can be repainted (. . .) but a facade is a more expensive kettle of fish. The worst of all seems to be the argument that neo-Gothic constructions were originally painted in that color! I don't know when it was built but my layman's eye tells me at a glance that it can't be early nineteenth-century neo-Gothic (in other words built a couple of years after the completion of the château) but that it is a pseudo-Gothic structure from the late nineteenth century, just like most of our beautiful railway stations, town halls, and so on. Was everything at the beginning of this century painted in that disgusting bright yellow color? And even if it were genuinely neo-Gothic, and if neo-Gothic structures were originally painted that color, why in God's name should that matter to us? Why should we have to look at yet another hodgepodge just because of convention? None of those concerned with this have to live here for three months at a time and look at the château every day, so let them at least take the opinion of the observer into account. (. . .)

(October 4, 1993)

(. . .)

9) Please have Mrs. M. or E. prepare the pike from Lány that was given to me, in some very original way, with unique spicing, so the parliamentary five will not soon forget it. (. . .)

There was a time when your financial circumstances aroused a great deal of interest. Do you wish to comment on it here?

I don't want to, but I must. Again I'll begin chronologically. As I was a son of an entrepreneurial and therefore bourgeois family, my childhood was comfortably affluent. Then came the communist putsch in February 1948; all my family's property was confiscated and class war was waged against us. At that period I really had no money at all. But in the 1960s, when they started performing my plays in different parts of the world, our situation changed. It doesn't bear comparison with the wealth of today's Czech entrepreneurs, but at the time, and in the circumstances, I was relatively well-off. Oddly enough that lasted all through the 1970s and 1980s. Although I was persecuted, banned as a writer, and ultimately imprisoned for a long period, I still had money, thanks to the fact that my plays were performed and my essays were published in the West, something neither the regime nor I could prevent from happening. The most interesting thing, of course, came later. I had never given much thought to the fact that the democracy we were struggling for, and which was still in the invisible future, would return people's confiscated and nationalized property, and even less did I think that it might one day involve me. That idea, which was completely absurd to me, was only kept alive over the years by official communist propaganda. In all the inflammatory articles written against me, their propagandists claimed that I was fighting against the socialist regime chiefly to get the family property back. Of course, I found the whole idea laughable.

And now comes the paradox: after 1989, nationalized property really did start to be returned, and family businesses were also gradually restored to my brother and me as the heirs of our deceased parents. Those properties became a great cross to bear—there's no other way I can describe it. In short, as many times before, history laughed and stuck out its tongue at me.

Do you think that property ought not to have been returned to people?

I don't think that. There was a deep longing for property restitution. I myself, however, didn't anticipate that it would be such a painful subject and, somewhat arrogantly, I scorned the notion that it might. But in this country there were tens if not hundreds of thousands of tradesmen and small businessmen for whom the communist program of nationalization had been a catastrophe. The trauma they had experienced after 1948 was clearly passed on from generation to generation, and if our parliament, or rather our parliaments, passed the relatively generous restitution laws so quickly, they were not acting on a whim but rather were responding to the general will to right those earlier economic wrongs.

On the other hand, a large role was played here by prejudices cultivated over the years, so that to this day some people shake their heads because a château that used to house a nursing school was returned to a count who had come back from God knows where. But even that was the right thing to do. If it's justice you want, then it has to be for everyone. Moreover, it has turned out that the aristocracy—who have in their blood a centuries-old tradition of stewardship of family property and regard for the future generations of owners—are incomparably better and more sensitive at maintaining their family estates than the state or other public institutions were. Sometimes they even leave those schools where they were, but with much more pleasant premises than they had been forced to operate in before. This is not true in every single case, but the law can't be selective, otherwise it wouldn't be a law, it would be a decree.

And so you too accepted property under the restitution law?

How could I not have accepted it? Could I have said that it should go on belonging to the Regional Committee of the Communist Party, as had been the case up to that point? Or that the National Property Fund or the Ministry of Privatization should keep it and do with it what it pleased? That would have been absurd and, moreover, in my case, it would have been a denial not only of my family's achievements but also of the very principle of restitution, which was one of the pillars of the transformation of our economic order.

The core of the property returned to you was Lucerna, one of the most marvelous complexes in the middle of Prague, with many commercial uses; and the Barrandov Terraces, a formerly famous upscale watering hole on the outskirts of Prague. You and your brother, Ivan, each received a 50 percent share of these properties. What happened then?

Ivan immediately transferred the ownership of everything to his wife, Dagmar; he's a philosopher and mathematician and he clearly could not imagine becoming an entrepreneur at that stage in his life. Unfortunately, I couldn't come to any rational agreement with his wife on the future of Lucerna. The building was in a dilapidated state, and I wanted to lease it for a long term to a big, smart Western firm that would commit to restoring it (an investment of at least a billion crowns) or have it be turned into a public company in which a single such partner—and there were plenty of interested parties at the time—would hold a significant portion of the shares. But she wouldn't agree, and as the owner of exactly 50 percent of the property, I could do nothing. And so, rather than look passively on as Lucerna inevitably deteriorated, and bear responsibility for that in the eyes of the world, and ultimately become—as president—an example of a bad custodian, I thought it would be better to sell my share. It was an evil, true, but a lesser one. The company that bought it was one of the biggest firms in the country and it clearly wanted to improve its image by restoring Lucerna. But it was unable to do anything of the sort, because it ran into resistance from my sister-in-law and later went bankrupt. Like so many other companies, it was, so I was told, stripped of its assets by unscrupulous owners. As far as I know, no one was ever found guilty of this, but in our circumstances, that does not mean that it didn't happen.

I transferred my share of Barrandov to my wife, who, of course, is a better entrepreneur than I am. She managed to buy the other half and then sold this once famous and now rather decrepit structure for a profit, to a company that I hope turns out better than the one that bought my half of Lucerna from me. To round the story out, I should add that most of my own money, and the money I gained through restitution—an amount that exceeds one hundred million crowns—I put to very good use: I gave half to our foundation, Vize '97, and half to other nonprofit organizations. But I really don't like releasing this information, and have done so only after serious consideration: for I have discovered that in the Czech lands—oddly enough—such matters arouse hostility. People will say: if he gave so much to humanitarian causes, how much does he really have? He must be filthy rich! And as a rich man, in the prevailing opinion, he clearly deserves to be treated with hostility and contempt. In a period when capitalism is being restored and when the party with the greatest support has in its program the slogan "Capitalism Without Adjectives," it is truly strange. But I guess it's just another one of our postcommunist paradoxes.

Your brother, Ivan, has complained that when you were in prison he and your wife would visit you four times a year, and now a whole year might go by when you don't see each other once. Is this because of the conflicts you had over property?

I respect Ivan. We understand each other and we enjoy talking about all kinds of things that have nothing to do with his wife and the family property; for example about who should receive the prize awarded by our foundation Vize '97—he's on the jury. But otherwise it's true we seldom see each other—either with our families or just the two of us. The reason is obvious. We are far from being the only family to which property restitution has brought conflict. I read of a survey that said almost half the families that had property returned have had a similar experience.

Do you regret not having children, and thus no heirs?

The Good Lord did not give me children and he probably knew what he was doing: they would not have had an easy life. But I regret it, of course. As far as inheritance is concerned, you have reminded me that for some time now Dáša and I have been getting ready to write some kind of will. After all, an airplane could go down with us aboard at any time! But it occurs to me that not having one's own children might in some matters be countermotivating, at least to someone as old as I am. If I were younger and had children, I'd probably build a nice, small, modern family house in Barrandov. I have it exactly thought out. And then we could sell this miserably renovated house of horrors in which we live. But where can a childless septuagenarian with health problems and who, moreover, is interested mainly in politics and philosophy, burdened with many public responsibilities, and incapable of raising his voice at anyone, find the energy to put up a house in Bohemia?

Hel, August 28, 2005

All my life I've longed to write a brutally honest diary, something in the style of Henry Miller, Charles Bukowski, Anaïs Nin, or of my late friends Jan Zábrana and Pavel Juráček. We were very close friends and I had no idea that over the years they had written detailed and ultrafrank diaries. They may be the best things they ever wrote. I was never able to do anything like that; I always preferred to hide behind the characters in my plays. Clearly my shyness was what stopped me. But those two were also shy. I don't know. Let these few diary entries about this and that, and, in fact, this whole little book I'm writing, be a distant echo of that ancient ambition of mine, and let that line of thought in it represent in part the motif of a "book about itself," or rather about the

process of writing it. I love that genre. I have often wondered if it would be pos-
sible to write a play in which the thoughts that ran through the author's head
while he was writing a bit of dialogue, or his ideas and experiences during the
writing, or his comments on what he's writing about, would appear in the
characters' speeches during the course of the play. But so far I haven't come
upon a way to do it that would make it comprehensible to an audience. A
small hint of this attempt may be present in my play Tomorrow.

A while ago I spoke about my staff, and I wonder if what I have said, along
with the samples of my memos, may not have created the impression that they
only gave me grief. That's not the case. They pulled that dangerous wagon
along with me, and I could not have managed without their help. It was to
their credit as well that the Prague Castle, of all the offices of the state admin-
istration, was traditionally the friendliest, and had by far the most pleasant
atmosphere. People from the ministries and elsewhere would come to us for a
breath of fresh air. Nowhere else were there so many young and new people. I
know that to this day many say that the years they spent in the Castle were the
best years of their lives. And even though all of those who worked at my side
are today living under a curse, it can't be said that they have vanished com-
pletely: for example, almost all those who were working on foreign policy
issues are now employed somewhere as our ambassadors. I meet with them all
once a year; in fact, the next meeting is in a week. I can't name all my staff, of
course, nor can I pick them out at random and therefore, for simplicity's sake, I
will mention only my chiefs of staff since my first election by the freely elected
parliament in June 1990: Karel Schwarzenberg, Luboš Dobrovský, Ivan
Medek, and Ivo Mathé. There have been disagreements and friction with all of
them from time to time, but they all served faithfully and they all deserve my
thanks. Without them I could not have accomplished even the little I may have
achieved.

**For years your mistakes have been written about. Sometimes more,
sometimes less. So tell me about those mistakes. How do you see that
today?**

We've already talked about how, after the era when I was revered as
a national hero, a martyr, a leader of the revolution, and ultimately the

president-philosopher, the inevitable hangover arrived and the journalists felt the need to find some fault with me so they wouldn't look like mindless cheerleaders. In 1993, for instance, when I first ran for the Czech presidency, a certain television newsreader said something about me and, to my name, automatically added the comment that I had made many mistakes. It was a cliché at the time, uttered without thinking, almost as though it were a part of my job description or my title. If you had asked that newsreader, who by the way is an acquaintance of mine, what specific mistakes she had in mind, she would probably have been embarrassed, because she'd never really thought about it, nor had anyone ever asked her. As a joke I printed a business card on my computer that said *Václav Havel, Author of Many Mistakes and Errors,* and I sent it to her. Apparently she was spooked by it.

I really don't know what people have in mind when they say that. Probably everyone means something different, and if you added it all up, they're blaming me for the general misery of the world. Given my character and my everlasting self-doubts, however, I would be uncomfortable creating the impression that I think I have never made any mistakes at all. Undoubtedly there have been many. Once a reporter asked me about my mistakes and wanted me to list them: he obviously needed to know himself what was behind the cliché. I told him that I had my own idea about what those mistakes were, but I wasn't about to make his work easier for him by telling him. Let him come up with his own list; that's his job as a reporter. After that response, which somehow stuck in people's memory, the media clichés about me were enriched by the accusation that I was trying to hide my mistakes. And so I was challenged to admit to them even more frequently.

The whole thing is a kind of game of interrogation and confession. In fact, I'm meant to confess that I'm not a walking legend or a fairy-tale prince but an earthling who—like anyone else—leaves a mess of failures, gaffes, and errors scattered behind him along his path through life. But of course you don't have to force me to make such a confession: I freely admit it wherever I go.

But seriously: if I've made any mistakes, then they probably all derive from my awkwardness, my indecisiveness, politeness that slips easily into compromise—see the incident with Rushdie. I didn't know how to make proper use of the authority I had, particularly in that first period—and I didn't know how to maintain that authority. I found myself often watching in embarrassment as something happened that I might have prevented; not by making better use of my constitutional authority, but better deploying my informal, personal authority, the kind that would make others take my words more seriously. Think of how many critical and yet highly constructive speeches I have given; the politicians always clapped politely, and some of them even patted me on the back when no one was looking, but none of them took any of my words to heart. That may have been one of the reasons why some journalists called me a utopian, a dreamer, an idealist. But I can't be anything other than what I am. Of course, I might theoretically at one time have taken over the Civic Forum, turned it into the most powerful political party in the country, raised money for it, appealed to the majority's instincts, and then governed with its help. But had I done that, would I still be me? And would I have even known how to go about it? Can you imagine me in such a role?

For years you were attacked from both the right and the left. Those on the right criticized you for being a leftist, those on the left for being right-wing. Some criticized you for being against the wealthy, others for having no understanding for the poor. Some criticized you for not having your own party, others for having little regard for the other parties, and so on and so forth. How did you bear all that? How did you respond? And mainly, how did you respond to all these campaigns against your wife, or yourself, or all the disinformation spread about you?

It's an eternal dilemma: to respond or not to respond? Some say that with every lie or attack, the perpetrator must be immediately rapped over the knuckles so he will never do it again, and to prevent people thinking that the perpetrator is right because the person attacked did not speak up. Others say that one should never respond because in doing so you merely give more publicity and credence to something not worth the attention.

It's a difficult decision. Some time ago, they wrote that Dáša was spending one hundred and fifty thousand crowns a month on her appearance. It was absolute nonsense, of course. Dáša is very frugal; she's perpetually repairing or refashioning her clothes so that they will always look new, and as an actress she knows how to put on makeup and she does it all herself. I've never ever seen a beautician in the house, nor do I even know exactly what that is; probably a makeup artist. That gigantic headline and the pseudo-news item that followed would truly not have been worth paying attention to had it not harmed the work of our foundation. Some people were scandalized and wrote that such an extravagant woman has no right raising money for charity. That was why Dáša sued the newspaper in question. And you know what the verdict was? Her demand for an apology was denied because, it was said, it would merely mean giving further publicity to a meaningless lie! Even the court, which is meant to issue a clear "yes" or "no" verdict, had obviously succumbed to some kind of strategic public relations thinking, which I consider to be a great victory for the tabloid press, even greater than had the court concluded that my wife really had spent that much.

In other words, deciding to respond or not is a never-ending process. We were constantly dealing with this in the Castle. On the one hand, I view it all with a certain dispassion; after all I have schooling in such things: the communists wrote lies about me all my life. On the other hand, the stuff that flows in my veins is not water but blood, and sometimes I get angry. A couple of times I responded in writing to various outrageous attacks, sometimes against the recommendation of my office. The newspapers are happy to print such a response because they can run it under a big headline from which it follows that the president reads their paper and takes it seriously. For the most part, however, I did not respond. There's no general rule of thumb; it's clearly something that has to be decided case by case. But all that is over and done with and it's not that interesting. What is interesting is something else: no matter which politician I speak with privately, anywhere in the world, sooner or later they bring the conversation around to this subject. All of them struggle with it, all of them are bothered by it. It's a testimony to the gigantic power of the media in the world today.

A German reporter once said to me that you were like François Mitterrand—you love gesture and theater in politics. That was often evident in how carefully you monitored the preparations for various negotiations, and the arrangements for gala events, state dinners, etc. How important is ritual in politics?

First, if you'll allow me, I'll speak about politics and drama. Politics, like life itself, simply plods on; at first sight it doesn't seem to be articulated in any comprehensible way; there are not many clear beginnings, entr'actes, interruptions, moments of catharsis, climaxes, or endings. It seldom happens that politics is fixed on a clearly defined goal. Drama is an attempt to deal with this fundamental amorphousness of life, to uncover something like the structure of Being, to display in vivid terms its internal weave, its hidden structure, and its real articulation. Drama's job is to visibly define the beginnings, the interruptions, the pauses, and ultimately the end, or the point of it all—in other words, all the things that are so hard to see outside of drama.

People like to understand the world in which they live; their effort is always, in one way or another, guided by an attempt to understand the inner logic, the architecture, of Being. They like recognizable beginnings and endings; they like to know what came "before" and what came "after," what came out of what, or what is related to what, and they like to experience all this in some kind of vivid abbreviation.

Politics—as an area of activity that demands general support—requires, more than anything else, that people understand it, that they grasp what the purpose of it is in any given moment, how what follows comes out of what went before, and why everything has the kind of tempo that it has. But as I've already suggested, politics, by its very nature, resists that kind of understanding. It's true that here and there a policy may succeed or fail, and everyone recognizes that at once. But for the most part that's not how it works. Politics is more of a strange, never-ending process with no clear turning points and no unambiguous and immediately recognizable outcomes. It seems to me particularly important, therefore, that politicians have an elementary dramatic instinct, that is, a sense of how to make distinctions between various acts or events, how to order them, stack them up, give them a meaning ful sequence, gradation, or structure. A basic danger facing politics in the modern world is that it will appear to be hopelessly boring, a gray, dull, daily administrative grind, enlivened occasionally by a scandal or pseudo-scandal that is forgotten as soon as it's over; in other words, something that has no point, and thus no thinking behind it. Naturally, it's in the general interest to confront this danger.

A second theme is loosely related to this: politics and theater. Of course, politics works, and has to work, with signs, symbols, rituals. It's always somewhat theatrical. The language of symbols and signs often conveys the meaning of what is happening more exactly and vividly than the most thorough intellectual explanation. Political concepts need visualization. Shared and commonly experienced signs and symbols join human societies together in an understandable way; they are a society's mortar, the emotive and focused expressions of its identity; they give presence to its common history, its common traditions, its common culture, and its models of relationships and behavior. They point to the victories and defeats of our forebears, to shared ideals and to the memory of those who died for them. Respect for this language of symbols, if it is to serve a good cause, requires a highly refined sense of moderation. In many cases you have to go only a tiny step further than is appropriate in a given human and social context, and you can awaken demons, nationalistic or otherwise, that are very difficult to tame. In a way, it's like playing with fire. If a certain kind of exaggerated emphasis on the ritual dimension of politics can evoke in people obsessions that are connected with hatred of everything that is different, then at the same time such a politics—at least in more enlightened eyes—can also become ridiculous and absurd: exactly what Karel Teige referred to as "Super-Dada."

But finally, to the heart of your question: it is true that I paid a lot of attention to what we might call the aesthetic side of politics. There are at least three reasons for this. In the first place, I am fully convinced of what I have just tried to explain, that is, the profound importance of this dimension of politics.

In the second place, there weren't many traditions in our country that could be drawn upon; we had to invent everything for ourselves. What we inherited from the communists was for the most part unusable. And so we had to apply our creativity to all kinds of things: from the state honor rolls to the ceremonies at which the decorations would be awarded; from furniture to writing paper; from the location and style of state lunches and dinners to ceremonial uniforms and the waiters' dress; from flags, standards, flagpoles, and dishes, to the decoration of halls and offices with sculptures and pictures. At the beginning I even had to bring paintings for my office from home!

The third reason is perhaps obvious: I enjoy such things, and perhaps I have a more developed feel for this approach than others do, or at least I experience them more intensely. This sensitivity of mine is in fact increasing: the older I get, the more pedantic I become. Before state dinners, I even took to rearranging the cutlery myself—I have my own standards in certain matters that come from my bourgeois restaurant background—and when they served half-cooked potatoes at a lunch for the Japanese emperor I almost had a nervous breakdown. Fortunately he understood this to be a Czech culinary specialty.

(May 18, 1997)

Five months after my wedding it appears that the Office of the President of the Republic, the Czech Republic, and its existing legal order are incapable, in any reasonable way, of responding to the fact that the president of the republic has gotten married. The state, which is allegedly democratic, is staring at this fact like a calf staring at a new gate and it doesn't know what to do. My wife is not a civil servant, and even less is she a state official; she is apparently a completely private citizen. At the same time, however, she is expected to be the crowning glory of the president's visits at home and abroad, and in some instances she is even expected to directly represent the president, in the name of the state, but without the state's help. A small example: everyone wants her to open the Czech Center in Paris, but no one is capable of organizing this trip, arranging the details, paying for it, preparing for it, setting it up. (. . .) In short, all kinds of demands are made on "the first lady": protocol demands, political, state, social, public, charitable, cultural, and other wise; she has to deal with a large volume of correspondence, to accept or reject patronages, to accept or reject invitations, and at the same time she has no staff to deal with all of this for her, and on her behalf. So far it's been me who has spent the most time dealing with all of this, which is, as everyone will recognize, systemically inappropriate. (. . .)

The OPR, it would seem, has been no help at all, and if it has, it has offered ideas, not action. The state has simply not recognized that the president has a wife and that the wife is a public figure, influencing not only the image of the state in the world but also the political position of the president. Dagmar must find a form for her public existence, for her charitable and foundation work, and for her natural interest in culture. All this represents a not insignificant nut to crack: after the bland era of communist hausfraus, who were permitted to do everything and did nothing, came Olga, who had her own place in the Committee of Good Will (nineteen employees); Dáša has no Committee of Good Will. Today she has a single secretary, who is goodhearted and works from dawn to dusk, but with all the complicated responsibilities that have piled up on her desk she has not been able to do the simplest of all tasks, drawing up and printing out Dáša's schedule. What are we going to do about it? (. . .)

(February 8, 1998)

(. . .)

Whether anyone likes it or not a married couple is once again installed in the Prague Castle, and has been for over a year now. That is to say one state official elected by parliament, and one wife, whom he himself has elected (and naturally she him). This wife has fought for a year for her place in the sun and today she feels that she is worse off than she was a year ago. It is true that she now has two secretaries, that she was given a nice office and not long ago she was even given the services of Mr. Š. During that year she has accomplished many good works: she established a charitable foundation; she changed her way of life to suit that of her husband; she has given up her own profession; she has successfully represented us in the world; she has taken on many sponsorships and honorary chairmanships; she has visited—as the wife of the president—many social, medical, and cultural institutions; she has, with her own hand, answered many hundreds of letters from citizens, etc.,

etc., etc. In her new position she has given of herself to the full, and at the same time, oddly enough, she has not made any serious mistakes. And the results? Very sad: from being one of the best-loved actresses in the country, and from being a woman whose marriage to a sick president was highly popular with perhaps 80 percent of our citizens, she has become the butt of countless vulgar jokes, a favorite target of ridiculing commentators, of attacks and insults from a large number of reporters, the object of a year-long stream of almost daily insults from the private television network Nova, and ultimately—in the eyes of the public—she has practically become the bane of the nation's existence. I'm not going to go into all the tangled sociopsychological reasons for this strange phenomenon, nor attempt to examine the degree of guilt to be borne, one way or another, by many people, including myself. But the OPR bears its own share of the responsibility, because a not insignificant part of it has never, internally, come to terms with my marriage, which unfortunately is reflected in how Dáša is assisted by various people, and which naturally is reflected in the way that I am accepted.

(. . .) Therefore, the moment my new mandate as president begins I would ask all of my colleagues to work sincerely for my wife and her good public image as well. It does not demand a lot of work. It just demands goodwill. (. . .)

(Undated, 1999)

I have just caught a whiff of the old atmosphere from January 1997, when I married, when the OPR felt that my new wife had no need, in the Castle, of a secretary, or a desk, or an office, because she was only my wife, someone whose place was clearly in the home by the washtub. The piles of letters, invitations, suggestions, requests, pleas, etc. she received ought clearly to have gone straight into the wastebasket, for in the law governing the OPR there is nothing about any service to be provided for the wife of the president. What followed were the notorious squabbles and Dáša's struggle, the result of which was her own (. . .) secretariat. (. . .) It would appear that the situation had more or less finally stabilized. And what do I suddenly discover? That my wife has gone, totally unprepared, not on a private visit, nor on a foundation visit, but on an official visit (representing me), even though the OPR has known for at least half a year that she was going. (. . .) Dáša keeps calling me in desperation from Japan, saying that she doesn't know how many times I have already been there, where I have been and why, and what I did there, (. . .) that she knows nothing about the relationship between Buddhism and Shintoism, etc., etc. (. . .) And all that was needed was to provide her with (. . .) a little brochure (. . .). Why did that not happen? Why isn't the OPR, after all these years, when something serious is at issue, capable of taking into account the fact that I have a wife who occasionally has some state business? The situation is being corrected posthaste. I spent the day that I was meant to spend in convalescence and preparing for the visit of the Irish woman, looking up various articles on Japan and faxing them to Dáša. Such a situation must not repeat itself!

(August 21, 1999)

(. . .)

6) In the closet where the vacuum cleaner is kept, there also lives a bat. How to get rid of it? The lightbulb has been unscrewed so as not to wake it up and upset it. (. . .)

It's well known that you took a great interest in the Prague Castle and that many changes were made while you were president. What were the main changes, and what ideas were behind them?

As I've already said, the Prague Castle, or rather the Castle and the area that immediately surrounds it, is a special organism, a small city within a city. When we arrived it was a small, dead city. It was full of secret policemen; an entire unit, comprising several hundred state policemen, was based there. Everywhere there were walls, iron barriers, bars, metal doors, inaccessible rooms, inaccessible spaces, wires, microphones. With my friend the architect Miroslav Masák, who came with me to the Castle, I spent a lot of time thinking about what to do with it. We even held a small international architectural symposium on the subject. First we opened what we could to the public, and we moved out the state security police and the troops of the Ministry of the Interior. At the same time we tried to connect various spaces—the courtyards and the gardens—so that there would be uninterrupted walkways between them. We experimented with ways of desanctifying the enormous cathedral in the spirit of Bakhtin, which meant opening its precincts to jugglers, musicians, stall-keepers, the kind of people who had traditionally set up shop in the precincts of Gothic cathedrals and who balanced the finger pointing strictly toward heaven with an emphasis on all the profane sides of life.

A lot had to be restored and revitalized because the communists—as they had in everything—focused exclusively on the surface impression. They had constantly repainted the visible facades, but behind that there were often rare things that had been entirely neglected or untended. We quickly understood that if it were not forever to remain an enchanted Kafkaesque castle, the different functions of the place had to be intelligently interwoven: a place representing both entertainment and statehood; the esoteric connection of its main features; accommodation for students, a university faculty, places of amusement, art galleries, hospitality services, small shops, everything, in short, that belongs together if an architectonic or urbanistic space is to be genuinely alive, and not just a dead "realization" of someone's project.

It wasn't easy. We struggled with a lack of funds—the politicians thought that I was doing this for myself—and with a reluctant bureaucracy. In the end we were able to accomplish about 5 percent of what we had wanted to do.

In later years Masák was replaced by the architect Šípek, whose influence on the Castle is obvious. But we engaged other artists and architects as well. Naturally we made sure that there was a cultural life in the Castle; there were many important exhibitions, expositions, lectures, concerts, and performances. I really enjoyed tending to things like that. In this I tried, in my modest way, to follow in the footsteps of the emperor Rudolf II, who as a ruler was clearly eccentric and hardly successful, but under whom the Prague Castle, and ultimately the whole of Prague, became one of the most important cultural cities in Europe, which at the time meant in the world. He was a friend of schol ars, thinkers, astrologers, and mystics, a great collector of art, and a famous patron; the greatest personalities of his time, from Tycho Brahe to Arcimboldo, were connected with him. I had one of Rudolf's globes and telescopes set up in my presidential reception room to emphasize the intellectual and cultural dimension of this new period, and the sense of tradition. Whether these things are still there or not, I don't know.

What about the château at Lány? It's the traditional country seat of presidents and it's linked above all with Masaryk's name. What state did you find it in?

It had just been renovated a few years before, so it was in decent shape. The furnishings and the decor, however, were execrable. It's a style I knew from all communist residences: nothing but bathrooms, refrigerators, television sets, sound systems bought by the ton and never used, disgusting tiles, fake Persian rugs, flashy bourgeois furniture. Any trace of Masaryk had been removed; we found his writing desk somewhere in the fuel shed, and fortunately it was possible to restore it. There was no money to make any thorough changes, but Olga, with the help of Diana Sternberg, did what she could: they installed nice new drapes, real carpets, historically appropriate period furnishings, etc. Things were found in various Castle storage rooms. Dáša carried on their work, but most of the changes took place in the first period, when everything was easier and many people were cooperative. In the village of Lány, for example, mementos of Masaryk suddenly began surfacing, things that people had carefully hidden for decades and now let us use. We tried to bring Lány back to life. We opened the park to the public, and I held many political meetings in the château and received visits there. The Dalai Lama lived there whenever he was in Prague.

The Amálie villa belonged to Lány, didn't it?

Yes, but not completely. It is—like two other hunting lodges—a part of the Lány Woods, which is an independent organization under the

Prague Castle Administration. It's a very pretty villa, and right after I discovered it my colleagues and I, mainly Andulka Freimanová, and Michael Kocáb, began to organize informal discussions there. They were devoted to different themes or subjects from social life, and they took place on average once every three weeks. Over the years there were almost eighty of these get-togethers. Between twenty and thirty people were always invited. The discussions lasted four or five hours. There was a break during which dinner was served, and altogether several hundred people took part. It became an institution in itself. And the most interesting thing is that everyone respected the principle of confidentiality and discretion. The basic condition for a genuinely open and often very heated discussion was that no one would ever talk about what went on there anywhere else; in other words, no one was to speak for anyone else. Let those who wish to communicate something to the world do so in their own names. I don't recall that in all those years there was a single indiscretion—and yet Czech life is famously indiscreet; when something is known by more than one person, sooner or later the whole world knows it.

Hel, August 28, 2005

As I sit here in this marvelous Polish complex, writing about how the two seats of the Czech head of state have been cared for by the Czechs, I am overcome by a mild sense of melancholy. Poland has several such seats, all are wonderfully staffed, and after they were destroyed they were either completely rebuilt or were restored from their foundations up; together they must have a large number of employees, and enormous amounts of money must have been invested in them. Even the mere day-to-day maintenance must cost a lot of money. I don't say this because the little Czech Republic should desire the same as large Poland with its completely different historical tradition; still, I can't help but feel this melancholy when I remember the struggle we had over every crown spent on restoring a Gothic fresco, paving a courtyard, or repairing a roof. I would invite the budget committee to lunch at Lány and show them everything and explain everything in broad terms, but I always felt like a penniless student begging for support. They didn't seem to understand that Lány was their calling card as well, not to mention the fact that in two hundred years no one will know who Joe Blow the member of parliament, or President Havel for that matter, was, but everyone will see what we have left behind us in the structures that embody our statehood, or more generally, in the aesthetic appearance of our land.

But to other matters: I've just written about drama as a concentrated picture of the structure of Being, the world, life. Some may wonder why I am jumping from period to period in this book. It's for precisely the same reason that a playwright, or even more so, a novelist, does: everything is related to everything else; anything from a particular period points to something from the period that preceded it or the period that followed; everything is linked together in all kinds of ways, and one of the ways to touch on this hidden fabric of life is the collage, the combining of things that, on the surface, are unrelated, in such a way that they ultimately tell us more about the connections between them and their real meaning than any mechanical chronology could, or any other ordering principle that suppresses accident. That at least was my intention.

And one more thing about this book: for a long time I have observed with interest a particular television host who always invites guests to take part in a conversation on his public affairs program, while continually exhorting them to "Please be brief!" And I ask myself, why did he invite them on the show? These people are on television perhaps for the first and last time in their lives; they may have traveled from the far ends of the country to tell the nation something about their life's work, or about some crucial experience they've had, and the moment they arrive they are silenced and told not to speak at any length because the moderator has to finish in time for some idiotic commercial break. Naturally, his guests panic and don't say anything at all. How I would sympathize with them if they punished the moderator by deliberately talking on and on and refusing to be interrupted until the television set exploded! (By the way, in America I regularly watched Larry King and other talk-show hosts but I never saw them so shamelessly interrupt what anyone was saying.) And so I'm going to punish that moderator in the name of his unhappy guests by using his pet phrase as a title for my book.

On February 3, 2003, at midnight, your presidency came to an end, and you left the Prague Castle for good. What were you feeling? How did it take place?

Almost nothing in my life is normal, and so the atmosphere in the Prague Castle in those final weeks and days before the end was very strange. People who had gone through those long years with me and had gotten used to me suddenly found it very hard to grasp that everything was about to change. Some of them sensed that they could not remain there, and for a long time beforehand, in an unfavorable political atmosphere, they began looking for other jobs, though they were afraid to inform each other or tell me about it; others believed that a president would be elected who would keep them on. I kept claiming that my successor could be no one other than the one who was subsequently elected, but others claimed that it was impossible and didn't believe that it would happen. Anyone who didn't leave voluntarily was later fired. There may have been a few who adapted and found favor, but not many stayed on for very long either.

So even though they didn't know who would be elected president, my colleagues were, more than understandably, in a state of high anxiety. This nervousness entered into my own work and life as well: more than once, out of fear that a problem might arise during the handover, either for me or for them, they came to me with rather bureaucratic requests, for instance that I should return a particular chair, or a ruler that I had allegedly borrowed from the Castle. No one was interested in how many of my own things I had given to the Castle. Suddenly there were a thousand tiny decisions to be made about whether something belonged to me (in which case I could take it home) or the state. They didn't want to give me books that had been specifically dedicated to me, but on which some kind of official stamp had been placed; on the other hand I was meant to be given absurdly large sculptures, gifts that I had nowhere to put, but which had not been stamped. Perhaps it was my mistake for not allowing enough time to prepare for my departure in peace and quiet, thus making it necessary to do everything at the last minute in a state of considerable nervousness. With the best intentions, my faithful secretary of many years took away my computer because it was government-issue and provided me with another one which was far more modern, which means far more complicated: it is always asking me something, wanting something, scolding me for something, thinking about something, and offering me a choice of many possibilities. At the same time it uses a kind of incomprehensible language, a mixture of Czech, English, and computerese. If I happen to hit the wrong key it starts to play the Panamanian national anthem, or it shows me a colored picture of a biological cell. Before I'm able to return to where I'm supposed to be, it manages—or is it me?—to wipe everything out. It's not at all my secretary's fault, but I was naturally angry with him and with Bill Gates. And just as I had to become familiar overnight with a new computer, I had to quickly become familiar with a lot of other things, from my cell phone to the completely new arrangement of one-way streets in Prague. In short, it was quite tense in the Castle shortly before my departure. At times it was reminiscent of the sinking of the *Titanic*.

Later, when my successor was elected, some of my final documents—more or less private and literary archival materials—were quickly spirited out in the night. I had a farewell party for all the Castle employees in the Spanish Hall and I was touched by how many people were moved to tears, including various members of the cleaning staff, or gardeners, whom I had never met. We spent the final evening with friends from the theater and Dáša's colleagues in a pub very close to the Castle, and at midnight we went out onto the square to watch the presidential standard being lowered. My pistoleers came up to me and said that they were signing off, but that I wasn't to be afraid because they would continue to guard me until morning.

I felt a great sense of relief that night, and I am glad that I no longer have to bear that burden. I will not hide the fact, however, that the end was very strange indeed. It was naturally very inspiring for my *Lear*-like play about leaving one's post. I can't say that I wasn't thanked for my service to my country; in the first place, it was a decision of parliament, as the law provides, that I be given both of the highest state decorations, one of which I had created and introduced myself; in the second place, Dáša organized a great evening in the National Theater at which dozens of our most popular actors and singers saluted me and performed for me. It was a huge job. Dáša worked on it secretly for half a year, and in the end I didn't really enjoy it because I was sitting on pins and needles in the presidential box hoping that nothing embarrassing would happen; after all, the whole thing was one giant improvisation! But it didn't. And in the third place, the Czech musical underground said good-bye to me at the Czech Rock Café.

Can a statesman who has been elected president four times simply retire and have peace and quiet, or is it just you who doesn't seem to be able to do that?

Without even trying to, and often despite the fact that I resist this, it seems that I must go on being something of a pioneer. I foolishly thought that when this job came to an end, all my adventures would come to an end as well, and that, being well provided for and having no responsibilities, I could enjoy life, travel, rest, that I could think, and read the most important books I had missed out on. It was a purely utopian dream. Everything turned out differently. In the first place, I had to become a pioneer of Czech postpresidential life. We'd never had a president who had come to the end of his mandate in a simple, formal fashion. Masaryk resigned before the end of his term because of old age and poor health, and lived out the brief remainder of his life in Lány as a national saint. Beneš resigned twice and was never able to serve to the end of his terms. Hácha was swept out of office and died in prison. (He was, by the way, the only one of our presidents who went to prison after being president: more often it was the other way around.) Gottwald died in office. So did Zápotocký. Novotný had to leave office prematurely, and somewhat ignominiously. Svoboda was relieved of the office because of illness. Husák left it prematurely and in shame and defeat. So we're not used to presidents who serve their full terms and we're not entirely sure what to do with someone who has. I have to smile to myself when I realize that people don't know how to address me. Some say "Mr. President," others say "Mr. Former President," some say "Mr. Havel," and it's only a matter of time before someone addresses me as "Mr. Former Havel." I'm invited everywhere, under the impression that now at last I have time, and yet they are a little leery of me for fear that contact with me might somehow compromise them. Some people greet me almost surreptitiously, as they used to when we were dissidents. That has nothing to do with my uncertain status as ex-president, but is rather a result of our current political situation and my former political role. But I'm also often invited abroad as well, to various events, lectures, ceremonies, political visits, or working visits, and this happens perhaps even more frequently than before, because even abroad, people clearly assume that I must have more time now.

But hold on: I can't blame everything on others. I involved myself in so many international matters because I wanted to. There are certain tasks I simply have to take on, and would take on, even if I didn't want to. I simply have to speak out against totalitarian regimes or dictatorships, whether they be in Cuba, Belarus, Burma, or North Korea. I can't turn my back on dissidents from those countries who visit the Czech Republic and want to see me, and I cannot avoid meeting with foreign politicians with whom I experienced important events, and with whom I worked to have an impact on history. If I tried to avoid all that entirely, I'd be denying my entire life up to this point. In short, I can't even think about real leisure, traveling, thinking, and reading, nor do I have the time or the focus for these things.

Obviously, to a considerable degree it's my own fault, but to be fair, it's also a consequence of the very specific circumstances of the post-presidential phase of my life. I was the first democratic president the country had had in a long time; I was connected with our revolution and with the fall of the Iron Curtain; I was a very special case, and that explains a great deal. And on top of all that, I still appear to be, and to a considerable degree rightly so, in some kind of ongoing, latent opposition to current Czech politics and its morality. I can't imagine any other factors that would be less likely to make a peaceful retirement possible.

But could it be any other way? It's an immensely interesting and inspiring experience and it's very odd how again and again this experience relates to the theme of the play I'm trying to write. A small example: retired politicians always used to seem to me somewhat shabby, wrinkled, not as well dressed, worn out. I've only now come to understand why: they don't have to get dressed and spruced up every day for the television cameras and the photographers who dogged their heels when they were in office. Who would not give in to the temptation to relax about one's appearance? After all, you're no longer caught up in such a whirl, and people don't take such good care of you because everyone knows there's not nearly so much at stake.

And another thing: you suddenly realize that you can't speak about those who have replaced you as openly as you would wish. You would be immediately suspected of speaking out of a sense of injury or jealousy, or that you were being so talkative only because you were no longer burdened by responsibility. But it's also impossible to remain entirely silent. Willy-nilly one must constantly decide, yet again, between the greater and lesser evil, just as one had to do in politics. Moreover, you are president for a fixed period, five or ten years, but you are ex-president for the rest of your life. That was something else I hadn't thought of before.

One more point: in the past when I met someone, I was always provided beforehand with a brief but exhaustive explanation of who he was, what he did, why I was talking to him, and whether I had ever met him before and so on. Today, when I have a small office with a tiny staff, it's no longer that easy, and if it weren't for the fact that I still have a few friends and former colleagues in various ministries and offices, who knows how we would manage? I could go on listing such observations, but I repeat, I have nothing to complain about. On the contrary I enjoy life. And I'm trying to answer your questions truthfully.

CHAPTER SIX

Hrádeček, November 28, 2005

For the whole of September and October I never stopped. Yet what did I actually do? I visited several European countries, had a lot of meetings and visits and discussions, and made countless speeches—and all at a time of year when I'm usually under the weather. I'm quite surprised that I survived it all without any damage to my health. I'm at Hrádeček once more, but there's a lot of snow here now and the trees are beautifully cloaked in white. I'm really like a hermit here. (Hrádeček is off by itself and my only neighbor is my friend Andrej Krob, who has a cottage nearby, but he's not there now.) Yesterday I watched a thriller on television and then I realized that for the first time in my life I felt afraid here. The very thought that I might suddenly glimpse the movement of a human shadow gave me goose bumps and heart palpitations. I stopped getting the newspapers a while ago, and my news comes from television. I read the papers only when I happen across one. The last time that happened was several days ago on the plane from Budapest, when I discovered I was the subject of a scandal. The Czech media are up in arms because I have apparently supported our new prime minister. The whole thing obviously started a while ago, when he invited me for coffee, and as we were leaving we were waylaid by a journalist who asked me how I'd have gotten along with the current prime minister if I were still president. I said I thought we'd hit it off. By that I meant that I would not have been having constant public squabbles with the prime minister over how to interpret the constitution, as our current president does. I should have expressed myself more precisely or concretely, but still, why there should have been a controversy or even a scandal over this, I have no idea. But obviously I can't understand everything.

As president, you witnessed and participated in many important events. Which do you think were the most important?

Today there may be many people, particularly young people, who don't know what the Warsaw Pact was. For them it's just part of history, and some of them may tend to believe that this pact expired automatically, by itself, that it was just history taking its course. That's not how it was. The Warsaw Pact had to be dissolved, and it was not at all a simple matter. Soviet troops were stationed in our countries; our general staffs were more or less branch plants of the Soviet high command and bases from which the Soviet military intelligence could operate; the basic and unquestionable dogma, that this alliance was vitally necessary, had been drummed into the general consciousness for decades. During the revolution we demanded and got free elections, we demanded that the leading role of the Communist Party be removed from the constitution, we called for freedom of the press and for a market economy, but the idea of dissolving the Warsaw Pact, that fundamental instrument of Soviet hegemony, seemed too dangerous even to the radicals among us. Even in his wildest dreams, I don't suppose it occurred to Gorbachev that anyone might want such a thing.

When the subject was finally broached it must have put him in a tight spot: he couldn't intervene forcefully because it would have been a blow to his whole notion of perestroika; but at the same time he must have realized that the liquidation of this pact would necessarily result in the collapse of the Soviet Union itself. So we started by talking about a new pan-European security structure into which the Warsaw Pact would be smoothly integrated without prejudice. Then we talked about the liquidation of its military structures with a view to the new international situation, while preserving it as a political structure, by which it was clearly meant that it would have a purely symbolic existence. The total dissolution of the Warsaw Pact happened after several months, at the very end of this chain of proposals.

Today it would be hard to explain to anyone how risky these various feints and maneuvers were, and also how necessary they were, not only with a view to power relationships in the region but also with a view to public opinion and ultimately to our own thinking as well. We all knew that the Warsaw Pact had to be dissolved, but none of us knew at first exactly how to bring it about.

I recall that at the time we had a slight problem with the Hungarians: they didn't want to dissolve it because they wanted to exit from the pact with great pomp and circumstance, and they couldn't do this if it no longer existed. Their position had obvious historical roots: they realized the great symbolic meaning it would have for Hungarians if Hungary were to do now what it had tried to do in 1956 before its attempt was drowned in blood. I remember that at one Warsaw Pact summit in Moscow, the Poles, the East Germans, and the Czechs sat long into the night trying to persuade the Hungarians to change their minds, until they finally relented.

The whole matter took a great deal of effort; it was not simple, particularly since the Soviet troops were so slow and so reluctant to leave our country; but in the end, we were successful. I consider that moment, in the summer of 1991, when I ceremonially announced to the world—as representative of the presiding country at the end of the final summit of the Warsaw Pact—that the Warsaw Pact was now dissolved, as one of the strangest moments in my life. Moreover, it happened in Prague, the city that Warsaw Pact troops had invaded little more than two decades before. Many years ago, I had been a beleaguered and rather ridiculous private in the sappers, the traditional Soviet graveyard for the class enemy, and now, as liquidator of one of the two most powerful military alliances in the world, I was overwhelmed by the absurdity of it all.

Gorbachev did not attend that self-liquidating summit; he was represented by Gennady Yanayev, a morose drinker straight out of Dostoyevsky, who was clearly more easily rattled than Gorbachev; about three weeks after that, he attempted a putsch in Moscow. But in so doing, he definitely buried the Soviet Union itself, which truly could not long have survived the end of the Warsaw Pact.

With the pact's dissolution (today an almost forgotten historical step) the bipolar division of the world finally collapsed, and our civilization could begin the difficult task of finding a new and better order—

which, I must add, it has yet to find. Nor will it, as long as the political technocrats so massively outnumber the dreamers.

What are your thoughts and memories on the expansion of NATO and the Czech membership in it? Was that an easier job? Was it merely the logical consequence of the dissolution of the Warsaw Pact?

Not at all. I would say that it was even more difficult.

Why?

The struggle to expand NATO to include Eastern Europe essentially lasted for ten years. There were many reasons why progress was so sluggish, but the most significant holdup was a certain conservatism or caution on the part of Western members. They were afraid of expansion. They felt they hadn't investigated us thoroughly enough. They didn't understand how whole countries could suddenly appear to want the precise opposite of what they had wanted—or seemed to have wanted—not that long before. They were horrified at the prospect of suddenly sharing security secrets with their recent adversaries, those still rather incomprehensible postcommunist countries. No one properly knew what might become of them, or who the people who governed them were, or the unforeseen problems these unknown qualities might yet cause the whole alliance.

By way of illustration: shortly after the expansion of NATO a highly confidential luncheon meeting was held in Washington to which only the top representatives of the member states—that is, the presidents or prime ministers—were invited. President Clinton explained why he thought it would be right to invade Milosevic's Serbia. My immediate, private response was total astonishment that Clinton was speaking so openly about such an immensely delicate matter in front of me and my colleague, the Polish president, Aleksander Kwaśniewski. My response was laughable, as I soon realized, but I mention it to illustrate the situation at the time. We felt that there were probably good reasons why they couldn't completely trust us, and thus we were surprised to find that they suddenly did. By the way, Clinton's extemporaneous argument for armed intervention was long, detailed, and extraordinarily well informed and convincing; I don't believe that many of the European statesmen present knew as much about the situation in the former Yugoslavia as Clinton.

Tell us something about how you worked for the expansion of NATO, and why you put so much effort into it. It's my impression that among Western liberal intellectuals who are close to you, NATO has more opponents than supporters. Is it true that the decision to expand NATO was made at one of your private dinners with Clinton at Madeleine Albright's in Washington?

We had several such dinners, and they all revolved around that subject, and I was a great advocate of expansion. Nevertheless, none of those dinners in itself led to a final decision. The reason why I pushed so hard—at private functions but mainly in my public speeches—was simple: I felt that the expansion of NATO to the East would guarantee the irreversibility of the new conditions in these countries, and of peace in Europe. I could well imagine crowds of populists, demagogues, nationalists, and postcommunists who would exploit every delay to argue, with increasing urgency, that the arrogant, consumerist, and selfish West neither recognized us nor wanted us, and therefore we must go our own way.

Let us understand what that way would have entailed: it would have meant authoritarian governments flying, instead of the abandoned red flag, the flag of nationalism, beneath which it would hide its own Mafia-like practices, and the privatization of everything into its own hands. And reawakened nationalism would necessarily lead to a new danger of confrontation. Nationalists may well be as alike as two peas in a pod, but this doesn't necessarily lead to brotherhood; on the contrary: nationalist ideologies are essentially confrontational.

But that wasn't the only issue. I also thought that—unlike the technically long and complicated expansion of the European Union, however more feasible it might be politically—the expansion of NATO was, technically, a relatively simple matter, while at the same time very important politically. So the obvious approach was to try to expand NATO first, and thus create a calmer and more stable environment for the preparations for membership in the European Union. But you could also argue from the other side: who knows whether the more cautious and more self-centered European Union would have been willing to expand at all if NATO had not expanded first, and if its expansion had not been preceded by the security guarantee that the EU itself was unable to provide? The main trailblazer and the guarantor of the new order at the time was clearly the United States. We felt this and we made our position clear. That may be why, from that time on, our country has been accused of excessive pro-Americanism.

Are you sure that the representatives of the other Eastern European countries saw it the same way?

I think so. One small example: when Clinton announced his Partnership for Peace initiative in Prague, in the presence of the top Polish, Hungarian, Czech, and Slovak representatives, we all said at once, without hesitation, that while we understand that as a step in the right direction, it must not be a substitute for full membership in NATO. At the time—it was in 1994—I wrote a draft of our common declaration, and I remember that the Visegrad countries approved the text in a matter of minutes.

And what would you say to all the critics of NATO who consider it an instrument of Western imperialism and an association of politicians and generals who serve the expansion of mighty multinational corporations, or at least defend their current territories?

As a traditional critic of many aspects of globalization, including the deepening dependence of politics on powerful companies and corporations, I have a natural understanding of this criticism. Nevertheless, I have long ago come to realize that rather than simply rejecting the alliance without offering a better alternative, it makes far more sense to remind it again and again of its founding values, and to do everything to ensure that the alliance serves those values above all. That means to emphasize over and over again, and to project over and over again into its practical decisions, the idea that gave NATO birth—in other words, the idea that freedom and democracy need to be defended, if necessary by force. I repeated until I was blue in the face that NATO is meant to serve citizens and not just generals.

(May 1, 2001)

(. . .)

3) (. . .) In the first months after the revolution I felt a strong inclination to meet privately with one or other of the top officials in the former regime, to try to learn from him how he saw everything from his place at the center of power, what he was actually thinking then, what he thinks now, how that regime actually worked, who was afraid of whom, who tapped whose conversations, etc., etc., etc. I am, after all, an unusually curious person. But nothing of the sort ever happened and for two very good reasons: (1) If the public had ever learned of such a meeting, however private—and that would certainly have happened, since I would never have set it up in any conspiratorial way—I would have been eaten alive, and above all, by our freshly minted post-November anti-communists. That wouldn't have bothered me so much personally, but such a conflict would not have done much to help our still quite fragile postrevolutionary democracy, all the more so because such a meeting would certainly have been interpreted as proof of some secret conspiracy between the dissidents and the communist rulers, which was a relatively popular theory at the time. (2) I was persuaded by connoisseurs of power that such a meeting would have been a total waste of my time: I would, they say, have learned nothing interesting from the former rulers; I would only hear various lies and clichés. (. . .)

(February 10, 2002)

(. . .)

2) A very preliminary draft of a letter to Put'ek. (. . .) I would like to say now how happy I would be if we could welcome you in Prague to the November summit of NATO. It will be, as has become the custom in recent years, held in conjunction with a session of the North Atlantic Cooperation Council, the NATO-Russia Council, and the NATO-Ukraine Commission. Parallel with these official meetings there will be many events held by nongovernmental organizations dealing with questions of the future political and security ordering of the world. I believe that at the joint session of NATO and the Russian Federation, a new quality of relations between that alliance and Russia will be officially confirmed. I think that a future world is unimaginable without a solid partnership between these two large and powerful entities, something I have said in public many times. The meeting I refer to will be taking place for the very first time on this side of the former Iron Curtain. It seems to me all the more important, therefore, that Russia be represented in Prague by its highest official. Your personal participation in it will be perceived by the whole world not only as the clear and final agreement of your country to the end of the bipolar division of the world, but above all, and mainly, as an expression of Russia's clear intention to seek a new world order based on the equal partnership of many political, or cultural, or geographical entities, whether made up of country, regional, or continental groupings. Of course, you will be officially invited by the secretary general of NATO. Please understand my letter as a personal intercession by a representative of the host country. (. . .)

(August 21, 1999)

(. . .)

6) In the closet where the vacuum cleaner is kept, there also lives a bat. How to get rid of it? The lightbulb has been unscrewed so as not to wake it up and upset it. ( )

The Czech entry into NATO, however, did not have a lot of support at home. The Social Democrats wanted to hold a referendum on the subject.

You're right, it didn't have a lot of support, and a referendum would probably have ended up not endorsing it. It's easy to understand why this would be so: after so many decades of ideological massaging, many people may still have suspected that NATO was a rather dubious organization run by capitalists and imperialists. And if they didn't feel this way, they may have feared that NATO could involve us in some international adventures that would prevent us from looking after ourselves properly, something that should be our primary goal. After the dissolution of the Warsaw Pact, some may also have thought that having liberated ourselves from one alliance and become an independent country, it made no sense to don another yoke, even one of clearly opposite intent. Not many made the distinction that one of those pacts was an instrument of foreign domination and the other, on the contrary, was a means of defending its members against such domination.

So, although I'm in favor of referenda, I was against one in this case. Without a massive yes-campaign it would have turned out badly, which would have been to the detriment of our country and the whole of Central Europe. In a representative democracy, politicians sometimes have to take responsibility for unpopular decisions, or for supporting a minority opinion. If, for example, we had had a referendum on the Criminal Code, we would still have the death penalty. But my main argument against a referendum in this case was a different one: the task of politicians is to guarantee, through agreements, the security of their country; it is part of their mandate, and if democratically elected representatives do not act against the sovereignty of the state—which in this case was demonstrably not so—holding a referendum would call in doubt their mandate, and amount to an expression of nonconfidence. In that case, however, a new election should have been called, not a referendum.

This, however, was not a controversial subject about which there could be various opinions, as though it were simply a matter of deciding whether or not a superhighway should be built; what was at issue was a principle: whether or not the state has a right, through agreements, to defend its independence in a way that it considers best.

Were there many disagreements among politicians about the entry into NATO?

There were. The communists were naturally against joining NATO and probably many Social Democrats were as well. The ODS was for joining, although Václav Klaus was not enthusiastic, but in the end he did not dare go against his own party.

Miloš Zeman was also very strongly against it, was he not?

At first he was. But later he very generously retreated from his position and also gave up his support for a referendum and ultimately became a supporter of NATO. Nevertheless, he added that he was doing it only out of gentlemanly consideration for me—a typical quasi-joke on Zeman's part.

What about the Russians? A very serious reason for hesitation on the West's part was, after all, fear of the Russians.

You're right. I almost forgot about that. However—like many others—I knew very well that it was a groundless fear. Of course the Russians didn't like it, particularly later when the inclusion of the Baltic republics became an issue. Naturally, the Russians protested loudly and made threats, but it was only one of their traditional rhetorical exercises. They would have had to think very carefully about any more serious response to the expansion of NATO. They were already too much in need of Western economic assistance; after all, their country was on the brink of collapse.

By the way I have an interesting recollection on that score: when Yeltsin, with whom I had a very friendly relationship, was in Prague, I asked him if it bothered him much that we were trying to enter NATO. He said that that was our business. I asked him to repeat it at a press conference, and he did, and as we were leaving the press conference, he asked me if he'd put it well, and whether I was satisfied. That was typical: he had the manners of a grandee. Two weeks later the Russian Ministry of Foreign Affairs sent a memorandum around to all Western governments stating that Russia would consider the expansion of NATO a hostile act. That kind of thing is an Oriental mode of behavior— declaring something loudly for ritual purposes without actually believing it.

Shortly before you left office, a NATO summit was held in Prague, in late November 2002. This is a large and demanding event that is held once every two years, in which up to fifty heads of state take part. Was it your idea to bring this summit to Prague? Wasn't it a big security risk? Didn't it cost a lot of money? Did it not provoke protests from Czech society?

I happen to know precisely when and where that idea came up: it was about a year before, on a plane from Istanbul, when we were returning from the summit of the OSCE. I don't know any longer who first suggested it, but I know that I immediately took it up and persuaded the minister of foreign affairs, who was flying with us, that we should do it, and then I began to work on it systematically. Ultimately a formal decision was made to hold it in Prague. It was the first NATO summit to be held in a new member state, and its significance was decisive because it was at this summit that NATO was expanded to include other Eastern European states, including the three Baltic republics. From the point of view of the future political structuring of the world, this expansion was probably even more important than the preceding expansion that had included the three Visegrad countries. It was no longer just a small compromise, but a clear indication that the spheres of interest once defined by the Iron Curtain had come to an end. Yeltsin had generously supported Czech membership in NATO, but the Baltic republics must have been very hard for Putin to swallow. Of course in the end, Putin did not come to the Prague summit. It was a distant echo of Gorbachev's absence in Prague in 1991: Gorbachev had to come to terms with the end of "their" pact, Putin with the expansion of "that other pact" right to their borders. Very few people may have noticed that both these events of fundamental historical significance happened in Prague, a place where—as I have said so often—history is traditionally raveled or unraveled.

I devoted a great deal of energy to the preparation for the summit. I wanted a visible representation of what I spoke about a while ago, which is that NATO must not be, and does not wish to be, an association of traveling politicians and generals but that it is, must be, and wishes to be one of the guarantors of human and civic freedom in the whole sphere of Euro-Atlantic civilization. I also wanted this summit, in particular, to stand out from all the others in the memories of the politicians who took part, one that, thanks to its dramatic structure and atmosphere, they would remember as a truly historic meeting.

I think we succeeded. Whenever I meet a president or a foreign minister or another official who was there, they always remark on how extraordinarily successful that meeting was. Its climax was a gala dinner for several hundred people in the Gothic Vladislav Hall in the Prague Castle. We relied on my Castle architect, Bořek Šípek, to design an inventive lighting scheme and decor for the hall; I commissioned an original work from the musician and composer Michal Pavlíček: it was called *A Celebration of Freedom* and it was a medley of Schiller's "Ode to Joy," the "Marseillaise," the American spiritual "Freedom," John Lennon's anti-establishment song "Power to the People," and Smetana's *Vltava Suite*. It was played by symphony orchestra musicians, rock musicians, and sung by both opera and rock singers; it was performed at the end of the dinner and lasted not quite half an hour, and everyone present was wildly enthusiastic, from presidents Bush and Chirac to my friends Adam Michnik and Bronisław Geremek. Prague, the Czech public, and the state treasury survived the summit intact.

They also presented me with a diploma signed by the heads of all the NATO member states in recognition of my services. I didn't know that this was going to happen and I was very moved. This diploma is, I hope, hanging in my underground "corridor of fame" at home, where I put all my diplomas.

Hrádeček, November 30, 2005

In ten months I will be seventy. I'm quite focused on that date. I would like to be able to put a full stop after one stage of my life, or at least a semicolon. I'm someone who needs deadlines or horizons to aim for; otherwise I flounder in an endless wash of time. I'd like not only to finish writing what I'm writing now by that birthday, but, if possible, to write the play as well. On my birthday it's become a tradition to award the prize of our foundation Vize '97; this time we are presenting it to the marvelous Oxford-based Anglo-Polish thinker Zygmunt Bauman. Shortly after that, we will celebrate the tenth anniversary of Forum 2000, an annual conference on the present state of the world that I started and that takes place every year in Prague. Immediately after that, Dáša and I would like to go for another extended trip to the USA. At this point I would have no immediate tasks ahead of me. I would get out of many of my responsibilities, and I would try to observe the world quite freely.

The last time I saw Jan Patočka, the great Czech philosopher, in a kind of waiting room in the Ruzyně prison where we were both being interrogated about Charter 77 and where they kept me overnight, he told me: you're not going to believe me, but life is awfully long. I was somewhat surprised at the time, but now that I'm approaching Patočka's age, I have the same feeling, and it's a feeling I've had rather often in my life. Yesterday, as I was looking up one of my juvenile poems in my collected works, I got to reading other bits of that particular volume and suddenly the 1950s came back to me, along with vivid memories of my literary beginnings. In my mind's eye a procession of my closest friends paraded by, led by the poet Jiří Kuběna. And I felt as though I were back in that period; I began to breathe its air, touch its realities, its illusions, and its truths, and I saw not only those times, but my self, my self both as I was then and as I am now. I was quite derailed. Suddenly I was fifty years younger! Suddenly a thousand long-forgotten things arose in my mind, and I experienced again my own long-forgotten torments with the mystery of space-time to which I devoted so many of my early poems. Yes, everything is somehow strangely connected to everything else: the play that I'm constantly thinking about, this digest of my recent experiences and current thoughts, the glance into my ancient poems, the feeling that I will never complete anything because it's getting too late; and naturally the terrifying list of everything in my life that I could have done differently and better, or that I might have done but didn't. And along with that is the contrary feeling that no more could have been accomplished, that what's done is, in fact, enough, and that everything fits together rather well and there's no more to add to it, that I have nothing to complain about, and that every complaint is really an expression of disgusting vanity. But, not to rattle on: what will Mr. Hvížďala ask me about now? Aha! The European Union.

Let's move on to the European Union. You're known as a great friend and proponent of this institution, and, in fact, you could even be called a Euroenthusiast. Doesn't it seem to you that Europe is in a deep crisis, particularly after the rejection of its constitution by France and Denmark? Or that it might even be a great historical mistake based on the illusion that you can unify the un-unifiable?

In one of his books, Ortega y Gasset argues persuasively that Europe is, and has always been, a single political entity, regardless of how complex it may be internally. But who created its internal political order? Naturally it has always been the larger, the more powerful, the stronger entities, and that order was always imposed by force, usually on battlefields, and frequently with other kinds of pressure or blackmail. So these several postwar decades—during which Europe has tried to build its internal political order voluntarily, on just and democratic foundations, on the principle of equality, mutual respect, following the path of dialogue, not the path of violence—can therefore be seen as a truly unique period in history. Obviously it's an immensely important effort, not only for Europe but for the whole world. Two of the worst wars in the history of humanity had to break out on European soil, and Europe had to drag the whole world into these conflicts, before it finally understood that this way leads only to hell. The great men who started the unification process in Europe understood that this unique and richly variegated political entity must be structured in a different way, which meant, among other things, shifting the debate about its structure from the battlefield to the congress halls. More often than not these men may have found themselves in a minority, or they may not have acted in harmony with the will of their majorities, but at the time they were able to get away with it, perhaps because they were not, as today's politicians are, in thrall to the all-powerful mass media and to daily opinion polls.

I am not, as you have suggested, a Euroenthusiast. I am merely aware of the enormous historical importance of what has been going on in Europe for a long time. Viewed against the backdrop of these historical facts, the question of whether the common constitution—and it's clear that there has to be one sooner or later—will be approved now or in ten years, and in which form it will be approved, is, on the whole, a trivial detail.

By the way, I would like to see a different constitution from the one that is currently stalled. It should be ten times shorter, it should be written in a human, nonbureaucratic language, and it should be easy enough for children to learn in school. In this sense, America could provide an example to Europe. Of course, it is important that the tons of agreements that make up the union today be boiled down into a single text, though it would be almost unreadable. Nevertheless, in my opinion, that text should form an adjunct or an appendix to the constitution, something to which the constitution could refer, but which would not necessarily be the same as the popular version.

But I would also see the institutional structure of the European Union somewhat differently, as something simpler and more transparent than it is today. I have spoken about this on various occasions, and it was always positively received, be it in the European, French, or Italian parliaments, yet I admit that my notions are still somewhat utopian. But it's interesting that the "shadow" foreign minister of the ODS, who once criticized my suggestions, recently expressed agreement with them.

Am I to understand that you have no reservations about the present work and direction of the European Union?

Not at all! I have very fundamental reservations, but they are completely different from the reservations of most of today's Euroskeptics.

What are they?

I can't help feeling that the European Union today is letting itself be dragged, with no resistance, in the same general direction as the rest of global civilization; it's driven by the idea of growth, growth for the sake of growth, the creation of profit at any price, development and prosperity, although unfortunately utterly one-dimensional. The main goal of Europe today is to catch up with and surpass the United States. This seems to me to be a very poor choice of goals. Modern technology and consumer civilization have their deep origins in Europe; Europe once aggressively imposed its modern values on the entire planet, and thus it set in motion the ambiguous momentum that today we call globalization. Europe no longer has a mission to impose anything on this planet anymore, and anyway, it's beyond its powers to do so. But Europe could certainly do more than just blindly keeping step and trying to "catch up to and surpass" someone in matters common to everyone. Europe could be an inspiration, an example of how to try to think not only of quantity but also of quality, how not to think merely about momentary short-term material success but also about qualitative, indirect, long-term success, to revive the tradition of responsibility for the world that its culture once helped to articulate.

In short: the European Union today seems to me terribly technocratic and materialistic. Perhaps there is within it—or rather within its western half—more regard for civic culture, for human rights, for economic justice, for nonrenewable resources, or for the environment in general, than there is in our country. But even there it falls very short of what we should appropriately expect. It can't create an identity by chasing after global economic success, or even just by lagging behind. I think it has more to contribute. It might provide an example, not only of a peaceful and just political system within one continent, but also of how to treat one's own traditions, one's own culture, one's own landscape, one's own resources, with intelligence and sensitivity. It seems to me that Europe is in danger of losing its spiritual dimension in a flood of trivial concerns, such as what kind of tariffs ought to be imposed. It's as though some fundamental discourse about the direction of the world today were lacking, a discourse about the dangers inherent in that direction, and the role that this unique community of nations can play against this planetary background.

Aren't you afraid that in the unifying European environment there will be a loss of national identity?

It doesn't seem to me that the individuality of towns, cities, regions, or national customs is somehow vanishing from Europe. Portugal is and always will be different from Sweden, for example. And the European Union and its institutions are certainly not trying to suppress individuality; in fact, I would even say that its norms protect such differences. If anything threatens uniqueness today, it's modern civilization as a whole. After all, at moments it's almost impossible to know whether you're in an airport in Tokyo, a hotel lobby in Los Angeles, or a hypermarket on the outskirts of Prague. The pressure toward soulless uniformity that is perceptible everywhere today—despite the seemingly endless array of choices among a seemingly infinite array of products pretending to be different from one another—poses a great threat to all forms of uniqueness. Without even being aware of it we are subtly made more alike and, at the same time, through modern technology (both in transportation and information) we are all pushed closer together, which can lead to revolts by those who feel their uniqueness threatened, and these revolts are—often by proxy—sorted out through regional or local conflicts or by terrorist attacks. But let's call the causes of all this by their proper names. We can't very well uncritically applaud the consumer society and its omnipresent dictatorship and at the same time blame the decline of diversity on the European Union. The EU can be admonished only for doing what everyone else is doing: succumbing to the dictates of civilization, whose best-known representative is the multinational corporation.

Do you think that Turkey or Ukraine belong in the European Union?

In the past, Russia caused a great deal of suffering to many nations and ultimately to the entire world by, among other things, never knowing precisely where it began and where it ended. I think that the European Union should not repeat this Russian error, and that it should very quickly clarify how far it wishes to, or can, reach.

The EU is defined not merely by values but also by geography. In my opinion it ought to be open to the Western European countries that have still not been included, to all the Balkan states, to Belarus and Ukraine. And, if the European Union is not to become another United Nations, that is where it should end. Of course it's another question as to whether these countries will wish to join, and of course, whether—and when—they will fulfill all the requirements of membership. But it seems to me that from the Baltic states, which are already members, there is a clear line along the Belorussian-Russian and the Ukrainian-Russian borders. Russia is clearly an entity unto itself, an enormous Euro-Asian empire, practically as large as two Europes put together. This entity needs to have an excellent partnership with the European Union, but it's nonsense to talk about Russian membership in it. That would destabilize and ultimately destroy the union. And by the way, it is no disgrace not to belong to the EU, just as it is not a disgrace not to be in NATO. New Zealand is not in the European Union, but this doesn't bother it in the slightest, even though it is closer in its values than many new members or candidate members. But that can't be helped: along with the yardstick of values there must also be a generally respected yardstick of geography, otherwise it would be an invitation to misfortune.

And what about Turkey?

I don't like the way Turkey is always being led about by the nose. For several decades, it was good for the West because it was an important co-defender of its security—it was not without risk that Turkey allowed rockets aimed at the Soviet Union to be based on its soil—and for several decades, as a member of NATO, it has shared Western values. Now that the danger has passed, it's suddenly not good enough for us. The fact that it's an Islamic country is an issue I wouldn't bring into it. The European Union is not a religious community, and there was a time when Islam played a part in creating European cultural traditions. I think that it should continue to be a strictly technical question: when Turkey fulfills all the conditions of membership, it will simply become a member.

The old member states have contributed significantly to the development of the new members who are all less evolved because of long years of communist rule. Do you think that we can ever pay them back? What do you say when you are reminded of this subsidization?

I think that we have an opportunity to pay them back in a certain way already, and one can even see situations in which we are already doing this. I'm thinking about our political voice. The European Union occasionally still suffers from the old European disease, which is the tendency to make compromises with evil, to close one's eyes to dictatorship, to practice a politics of appeasement or even of accommodation, vis-à-vis totalitarian systems, that is determined by economic interests. Some politicians, those who have not experienced fascism or communism, are incorrigible in that regard. I think that the new members of the European Union, who have a relatively recent experience of totalitarianism, are perhaps duty-bound to take a more principled position—should it occasionally be necessary—and to monitor the European Union in that regard, or educate it. It's in everyone's interest. Accommodating evil has, so far, never forced evil to retreat, or to become more humane; on the contrary, it has always made life easier for it. In the end, when confrontation came, the price that everyone had to pay was infinitely higher than the cost of a firm stance.

(April 5, 1998)

1) For two days I have carefully studied a suitcase full of correspondence and expert opinion concerning the drug law. In places it was incredibly interesting reading and in places quite boring and stereotypical, and it was definitely harder for me to decide after I'd done the read-

ing than it would have been without it. Nevertheless, I have finally decided what I thought I would decide from the very beginning: I am against the law. Naturally I'm not going to go through all the arguments here; that would mean adding another kilogram of paper to the pile. Just one interesting, though perhaps marginal, observation: from the many letters (. . .) if not from all of them, that argue for voting down the law, there radiates an enormously sympathetic spirit of tolerance, interest in the matter, concern for young people, understanding of the life of minorities, and of unconventional lifestyles, a spirit of compassion, a spirit of respect for human rights and the dignity of human beings, etc., etc., etc. From letters and viewpoints that favor the law (and they are a tiny percentage of the whole, and mainly positions expressed by the executive branches including the police) there radiates quite a different spirit: anger, hatred, reactionary sentiments. Example: while the former never attack anyone, the latter are constantly referring to "pseudo-experts who have conspired with the narco-mafia" and have "unleashed a campaign." The writing was bad. It was bureaucratic, communistic, journalistic hate-mongering—and left you with the impression that if anyone has conspired with anyone, it's been the clerical reactionaries conspiring with the police, who want to make life easy for themselves: they clearly imagine that they can perform an endless series of personal searches around schools, or in alleyways, or in discotheques, that they will occasionally find something on someone and be able to demonstrate statistically the success of their war on drugs. In reality, however, it will all be completely counterproductive; it will drive a third of the young people away from the state and into some seductive underground catacombs, and the results are not hard to imagine: in a couple of years the patriotism of the next generation will sink to a historic low. The dealers will only mock us and go on merrily raising their prices and buying off the police.

Now the only concern is how my veto should be formulated for the Chamber of Deputies and how the press release will be worded. On the first question: perhaps it would be enough for me to write that, after a thorough consideration of all aspects of the given amendments, I have come to the conclusion that the dangers that will accompany the law's application will outweigh the advantages it will bring. And that it could lead to the prosecution of the victims rather than the perpetrators. And that it also has some legal faults (one example may stand in for all of them: another substance has been slipped into the list of weapons and radioactive materials, the mere possession of which can be criminal; this is too abrupt a departure from the legal relations and the system of rights and freedoms of the citizen to be simply smuggled in in this underhanded way). (. . .) As far as the press release is concerned, that should not be published until the matter is with the Chamber of Deputies. It should probably be somewhat longer. For example: after a detailed study of all the relevant expert reports, official positions, transcriptions of the debates in both houses of parliament, and the correspondence which he has received, the president has decided to return the amendments to the Chamber of Deputies. He believes the law will cause more harm than good, that it's a deviation from the Czech conception of antidrug policy, and that it represents too abrupt a departure from the existing system of civil rights and freedoms, that it puts users and addicts at a disadvantage without strengthening the sanctions against the genuinely guilty parties, and that it has not been formulated properly. The president is in favor of an amendment to the Criminal Code in this matter, and he is even in favor of increasing the sentences for drug dealing, or rather for dealing, importing, and exporting, etc., but at the same time he is in favor of doing it properly. (. . .)

(April 11, 1999)

(. . .)

8) We need a longer hose for watering. (. . .)

(July 10, 1996)

Preliminary ideas: (. . .)

3) The framework program: Wednesday: the guests arrive, check in. Thursday, Friday, Saturday: during the day the conference sessions, late afternoon and evening, the cultural program: a reception (Vladislav Hall), a multicultural concert (Vladislav Hall or the Municipal House), a tour of the Castle, a tour of Prague, etc. Sunday morning: a multireligious "mass" in the cathedral. Afternoon, departure.

4) The participants: (a) fifty to a hundred main guests from around the world. (b) a certain number of delegates to accompany them (wives, assistants, etc.). (c) fifty Czech participants, political scientists, sociologists, etc. (most likely as observers). (d) an undetermined number of journalists and representatives of the media from around the world and from home. Accommodation and travel will be paid only for the main guests, and if necessary to those accompanying them.

5) Title: Forum 2000. (Commission a logo from Skalník as soon as possible!)

6) Place: everything will take place in the Castle. Here is how I see it: the main locale throughout the conference will be the Spanish Hall, appropriately decorated by Bořek Šípek. In the center will be the first circle, or rather oblong (tables, chairs, microphones). Only the main guests will sit here. Around this first circle will be a second circle (on risers, with a podium). This is for the assistants and their delegations and the Czech observers. Around the second circle there will be a third and highest circle where the media will be located (for the entire conference). Throughout the event, the Rudolf Gallery will be set up as a large restaurant (many small round tables), where the guests will have lunch, and confer. (. . .)

10) The themes or questions to be addressed by the conference: (a) Ecological dangers facing humanity and the planet. (b) Population explosion. (c) Social disparities in the world. (d) The boom in armaments. (e) "Conflicts of civilizations and cultures"; religious and national conflicts. (f) All of these subjects are dealt with in huge thematic summits in the U.N. and hundreds of other conferences. What do these various threats to the world have in common? What connects them? Can they be dealt with in isolation? (g) Is it true that the most profound key to the human ability to somehow confront these threats lies in the area of the spirit, of human consciousness, of the creation of a global sense of responsibility? (h) Is it true that in the roots of all civilizational, cultural, and religious spheres or worlds there is something common, to which attention can be drawn and out of which a spirit of global responsibility may grow? Is it true that the deepest root of such responsibility is metaphysical? (i) Human rights: To what degree are they universal and to what degree can we demand respect for them from everyone? (j) The world order as a "technical" expression of this new spirit of global

responsibility: the importance of regional structures (between the nation-state and worldwide associations), such as the European Union, the Commonwealth of Independent States, NATO, the Association of Southeast Asian Nations, the Asia-Pacific Economic Council, etc. Reform of the U.N.: the significance of other world organizations. (k) What can concretely be done to stimulate a new and more responsible relationship of people (politicians, governments, nations) to the fate of the planet as a whole? (. . .)

12) Conclusion: the whole conference might later be published as a book. If the conference is successful, it might be decided to hold it regularly in different places in the world. A manifesto, or declaration, could be quietly prepared. It would be secret. Only if the proper situation for it arose, and most participants expressed the willingness to support some kind of final appeal, could we then come out with it and begin to edit it in a small circle of people.

You've always had a reputation for being a very peace-loving and tolerant person, almost a pacifist—as an author of essays, as a dissident, as a leader of the Velvet Revolution, and as president. But in our conversations you have made it clear, for instance, that you supported the NATO intervention against Milošević's rump Yugoslavia, and the more recent attack of the international coalition on Iraq. How do you reconcile these things?

You are right that all my life, both in fundamental matters and in day-to-day affairs, I have always preferred consensual resolutions, conversations, even compromises. Olga, in her time, held this against me and called it cowardice, and so does Dáša, and I have been criticized from different sides. Perhaps there is some truth to the notion that my distaste for confrontation is almost chronic. But I must add that I have always thought that my tolerance has limits, and at some point to refuse to cross that line might easily mean the betrayal of my own principles, the betrayal of friends, and the betrayal of myself. There are simply moments when you have to cry out "Enough!" and be prepared to use force to protect yourself against evil. It's unfortunate, but as long as people are merely people, it will obviously be necessary.

I recall how for a long time I was critical of the apathy of the international community to the events in Yugoslavia. I felt that an intervention would be necessary sooner or later, and that the sooner it was carried out, the fewer the sacrifices it would mean. I condemn the politics of appeasement; Czechoslovakia, and ultimately the whole world, had a direct experience of the suicidal nature of appeasement in the mid-twentieth century. A timely, well-coordinated, and decisive attack against Hitler could have saved millions of lives. I know how hard it is for a responsible person to decide whether to fight or not: the risk of suffering, pain, and the loss of life is something that he imposes upon others by his decision, very seldom on himself. Still, if you can't stand the heat, you shouldn't go into the kitchen. I will never forget my visit to Kosovo years ago: tens of thousands of families with their children, their animals, their bedding, and their wagons were returning over mountain roads, back to the homes from which they had been driven. Their gratitude to those who had intervened on their behalf was enormous. How often does it happen in history that half a million people who have been driven out of their homes return en masse six months later? In the matter of Bosnia and Herzegovina, as in other Yugoslavian conflicts, I was mostly in favor of timely intervention. To some I might have seemed at the time like a militarist, but I felt that intervention was the only way to prevent an infinitely greater misfortune. A certain kind of intervention is not only an expression of solidarity with one's suffering fellow citizens of this planet, but also an act of self-defense; we never know how great a conflict may grow out of a military confrontation, and who might ultimately be drawn into it. Let us recall that the First World War began in Sarajevo.

In your speeches, above all on the international scene, you've often dealt with questions like the so-called clash of civilizations, coexistence in the modern world, multiculturalism. Would you be able to briefly and simply formulate what in those matters would be your message to the world?

I have always thought about such questions, and I have enjoyed reading intelligent books dealing with them. In the last sixteen years, naturally, my interest in these themes has grown considerably, for the same reasons that I accepted a political position in Czechoslovakia. I knew that our task was not finished with the fall of the Iron Curtain and the end of the bipolar division of the world. On the contrary, it was only then that the main work began: seeking and creating a new order that would correspond to the real state of affairs in the twenty-first century. In other words: anyone who said A must also say B. And that was the reason for my endless ruminations on those themes.

I can understand that. But what is the gist of your thinking?

I think—and countless official travels around the globe have merely confirmed this—that the era in which the West, or the Euro-American sphere of civilization, could consider itself superior to other spheres has ended, or must end. Neither America, nor Europe, nor both of them together, can be masters of the world and the sole authors of how the planet is organized. It is true that it was in this sphere of civilization, and mainly from its traditions, that the present global civilization has grown; by which I mean the thin skin of it that covers the world. But that does not give anyone the right to hegemony.

The world today consists of several large civilizational or cultural spheres—which are at the same time geographic spheres—that share this "skin," which is partly an instrument of progress and development for everyone, and partly a tragic source of great misfortune for many. Be that as it may, if humanity is not to be decimated by enormous man-made catastrophes, it must—among other things—understand and accept the principle that all these cultural or civilizational spheres—what [Samuel] Huntington calls "civilizations"—are equal and enjoy the same rights.

Apart from the fact that I was constantly circling back to these themes in my speeches, I tried symbolically to indicate what I think in other ways as well. For example, in some distant countries, before visiting the seats of the local Europeanized or Americanized governments, I would always try to visit the original inhabitants—the Aborigines in

Australia, the Maoris in New Zealand, the Indians in Brazil, and the inhabitants of Easter Island during my visit to Chile. In addition, on state visits to some countries, I tried to leave the beaten path and explore places that were important or sacred to the local populations, though they were not often shown to foreigners, places like Benares in India. I believe that the only possible way to establish the fundamental principles of peaceful coexistence on our planet—the coexistence of citizens, their institutions, countries, and supranational regional associations and groupings—is on the basis of mutual respect on the part of these "civilizations," and respect for their absolute equality. Such principles, I believe, can be created only within the framework of a common moral minimum, that is, within the framework of moral principles that are common to all cultural and religious traditions. And there are more than a few of them! After all, the injunctions not to steal or kill apply everywhere, and everywhere the moral order is in some way related to the idea of eternity. In any case, it's been shown time and again that without that relationship to eternity, any moral order will always necessarily collapse.

Have you ever tried to put these basic ideas, which are certainly shared by many others besides yourself, into a political document that would carry more weight than a speech? I heard that you tried unsuccessfully to do something like that in the U.N.

I myself never tried to do anything on my own initiative. Nevertheless, in 1995, when the fiftieth anniversary session of the U.N., to which all the heads of state would be invited, was approaching, Madeleine Albright asked me in confidence to try writing a short, inspirational manifesto that the U.N. might adopt on this occasion, and which would be an expression of a general agreement on how we ought to go forward living together on this earth. So I tried to summarize my ideas in a short text which, of course, if I remember correctly, concluded with several concrete suggestions for the U.N. Madeleine liked it a lot and she said that other people from different countries to whom she showed it privately liked it as well, but they all agreed that there was no hope of its ever being adopted. Each of the almost two hundred member states of the U.N. would want to add something of their own—many merely for reasons of prestige—so that the outcome could only be a large pot of amorphous porridge that wouldn't be worth struggling for.

This otherwise meaningless little anecdote says something about the complexities, not just of the U.N., but probably of all international organizations. Just for the sake of order, please don't confuse this confidential and unsuccessful initiative with my speech at the same plenary session of the U.N., in which I presented very daring and very concrete suggestions for reforming the U.N.

Hrádeček, December 2, 2005

I write and I write and I try to reply to questions, questions that I edit in my own way, and I try to find ways to say something complicated concisely. I think about how often I have said the same thing, and how much more precise it was when I said it before. I write and I write and I think, and at the same time I think most about Dáša, who is ill and in Prague. She has something wrong with her thyroid gland. She's exhausted, but at the same time she has fits of frantic activity and fits of disgust with me, which are often quite understandable and quite justified. It's a strange thing: of all the people that I'm close to or that I've ever known, Dáša has the biggest heart; she would give me, if I needed it, not only her kidney, not only her liver, not only her lungs, but even her leg. Her care for me, for Nina, for her mother, and for all those both close and farther away, has been limitless. But the bigger her heart is, the more I seem like a clod beside her. What's to be done? Dáša is my guardian, not only in that she's constantly pulling me back from my deathbed, but also her very existence and her radiance is constantly urging me on to further efforts. I'm afraid that if I didn't have her, I'd just be lying around staring at the ceiling.

(November 16, 2002)

(. . .)

g) In the name of the Czech Republic, I am happy to declare that we agree, fully and without reservation, that membership in NATO be today offered to these seven countries: Bulgaria, Estonia, Latvia, Lithuania, Romania, Slovakia, and Slovenia. We consider this expansion very important, not only because several medium-sized or smaller European countries will be given new guarantees for their defense and security or because these countries will accept their share of responsibility for peace and freedom in the large Euro-Atlantic sphere of civilization. Even more important is what this expansion means indirectly: it is a clear indication, not only for all Europeans but for the whole world, that the era of the violent division of the world into two spheres of influence, or even the subjugation of the weaker by the stronger, has definitively come to an end. The expansion by seven new members will be a great expression of confidence in the right of nations to freely decide which part of the world they wish to belong to and what relations they wish to form and cultivate.

i) (. . .) I have the honor and the delight at this moment to announce to you, in the name of the North Atlantic Alliance, that your countries have been summoned to membership in this defensive pact. Friends, I congratulate you, and I welcome you among us. I have the same feeling of joy as I had three years ago in Madrid when the alliance summoned my own country to membership. (. . .)

(October 4, 1993)

(. . .)

9) Please have Mrs. M. or E. prepare the pike from Lány that was given to me, in some very original way, with unique spicing, so the parliamentary five will not soon forget it.

How would you describe the basic experience you acquired during your thirteen years in the highest political office? Or what basic insights did you have?

Like most people, I suppose, I have always had a kind of irrational respect for people in high office. It is as though the position itself invested its holder with a special aura or magic halo. I even felt, somewhere deep within myself, a certain respect for the stupidest communist functionary who merely spouted rubbish. I felt he couldn't just have fallen into that position, that behind those idiotic speeches there must have been something I couldn't see, some very important skill that was invisible from the outside, otherwise he would never have made it that far. Sometimes this automatic deference went so far that when I myself appointed one of my friends or acquaintances as minister, willingly and on my own initiative—and that was how things happened in those early postrevolutionary days—I suddenly began to behave more politely toward him and take him more seriously.

If it is not taken to extremes, this respect for authority can be something of a good thing, especially today, when the media play such a decisive role and are willing and able to destroy reputations, even of those who don't deserve that kind of treatment. In fact, it may be the case that it's only thanks to this respect that some countries can still go on existing.

But why am I saying this? One of the first surprises when I found myself president was that the people I dealt with, whether in domestic politics or abroad, were exactly the same as anyone else, were in no way outstanding and sometimes were even more naive, less educated, and less civil than their fellow citizens who did not hold public office. There are a lot of things politicians don't know; they speak mostly about things that they have learned a short time before from briefing notes; they are jealous of each other; they're always looking around to see where the photographers are standing; and they subtly position themselves within range of their cameras, pretending that they just happen to be standing there; in places where there are a lot of them gathered together—for example, at various summits—those who are less famous and powerful jostle to be close to those who are more famous and powerful because they want it to appear at home as though they are having a friendly conversation. More than once I've seen how, at a reception, there has been a huge knot of people around the American or the Russian president, while other presidents were standing alone in a corner, either because no one knew them or because they didn't know anyone, or because there was no language in which they could converse with anyone, or simply because they wanted to have a quiet moment.

Another observation is related to that: not only are politicians quite ordinary people but their personal relationships play an immense role—perhaps greater than they should. When someone is drawn to someone else, when someone has a fond memory of being with someone else, perhaps at a party or in a pub, when they know a common language well enough to have a conversation without an interpreter, and when they have a common complaint, let's say, about someone, then the conditions are ideal for improving relationships between those two countries. Sometimes it even reminded me a little of the Middle Ages, when friendship or family ties between rulers could guarantee peace between their countries, or lead to their close cooperation, or even to their integration, whereas enmity, jealousy, or an unfortunate memory of a personal slight, on the contrary, could easily lead to military confrontation.

In all this, of course, I do not wish to say that I did not meet a lot of extraordinary people in the highest political spheres, people who were wise, brave, erudite, generous, and entertaining. It merely seems to me that there are no more and no less of such people in politics than anywhere else.

Do you have any real personal friends among politicians on the international scene?

I think that there are some whom I can consider my friends. Some of them are no longer in office, but we know each other well from those long-ago postrevolutionary times. Along with Bill and Hillary Clinton, George Bush Sr., the late President Mitterrand, Queen Beatrix, King Juan Carlos, Árpád Göncz, Mário Soares, and others, I would probably put Richard von Weizsäcker in the first place. He helped me a lot in the early days and I took him somewhat as my presidential mentor. One typical example: after everything that had happened between the Germans and the Czechoslovaks, and after years of so many sensitive taboos, it seemed to me that it would be a good thing to demonstrate in some highly visible way that a new era was beginning in our mutual relations. And so in February 1990, I came up with the idea of having President Weizsäcker come to Prague on March 15 for the anniversary of the German occupation and Hitler's arrival in the Prague Castle. My idea was to organize a large meeting in the Vladislav Hall, where I would say that, whereas fifty-one years ago an emissary of war stood in these precincts, today we welcome an emissary of peace. I telephoned Weizsäcker and suggested it to him and explained the reasons for it. He immediately recognized the symbolic significance of such a visit and agreed, without consulting any advisers or studying his schedule. It may not have been easy for him to do, politically, because after all, he would be recalling something that many would rather have forgotten, but he never hesitated for a minute, even though in normal countries an event in the presidential program is not scheduled like this at the last moment.

I remember that telephone conversation well because I had to make it from a bathtub. For reasons that were unclear, the former president's office was surrounded by several bathrooms that my secretariat was using as offices until the appropriate renovations could be done, and that phone call was put through to one of those bathrooms.

The visit was, I think, very successful, and it included a walk through Prague and a grand reception for just about everyone. For citizens accustomed to state visits with bulletproof cars streaking from the airport to the Castle and back with hundreds of policemen in attendance, Weizsäcker's visit was a mild sensation.

Did you discover something in office, something important in the political process, that you hadn't been aware of before? Or, to put it another way: what was your most interesting personal experience in your political dealings, either at home or abroad?

Again and again I realized how important it is to have a very ordinary thing: good taste. It's good taste above all that determines how long one should speak, how much one should reveal, how deeply one should probe; when to make a joke and when to speak seriously; when one should speak indirectly and when one should speak fully what one has in mind; how to make sure that the conversation does not languish and that your partner is comfortable.

None of that is easy. Sometimes you may be in a foul mood, or feel depressed, or have a hangover, and can only with great difficulty bring yourself to say something more or less coherent, anxiously awaiting the moment of salvation when the time allotted for the audience will finally be up. It's particularly difficult when your partner is laconic and you are speaking only to avoid a silence, or during audiences that are completely formal, when the only reason you're meeting someone at all is because protocol demands it, not because the two of you have something to discuss. Nonetheless, I must add that even during such boring and essentially disruptive visits, you may suddenly discover to your surprise that protocol has brought you together with an extraordinarily interesting person whom you would otherwise never have met.

It's not good, however, to have several such visits in quick succession and have no time in between to read or brush up on your briefing notes. In that case you can get your visits and their agendas mixed up, and it's very easy to make a faux pas, such as, for instance, when you ask the Spanish foreign minister to give your greetings to the Portuguese president, or the Cambodian ambassador to give your best wishes to the king of Thailand. On one state visit in a nearby European country, I had the opposite experience; my host filled a meeting scheduled for an hour with fifty-five minutes of introductory remarks. It was impossible to interrupt him. It was easier for me to remain silent and not try to make conversation, but something like this should not happen. But the whole thing was nothing more than a lack of taste on the part of my host. If I speak of "taste" in these circumstances, I obviously have in mind "taste" in the broadest sense of the word, and not just taste in ties.

(Undated, 1999)

Regarding the upcoming publication of my collected works:

(. . .)

4) (. . .) In general, regarding the speeches from the revolution: somewhere in the notes it should say that I wrote many of the collective texts (among them the introductory declarations of Charter 77 and VONS, several Charter documents, "Democracy for Everyone," i.e., the introductory declaration of HOS, "Several Sentences," etc.), but on principle I have never published them as my own work, and have never declared my authorship of them. In the case of the Civic Forum, however, it's different: it's impossible to draw a dividing line between what is "collective" and what is merely mine, because there was never any time to discuss these things and I had something like a "blank check"; I was the unofficial spokesman of the Civic Forum, so it's difficult to distinguish between what is an official document of the Civic Forum and what is a personal speech of mine. For the sake of historical logic and transparency, therefore, it is all being included. I think that such a note must be there, otherwise there will be objections that I have included the position of institutions in my own writings. I don't need to emphasize this in the case of the declarations from August 1968 because I've already revealed elsewhere, for example in *Disturbing the Peace*, that I wrote them, and in any case, everyone knew that and understood them to be my texts. (. . .)

5) The third volume seems to me the most problematic. I'm truly astonished that in my youth I used concepts such as "socialist art," "socialism," "capitalism," etc., and that I had made reference to various writers and party congresses, etc. Today it seems absurd. Perhaps a few words could be written about this in the notes. It occurs only in texts that were intended for publication (some of them were published, some were not). And that way of speaking or arguing was clearly a condition for publication; as a matter of fact it wasn't even possible to speak in public using any other language. By the expression "socialist art" I meant nothing more than art that was made in a communist state. But at the time no one worried about whether or not it represented a conceptual confusion. It was a kind of game people played. I don't really much understand it anymore, and as I read it, I was instantly shocked and my first reaction

was that it should be taken out. That, of course, was an improper response. Let it remain as a document of the time. And by the way, the thing I'm talking about appears only in texts from the late 1950s, and it belongs to that time. Before that, in the Dark Age, none of us felt the need to use these official words, and by the early 1960s, that was the case again. It was characteristic of that strange time, after the revelations about Stalin, which was such an incredible event that it clearly confused quite a few people. (. . .)

(June 7, 1994)

(. . .)

5) I would ask Mr. Řechtáček to repair and refill my lighter and send it back. (. . .)

We've already touched on so-called nonpolitical politics. As far as I know, this term was first used by President Masaryk, who had in mind the various small civic or public activities that citizens engaged in for the public good. You have explained your understanding of the term many times, but your notion of nonpolitical politics is still being held against you. Your critics clearly understand it as a kind of impractical dreaming, the invention of something new, as a lack of faith in political parties and standard approaches, as a kind of moralizing, and God knows what else. Would you like to come back to this subject at the end of our conversation? Can you, in a few sentences, formulate your general political credo, regardless of what anyone calls it?

What is meant by that much-used notion, "standard approaches"? I suspect it means turning the mediocre, the substandard, the banal, into an ideology. It's as though the ideal of good standard behavior were adaptation to the status quo, whatever that may be, because the mere existence of a status quo, and the fact that the majority is inclined to accept it, means in and of itself that it is good. At the same time, what we have here is resistance to any kind of independent thinking, and to the willingness to make sacrifices for one's ideals, or to take any risks whatsoever. The behavior that most people displayed during the "normalization" of the 1970s and 1980s—when people pretended to agree with the system in exchange for being allowed to enjoy small homey pleasures—has been made into a norm in the name of which everything that does not fit that norm becomes a target for ridicule. That's where the aversion to dissidents comes from. Dissidents did not behave like the majority; they were willing to speak the truth aloud and thus maintain the continuity of freethinking; they were not speculating about successful outcomes but were risking sacrifice and defeat. That kind of nonstandard behavior is not forgiven!

You ask about my political credo. I am an opponent of every obsession, because I consider obsessions the most dangerous of social phenomena. Thus I am also an opponent of market fundamentalism and dogmatism, for which the snide brigade have branded me a left-winger. But the law of profit does not guarantee anything meaningful in itself. I mention it here because market dogmatism is the part of the ideology of "standardness" that we've been talking about. I really don't know why I should, on the basis of an injunction from on high, choose a standard wife, a standard flat, amass money and material goods in the standard way, and think in a standard fashion. And I don't know why, as a politician, I should have a duty to fly the flag of standardness. Either I persuade the public that my minority opinion is meaningful, and so gain their confidence, or I will go my own way and not be hurt.

I could formulate my credo another way: I think that the moral order stands above the legal, political, and economic orders, and that these latter orders should derive from the former, and not be techniques for getting around its imperatives. And I believe that this moral order has a metaphysical anchoring in the infinite and the eternal.

In this connection, I cannot avoid asking you how you see the political situation in the Czech Republic.

The leading role of the Communist Party, imposed by force and accorded allegiance everywhere, has left deep grooves in the social consciousness, and many people—without realizing it—still harbor some respect for this principle, which means that they are always seeking a political institution that will ease their way to success. Today, of course, the situation is radically different: we have more than one large and influential party; there is a choice, and there is no direct or open demand that you belong to one party or another. Nevertheless, residues of this old principle undoubtedly survive both in the system and in people's feelings: first you have to join a party, and once you're there, you get close to someone, and then you look around for a better position.

The party that entered this groove most smoothly was the ODS. People are always telling me how cleverly former communist managers were sometimes able to take control of local ODS organizations, and how many careerists from the period of normalization have continued their careers under this new banner. The size and strength of the ODS derive, among other things, from the fact that its founders sensed where to position themselves at the crucial moment and what to offer. In saying this, of course, I don't want to impugn the numerous achievements of hundreds of members of this party; who knows how much worse things might have been in this country had there been no ODS. It offered the country an unsentimental capitalism, which was, perhaps, good at a certain moment.

But now the situation is different. A younger generation is growing up for whom the language of our politicians is quite alien. Not only that: many people today are tired of those same big parties, the same faces, the same squabbles, the same deals; they don't want to vote and they are losing interest in politics. Anyone who offered these people a genuinely interesting and persuasive alternative could easily get at least 20 percent of the vote in the next general elections. But that probably won't happen. People who would like to go that way, and who have so far supported small extraparliamentary parties, be they liberal or green, on the one hand, or have gotten involved in the rich spectrum of civic initiatives on the other, are obviously incapable of working together. Too bad. The revolt against postcommunism has been postponed.

You've spoken a lot about postcommunism. In your essay "The Power of the Powerless," written almost thirty years ago, you used the word "postdemocratic." What did you mean by that?

It's something like "nonpolitical politics." I used the word only once, in quotation marks, in a particular context, and, in fact, metaphorically. It was the opposite of a similarly situational concept I used in that essay, that is, "post-totalitarianism." By postdemocracy I meant nothing more, and nothing other, than a democracy that has once again been given human content, which is to say that it is not just formal, not just institutional, not just an elegant mechanism to ensure that although the same people govern, it appears as though the citizens are themselves choosing them again. I may have been naive, but I was merely explaining then what I still think to this day, and more urgently than ever: that if everything is not to turn out badly for us, we will need a revolution of "heads and hearts," as Masaryk called it, a kind of general awakening, an emphasis on seeking an alternative to the established and already shopworn and very technocratic political parties, or at least a crying out for their inner renewal; an effort to rid them of their hidden, subtle, and omnipresent power, which itself is a denial of the principles of representative democracy; an emphasis on the development of an open civil society and on the reconstruction of transparent human communities as an instrument of human solidarity and self-regulation; an emphasis on long-term interests and on the spiritual and moral dimensions of politics—all of those are simply aspects or consequences of the same fundamental ideal, which of course is not complicated in the least. It is simply the extrication of the human race from the self-destructive and automatic collapse of civilization.

CHAPTER SEVEN

Hrádeček, December 5, 2005

I'm running away. I'm running away more and more. I find various excuses to run from my study, downstairs into the kitchen where I tidy up, listen to the radio, wash the dishes, cook a meal, think something over, or simply sit in my old place by the window and stare out. What I'm running away from is writing. But it's more than that. I'm running away from the public, from politics, from people. Perhaps I'm even running away from the woman who saved my life. Above all, I'm probably running away from myself.

What am I actually afraid of? Hard to say. What's interesting is that although I am here alone—and will continue to be here alone because no one that I know of has plans to visit—I keep the house tidy; I have everything in its place, everything has to be aligned with everything else, nothing can be left hanging over the edge of a table, or be crooked. At the same time the refrigerator must always be filled with a variety of food that I can scarcely eat myself, and there must be fresh flowers in the vases. In other words, it's as though I were constantly expecting someone to visit. But who? The unknown and unannounced guest? A strange and beautiful woman who admires me? My savior, who likes to show up unannounced? Some old friends? Why is it that I don't want to see anyone, and at the same time I'm always expecting someone, someone who will really appreciate that everything is in its proper place and properly aligned?

I have only one explanation: I am constantly preparing for the last judgment, for the highest court from which nothing can be hidden, which will appreciate everything that should be appreciated, and which will, of course, notice anything that is not in its place. I'm obviously assuming that the supreme judge is a stickler like me. But why does this final evaluation matter so much to me? After all, at that point I shouldn't care. But I do care because I'm convinced that my existence—like everything that has ever happened—has ruffled the surface of Being, and that after my little ripple, however marginal, insignificant, and ephemeral it may have been, Being is and always will be different from what it was before. All my life I have simply believed that what is once done can never be undone and that, in fact, everything remains forever. In short, Being has a memory. And thus even my insignificance—as a bourgeois child, a laboratory assistant, a soldier, a stagehand, a playwright, a dissident, a prisoner, a president, a pensioner, a public phenomenon, and a hermit, an alleged hero but secretly a bundle of nerves—will remain here forever, or rather not here, but somewhere. But not, however, elsewhere. Somewhere here.

It's still not clear to me whether or not you regret having accepted the highest office in the land sixteen years ago.

I don't know if I regret it. It depends. Sometimes I try to imagine all the things that might have been had I not accepted the post. For example, I might have read dozens if not hundreds of interesting books that came out during that period. I could have traveled and seen a great deal; I could have kept much more closely in touch with what was going on in the theater and literature; I could have written some more plays; I could have expressed my opinions on things much more freely without being burdened, twenty-four hours a day, by the very special responsibility that comes with that job; I would not have had a notoriously recognizable face, which has compelled me to check myself all the time and think about what someone might say or write about something I have done; I might have been in better health, and so on, and so on. That's the way I think in my weaker moments, of course, when—justifiably or not—I'm in a bad mood.

At other times, when I'm feeling better, I keep reminding myself that my thoroughly improbable life has been an enormous gift. I think of the many interesting people I have known from up close, from politicians who are making history, to the most famous Hollywood stars, to astronauts; of the many historic events I have been able to see into from up close and perhaps even directly influence; and of how essentially undeserved it all was.

If you had known in November 1989 that you would be president for such a long time, and what it would entail, and what awaited you, would you still have agreed to be a candidate?

Of course, I would have laughed at the whole idea.

Is it a good thing you didn't know?

Whether it was a good thing for the country or for the world is really a question that others must answer. For me, it was an immensely interesting experience interwoven with so many strange tribulations that I'm simply unable to describe them. In the end it's not important.

Hrádeček, December 8, 2005

The day before yesterday I had heart palpitations. They were quite strong and lasted a long time and were very unpleasant. My pulse rate was 160. Then yesterday, for a change, I couldn't sleep, and in fact I lay awake all night, but at the same time I couldn't read or write, so I tossed and turned and suffered. Moreover, the weather here is miserable, certainly no winter wonderland. The worst of it all is, of course, that Dáša in Prague is sicker than I am. She feels awful and she also has heart troubles and she is supposed to be staying in bed, something she is incapable of. Tomorrow I'm going back to be with her. But why, in fact, am I describing the state of my health? Perhaps because I keep thinking how absurd it is that a wreck like me is the laureate of dozens of the highest state honors from various countries in the world, with honorary doctorates from the most prominent world universities. It's strange, but ulti-

mately it must have had its own logic—after all, no one was incredibly upset by it.

(Undated, 2001)

1) Find out if Kraus got his—he hasn't replied—
2) Send new people the old invitation—
3) Send a new invitation to old invitees, apart from Kraus—
4) When the newly invited reply, send them the old invitation—
5) A nicer list—

Recently, there was speculation that you might run for president again in 2008. What do you make of that?

Of course I'm pleased that there are people who still have confidence in me and would like to see me in the Castle once again. I don't understand this as a consequence of some exceptional love they have for my person, but as a way of identifying with the values I represent, which means they have a somewhat different concept of the world and politics from what prevails today. Theoretically, I might be able to stand for the presidency. According to the constitution no one can hold the presidential office more than two consecutive terms, but after a hiatus he might actually come back for another term; I know that it's happened in several other countries. In reality, however, it's out of the question. If, after having run for this office several times with great hesitation, and only after intense efforts to persuade me, and having clearly said that I was leaving office for good—really and truly—I would be an absolutely absurd figure were I once again to broach that possibility. It would simply be too laughable.

But that's not the main reason. I really think that political conditions in this country have gone stale, and one of the ways out of this is to clear the way for younger, newer, fresher, and uncompromised people, to open politics to new blood, to a fresh wind and new ideas. The Klauses, the Zemans, and the Havels, as members of a generation that was deformed in one way or another by communism, and as the main figures in the long phase of Czech postcommunism, now deservedly belong in retirement. Something has to change. When I spoke about this several times in the newspaper or on television I named people I thought might be able to fill the presidential office: Rut Kolínská and Simon Pánek. These are people who, for years and years, have worked without personal gain in the nonprofit sector, and who, with no claim to fame, are helping their fellow human beings at home and around the world; they obviously have all the necessary qualifications, such as an appropriately broad view of things; they know languages; they have the social graces, etc. At first the idea was ridiculed as purely utopian, or as a provocation—after all, orthodoxy would have it that not only the president, but every public official as well, must come out of the womb of some political party. Nevertheless it's changed a little over time, and fewer people are laughing at the idea now. In any case, it seems far less insane than the idea that I should be president once was, back in 1989.

But there are other factors: my age, my health, my general state of exhaustion. Not to mention how improbable it is that today's parliament, or any other parliament with a similar makeup, would ever elect me.

I still don't understand how someone with so many doubts about himself, so little self-confidence, who constantly subjects himself to self-criticism, could achieve so many things in life, and be generally considered as an incisive, forceful, active, and successful individual.

"I sometimes ask myself whether I did not originally begin to write, and in general to try to achieve something, only to overcome my essential experience of inappropriateness, or of embarrassment, or of not belonging, or simply of absurdity, and in order to be able to live with those feelings." That, as you will recognize, is a quote from *Disturbing the Peace*. Both there, and mainly in my letters from prison written a few years before that, I deal with this subject in a broad way. I talk about how as a little boy I was awkward and clumsy, and therefore always straggled along behind the others, about how intensely aware I always was of the various social barriers between myself and my environment, and that, in fact, the main motor of my efforts and the drive behind my activities was an attempt to find my place among others, to be their equal, and not to suffer from being different.

As you can see, for years I've been asking myself the same question you're asking me now. Rather than having to repeat myself, or risk saying things less articulately now than I did then, but also to emphasize a certain continuity in my thinking, not only about the world but about myself, I will, if you will allow me, quote a little more from *Disturbing the Peace*. (. . .) "[M]y life, my work, my position, everything I've done, seems intertwined with a suspiciously large number of paradoxes. Take this one for instance: I get involved in many things, yet I'm an expert in none of them. Over the years, for example, I've become known as a political activist, but I've never been a politician, never wanted to be one: I don't have any of the necessary qualities for it. Both my opponents and my supporters see me as a political phenomenon, though nothing I do can be considered real politics. Every once in a while I philosophize—yet what kind of a philosopher am I anyway? Certainly I've enjoyed reading philosophical books since my youth, but my philosophical education is more than shaky and thoroughly piecemeal."

(October 30, 2000)

(. . .)

2) Clean the disgusting rugs by the elevator from the tunnel. Prince, when he saw it, vomited—

"I occasionally write about literature—yet if there's anything I most certainly am not, it's a literary critic. . . . Even in what I would consider my chief, original vocation, the theater, I'm not really an expert. . . . And rather than be a dramaturge in any old theater just because I've been trained to be one, I'd prefer to go back to working in a brewery. In any case, as a dramatist I'm somewhat suspect: I can write in my own highly particular way, within the limits of my narrowly defined poetics, but if I had to write something that even slightly departed from that I would probably fail miserably.

"In general, then, though I have a presence in many places, I don't really have a firm predestined place anywhere, in terms of neither my employment, nor my expertise, nor my education, nor my upbringing, nor my qualities and skills. . . . The list of my private paradoxes, however, doesn't end here. It's just the beginning. Some others, at random: I have chosen a rather agitated way of life and I myself am always ruffling the surface somewhere, yet I long for nothing more than peace and quiet. I have an extraordinary love of harmony, comfort, agreement, and friendly mutual understanding between people. . . . Tension, conflict, misunderstanding, uncertainty, and confusion upset me; yet my position in the world has been, and continues to be, deeply controversial. I've been in conflict with the state . . . all my life; my reputation is that of an eternal rebel and protester, to whom nothing is sacred, and even my plays are anything but a picture of peace and harmony. I am very unsure of myself, almost neurotic. I tend to panic easily; I'm always terrified of something, scared even when the telephone rings; I'm plagued by self-doubts and I'm always masochistically blaming or cursing myself for something; yet I appear to many . . . as someone who is sure of himself, with an enviable equanimity, quiet, levelheaded, constant, persistent, down-to-earth, always standing up for himself. I am rational and systematic; I love order and orderliness; I am disciplined and reliable, at times almost bureaucratically pedantic; at the same time I am oversensitive, almost a little sentimental, someone who's always been drawn by everything mysterious, magic, irrational, inexplicable, grotesque, and absurd, everything that escapes order and makes it problematic."

(October 30, 2000)

(. . .)

2) Clean the disgusting rugs by the elevator from the tunnel. Prince, when he saw it, vomited—

"I'm a sociable person who likes being with people, organizing events, bringing people together; a cheerful fellow, sometimes the conversational life of the party, one who enjoys drinking and the various pleasures and trespasses of life—and at the same time I'm happiest when alone and consequently my life is a constant escape into solitude and quiet introspection. . . . I write mercilessly skeptical, even cruel plays—and yet in other matters I behave almost like a Don Quixote and an eternal dreamer, foolishly struggling for some ideal or another. At my core I'm shy and timid—and yet in some forums I'm notorious as a rabble-rouser who is not afraid to say the toughest things right to someone's face."

Hrádeček, December 9, 2005

I remember my friend the great but little-known Czech philosopher Josef Šafařík, who spent about twenty years writing his last book—it was called The Journey to Final Things. *He wrote it, you might say, in blood; he was always rewriting it and he was never finished. His other friends and I tried to persuade him to let it go, that it was important that it exist and circulate, but he wouldn't listen. Meanwhile conditions changed and his book was actually able to be published by a proper publisher. On the very day that they brought him the first copy from the publishers, he died. Clearly, the moment he had completed his life's work, his life lost its meaning. Perhaps unconsciously, he*

had held back from completing it so that he would still have a reason to live,
and therefore he went on living.

(November 14, 1993)

(. . .)

5) On the door to my office there is the name of a secretary who hasn't
worked for me for months, and the name of Lenka Š. is not there. Please
change it immediately! In one of the most public places which heads of
state and all the delegations pass when coming to see me, that is, by the
pistoleers' table in the corridor at the entrance to the Plečnik Room,
there are three (why three?) disgusting old-fashioned telephones—each
of them, moreover, different—as well as an ugly table lamp. Please get
rid of them immediately. I don't understand why there are hundreds of
beautiful new telephones all over the Castle (many of them in rooms that
no one uses) and that in the only place that absolutely everyone can see,
there are these antediluvian monstrosities. Let there be one new, nice
telephone in the place of the existing three monstrosities. Let E. install
some pleasing lamp that would go with the decor. That corner mustn't
look like a waiting room in a regional police station circa 1971. (. . .)

(October 19, 1996)

(. . .)

10) (. . .) (b) The prime minister told me at Baryshnikov's ballet performance that we should certainly meet in the coming week; he says it
needn't involve lunch or dinner (for simplicity's sake). It appears from
my schedule that I don't even have a minute of time for the prime minister! This is a typical example of the systemic nonsense of my schedule.
Do it any way you want, but after November 1, something like this should
be absolutely unthinkable. I must, in principle, have one or two afternoons a week free for political meetings that cannot be planned in

advance and that are incomparably more important than most of the other items on my program. (Zieleniec, for example, wants to meet confidentially with me from time to time and I occasionally have to meet with Výborný, etc., etc. Sometime I ought to attend a cabinet meeting; we've had a new government for half a year now and I still haven't been there!) (c) Sometime we have to have a twenty-minute meeting in the Dalibor Oubliette (. . .) to agree on some of the details for the new furniture. (. . .)

"Or something else . . . for many people I'm a constant source of hope, and yet I'm always succumbing to depressions, uncertainties, and doubts, and I'm always having to look hard for my own inner hope and revive it, win it back for myself with great difficulty, so that I scarcely seem to have any to give away. So I'm not really comfortable in the role of the distributor of hope and encouragement to those around me, since I'm always on the lookout for some encouragement myself. I come across as one who is steadfast and brave, if not hardheaded, who did not hesitate to choose prison when far more attractive options were offered him—and there are times when I have to laugh at my reputation. The fact is I'm always afraid of something and even my alleged courage and stamina spring from fear; fear of my own conscience that delights in tormenting me for real and imagined failures. And all that heroic time in prison was in fact one long chain of worries, fears, and terrors: I was a frightened, terrified child, confusedly present on this earth, afraid of life, and eternally doubting the rightness of his place in the order of things; I probably bore prison worse than most of those who admired me would have."

(Undated, 2001)

1) Find out if Kraus got his—he hasn't replied—
2) Send new people the old invitation—
3) Send a new invitation to old invitees, apart from Kraus—

4) When the newly invited reply, send them the old invitation
5) A nicer list—

"Whenever I heard the familiar shout on the range, 'Havel!' I would panic. Once, after hearing my name yelled out like that, I jumped out of bed, confused, and cracked my skull on the window, and with all this, and despite all this, I know that if it were necessary I would go back to prison again, and I would survive.

"How does it all fit together? How are all these things related? Why don't these paradoxical qualities cancel each other out instead of co-existing and cooperating with each other? What does all this mean? What should I think about it all? How can I—this odd mix of the most curious opposites—get through life and, by all reports, successfully?"

So much for the quotation: what can I add to it after almost twenty years? Perhaps only to admit to astonishment that I can quote this today without feeling awkward about it, and more or less agree with it. And of course, astonishment at the wild twists and turns that my life took after that, the incredible things I encountered, and how all those paradoxes that I once talked about deepened. Yes, today I feel torn apart by the contradiction between my nature, my spiritual and nervous state, on the one hand, and the role that I play for so many people on the other. Isn't this something in the nature of a confidence trick? Perhaps not; perhaps one unwittingly supports the other: doubts grow out of actions, actions out of doubts.

Hrádeček, December 9, 2005

A new book by Madeleine has just arrived in my hermitage, and I'm bowled over: I simply don't understand how she can fulfill all her many public respon-sibilities, lecture at a university, travel about the world, and simultaneously, quickly write two thick and highly interesting books, full of quotations, exact memories, and references. Of course, she certainly has assistants. But I could have them as well without ever being able to achieve something like that. I'm from a different country, a different culture, a different tradition, I've had a different education. I have often said what a pity it was that from the first days of the revolution I didn't take time each evening to tape-record the things I had experienced that day and what I thought about them. Now I remember nothing, and so I leave it to historians to come up with a description and an analysis of the political events that I went through.

But what surprises and pleases me most is that I can find the thoughts I have today in things I wrote fifty years ago. Of course the younger I was, clearly, the more audacious I was, and also the unfortunate influence of a long and closely watched sojourn in the political limelight also plays a role here; after all, for years I was corseted with all kinds of diplomatic considerations, as well as looking over my shoulder at the crowds of those prepared to analyze my every word, and, justifiably or unjustifiably, criticize it. If you have to write a lot and can't play around with it too much, you inevitably give in to the temptation to take the easy way out, which is a constant reminder that it is always fundamentally easier to express oneself neutrally and blandly, than to express a sharp opinion colorfully. For anyone with creative ambitions, this is utter hell. For example, the agony I went through with the traditional New Year's speeches! The immense demands and expectations—having to balance praise with criticism and make reference to various areas of human activity—always overwhelmed me. If I had tried to fulfill every expectation, the speech would have lasted two and a half hours and no one would have been able to listen to it for more than a minute.

But at the same time, reading my old texts brought home to me in very interesting ways the different stages of the life of our country and its atmosphere, as well as that of my own personal life. Suddenly—after many years and decades—I realize how profoundly things differed between the first and the second half of the 1950s, or the first and the second half of the 1960s, and of course later, during the era of normalization after the Soviet occupation—differed in ways that included hundreds of inexpressible aspects, movements, tones, subtones, illusions, revelations, tendencies, or characteristic emotional coloring. I am not, nor have I ever been, a chronicler of my time; yet all of that atmosphere mysteriously, unintentionally, somehow soaked into those ancient texts. To me, that was an interesting insight.

I also realized how many people played an important role in various stages of my life, and what important lessons I learned from them in the matter of creative independence and civic morality, regardless of the route that many of them later took. It's important to say that none of them ever took the route of real betrayal.

So far in our conversation you have been rather critical of political conditions in the Czech Republic. Do you see hope anywhere?

Yes. I see it clearly in the younger generations. Not because better people are being born today than before—naturally young people today exhibit the same differences in character, morals, and life trajectories and skills as you could see in their parents, their grandparents, or anyone else. Nevertheless they are significantly different in one way: they are no longer deformed by communism. They have not grown up in circumstances that demand hypocrisy and spinelessness, conditions that support selfishness, indifference to others, and xenophobia, under a regime that was always talking about the working class, which was meant to be in charge, while in reality cultivating the basest forms of petit bourgeois values in its citizens. All of us who grew up under communism, including those who openly opposed it, have been marked by it in one way or another; the miserable moral atmosphere poisoned us more than we realized. Young people have grown up in freedom; they have learned to handle a greater degree of independence; if they wish they can study abroad, and in this they hardly differ from young Belgians or Americans, and therefore have no need to feel inferior to them, to fear them, or, on the contrary, to envy them. The growing influence of these generations on public life gives me hope that circumstances will change for the better. It seems to me that in politics today, the generation that grew up in the era of so-called normalization—possibly the most deformed generation of all—exercises a very large influence. Under normalization, no one believed in any ideal any longer, and the most successful were simply the most cynical.

(October 19, 1996)

(. . .)

6) What happened to the million crowns that some woman is supposed to have brought me in a suitcase? If it was a gift to me as an individual, then I would have to pay an absurd gift tax on it. Please try to persuade the lady in question to make it a gift to my foundation (something I would have done with it anyway, except that it would have been substantially less money). (. . .)

7) What are we going to do about the St. Wenceslas relics? Please decide whether they should really remain with me, in my personal safe, as some say, or whether they should be deposited with the other remains in the St. Wenceslas Chapel. Please get the opinion of E. and other competent people. At the same time please prepare a nice thank-you letter to the donor, which I will then approve and sign. There should be something in the letter to explain what I will do with the relics. If they will remain in my possession then we should say in the letter that I will bequeath them to the Czech state in my will. (. . .)

(January 22, 2003)

(. . .)

I'm wondering whether I shouldn't do something about the Mašín brothers before I leave office. But what? Can I grant them a pardon? Probably not, but even if it were technically possible, they would demonstrably reject that, and I would be mildly humiliated just before leaving office. Or should I, in an open letter, invite them to the Czech Republic, giving them my personal guarantee of safety? But that's rather strange. What kind of a legal system would it be in which former presidents could decide who would be safe and who not? Please give some thought to this—as to whether and how it might be done. It's not about the act itself but about its significance, which would initiate an informed public debate about whether or not the communist regime in this country ought to have been opposed by the same means as Nazism was, or not. I myself don't have a very clear opinion about this, but I incline to the position that different times require different means. That, however, would be the subject of a book. I would not award them a state medal of honor though, because that would not initiate the debate, but rather end it. Or more precisely, it would turn it into a free-for-all.

(August 21, 1999)

(. . .)

6) In the closet where the vacuum cleaner is kept, there also lives a bat. How to get rid of it? The lightbulb has been unscrewed so as not to wake it up and upset it. (. . .)

Do you have some experience with the young people you speak of? Do you associate with them? Do you know them? Do you think they understand you?

I certainly don't know an entire generation, at least not very well. Nevertheless, I occasionally take part in discussions at universities or high schools; I sometimes meet with young people at festivals or concerts, and I have the impression that they quite respect me and are interested in my opinions. I feel they understand those opinions and sometimes even share them. But that's not the deciding factor. What is important is that they simply use their own minds. I am always surprised, for instance, when I read various weeklies or monthlies, at how many new bylines appear—and for the most part these are students— and how many interesting things these new or future journalists, or scientists, or literati know and how well they understand what they write about it. That for me is the main source of hope.

Hrádeček, December 10, 2005

I've just quoted my answers from the conversation in Disturbing the Peace. I remember very vividly the period twenty years ago when I was writing those replies. It was here at Hrádeček as well. At the time I didn't have a computer, so I wrote them directly on a typewriter, which, given my pedantry, meant that every time I made a typo or a correction, I felt I had to type the whole page over again. I made four carbon copies of every text. Once, I was writing at night, as I am doing now, and at the very moment I was describing the biggest nightmare of a writer whom the totalitarian regime does not like—that is, fear that the police will search his house and confiscate his unfinished manuscript— Olga came into my study and told me that the police were snooping around outside, and she suspected they were getting ready to search the house in the morning. I was alarmed and quickly wrapped the entire manuscript, along with the carbon copies, in something and snuck out into the woods, where I hid it. There was no house search, and the next day I returned to the woods and recovered the manuscript.

I mention this not because of the strange coincidence—that I just happened to be writing about the fear of losing a manuscript when it turned out that I might have good grounds for that fear—but because I've realized that, even today, I feel fear as I write. It's not fear of a house search, of course, but fear that for one of several other reasons—having to do with time, with work, with health, or with my psychological state—I will not manage to finish writing this thing, or I will lose the manuscript, or that I will throw it out. I think that every writer who is not just a craftsman knows this fear. At one point it might take the form of fear of the police, at another time fear of fire, or of one's own inadequacies, or it may be a secret or acknowledged fear that one might not manage to finish writing something in one's lifetime. The whole thing is somewhat ridiculous because it assumes that the world desperately needs the work in question, and that it will fall apart if it doesn't appear. It's a ridiculous notion, but in its own way, that's how it ought to be. We should, after all, do everything seriously, as though the future of the world depended on it, and, as a matter of fact, in some ways it does. Even with this book—however it turns out—the world will be forever different than it would be without it. You *might even say that we don't know for sure that the world did not come into existence so that this or that book could be written and completed. Who can show that this is not the case? Not to forget: today is Human Rights Day, and I am recalling various events from my life connected with this date.*

(February 7, 1996)

(. . .) Further I would ask that the upcoming meeting try to think clearly about the relationships in areas of competence between the various interested people and institutions (the secretariat, the administration, the Castle police, the FAO, the friendly liquidators of the inheritance, the friendly food purchasers, etc., etc.). I am very moved at how many people are concerned about me and about Ďula; still, there are so many of them that I don't know what I can ask of whom and whether or not I have the right to ask one or the other of these people about something or other. I would welcome it if you could clarify everything and make it, as they say today, transparent.

(April 11, 1999)

(. . .)
8) We need a longer hose for watering. (. . .)

I can't do otherwise at the end of all this than ask you the same question that I asked you in 1986. How do you see your future? What do you think is awaiting you? What do you hope for and what do you expect?

And I can do no other than once again repeat my answer: "The paradoxes will continue. I'll go on, as I always have, sitting down in front of a blank piece of paper with distaste; I will try everything to avoid writing, always terrified of those first words on the page. I will continue to find artificial ways of giving myself courage to write. I will despair that it's not coming. Yet I'll always manage to write a new play. The mysterious inner furies who have invented these torments will probably not leave me in peace and will have their own way in the end. As always I will be upset by all the expectations (many of which are out of proportion and even foolish) with which I am burdened, and all the roles from the representative to the Good Samaritan that are prescribed for me. I will continue to revolt against them and claim my right to peace—and I will ultimately carry out all these tasks and even find sincere delight in doing so. I will go on being bothered by things, fearing some things, getting into states, blaming myself, cursing, and despairing—and, as always, I will be found reliable, and will be seen where my place is."

(January 16, 1997)

(. . .) (c) For me, my many near-death experiences are in the past. And it interests me today as little as those several car accidents long ago that I miraculously survived without a scratch, or getting baked in the sauna that couldn't be opened, when I finally managed, thanks to strength given to me by all the gods including Allah, to kick the door down and thus save myself (that happened a few years ago in Lány). In other words, I'm not blaming anyone, I'm not angry at anyone, and the whole thing is of absolutely no interest to me—as a patient, or the physical object of this story. (. . .)

(October 4, 1993)

(. . .)
9) Please have Mrs. M. or E. prepare the pike from Lány that was given to me, in some very original way, with unique spicing, so the parliamentary five will not soon forget it. (. . .)

Hrádeček, December 11, 2005

The beauty of language is that it can never capture precisely what it wants. Language is disconnected, hard, digital as it were, and for that reason, but not only for that reason, it can never completely capture something as connected as reality, experience, or our souls. This opens the door to the magnificent battle for expression and self-expression that has accompanied man down through history. It is a battle without end, and thanks to it, everything that is human is continually being elucidated, each time somewhat differently. Moreover, it is in this battle that man in fact becomes himself. As an individual, and as a species. He simply tries to capture the world and himself more and more exactly through words, images, or actions, and the more he succeeds, the more aware he is that he can never completely capture either the world or himself, nor any part of the world. But that drives him to keep trying, again and again, and thus he continues to define himself more and more exactly. It's a Sisyphean fate. But it can't be helped: man will carry the complete truth about himself to the grave, though someone, in the end, will know that truth after all: if not the Lord God, then at least the great memory of Being.

(June 7, 1994)

(. . .)

5) I would ask Mr. Řechtáček to repair and refill my lighter and send it back. (. . .)

(August 21, 1999)

(. . .)

6) In the closet where the vacuum cleaner is kept, there also lives a bat. How to get rid of it? The lightbulb has been unscrewed so as not to wake it up and upset it. (. . .)

"I'll always end up paying for it, but oddly enough I'll survive and be there causing disruption wherever necessary. I can only conclude this prediction and our conversation by attempting to articulate the final and, obviously, the most paradoxical paradox of my life: I suspect that somewhere deep down I find this paradoxical life of mine terribly entertaining." And now, with this old prediction and suspicion of mine, I can only conclude as well this conversation of ours. Because what else can I add to it, except to say that today I am older and thus—I hope—more modest.

Prague, January 5, 2006

This year did not begin well either, at least for our family. Dáša is ill, and what's worse, it's at a time when she is starting to rehearse for the theater again for the first time in eleven years; I'm overcome by a strange lethargy, and I am constantly tired; and the worst of it all is that yesterday our faithful boxer Sugar died. Fourteen years ago, Dáša found her in a Dumpster when she was probably a two-day-old puppy. She saved her life and from that moment on they were inseparable friends and have experienced quite a bit together (for instance, how many Czech boxers can say they've been to America?). Her long dying and her ultimate death took a lot out of us. Now Madlenka is the leader of the pack, though years ago I suspected that she was a little superficial. But I've had to change my opinion, and I apologize to Madlenka for my mistake.

As far as the world is concerned? There was no new tsunami but humanity has endured many typhoons and earthquakes, which gives the impression that the weather has gone somewhat mad. The heaviest snowfalls in living memory, cold, thaws, rain, wind; nature, in short, is behaving just like my computer sometimes behaves—that means irrationally. I'm glad that I'm finishing this book; I wrote it over no more than a few days, but they were scattered throughout almost an entire year. Sugar died not only on Dáša's and my ninth wedding anniversary, but also at the moment when she was certain that this testimony of mine was finished.

Dear Dáša, thank you for bearing faithfully with me the weight of the years that this book covers. But was it really only a weight? Was it not also suspenseful, exciting, exhilarating, and occasionally full of laughter?

(April 11, 1999)

(. . .)

8) We need a longer hose for watering. (. . .)

ACKNOWLEDGMENTS

I would like to thank Karel Hvížďala for his questions and for gracefully accepting the role in which I cast him in this book. I would also like to thank Jaroslav Kořán, the director of my Czech publisher, Gallery, and my editor, Jan Zelenka, for their interest and the work they have done to expedite the publication of this book in Czech, as well as Joska Skálnik for his graphic design. Thanks as well to my assistant, Martin Vidlák, for his help in the electronic editing of the book; to Jiří Srstka, director of Dilia, Theatrical, Literary, and Audiovisual Agency in Prague, for setting the relevant agendas; and to Paul Wilson, for his translation into English, and for preparing the notes.

—Václav Havel

TRANSLATOR'S ACKNOWLEDGMENTS

Of the many whose advice or assistance helped lighten the work of translating and preparing this book for publication (chief among them Louise Dennys, Andrew Dorko, Ash Green, Vladimír Hanzel, Jakub Hladík, Martin Palouš, Michael Schellenberg, Sara Sherbill, Martin Vidlák), I want to single out two for special mention: Jan Zelenka, the book's coordinating editor in Prague, who spent countless hours finding answers to my queries and then subjecting a draft of my translation and notes to a close and careful reading; and my wife, Patricia Grant, who transcribed and tidied up the first draft and ran her eagle eye over subsequent versions. To all, my deepest thanks. Let any flaws that remain be on my head alone.

—PW

NOTES

Given the large number of names and events referred to in the book, the notes are not, nor are they intended to be, exhaustive.

CGW	Committee of Good Will
CSC	Czech Securities Commission
ČTK	Czech Press Agency
DDP	Department of Domestic Policy
DFP	Department of Foreign Policy
FAO	Family Affairs Office
HD	Heritage Department
IMF	International Monetary Fund
MFA	Ministry of Foreign Affairs
MOPR	Military Office of the President of the Republic
OPR	Office of the President of the Republic
OSCE	Organization for Security and Cooperation in Europe
PCA	Prague Castle Administration
PD	Political Department
PSS	Presidential Security Service
SSC	State Security Council
StB	State Security–Police

Czech and Slovak Political Parties by Initials

ČSSD	Czech Social Democratic Party
HZDS	Movement for a Democratic Slovakia
KDÚ-ČSL	Christian Democratic Union–Czech People's Party
ODA	Civic Democratic Alliance
ODS	Civic Democratic Party
OF	Civic Forum
ÚS	Union of Freedom
VPN	Public Against Violence

Currency

$1 U.S. = 25 Czech crowns (based on a 5-year average)

CHAPTER ONE

3 Dáša: Dagmar Havlová, neé Veškrnová. Havel's second wife. They were married in January 1997.

3 Karel Hvížd'ala: Czech journalist and broadcaster. See the note about the interviewer following the index.

3 John Keane: Author of *Václav Havel: A Political Tragedy in Six Acts*. He is a professor of politics at the University of Westminster, London, and the Wissenschaftszentrum Berlin.

4 "protected species": An ironic phrase meant to describe a class of dissident intellectuals whom the regime allegedly treated more leniently because they were known in the West.

5 "our book, *Disturbing the Peace*": In the mid-1980s, Karel Hvížd'ala, who was living in exile in West Germany at the time, conducted a book-length interview with Václav Havel. Called "Long-Distance Interrogation" in Czech, it was published in English in 1990 by Knopf under the title *Disturbing the Peace*.

5 Milan Kundera (1929–): Czech novelist, living in Paris since the early 1980s. Author of, among other books, *The Unbearable Lightness of Being* and *The Book of Laughter and Forgetting*.

5 Václav Bělohradský (1944–): Czech-Italian philosopher and professor of sociology at the Universities of Genoa and Trieste.

6 Pavel Tigrid (1917–2003): Czech journalist and founding editor of the influential Paris-based exile journal *Svědectví* ("Witness"). He was an adviser to President Havel from 1991 to 1992 and served as the Czech minister of culture from 1994 to 1996.

6 Michael Kocáb (1954–): Musician, founder of the rock group Pražský výběr (Prague Choice); in 1989, he negotiated the first contacts between Communist Party officials and the Civic Forum.

6 *The Memorandum*: Havel's second full-length play and the first of his dramatic works to be produced abroad. The play concerns the compulsory introduction of a new, artificial language into the workplace. Paul Wilson has recently retranslated it as *The Memo*.

7 Jiří Voskovec (1905–1981): Co-founder with Jan Werich of the Liberated Theater in Prague in the 1930s. Before the outbreak of World War II Voskovec and Werich fled to the United States, where Voskovec lived until his death. He played character roles in over seventy movies, the most famous of which was *Twelve Angry Men*, starring Henry Fonda. (Werich returned to Prague after the war and became one of Havel's early theatrical mentors.)

7 Hrádeček: A small farmstead in northeast Bohemia and Havel's country home since the mid-1960s. The name means "the little castle."

8 Josef Zieleniec (1946–): Co-founder with Václav Klaus of the Civic Democratic Party (ODS); minister of foreign affairs (1993–1997).

8 Lány: The official presidential weekend retreat, located in a town of the same name about thirty kilometers east of Prague.

9 Helmut Kohl (1930–): Head of the German Christian Democratic Party and chancellor of Germany from 1982 to 1998. One of the main architects of German reunification.

10 Litomyšl: The first meeting of the seven Central European presidents (representing Austria, the Czech Republic, Germany, Hungary, Slovakia, Slovenia, and Poland) took place in this town in the Czech Republic on April 14 and 15, 1994, at the initiative of Václav Havel. They discussed matters of common interest, in particular, the expansion of the European Union. At the end of the meeting, they issued a declaration.

10 "foreign policy eleven": A short-lived advisory group consisting of the president, the prime minister, the ministers of foreign affairs and defense, and seven other members.

10 Reduta: A legendary jazz club in central Prague.

11 Josef Lux (1956–1999): Head of the Christian Democratic Union–Czech People's Party coalition (KDÚ-ČSL) from 1990 to 1998; he was deputy prime minister from 1992 to 1998.

11 Jan Kalvoda (1953–): Head of the Civic Democratic Alliance (ODA) from 1992 to 1996; deputy prime minister, 1992–1997; minister of justice, 1996–1997.

12 the prince: Karel Schwarzenberg (1937–), the twelfth prince of Schwarzenberg. He was President Havel's chief of staff from 1990 to 1992.

12 "Michael Ž": Michael Žantovský (1949–): A founding member of the Civic Forum in November 1989, he became President Havel's spokesman and press secretary (1990–1992). From 1992 to 1997 he served as his country's ambassador in Washington.

13 "something I wrote in an essay": The quotation is from Havel's 1984 essay "Politics and Conscience," in Open Letter, Knopf, 1991. The "simple electrician" referred to by Havel in the essay is Lech Wałęsa.

13 Lech Wałęsa (1943–): The Polish shipyard electrician who spearheaded the strike in 1980 that led to the foundation of the revolutionary trade union Solidarity. He was awarded the Nobel Peace Prize in 1983 and served as the president of Poland from 1990 to 1995.

13 Mikhail Gorbachev (1931–): General secretary of the Communist Party of the Soviet Union (1985–1991).

14 "the Czech Republic has a prime minister": Havel is here referring to Stanislav Gross (1969–), a member of the Czech Social Democratic Party (ČSSD) who was prime minister from August 4, 2004, to April 25, 2005.

17 Ivan Kočárník (1944–): A member of the ODS and minister of finance and deputy prime minister from 1992 to 1997.

17 Radomír Sabela (1958–): Deputy minister for industry and trade.

18 ptydepe: A word invented by Havel's brother, Ivan, for the incomprehensible bureaucratic language that is the subject of an early Havel play, The Memorandum. The word has gradually entered the vocabulary of many Czechs.

20 Charter 77: The human rights movement launched by Havel and others in January 1977, hence the name. Initially signed by about three hundred people, the Charter became a focus of human rights and other dissident activities inside the country for the next twelve years. Havel was appointed spokesman several times, and many Charter 77 signatories were active in the creation of the Civic Forum in 1989.

20 Václav Benda (1946–1999): As a student of philosophy, Czech language and literature, and mathematics, Benda was a leading student politician in 1968. He later became a founding member of Charter 77 and the Committee to Defend the Unjustly Prosecuted (VONS). He was imprisoned, along with Havel, from 1979 to 1983. After the Velvet Revolution he became active in electoral politics in the Christian Democratic Union (KDÚ).

21 Petr Uhl (1941–): Journalist and political activist. A founding member of Charter 77, Uhl was instrumental in creating VONS and in reporting on human rights abuses in Czechoslovakia during the 1970s and 1980s. After 1989 he became head of the Czechoslovak Press Agency (ČTK) and served as a member of parliament.

21 *nomenklatura*: A special, elite category of membership in the ruling Communist Party. Only those who belonged to the *nomenklatura* could occupy key posts in the government and the economy.

21 "Zakaria's distinction between democracy and freedom": A reference to Fareed Zakaria (1964–), editor of *Newsweek International* and author of *The Future of Freedom* (2003).

21 "Popper's analysis of open and closed political systems": Karl Popper (1902–1994) was an Austrian philosopher whose best-known work of political science is *The Open Society and Its Enemies* (1945).

22 Mečiarism: Havel is referring to the authoritarian leadership and governing style of the first prime minister of an independent Slovakia, Vladimír Mečiar (1942–), who dominated Slovak electoral politics until 1998, when his party, the Movement for a Democratic Slovakia (HZDS), was voted out of office.

23 "I won my first two Obies": Havel was awarded the Obie—presented by *The Village Voice* for outstanding merit in off-Broadway theatrical productions—three times in all; in 1967–68, in the Best Foreign Play category, for *The Memorandum*; in 1969–70, in the Distinguished Plays category, for *The Increased Difficulty of Concentration*; and in 1983–84, in the Playwriting category, for his three one-act plays, *Audience, Private View*, and *Protest*.

27 Jan (Honza) Ruml (1953–): Politician and journalist. A member of Charter 77 and active in VONS, Ruml co-founded several samizdat publications, including the samizdat revival of the daily *Lidové noviny* and, later, the weekly *Respekt*. In April 1990 he was appointed a deputy to the minister of the interior and later, from 1992 to 1997, he was minister of the interior for the Czech Republic, and from 2000 to 2004, deputy chairman of the Czech Senate.

28 "the nuclear power station at Temelín": Construction on the station was begun under the communist regime, in 1984, and after 1989 it became the target of environmental protests.

28 Vladimír Dlouhý (1953–): Deputy prime minister in the first postcommunist Government of National Understanding, and chair of the National Planning Commission. As a member of the Civic Democratic Alliance (ODA) he was minister of industry and trade from 1992 to 1997.

33 Little House: Until the completion of his own residence in Dělostřelecká Street, Havel and Olga lived in the official presidential residence in the Royal Gardens, within the Castle precincts.

33 Václav Klaus (1941–): Czech economist, member of the Civic Forum, later its chairman, and co-founder of the Civic Democratic Party (ODS). He was Czechoslovak

minister of finance until 1992, when he became Czech premier from 1993 until his resignation in 1997. He succeeded Havel as president of the Czech Republic in 2003.

33 Miloš Zeman (1944–): Former leader of the Czech Social Democratic Party (ČSSD). He succeeded Josef Tošovský as prime minister in 1998 and remained in office until 2002. In 2003, he made an unsuccessful bid to succeed Václav Havel as the Czech president.

34 "the Conversations": Havel is referring to *Conversations from Lány,* a weekly radio "chat" that he recorded each Friday. They were broadcast each Sunday from March 1990 to February 1, 1998.

38 Petr Oslzlý (1945–): A dramaturge, theater director, and writer. He was an adviser to Havel from 1989 to 1992.

38 Alois Rašín (1867–1923): Czech economist and politician. He was active in the movement for Czechoslovak independence and became the new country's first minister of finance. He was assassinated in 1923.

39 Richard von Weizsäcker (1920–): President of Germany from 1984 to 1994.

39 Roman Herzog (1934–): President of Germany from 1994 to 1999.

40 Sudeten German claims: After the end of World War II, on the basis of the so-called Beneš Decrees, the Czechoslovak government expelled to Germany (or "transferred"—there is debate over the proper term) almost two million ethnic Germans living in the Sudetenland region of Czechoslovakia, which was annexed by Germany in 1938 after the notorious Munich agreement. Their property was confiscated, and from the early 1990s the surviving Sudetenlanders lobbied for redress.

40 "I set in motion a daring initiative": In a visit to Bonn in 1991, Havel proposed offering Czechoslovak citizenship to surviving Sudeten Germans and allowing them to participate in the reprivatization process through which property confiscated by the communist regime was returned to its legal owners.

40 Landsmannschaft: Literally an "association of compatriots." Havel is referring here to the Sudetendeutsche Landsmannschaft, formed in 1950 to bring together Germans expelled from Czechoslovakia.

41 Richard Holbrooke (1941–): American diplomat who, during the Yugoslav civil wars in the 1990s, brokered the agreement in Bosnia that led to the Dayton Peace Accords in 1995.

42 "the prime minister": At the time, it was Václav Klaus.

44 the cardinal: Refers to Cardinal Miloslav Vlk (1934–), who has been the archbishop of Prague and the Czech primate since 1991. In 1994 he was named a cardinal by Pope John Paul II.

45 "the Lytomyšl meeting in Hungary": Another meeting of the seven Central European presidents, this time held in Hungary. The first one was held in April 1994.

46 "the anniversary": Havel is referring to the anniversary of the end of World War II in Europe, celebrated in Russia on May 9.

46 Alexander Lebedev (1938–): Russian ambassador to Czechoslovakia and then the Czech Republic from 1991 to 1996.

47 Gustav Husák (1913–1991): General secretary of the Communist Party of Czechoslovakia during the period of "normalization" after the Soviet invasion of Czechoslovakia. He was president from 1975 until December 10, 1989, when he resigned.

49 "Wiesel's foundation": The Elie Wiesel Foundation for Humanity.

52 Plastic People of the Universe: A rock band that became the focus of an underground music scene in Czechoslovakia in the 1970s. When members of the band, and other underground musicians, were arrested in 1976, and seven people were sent to jail, their case became a catalyst for the creation of Charter 77. The band, minus its original bass player and composer, Milan Hlavsa, who died in 2001 at age forty-nine, is still playing today.

52 Saša Vondra: Alexander Vondra (1961–), a dissident of the younger generation, a spokesperson for Charter 77, and a founding member of the Civic Forum in 1989. Vondra was a foreign policy adviser to Havel (1990–1992), deputy foreign minister (1992–1997), and Czech ambassador to Washington (1997–2001).

52 Jiří Křižan (1941–): Screenwriter, activist, adviser to Havel after 1989, and deputy minister of the interior from 1992 to 1994.

52 "Several Sentences": A petition released in June 1989 and signed by tens of thousands of people demanding, among other things, the immediate release of all political prisoners, the reinstatement of the rights of assembly, the lifting of censorship, and the cessation of repression against civic initiatives like Charter 77.

53 "Anti-Charter of 1977": The regime's response to the appearance of Charter 77 in early 1977 was to create a counterdeclaration of loyalty to the existing regime and then compel prominent cultural figures—actors, singers, writers—to sign it. It was dubbed the anti-Charter by the opposition.

53 "Most": The word means "bridge" in English.

53 Ladislav Adamec (1926–): Prime minister of the Czechoslovak Socialist Republic from 1988 to 1989. After November 17, 1989, he conducted roundtable meetings with the Civic Forum. He resigned on December 7, 1989.

CHAPTER TWO

59 "Velvet Revolution": The epithet applied by foreign journalists at the time to the rapid, nonviolent regime change that took place in Czechoslovakia during November and December 1989, when the power of the ruling Communist Party collapsed. The Czechs and Slovaks quickly adopted the phrase, and it has been used as a shorthand description for that event ever since.

59 Milan Machovec (1925–2003): Czech philosopher who, in the 1960s, initiated a dialogue between Marxists and Christians. His best-known book, called "Jesus for Modern Man" in Czech, was translated into English as A Marxist Looks at Jesus.

60 Civic Forum (Občanský forum in Czech, sometimes referred to by its Czech initials, OF): A steering committee consisting of the leading members of Charter 77 and many of the opposition groups from the late 1980s, along with representatives of the churches, students, artists, and other individuals. The group was formally established at a meeting in the Činoherní Klub, a small Prague theater, on November 19, 1989. Havel was appointed the group's unofficial leader. A parallel organization, the Public Against Violence (VPN), was created about the same time in Slovakia.

60 Jiří Suk (1956–): Czech historian. The book cited, *Through the Labyrinth of Revolution: The Actors, the Plots, and the Turning-points in a Political Crisis*, is the most thorough study of the Velvet Revolution in Czech. It covers the period from November 1989 to June 1990.

61 Valtr Komárek (1930–): Economist, served as deputy prime minister in the transitional government appointed in December 1989.

62 "my rabble-rousing speech on Wenceslas Square": The speech marked the twenty-second anniversary of the Soviet invasion of Czechoslovakia. In it, Havel addressed the problem of persistent communist influence in the country.

63 Letná: The name of a large open park in Prague where many of the mass demonstrations were held during the Velvet Revolution.

64 "a compromise of the Polish type": In Poland during the transition from communism earlier in 1989, the communists were temporarily allowed to retain the presidency, which at the time was held by General Wojciech Jaruzelski (1923–), while a representative of Solidarity, Tadeusz Mazowiecki (1927–), became prime minister. Jaruzelski remained president until December 1990; he was succeeded by Lech Wałęsa.

65 Zbigniew Brzezinski (1928–): Served as national security adviser to President Jimmy Carter from 1977 to 1981.

66 "the first negotiations of the so-called decision-making political forces": On December 8, 1989, there was a meeting of different political organizations to decide on the composition of the new federal government. There were representatives of the Civic Forum (and its Slovak counterpart, the VPN), the Communist Party, the Union of Socialist Youth, and the other "shell parties" that had been a part of the National Front through which the communists had governed. All of the Civic Forum's and the Public Against Violence's demands were met.

69 Thomas Klestil (1932–2004): President of Austria from 1992 until his death.

69 Zdeněk Mahler (1928–): Czech screenwriter, actor. He was a coauthor of the screenplay for Miloš Forman's film *Amadeus*. He also made a television documentary called *Cathedral in Three Acts* (1995) and wrote a popular book on the Prague cathedral.

73 Petr Pithart (1941–): Lawyer and political scientist. He was active in the reform process of 1968 and later in Charter 77 and the Civic Forum. He was premier of the Czech government (1990–1992) when Czechoslovakia was still a federation. He served two terms as chairman of the Senate (1996–1998 and 2000–2004).

74 "Nazi execution of Czech students": In demonstrations by Czech students on October 28, 1939, to protest the Nazi occupation of their country, a Czech student was shot and later died. Two days after a mass funeral on November 15, the Nazis shut down the universities and executed nine students. After the war, November 17 became a memorial day for Czechoslovak students.

75 "exodus of East German refugees from Prague": During the summer of 1989, several thousand East Germans came to Prague and took refuge inside the walled compound of the West German embassy. After six weeks of tense negotiations, they were allowed to leave to the West, while the Czechs looked on. This incident, and similar events in Hungary, dramatically increased the tension in Czechoslovakia and were later seen to have been a precursor of the Velvet Revolution a few months later.

76 Jan Urban (1951–): Journalist and politician who was active in the Civic Forum in 1989 and then became the head of the Civic Forum's Coordination Center.

76 Joska Skalník (1948–): Painter and graphic artist who has done a great deal of design work for Václav Havel.

77 Zdeněk Mlynář (1930–1997): Reform-minded member of the Central Committee of the Communist Party during the Prague Spring and author of an autobiographical account of the Prague Spring (*Nightfrost in Prague: The End of Humane Socialism*, New York, 1980, translated by Paul Wilson).

79 Barnabas: A character in Franz Kafka's novel *The Castle*.

81 "Henry": Henry Kissinger.

82 Mikhail Bakhtin (1895–1975): Russian philosopher, linguist, and literary critic who was exiled to Kazakhstan by Stalin in 1929. He gained worldwide recognition after his death. His best-known work is *Rabelais and His World*.

84 *Summer Meditations*: In the summer of 1991, Havel wrote down and later published what he called "a series of spontaneously written comments on how I see this country and its problems today, how I see its future, and what I wish to put my efforts behind." Published in 1992 by Knopf, translated by Paul Wilson.

86 Alexander Dubček (1921–1992): Slovak communist politician who became general secretary of the Communist Party in January 1968 and whose name is most commonly associated with the Prague Spring reforms. After the Soviet invasion, Dubček was forced into internal exile, and he remained silent until the late 1980s. He was chairman of the Federal Assembly from 1990 to 1992. He died in November 1992 from injuries sustained in a road accident.

87 Ivan Dejmal (1946–): An ecologist who spent four years in prison in the 1970s for activism. He was later involved in the pre–Velvet Revolution ecological movement. He was the Czech environment minister from 1991 to 1992.

87 Alois Indra (1921–1990): A member of the faction of the Communist Party of Czechoslovakia that signed the notorious letter "inviting" the Soviet Union to invade the country in August 1968. He was chairman of the Federal Assembly from 1970 to 1989.

88 *Ubu Roi*: An absurdist drama by the French writer Alfred Jarry. First staged in France in 1896, it influenced Czech theater in the 1960s.

94 Otakar Motejl (1932–): A lawyer who, in the 1970s and 1980s, defended many who ran afoul of the regime. He served as chief justice in the Supreme Court, first of Czechoslovakia from 1990 to 1992 and then of the Czech Republic from 1992 to 1998. He was the Czech minister of justice from 1998 to 2000. In December 2000, he became the first Czech ombudsman.

94 Pavel Rychetský (1943–): A lawyer and founding signatory of Charter 77, he served in many government posts until his appointment as chairman of the Constitutional Court in 2003.

95 Dagmar Burešová (1929–): A lawyer. In the 1970s and 1980s she represented dissidents who were being prosecuted by the regime. She was the minister of justice from 1989 to June 1990, and from then until 1992 she was chair of the Czech National Council.

95 Zdeněk Jičínský (1929–): A reform communist, lawyer, author of the 1960 Czechoslovak constitution, and signatory of Charter 77. Since the Velvet Revolution, he

has served almost continuously as a member of the Chamber of Deputies for the Social Democratic Party (ČSSD).

98 "A majority of Czechs . . . connected the notion of Slovak independence with fascism": On March 14, 1939, just before the outbreak of World War II, the separatist, Nazi-influenced Slovak People's Party, led by Monsignor Jozef Tiso, and with Adolf Hitler's blessing, declared independence. The following day, what was left of Bohemia and Moravia (the Sudetenland having been annexed by Germany in 1938) was occupied by German troops. Slovakia's nominal independence lasted until the end of the war, six years later.

99 "Just recall our weeping presidents, or presidents obsessed with explaining the meaning of their capitulations": Several times in modern Czech history, top officials have found themselves surrendering to enemy forces and then excusing their actions by claiming that resistance would be disastrous for the nation. In 1938, during the Munich crisis, President Edvard Beneš abdicated and left for England, abandoning his country to Nazi occupation a few months later. Again, in 1948, the same president acceded to the resignation of the noncommunist cabinet ministers, preparing the way for the communist takeover. Yet again, on August 27, 1968, Alexander Dubček (who was the communist general secretary, not president) returned from Moscow to announce, through barely suppressed tears, that he had signed an agreement effectively legitimizing the Soviet occupation of his country.

99 Milan Kňažko (1945–): Slovak actor and politician. He was a founding member of the Public Against Violence in Slovakia in November 1989 and later became one of Havel's chief advisers.

103 "the floods": In the summer of 1997, there was severe flooding in Moravia, the eastern region of the Czech Republic, and along the Oder in Poland.

103 Bořek Šípek (1949–): An architect and friend of Havel who succeeded Miroslav Masák as chief architect of Prague Castle in 1993.

105 "Bratinka's Roma material": In August 1997, thousands of Czech Gypsies, or Roma, sought political asylum in Canada, Great Britain, and elsewhere on the grounds that they were suffering grave discrimination in the Czech Republic. Pavel Bratinka (1946–) was then a minister without portfolio in the Klaus government and chair of the Council for National Minorities. He was the first person at cabinet level to publicly admit that the Roma people were victims of discrimination by the police and the public. His reports, among others, were used by the Immigration and Refugee Board of Canada to help in evaluating the refugee claims they were processing. Bratinka was also sent to England as an envoy to confer with British officials.

106 Josef Bartončík (1943–): Chair of the newly reconstituted Czechoslovak People's Party (ČSL) from November 1989 until September 1990. The law referred to in the question is one that places a moratorium on all political campaigning for the two days before the polls open. The revelation of Bratinka's complicity with the old regime was highly controversial at the time and exposed Jan Ruml and Havel to accusations that they had broken the law.

108 MFD: Short for MFDnes, or Mladá fronta Dnes, a postcommunist version of the former Mladá fronta that was originally the daily organ of the communist youth organization. Today it is an independent daily.

111 Josef Tošovský (1950–): Czech economist and governor of the Czech National Bank from 1993 to 2000. From January to July 1998 he was the prime minister in a caretaker government appointed by President Havel after the resignation of the Klaus government.

112 "arrange for Lou to play in the White House": Lou Reed (1942–), a founding member of the New York rock group the Velvet Underground. The informal concert in the White House actually took place on September 17, 1998; Reed played with Milan Hlavsa, founding member of the Plastic People of the Universe, who had been inspired by the Velvet Underground.

113 "In Austria there was Waldheim": Kurt Waldheim (1918–) was president of Austria from 1986 to 1992. Havel's reluctance to pay one of his first state visits to Austria had to do with the controversy surrounding Waldheim, who was accused of falsifying his past as an officer in the German SA Cavalry Corps and of having participated in war crimes during World War II. While president, Waldheim was deemed persona non grata by many countries, and the United States had him placed on a watch list.

113 "a journey to a dramatically transforming GDR, intended to support their roundtable discussions": When the head of the ruling Communist party (the SED) in the German Democratic Republic stepped down in December 1989, the Berlin Wall had already been breached. On December 7, roundtable discussions, analogous to the talks between the Czechoslovak Communist Party and the Civic Forum and the VPN, opened up between the SED and East German opposition groups, and the discussions continued on into January, when Havel made his visit.

117 Jan Lopatka (1940–1993): Czech literary critic, dissident, founding member of Charter 77, and editor of several of Havel's samizdat publications, notably *Letters to Olga*, Havel's prison letters to his first wife.

118 Václav Černý (1905–1987): Influential Czech literary critic and literary historian.

118 Battle of the White Mountain: A decisive battle (November 8, 1620) in the Thirty Years War in which Bohemian Protestant forces were defeated, ushering in an era of Catholic, Austrian dominance that lasted for almost three centuries.

118 "during the time of Maria Theresa": Maria Theresa (1717–1780) was the archduchess of Austria and queen of Hungary and Bohemia from 1740 to her death.

118 Božena Němcová (née Barbara Betty Pankel, 1820–1862): One of the most influential writers of the Czech National Revival movement in the nineteenth century. *Babička* ("Granny"), first published in 1855, is her most famous novel.

118 "the post-Munich period": "Munich" is shorthand for the notorious agreement, signed in that city, whereby the British prime minister, Neville Chamberlain, agreed to allow Hitler to annex the Sudetenland region of Czechoslovakia in 1938. The word has become synonymous with "appeasement."

118 "the Protectorate": The period covering the Nazi occupation of Bohemia and Moravia, 1939–1945.

CHAPTER THREE

124 "the long-abandoned Masarykian idea of a single Czechoslovak nation": A reference to Tomáš Garrigue Masaryk (1850–1937), the first Czechoslovak president, who led the Czech and Slovak independence movement that resulted in the creation of Czechoslovakia in 1918. Masaryk favored a unitary state, that is, a single nation—the Czechoslovaks—rather than a federation of two nations, each with its own separate national government. In the minds of many Slovaks, this constituted a failure to see Czechs and Slovaks as separate ethnicities. The frustrations the Slovaks felt under this arrangement may have fueled the drive for independence.

125 "the asymmetrical model": The Union of Czechoslovak Writers was a statewide organization. At the same time, the Slovaks had their own, separate Union of Slovak Writers, which had no equivalent in the Czech lands until the country officially became a federation in 1969.

126 Edvard Beneš (1884–1948): The second Czechoslovak president, succeeding Masaryk in 1935. Beneš spent the Second World War in England as head of a provisional Czechoslovak government in exile. He was in office when the expulsion of the Sudeten Germans took place.

126 Karel Čapek (1890–1938): The Czech playwright, journalist, and novelist was a vigorous opponent of both communism and fascism and was strongly against the German annexation of the Sudetenland. He was devastated by the capitulation after Munich and died a few months later.

133 Vize '97: A charitable foundation (its full name is the Dagmar and Václav Havel Foundation Vision '97) created in 1997 to provide assistance in the fields of health, education, and culture.

133 Terezín (also known as Theresienstadt): A concentration camp established by the Nazis in the northern Bohemian garrison town of the same name. Tens of thousands of Jews, mainly of Czech nationality, died there, and many more passed through on their way to death camps in Poland.

135 George Soros (1930–): Hungarian-born financier and philanthropist who has been active, through his Open Society Institute, in promoting open and democratic societies throughout the world, with a special focus on Central and Eastern Europe since 1989.

136 Jan Kavan (1946–): A student leader in the 1960s, Kavan went into exile in the West after the Soviet invasion and spent the next twenty years based in Great Britain. On his return after 1989, his career was dogged by a scandal involving allegations that he had collaborated with the Czech secret police while abroad. He was foreign minister from 1998 to 2002 and served as chairman of the United Nations General Assembly from 2002 to 2003. He is a member of the ČSSD.

137 Amálie villa: A small villa about ten kilometers outside Lány used by Havel as a venue for informal, off-the-record discussions. Havel took part mainly as an observer and listener. The discussions, to which people of widely varying opinions were invited, served partly to keep Havel up to date on the latest thinking.

137 Rudolf Schuster (1934–): President of Slovakia from 1999 to 2004, the first president to be elected by popular vote (rather than being elected, as the Czech president is,

by parliament). He was ambassador to Canada for Czechoslovakia from 1990 to 1992.

137 Smokovec Declaration: The meeting at which this declaration was to be signed was meant to have taken place in Smokovec, in Slovakia, but instead was held in Gerlach (also in the High Tatra mountains in Slovakia) on December 3, 1999. It was a meeting of the four Visegrad presidents (Václav Havel, Árpád Göncz, Aleksander Kwaśniewski, and Rudolf Schuster) for the purpose of urging the European Union to start discussions with Slovakia about its eventual membership. The declaration they signed was then called the Tatra Declaration.

137 Aleksander Kwaśniewski (1954–): President of Poland from 1995 to 2005.

138 Tomáš Halík (1948–): Before the Velvet Revolution, Halík was active in the "underground church." He was secretly ordained as a priest in 1978 and was a close associate of Cardinal Tomášek, the archbishop of Prague. Since 1989 he has been actively involved in public life and served as an "external adviser" to President Havel.

138 Milo Djukanović (1962–): Prime minister of Montenegro from 1991 to 1998, and again from 2003 to 2006. From 1998 to 2002 he was president. He was charged with involvement in organized crime by Italy but claimed immunity as head of a now independent state.

138 Organization for Security and Cooperation in Europe (OSCE): An outgrowth of the Conference on Security and Cooperation in Europe, the OSCE embraces fifty-one countries in the Northern Hemisphere. Its activities include a variety of military, social, and humanitarian objectives, including conflict prevention and resolution; work to prevent trafficking in drugs, arms, and people; and the promotion of education, media freedom, and building democratic institutions. The OSCE headquarters are in Vienna.

142 Martina Navrátilová (1956–): The championship tennis player defected to the West in 1975 and became a U.S. citizen in 1981.

144 Jiří Dienstbier (1937–): A journalist and broadcaster until 1969, he was active as a dissident writer and a member of VONS. Along with Havel, he spent four years in prison in the late 1970s and early 1980s. He was Czechoslovak foreign minister from 1989 to 1992, and he was a special rapporteur to the former Yugoslavia for the United Nations in the late 1990s.

144 Luboš Dobrovský (1932–): Journalist and politician. Soon after the Velvet Revolution, he helped to negotiate the withdrawal of Soviet troops from Czechoslovak territory. He was minister of defense from October 1990 to 1992 and served as President Havel's chief of staff from July 1992 to February 1996 and as Czech ambassador to Moscow from 1996 until his resignation in January 2000.

147 Zbyšek Bujak, Jacek Kuroň, Adam Michnik, Bronisław Geremek: Polish activists in Solidarity before 1989.

147 Václav Havel Library: Inspired by the example of several American presidents, its purpose is to "gather, archive, administer, and make available the life and work of Václav Havel."

148 Jiří Stívin (1942–): Czech jazz flautist, saxophonist, and composer.

148 Iva Bittová (1958–): Czech avant-garde musician, singer, violinist, composer.

148 Andrej Krob (1938–): A longtime friend of Václav Havel, and founding director of the Theater on the Move (Divadlo na tahu), which specializes in presenting Havel's plays.

149   Miroslav Šlouf (1948–): A former communist official and Prime Minister Zeman's chief adviser. He was the focus of the controversy over police handling of corruption cases and was accused, among other things, of trying to influence the appointment of police officials.

149   Václav Grulich (1932–): Minister of the interior from July 1998 to April 2000 under Prime Minister Zeman.

149   "Victorious February": A reference to the communist takeover in Czechoslovakia in February 1948. It was called "Victorious February" in propaganda slogans.

151   "the report by PSS": Presidential Security Service—the Czech equivalent of the American Secret Service, detailed to protect the president and foreign dignitaries.

153   James Wolfensohn (1933–): Seventh president of the World Bank, from 1995 to 2005.

153   Jeffrey Sachs (1954–): American economist known in the region for advocating "shock therapy" for the flagging economies of Central Europe, particularly in Poland and Russia, after 1989. Since 2002 he has been director of the Earth Institute at Columbia University, New York.

153   Zygmunt Bauman (1925–): Author and professor emeritus of sociology at Leeds University, England. Author of *Globalization: The Human Consequences.*

153   Constitutional Court: The Czech Republic has, in effect, two supreme courts, one to hear appeals from the lower courts and the other—the Constitutional Court—to adjudicate conflicting interpretations of laws relating to the constitutional structure of the country. Its seat is in Brno.

161   "Clinton looked very good after his operations": In September 2004, former President Bill Clinton underwent a quadruple bypass operation that required follow-up surgery.

163   "Your Royal Highness": Charles, Prince of Wales.

163   "the risky event in the Míčovna": The annual meeting of the IMF and the World Bank, held in Prague in September 2000, was marked, as elsewhere, by demonstrations against globalization. Havel organized a hitherto unprecedented meeting between protesting NGOs and representatives of the IMF and the World Bank. The session was held in the Míčovna—a Renaissance hall in the Prague Castle originally designed for handball games.

164   Pavel Mertlík (1961–): Economist, minister of finance (1999–2001), and a governor of the World Bank for the Czech Republic (1999–2001). He teaches economics at Charles University, Prague.

165   Vladimír Železný (1945–): A Czech media baron and former owner of the private television station TV Nova. He was elected to the Czech Senate in 2002 and to the European Parliament in 2004. He was sometimes referred to as "the Czech Berlusconi" because it was felt he used his media holdings to enhance his political career. He has been investigated for tax evasion. The Czech Senate suspended his parliamentary immunity in 2003.

165   Pavel Zuna (1967–): A newscaster for TV Nova from 1999 to 2006.

166   INPEG: Acronym for the Prague-based Initiative Against Economic Globalization. It organized nonviolent protests against the annual meeting of the IMF and the World Bank Group in Prague in September 2000.

CHAPTER FOUR

179 Milan Uhde (1936–): Czech playwright, signatory of Charter 77, later politician. He served as Czech minister of culture from 1990 to 1992, and chair of the Chamber of Deputies from 1993 to 1996.

180 "Hayek's idea of the division of functions": Friedrich Hayek (1899–1992): Austrian-born liberal political philosopher best known for *The Road to Serfdom* (1944). The notion of assigning a different legislative function to each house of a bicameral parliament comes from his three-volume magnum opus, *Law, Legislation, and Liberty: A New Statement of Liberal Principles* (1973–79). The Civic Democratic Alliance (ODA), claiming Hayek as one of their chief influences, proposed that the Czech Senate deal with "private law" and the Chamber of Deputies with "public law," as defined by Hayek.

183 JAMU: The Janáček Academy of the Arts, a postsecondary art school located in Brno.

183 *The Chairs*: Havel is referring to the play by Eugene Ionesco.

183 "the whole affair around Czech Television": In late December 2000, a sit-in by Czech Television news producers was prompted by programming and management changes at the public broadcaster. The occupation—which disrupted the popular evening television news—sparked a crisis that lasted several weeks and brought thousands of people into the streets in support of the producers, creating an atmosphere reminiscent of the Velvet Revolution. Havel sided with the striking producers. The crisis was settled in late January, 2001.

183 "Rudolfinum speech": The speech was published in English by *The New York Review of Books* on March 28, 1999, under the title "The Sad State of the Republic."

184 Dělostřelecká Street: Havel's private residence.

186 "the alleged and naturally secret wedding of our Nina": Nina is Dáša Havlová's daughter, from her first marriage.

188 Kurt Gebauer (1941–): Czech sculptor.

198 Gripens: Swedish multipurpose jet fighters.

198 "the Indonesian woman": Havel is referring to the Indonesian president at the time, Megawati Sukarnoputri.

200 *Tvář*: A monthly magazine published by the Union of Czechoslovak Writers in the mid-1960s. It had two runs, one from January 1964 to December 1965, when it was shut down by the union under pressure from the party, and again from the fall of 1968 (after the Soviet-led invasion) to June 1969, when the newly installed Husák regime shut it down for good, along with many other publications. Havel was actively involved in both incarnations; Václav Klaus contributed a total of eight articles and reviews on economics and politics, all of them in the second, postinvasion run.

200 Rita Klímová (1931–1993): Official press spokesperson for the Civic Forum in November and December 1989; Czechoslovak ambassador to Washington from 1990 to 1992.

201 Václav Valeš (1922–): Czech economist who was a member of the Civic Forum. From July 1990 to September 1991, he served as deputy prime minister of the federal government.

202 Tomáš Ježek (1940–): Czech economist; served as minister of privatization from 1990 to 1992. From 1992 to 1996 he was an elected member of the Chamber of Deputies for the ODA, and was part of a working group that drafted the new Czech constitution. From 1996 to 1998 he served as chair of the Prague Stock Exchange, and as head of the Czech Securities Commission from 1998 to 2002.

202 Dušan Tříska (1946–): An economist, he was deputy minister of finance of Czechoslovakia from 1990 to 1992. He is believed to have designed the technical aspects of the so-called coupon privatization by which much of the Czech economy was returned to private ownership.

203 Ivan Mikloš (1960–): Economist, Slovakian minister of finance and deputy prime minister (2002–06).

205 "Salman Rushdie's visit to Prague": In February 1989, a fatwa, or death sentence, was issued against the Anglo-Indian writer Salman Rushdie by the Ayatollah Khomeini, the ruler of Iran, because he judged Rushdie's most recent book, *The Satanic Verses*, as blasphemous to Islam. While under the protection of the British government, Rushdie was invited to the Czech Republic to attend a conference in September 1993. As a demonstration of solidarity, Havel invited him to the Prague Castle, and the next day Havel's press secretary, Ladislav Špaček, issued a press release announcing that the visit had taken place. Prime Minister Klaus reacted strongly, as Havel writes, publicly accusing Havel of acting behind the government's back. Havel declined to respond in kind to Klaus; Špaček issued a second statement saying that Klaus's ministers had certainly known of the visit, and if he, Klaus, had not known about it, then it was, in effect, a government problem. In his subsequent "midnight" visit to the Castle, Klaus demanded that Havel retract this statement and fire Špaček. Havel compromised, and formally distanced himself from Špaček's statement, but did not fire him.

206 Frank Zappa (1940–1993): American musician and composer, founder of the Mothers of Invention. In 1990, Zappa came to Czechoslovakia and Havel suggested that he be appointed special envoy for Czechoslovakia for culture, trade, and tourism. The idea was rejected by the first Bush administration, so Havel made the appointment unofficial. Zappa died two years later of prostate cancer.

208 Ivan Medek (1925–): Czech journalist, lived in exile in Vienna from 1978 until his return after 1989. He was President Havel's chief of staff from 1996 to 1998.

212 "Pavlíček's music": Michal Pavlíček (1956–): Musician and composer. Havel commissioned him to write a special piece of music for the NATO summit, held in Prague later in 2002.

213 Vladimír Špidla (1951–): Czech politician who became leader of the ČSSD party in 2001 and was prime minister from 2002 to 2004.

215 Jiří Skalický (1956–): Chairman of the ODA party; environment minister and deputy prime minister from 1997 to 1998.

219 Jiřina Bohdalová (1931–): A popular actress who figures as an offstage character in Havel's one-act play *The Audience* (1975).

221 "The one I remember most proudly was the one at Harvard": Havel spoke at the Harvard commencement on June 0, 1995. The speech, which he delivered in English, is reprinted in *The Art of the Impossible: Politics as Morality in Practice*, published by Knopf (1997).

224 "Ukraine under Kuchma": Leonid Kuchma (1938–) was president of Ukraine from July 1994 to January 2005.

227 "a period of mass petitions": Havel's second term coincided with the tenth anniversary of the Velvet Revolution in 1989, and at the time, a number of petitions circulated that demanded a return to the values embodied in that revolution. The "Dřevičská Appeal," issued in 1999, called for the revival of the Czech economy, signed by leading representatives of the media and the economy, including Karel Schwarzenberg, at whose château in Dřevič the appeal was signed. "Thank You, Now Leave!" was a petition circulated by the former student leaders on the tenth anniversary of the November 17, 1989 demonstration. "Television: A Public Affair" was a citizens' petition set in motion in late December demanding a resolution to the crisis in Czech Television in favor of an independent public broadcasting model. "Impulse '99" was a manifesto issued in 1999 and deliberately named to recall Charter 77. It suggested that the process of transforming society had "stagnated." It was signed by some people close to Havel, giving rise to unfounded speculation that he was behind it.

230 V Luhu: A cottage within the grounds of the presidential country seat in Lány and belonging to the complex.

CHAPTER FIVE

233 "President Fischer" (1938–): Heinz Fischer became president of Austria in 2004, following the death of Thomas Klestil.

234 Charles IV (1316–1378): Born in Prague, son of Elizabeth I of Bohemia and John of Luxembourg, he became Holy Roman Emperor in 1355 and made his permanent seat in Prague, where his enormous legacy is still visible in the architecture (Charles Bridge), the town planning (the district of Prague II, centered on Charles Square), and the institutions (Charles University).

235 "your first wife, Olga": Olga Havlová (née Šplichalová) (1933–1996). She married Václav Havel in 1964, and was active in the dissident community during the 1970s and 1980s, in particular in samizdat activities and in the underground video project Original Videojournal. She became the first postcommunist first lady, and founded a charity to support the handicapped called the Committee of Good Will.

237 "my Philadelphia speech": Havel was awarded the Liberty Medal in Philadelphia on July 4, 1994. See *The Art of the Impossible* (Knopf, 1997) for the acceptance speech in English.

238 "Professor Klener": Pavel Klener (1937–), head of the oncology clinic where Olga Havel spent her final days.

238 Z line: A special internal, closed-circuit telephone system, a relic of the communist era and available only to the highest state officials. The "Z" comes from the Czech designation "Zvlaštni," or "Special."

242 Jiří Suchý (1931–): Popular actor, songwriter, poet, and, together with Jiří Slitr (1924–1969), founder of the Semafor Theater in Prague in 1959, which provided a forum for satirical cabaret.

243 "theater strike": Immediately after the events of November 17, 1989, the theaters across Czechoslovakia went on strike and opened their auditoriums for public meetings and discussions. The Civic Forum was created in one of these theaters, the Činoherní Klub.

243 Lucerna: A large entertainment and commercial complex on Wenceslas Square in Prague. Its centerpiece is a hall that is the venue for concerts and balls. The complex was built between 1906 and 1920 by Havel's grandfather Václav Havel (1861–1921).

246 Professor Pafko: Dr. Pavel Pafko (1940–), head of the Department of Thoracic Surgery at the University Hospital Motol in Prague; he was the first Czech surgeon to carry out a successful double-lung transplant.

251 Hel: A town at the end of the Hel Peninsula, Poland, extending into the Gulf of Gdansk in the Baltic Sea. It is the seat of the Polish presidential retreat.

252 Anna (Andulka) Friemanová (1951–): A close associate, and literary secretary of Václav Havel while he was president. She was in charge of the meetings in the Amálie. Married to the director Andrej Krob.

252 "Žižkov town hall": Žižkov is a district of Prague.

256 "Now she's starting to rehearse": In early 2006, Dáša Havlová returned to the stage in a Czech-language production of Israel Horovitz's *Park Your Car in Harvard Yard* at the Vinohrady Theater in Prague.

256 "why I refused to come back from Portugal when there were floods at home": In the summer of 2002, there was serious flooding all along the Vltava River, and Prague was especially hard hit. Havel was convalescing in Portugal at the time, and the press took him sharply to task for delaying his return until Wednesday, when the waters were already receding.

260 Zdeněk Urbánek (1917–): Czech writer and translator, famous for his renditions of Shakespeare and works by Walt Whitman and Edgar Lee Masters, among others, into Czech.

260 Jan Tříska (1936–): Czech actor, living and working in the United States since 1977.

260 Pavel Landovský (1936–): Czech actor and playwright; from 1979 lived in Austria and was associated, until 1987, with the Burgteatre in Vienna.

261 Klaus Juncker: Havel's literary agent and publisher (with Rowohlt Verlag) from 1964 to 1989.

262 "that dramatic October of 1956": In Poland, months of ferment on the streets and within the ruling Communist Party came to a climax in October 1956 when Władysław Gomułka was appointed general secretary of the party amid invasion threats from the Soviet Union. Khrushchev withdrew the threats when he became satisfied that Gomułka's "Polish road to socialism" would not undermine communist rule. October 1956 was also the month of the uprising in Hungary, which was crushed by Soviet tanks in November 1956.

262 "the song about 'The Lost Lvov'": From 1918 to 1939 the city of Lvov was part of Poland. Today, it belongs to Ukraine, and is called Lviv.

270 The Barrandov Terraces: Built on a cliff overlooking the Vltava River in the south of Prague, the Barrandov Terraces, along with the Barrandov film studios, were developed by Havel's father, Václav Maria Havel (1897–1979), and uncle, Miloš Havel (1899–1968), in the 1920s and 1930s.

272 Jan Zábrana (1931–1984): Czech writer, poet, and translator. Translated Russian and Anglo-American literature into Czech, including works by Isaac Babel, Ivan Bunin, Osip Mandelstam, Boris Pasternak, Ezra Pound, Sergei Jesenin, Graham Greene, Allen Ginsberg, Lawrence Ferlinghetti, and Sylvia Plath.

272 Pavel Juráček (1935–1989): Czech screenwriter and director, one of the avant-garde filmmakers who contributed to the famous Czech New Wave of cinema in the 1960s.

273 Ivo Mathé (1951–): Television producer and, after the Velvet Revolution, director of Czech Television from 1992 to 1998. He was Havel's chief of staff from January 1999 to February 2002.

277 François Mitterrand (1916–1996): Mitterrand was the longest-serving president of France (1981–1995).

277 "the structure of Being": In his writing, Havel frequently uses the word "Being" (bytí in Czech, which is a translation of the Heideggerian term "Sein," in German) in a way that is probably unique to him. It frequently occurs, as it does here, in phrases like "the memory of Being" or "the order of Being." The closest Havel has come to defining it was in his Letters to Olga, where he wrote: "Behind all phenomena and discrete entities in the world, we may observe, intimate, or experience existentially in various ways something like a general 'order of Being.' The essence and meaning of this order are veiled in mystery; it is as much an enigma as the Sphinx; it always speaks to us differently and always, I suppose, in ways that we ourselves are open to, in ways, to put it simply, that we can hear" (Letter 76, pp. 185–86, in Letters to Olga, Knopf, 1988).

278 Karel Teige (1900–1951): Czech art critic, journalist, and translator. In 1920 he became a founding member of the Czech art association Devětsil, along with writers such as Jaroslav Seifert, Vladislav Vančura, and Vítěslav Nezval.

282 "the visit of the Irish woman": Havel is referring to the Irish president at the time, Mary McAleese. She was elected in 1997, and reelected in 2004.

283 Rudolf II (1552–1612): Emperor of the Holy Roman Empire, king of Bohemia and Hungary. Rudolf attracted many internationally renowned artists and scholars to Prague. His reign is considered one of the high points of Czech history.

284 Diana Sternberg-Phipps (1936–): An interior designer. She reclaimed and refurbished a family château in Častolovice. Together with Olga Havlová, she was in charge of the redecorating of the presidential château at Lány.

286 "using his pet phrase": Please Be Brief is the title of the Czech edition of this book.

289 Emil Hácha (1872–1945): President of Czechoslovakia from 1938 to 1939, that is, from the annexation of the Sudetenland until the German occupation. He then served under the Nazis as a figurehead president of the Protectorate of Bohemia and Moravia until 1945.

CHAPTER SIX

292   "our new prime minister": Jiří Paroubek (1952–), chairman of the Czechoslovak Social Democratic Party (ČSSD). He was prime minister from April 2005 to August 2006.

293   Warsaw Pact: Formally called the Treaty of Friendship, Cooperation, and Mutual Assistance, it was an alliance of Central and Eastern European states (Albania, Bulgaria, Czechoslovakia, East Germany, Hungary, Poland, Romania, and the Soviet Union). It was signed in Warsaw in 1955, and although formally created in response to the establishment of NATO in 1949 and the rearming of West Germany in 1954, it was mainly an instrument of deepening Soviet control over Central Europe. One of its few joint military operations was the invasion of Czechoslovakia in August 1968. It was dissolved in Prague in July 1991.

294   Gennady Yanayev (1937–): Russian communist politician. At the time of the summit Havel refers to, Yanayev was vice president of the Soviet Union. During the August 1991 coup in Moscow, he was briefly the acting president, and was later prosecuted and sent to prison. He was released in 1994.

297   Partnership for Peace (PfP): A project established within NATO in 1994, as a prelude to expansion. Its purpose was to establish trust between NATO and neighboring states, in particular the former Soviet Union. Ten of the original PFP signatories eventually became members of NATO.

299   Puťek: Vladimír Putin.

299   Euro-Atlantic Partnership Council (EAPC): An organization within NATO, formed in 1997 to improve relations between NATO and non-NATO countries. The NATO-Russia Council was established in 2002 to facilitate communication between Russia and NATO; likewise, the NATO-Ukraine Commission was established in 1999 for a similar purpose.

302   "the three Visegrad countries": Poland, Hungary, and the Czech Republic. Slovakia, the fourth in the Visegrad group, joined NATO in 2004.

304   Jan Patočka (1907–1977): One of the leading Czech philosophers of his time. He was a student of Edmund Husserl and Martin Heidegger and a proponent of a Czech version of phenomenology that had a profound impact on Havel's thinking. He was banned from teaching and publishing for most of his life. Patočka was a co-founder and a first spokesman of Charter 77. He died of a heart attack shortly after the interrogation Havel refers to.

305   José Ortega y Gasset (1883–1955): Spanish philosopher. His best-known book in English is The Revolt of the Masses (1930). Havel may be referring to a lecture Ortega y Gasset delivered in Berlin in 1949 entitled "A Meditation on Europe."

314   Commonwealth of Independent States: An association of former Soviet republics created in 1991. It includes Azerbaijan, Armenia, Belarus, Georgia, Kazakhstan, Kyrgyzstan, Moldova, Russia, Tajikistan, Turkmenistan, Uzbekistan, and Ukraine.

321   Árpád Göncz (1922–): President of Hungary from August 1990 to August 2000.

321   Mário Soares (1924–): President of Portugal from 1986 to 1996.

324   HOS (Hnutí občanské svobody): The Movement for Civic Freedom, a more broadly based civic initiative than Charter 77, established in the late 1980s. Members of HOS took part in the establishment of the Civic Forum in November 1989.

CHAPTER SEVEN

339 "A new book by Madeleine": Madeleine Albright's most recent book, *The Mighty and the Almighty: Reflections on America, God, and World Affairs* (2006).

342 "St. Wenceslas relics": Havel may have been given a gift of bone fragments allegedly belonging to the remains of the Czech patron saint, St. Wenceslas (Václav in Czech), which he stored in his safe.

342 "the Mašín brothers": Despite their youth, the Mašín brothers—Ctírad (1930–) and Josef (1932–)—were active, with their father, in the anti-Nazi underground in Czechoslovakia during World War II, and were decorated after the war by President Beneš. They continued their armed underground struggle after 1948, this time against the communists. In 1953, they and three other members of their group fled to the West via East Germany, where two were caught, returned to Czechoslovakia, and executed. Ctírad and Josef and a third member of the group escaped to Germany and eventually to the United States. They remain controversial today, because in the course of escaping the country, they killed a total of six people—three in Czechoslovakia and three in East Germany.

345 Ďula: The Havel family dog at the time.

INDEX

Page numbers beginning with 354 refer to notes.

INDEX

ALSO BY VÁCLAV HAVEL

DISTURBING THE PEACE

In Prague in 1976 a quizzical playwright named Václav Havel agreed
to be the spokesman for a group calling for a more tolerant and open
Czechoslovakia. Thirteen years later, Havel became his country's president. These eloquent and probing interviews, conducted by Karel
Hvizdala, are at once Havel's political autobiography, a history of
Czechoslovakia under communism, and a guide for all people of conscience facing conscienceless regimes.

Autobiography/Current Affairs/978-0-679-73402-4

OPEN LETTERS
Selected Writings, 1965–1990

Spanning twenty-five years, this historic collection of writings shows
Havel's evolution from a playwright who had the courage to advise
and criticize Czechoslovakia's leaders to a newly elected president
whose first address to his fellow citizens began, "I assume you did not
propose me for this office so that I, too, would lie to you." Some of the
pieces in *Open Letters* are now almost legendary for their influence on
a generation of Eastern European dissidents; others appear in English
for the first time. All of them bear the unmistakable imprint of Havel's
intellectual rigor, moral conviction, and unassuming eloquence.

Current Affairs/Contemporary Politics/978-0-679-73811-4

SUMMER MEDITATIONS

Havel, president of the Czech Republic, addresses the legacy of communism as the euphoria of the Velvet Revolution gives way to a more
problematic reality. Yet even as he grapples with the challenges of a
political change, he affirms his belief in a politics motivated by moral
responsibility; in an economy tempered by compassion; and in the central roles of art and culture in the transformation of society. *Summer
Meditations* is not only a timely testament of events in Eastern Europe
but a profound reflection upon the nature and practice of politics and
a stirring call for morality and openness in public life.

Memoir/978-0-679-74497-9

VINTAGE BOOKS
Available at your local bookstore, or visit
www.randomhouse.com